They Rode with Forrest and Wheeler

In memory of

my parents,
Will Stratton Fisher,
1895–1949,
and
Estelle Carr Fisher,
1898–1988;

my cousin,
James Carr Brown,
1925–1945;

and my niece,
Patricia Jo Fisher,
1951–1990

They Rode with Forrest and Wheeler

A Chronicle of Five Tennessee Brothers' Service in the Confederate Western Cavalry

by JOHN E. FISHER

McFarland & Company, Inc., Publishers
Jefferson, North Carolina, and London

The present work is a reprint of the library bound edition of They Rode with Forrest and Wheeler: A Chronicle of Five Tennessee Brothers' Service in the Confederate Western Cavalry, *first published in 1995 by McFarland.*

LIBRARY OF CONGRESS CATALOGUING-IN-PUBLICATION DATA

Fisher, John E., 1926–
    They rode with Forrest and Wheeler : a chronicle of five Tennessee brothers' service in the Confederate Western Cavalry / by John E. Fisher.
        p.   cm.
    Includes bibliographical references and index.

    ISBN 0-7864-2270-X (softcover : 50# alkaline paper) ∞

    1. Confederate States of America. Army. Tennessee Cavalry.
2. Confederate States of America. Army of Tennessee—Cavalry.
3. Fisher family.   4. United States—History—Civil War, 1861–1865—Cavalry operations.   5. Tennessee—History—Civil War, 1861–1865.   6. Forrest, Nathan Bedford, 1821–1877.   7. Wheeler, Joseph, 1836–1906.   I. Title.
E579.4.F57   2005
973.7'468—dc20   95-10935

British Library cataloguing data are available

©1995 John E. Fisher. All rights reserved

No part of this book may be reproduced or transmitted in any form or by any means, electronic or mechanical, including photocopying or recording, or by any information storage and retrieval system, without permission in writing from the publisher.

On the cover: Lieutenant General Nathan Bedford Forrest (left); Major General Joseph Wheeler.

Manufactured in the United States of America

McFarland & Company, Inc., Publishers
   Box 611, Jefferson, North Carolina 28640
      www.mcfarlandpub.com

Contents

Maps and Illustrations	vi
Preface	ix
Introduction	1
1 The Beginning, Secession through 1862	9
2 The Year 1863 through Streight's Raid, January 3–May 3, 1863	29
3 Through the Chickamauga Holocaust, May 4–October 29, 1863	45
4 Chattanooga, Knoxville, and into the Atlanta Campaign, October 30, 1863–July 22, 1864	61
5 The Siege of Atlanta and Wheeler's Tennessee Raid, July 23–September 2, 1864	89
6 The Fall of Atlanta, Sherman's March, and Surrender in the East, August 25, 1864–May 19, 1865	106
7 Hood's Tennessee Campaign: Debacle at Spring Hill, November 16–29, 1864	143
8 Hood's Tennessee Campaign: Disasters at Franklin and Nashville, November 30–December 16, 1864	158
9 Hood's Tennessee Campaign: Retreat, December 16–27, 1864	173
10 Redeployment and Wilson's Alabama Campaign, December 28, 1864–April 12, 1865	181
11 An Army in Bivouac; Surrender and Home, April 12–May 25, 1865	202
Epilogue	225
Appendix A	255
Appendix B	257
Notes	259
Bibliography	283
Index	291

Maps

Seat of War	2
Kentucky and Tennessee: Operations in 1861–1862	10
Middle Tennessee and Northern Alabama (Streight's Raid)	30
Chattanooga-Chickamauga and Environs	46
The Atlanta Campaign: Chattanooga to Atlanta	62
The Atlanta Campaign: The Siege of Atlanta	90
Sherman's March: Atlanta to Savannah	108
Sherman's March: Operations in the Carolinas	128
Hood's Tennessee Campaign: Middle Tennessee and Northern Alabama	144
Battle of Nashville	159
Alabama, 1865	182

Illustrations

Lieutenant General Nathan Bedford Forrest	17
Major General Joseph Wheeler	25
The Five Fisher Brothers After the War	141
Thomas Burr Fisher, October 1920	232

Preface

This study represents the culmination of an effort to flesh out the military service portions of memoirs written by Thomas Burr Fisher, 1844–1922, one of five brothers who, between them, served in the Fourth and Eleventh Tennessee cavalry regiments, C.S.A., during the Civil War.

Fisher wrote two memoirs, one in 1915, the other in 1921, but he dealt only in broadest outline with his and his brothers' service during the war. The author of the memoirs was my grandfather, and I first came across the original copies in my home when I was a child. The material very early suggested to me the possibility of a formal study.

As my efforts in research and writing proceeded, I enlarged the scope of the task to include a running record of the activities of all the soldiers of the two cavalry companies in which Fisher and his brothers served and added an analysis of company casualties and attrition. I also felt compelled to include in the study the efforts of the larger military forces of which the brothers and their units were a part as well as the strategic considerations of pertinent army commanders on both sides of the conflict. Of course, the politics of secession, military occupation and divided loyalties, and the aftermath of the war, including the economic disaster concomitant with military defeat, had to be dealt with in the study.

The Fourth and Eleventh Tennessee cavalry regiments served under Nathan Bedford Forrest, quite probably the ablest cavalry commander produced by either side in the war, and Joseph Wheeler, an able commander whose greatest successes were accomplished in close support of the Army of Tennessee. Forrest's military campaigns have received detailed attention in numerous studies. But Wheeler has been considerably less written about. Accordingly, the Civil War reader will likely find in these pages more detail that may be new or unfamiliar concerning Wheeler's campaigns than he or she will find in treatments of Forrest's campaigns. Since this study, however, proceeds from the point of view of company soldiers as much as from that of their cavalry commanders, Forrest and Wheeler, the reader will find new and hitherto unpublished material throughout the narrative.

The soldiers of the Fourth and Eleventh Tennessee cavalry regiments served in a variety of ways in support of the Army of Tennessee, as couriers, cowboys, guards, police, pilots, scouts, intelligence gatherers, mounted infantry, and dismounted on the line of fire. Wheeler's cavalry was virtually the only Confederate force in the field to oppose Sherman's November–December 1864 march through Georgia from Atlanta to the sea.

An analysis of manpower attrition in the two companies reveals something about the Civil War infantry's poor opinion of the cavalry and its belief in the cavalry's reluctance to fight and thus expose itself to the lethal combat that was a commonplace for soldiers of the infantry.

While this study deals primarily with military history, the family of Thomas Fisher and his brothers and their place in nineteenth-century American society, culture, and economy is not neglected. Since they came from a small slaveholding family, their relations with slaves and, after the war, freedmen and women are dealt with.

Thomas Fisher was the only one of the five war-veteran brothers who survived into the twentieth century. After the war, he attained a classical collegiate education, became a cleric, and was active vocationally through the Progressive era in America until after World War I. His surviving memoirs, sermons, and letters indicate that although he grew up in a rural community where the practices of frontier religion were the norm, he moved away from his bucolic roots to a modern, urbane, and progressive approach to socioreligious belief systems, scholarship, and ethics. His writings indicate that in his mature years he shared, in common with progressive churchmen both in the South and across America, a common faith expressed in an ecumenical Christianity with an emphasis upon social justice. Thus the evidence that Fisher left adds to a growing body of evidence that liberal religion indeed was indigenous to the South in the late nineteenth and early twentieth centuries. Studies made not many years ago mistakenly assumed that Southern churchmen during the period remained attached to a traditional theology of individual salvation and did not share in the development of liberal and informed theological, social, and cultural views.

Without the material help of the following people and institutional representatives, this volume would not have been possible:

I am indebted to Thomas Burr Fisher's late daughter-in-law, Estelle Carr Fisher, who recognized the value of and preserved, edited and transcribed accurate typescripts of Fisher's two memoirs, one untitled, written in 1915, and the other, "Life on the Common Level," written in 1921. Her personal acquaintance with Thomas Burr Fisher, together with her sympathetic understanding of what Fisher was trying to accomplish in his literary efforts, her editing skills, and her breadth of knowledge and interests combined to make her the ideal choice for the tasks. Without her initiatives, this volume would likely not be in print. She and her husband, Will Stratton Fisher, preserved Thomas Burr Fisher's memoirs, sermons, books, and collection of photographs following his death in 1922.

I am grateful to John Thomas Fisher of Columbia, Tennessee, who preserved and made available for transcription Thomas Burr Fisher's 1921 memoir, "Life on the Common Level."

I am indebted to Betsy Hammonds Fisher and the late Howard Boone Fisher of Dallas, Texas, for making available correspondence, newspaper clippings, books, records, and magazines of Thomas Burr Fisher, Howard's father.

I am grateful to William L. Jones of Milan, Tennessee, whose volume, *The Fisher Scrapbook, 1730–1972*, contains a transcript of William Stratton Fisher's wartime diary as well as other increasingly valuable genealogical detail of the Fisher brothers' family. His book is an invaluable resource.

I am indebted to the late Marshall Wilson Lovell of Nashville, Tennessee, for making available for publication the wartime diary of his grandfather, William Stratton Fisher; and to the late Lucian H. Boone of Dallas, Texas, for making available to me the genealogy of the Boone family.

I am immeasurably indebted to Professor Shung Wu Lee of the University of Illinois and Mary E. Fisher-Lee of Champaign, Illinois, for their generous and material aid in computer technology, advice, and counsel which facilitated and expedited the production of this volume.

I am also deeply indebted to librarians of the Library of Congress, Washington, D.C.; the Library of the United Methodist Publishing House, the Public Library of Nashville and Davidson County, the Tennessee State Library and Archives, and the Vanderbilt University Library, all in Nashville; the Virginia State Library in Richmond, the Fairfax City Regional Library, Fairfax, Virginia; the Mary Riley Styles Public Library in Falls Church, Virginia, and the Arlington County Public Library in Arlington, Virginia; to archivists in the Military Reference Branch of the National Archives and Records Administration in Washington, D.C.; and to William Jayne, Director of the Public and Consumer Affairs Service, National Cemetery System, Department of Veterans Affairs, in Washington, D.C., for their help in the course of my research.

Photographs of Nathan Bedford Forrest and Joseph Wheeler were obtained through the Prints and Photographs Division of the Library of Congress. Fisher family photographs are from the author's collection.

My efforts have been materially assisted by family members not otherwise acknowledged herein who have shared with me their recollections of people and events and thus have enriched the substance of the narrative related in this volume. They include the late Mary Fisher Boone of Dallas and Oklahoma City; Wilson Phillips Fisher, Thomas Waterston and Ethel Frensley Fisher of Nashville; and Commodore Bascom Fisher of Tehran, Iran, Maryville, Tennessee, and Grand Rapids, Michigan. Contemporaries include Will Stratton Fisher, Jr., of Cleveland, Ohio; Thomas Carr Fisher, Thomas Waterston Fisher, Jr., and Joyce Jean Fisher of Nashville. I am grateful to each of them.

I am deeply grateful to Nancy, Emmie and Andy, John and Sally, and Steve for reading the manuscript and for their critical comments and recommendations, as well as for their encouragement and gifts of valuable resource material during the extended course of my research and writing.

Finally, I am indebted to the late Professor Henry Lee Swint of Vanderbilt University, an inspirational historian, author, and teacher, who introduced me to American social and cultural history and encouraged my research and writing therein; and to the late Rhoda Lee Kennedy, my teacher and friend, whose interest and insights into American history encouraged me to pursue independent studies in the field. The influence of both Swint and Kennedy, who each taught more than a generation of students, continues to be instructive and inspirational to those whose lives they touched.

JOHN E. FISHER
Falls Church, Virginia

Introduction

Thomas Burr Fisher returned to his family's home in the Farmington-Verona area of Marshall County, Tennessee, on Sunday, May 21, 1865, after having served in Company C, the Eleventh Tennessee Cavalry Regiment, Confederate States Army, from September 30, 1862, to May 10, 1865.[1]

During the war, he had seen action with the Army of Tennessee beginning with Joseph Wheeler at the Battle of Murfreesboro, or Stones River, and ending with Nathan Bedford Forrest in Alabama in 1865 following John B. Hood's withdrawal from Tennessee after the disastrous battles of Franklin and Nashville. He returned home, one of five brothers who had served in the Fourth and Eleventh Tennessee cavalry regiments with remarkable fidelity.

Two of his brothers, Elisha Monroe Fisher and James Wesley Fisher, joined the Confederate army on November 16, 1861, and found themselves, on December 11, 1861, placed in the Eighth Tennessee Cavalry Battalion, a unit increased in numbers on May 26, 1862, and designated as the Fourth Tennessee Cavalry Regiment.[2]

Not until September 30, 1862, when their home was behind Federal lines, did he and his other brothers, John Franklin Fisher and William Stratton Fisher, take up arms. They joined a company of partisan rangers, organized at Chapel Hill by Captain T.C.H. Miller, which operated with Major D.C. Douglass's battalion until the organization of the Eleventh Tennessee Cavalry Regiment on February 25, 1863, in which their company was placed, along with Douglass's and Daniel W. Holman's battalions and two companies commanded by William Forrest (the general's younger brother) and James H. Edmundson, respectively.[3]

The five Fisher brothers were reared on a 275-acre farm between Farmington and Verona in Marshall County, Tennessee, in the midsection of the state in an area of diversified farming and livestock. The neighborhood they lived in included small slaveholding as well as nonslaveholding families amidst the bluegrass, limestone, and cedars of the northern portion of the county in the valley of the Duck River.

Cotton was *not* king in their part of the South. No cotton was grown on the family farm where they grew up, nor was any grown within their neighborhood, the growing season being too short. Corn and wheat were the

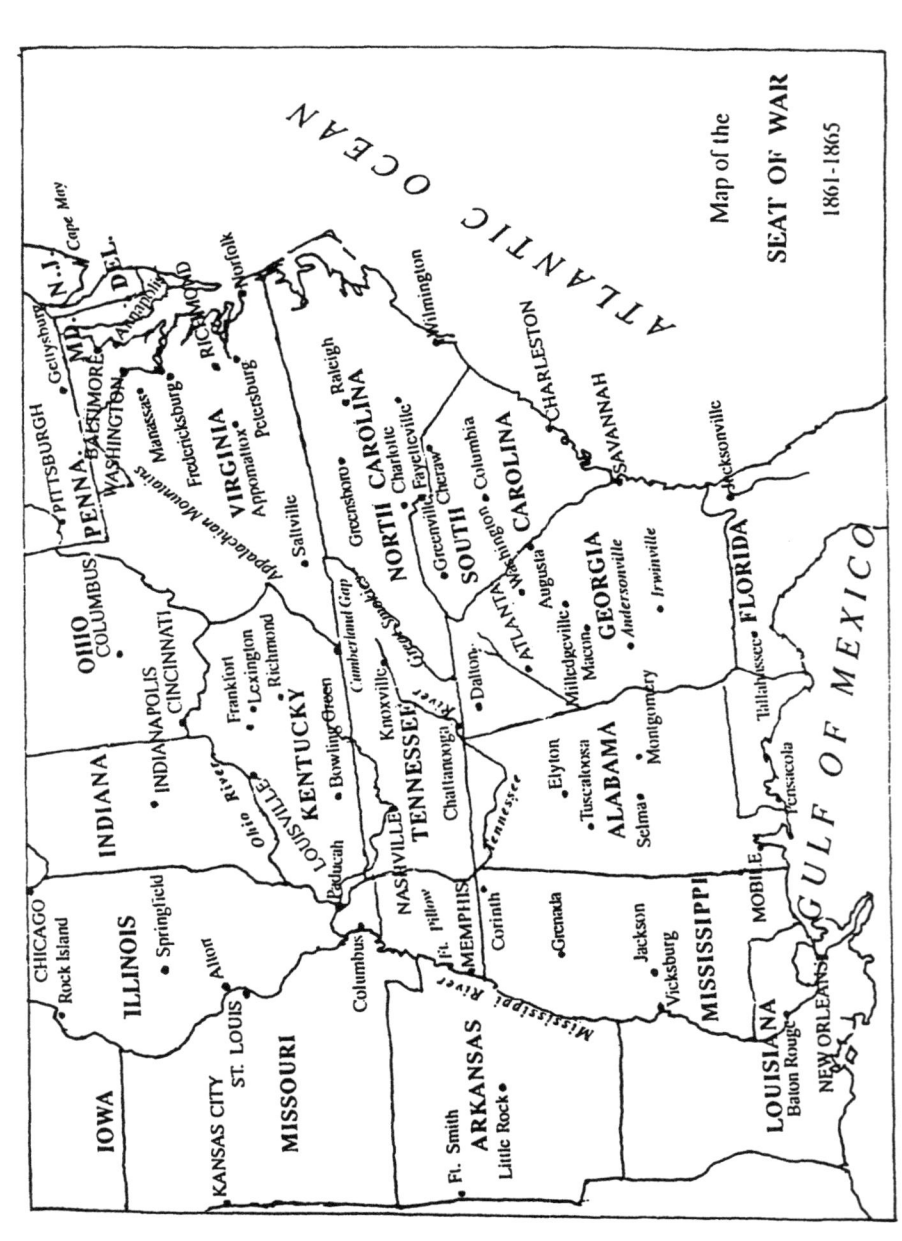

principal money crops, together with alfalfa, clover, rye, and timothy for silage.

Livestock raised included sheep, hogs, fowl, cattle, oxen, draft and saddle horses, and mules. The sheep and swine were of improved strains and were raised for sale, and both draft and saddle horses of blooded stock were raised for sale. About 71 percent of the family's 275-acre farm was woods and pasture.[4]

The brothers Fisher had an affinity for blooded horses, which they had grown up riding, so it was quite natural for them to join the Confederate cavalry.

They were descended from German and English immigrants, the male line of which had come to America and settled in Mecklenburg County, North Carolina, in the eighteenth century. Their great-grandfather, Frederick Fisher, had fought on the American side and was severely wounded in the Battle of Kings Mountain, South Carolina, on October 7, 1780.[5]

They were successors to several generations of a family which had rather single-mindedly followed agricultural pursuits. The isolation of their rural farm community caused them to think in terms of self-dependence, and they responded by being generalists as producers of crops, breeders of animals, mechanics with skills as blacksmiths and carpenters, and merchants in the combined production of their hand skills and soil.

They were ten miles from the county seat, Lewisburg, and since travel was slow and uncomfortable, they seldom had sufficient reason to go far from home.

After the war, Thomas and his brother, Monroe, broke the farmer pattern and undertook non-agricultural pursuits. Monroe became a teacher and schoolmaster. Tom became a clergyman.

The other brothers continued to pursue farming. At the beginning of the Civil War, they, their parents, and other forebears were what Thomas Jefferson described as "the chosen people of God, if ever He had a chosen people, whose breasts He had made his peculiar deposit for substantial and genuine virtue." They were, Jefferson believed, above corruption of morals for they were above dependence, subservience, and venality.[6] But they, like Jefferson, were not above being slaveholders.

Qualities of "dependence, subservience, and venality," so despised by Jefferson, the champion of independent small farmers, might characterize vulnerable individuals of twentieth-century generations in America who would live in cities, prosper, and work for employers to whose ideological bidding they might feel obliged to surrender regardless of the public morality thereof. This, of course, was precisely Jefferson's concern.

John Fisher, the father of the five brothers, was a small slaveholder, whose three adult slaves were women who were employed in a cottage industry, weaving and sewing. Between them, the two younger slave women had five children in 1860.

John Fisher likely raised sheep for sale as well as for their wool. Some of the latter he probably sold to factors in Nashville, where wool was transshipped to France in the 1850s. The remainder would have been used in his cottage industry. Fisher employed a 27-year-old white live-in employee, Nancy Grant, as well as the three slave women in 1860.

It is believed that the family tanned leather from its slaughtered animals and produced footwear, purses, headdress, harness and saddlery of good quality. In the 1840s and 1850s, however, the price and quality of purchased leather goods would have encroached upon this family industry until the war, with its shortages and higher prices, would cause family members to regain their skills in leather tanning, cutting, and stitching.

For family consumption, members of the family grew Irish and sweet potatoes, beets, carrots, and turnips, as well as peas and beans, and orchard products such as apples and peaches. With three milch cows and abundant pasturage, the family enjoyed milk, butter, and cheese of the highest quality. The women of the family had charge of poultry, chickens, turkeys, and a few ducks, all used for home consumption. The women helped in gardening and dairying.

Thus the only collectivism the family members knew was found in the home, which housed an extended family, including the slave women. Most of the family members never knew the strictly nuclear family of only parents and their children which became the norm in America after the Great Depression of the 1930s. Both before and after the Civil War, each of the Fisher brothers, with one exception, lived in homes with parents of their wives or other relatives and live-in servants, a collectivistic experience which emphasized a substantial degree of interdependence and tolerance.

John Fisher was born in North Carolina in 1806 and came across the mountains to Tennessee with his parents when he was a child. On the eve of the Civil War, the only thing that kept him from farming better than he ever had was the persistence of an area-wide drought in the second year of its three-year duration.

In 1860, Fisher was one of some 300,000 Southern whites who owned between one and ten black slaves. As previously noted, he had eight, five of whom were children. His personal estate, including his slaves, was valued at $7,285, and his real estate, 275 acres of land and buildings, was valued at $5,500, or $20.00 per acre. The value of his land per acre was considerably higher than the average valuation of land ($12 to $14 an acre, the highest in the state) in rural Middle Tennessee counties in 1860.

The value of John's farm implements and machinery was estimated at $90, which was about average for a slaveholder working 80 acres of improved land in 1860 in the area of Marshall County, Tennessee,[7] and testimony to show just how little capital was required to own and operate a moderate-sized farm on which general agriculture was practiced in that time and place.

Still, the efforts of family members, including those of the Fishers' extended family, permitted them to enjoy some of the accoutrements of culture which hitherto had been less plentiful. Even in leaner days, however, John and his second wife, Mildred Stratton Fisher, had spent a fair amount of their substance on a relatively lavish style of entertainment, according to their son, Thomas. They were counted among the most generous and hospitable people in the community. Their family was large and guests under their roof were numerous and frequent.

John Fisher joined neighbors to provide a rudimentary education for his children through subscription schools. Cities had them, but there were scant public schools in most of rural America until after the Civil War.

The civilizing influence of an informed Methodism, representing the most numerous religious family in the South at that time, was evident in John and Mildred's household. Part of the religious influence stemmed from John's parents, Jacob and Nancy Fisher. Jacob deeded land for the establishment of a church near Berlin, in Marshall County, on August 16, 1837.[8]

One might believe that family members subscribed to and read the *Christian Advocate* and the *Methodist Quarterly Review*, both out of Nashville, when Thomas was a boy. The women of the household may have received copies of the *Ladies Repository*, a quarterly art journal and one of the early periodicals for women published in the United States. Its publication, by the Methodist Publishing House in Cincinnati, began in 1841.

A religious influence played a role in the naming of the children. The first two sons born to John and Sarah Hurt Fisher were given names which combined scriptural and civic names of significance, John Franklin and Elisha Monroe. Two daughters received one scriptural name each, Mary and Elizabeth. A third son was given the name Wesley, which had an obvious connection with the family's church affiliation and the two eighteenth-century Anglican divines, John and Charles Wesley, who, with George Whitefield, another Oxonian priest, were the prime leaders of the incipient Methodist movement.

Of the three sons born to John Fisher and Mildred Stratton, the first was named for Mildred's father, William Stratton. But the second was given the surname of an esteemed member of the Tennessee Conference of the Methodist Episcopal Church, William Burr. And the third was given the surname of Bishop Henry Bidleman Bascom, 1796–1850, a native of New York, a popular speaker, editor, president of Transylvania College, and chaplain of the United States Congress, a man who had the reputation of being something of a dandy and man of the world as well as a spokesperson for the American Colonization Society and an apologist for the South in the abolitionist controversy which sectionally split Episcopal Methodism in 1844.[9]

John and Mildred Fisher may have first known of Bascom through his editorship of the *Methodist Quarterly Review*, originated in 1818 and now known simply as the *Quarterly Review*. It is the oldest of the church's periodicals in America.

Methodism was a progressive product of eighteenth-century Anglicanism. It originated as a movement at Oxford in the university, a point not lost on American Methodists who became prodigious and successful college and university builders. While the church's contribution to educating the underprivileged, blacks, and women has been extraordinary, the church has founded prestigious national universities such as Northwestern, Vanderbilt, Emory, Duke, et al. In 1892, the Methodist Episcopal Church established the University Senate, the first and now the oldest voluntary accrediting agency in American higher education.[10]

It diluted the importance of classical dogma and traditional usage by its preoccupation with the wellsprings of human consciousness and experience. It was part of a contemporary *zeitgeist* and helped to stimulate the Romantic movement in literature, poetry, the arts, architecture, social reform, and in accepted bases of intellectual understanding. It stimulated interest in one's inner life and thus contributed to the rise of the discipline of psychology.[11]

In philosophy, it provided, originally through Borden Parker Bowne, 1847–1910, of Boston University, a Methodist influence on personalism, a significant philosophical school in America. Its influence continues. Principal second-generation Methodist personalists include philosopher Edgar Sheffield Brightman, 1884–1953, theologian Georgia Harkness, 1891–1974, and social activist Bishop Francis J. McConnell, 1871–1953.

Personalism emphasizes the worth of individuals, of ethical values and of human freedom in a society so organized as to permit each person to achieve, through exertion and struggle, the optimum in personal growth and development. A theistic personalist sees God, whom one emulates, as a struggling hero working for lofty moral ends.[12]

By emphasizing the experiential element in religion, Methodism gave credibility to the insight that the essence of faith is manifested not so much in theological beliefs as in the daily living of one's life. It asserted the centrality in Christianity of personal character and the love and service of God in place of terms, opinions, creeds, and rites.[13]

In America, nineteenth-century Methodism's influence stemmed from its size and affluence, its perception of religious interests in their broadest sense, i.e., combining both sacred and secular, the primacy it accorded to humanitarian reform, and its pioneering use of congregational singing and revivalism as evangelistic tools and methods. It pioneered in the use of the printed word in its educational and missionary efforts. The Methodist Publishing House in Nashville, using the trade name Abingdon Press, is the oldest American book publisher and one of the largest and most prestigious. It was established in Philadelphia in 1789.[14]

The church required its membership to be disciplined, utilizing the class meeting to this end, a requirement which was on its way out by the Civil War era. Its religious life was marked by an aggressive episcopal policy which tended to become less incursive prior to the end of the century.

By making no exclusive or exclusionary claims for itself, avoiding doctrines which might be peculiar to itself, and manifesting a preference for empirical knowledge and ethically-informed pragmatic reason over convention and dogma, the church developed a number of catholic leaders including the cosmopolitan layman, John R. Mott, 1865-1955, whose efforts materially molded and defined the twentieth-century ecumenical movement.[15]

The interests and emphases of American Methodism affirmed that one might realize success and the good life through lofty human character, selfless motivation, and altruistic behavior. And the good life might be esteemed on the common level where one need not be anxious for the pursuit of conventional respectability expressed as acquisition of or identification with wealth and power, position and place. Thomas Burr Fisher divined as much when he titled his 1921 memoir, "Life on the Common Level." His predilection for commonality combined and embraced not only Judeo-Christian behavioral norms but American democratic values as well.[16]

The oldest part of the home in which the brothers Fisher were born had been built prior to 1810 when their forebears came to live on the land, a Revolutionary War land grant to John Fisher, a great-great uncle, who had served with Virginia troops both at Kings Mountain, South Carolina, and Guilford Courthouse, North Carolina, during the American Revolution.

The structure had been enlarged room by room until it was a commodious albeit obsolescent edifice by the time it was torn down in 1969, when the property was sold for the first time to people outside the Fisher clan. It was not an architecturally pleasing farmhouse. Its style was eclectic, primitive, and utilitarian. But the log and frame building had served several generations for over 150 years.[17]

Besides their parents and siblings, the brothers Fisher, of course, were a part of an extended family which included slaves, three black women and five children. The oldest of the three women, whose name has been lost, was given the task of carding rolls and spinning them on a wheel. More demanding physical tasks such as cooking, washing, ironing, and cleaning, or outside tasks such as hoeing and milking, were given over to the two younger women, Melinda and yet another whose name is now unknown.

All three women were what was known in the slave culture as "broad wives," that is, they were married to slaves of masters other than their own. The eldest of the three women, who had been married to a venerable slave of Jonathan Thomas, probably died in the 1860s, following her husband's death.

Thomas Fisher recorded that it had been the practice of her husband to come to John Fisher's home each Saturday evening to stay with his wife until Monday morning. He spent a good deal of time on Sundays reading his large-print New Testament with the aid of spectacles. When he died, his wife had his Bible placed under his head and buried with him in his coffin.[18]

In 1854, at the age of 70, Jacob Fisher, the Fisher brothers' grandfather, after a particularly severe drought-stricken year, removed to Johnson County, Illinois, near where a married daughter, Rebecca Fisher Helm (1808–1887), and her husband, Moses Watkins Helm (1806–1854), had gone to live in 1849. The latter was a brother of Jacob's second wife, Nancy Helm. Here Jacob resumed farming in the Grantsburg township and, with Nancy, continued to raise a second family.[19]

Owing to the removal to Illinois of Jacob with the younger members of his family, as well as his oldest daughter, Rebecca, it was virtually assured that family members would be arrayed on opposite sides in the Civil War. Indeed, one of Jacob and Nancy Fisher's sons, Franklin A. Fisher, born in 1837 in Tennessee, enlisted in Battery E of the First Illinois Light Artillery, U.S.A., on August 18, 1862.

Another son, Robert W. Fisher, born in Marshall County, Tennessee, in 1841, served in Battery K of the First Illinois Light Artillery. And a son of Rebecca Fisher Helm, James G. Helm (1833–1904), also a native Tennessean, served as Junior 2nd Lieutenant of Battery K beginning August 15, 1862.

Battery E of the First Illinos Light Artillery participated in the Battle of Nashville in December 1864. Previously it had seen action in Mississippi and West Tennessee. In the fall of 1864, it had joined in the pursuit of Confederate Major General Sterling Price after his threatened strike against St. Louis failed.

Battery K fought against Confederate incursions in Kentucky in 1862. On August 18, 1863, it went with Major General Ambrose Burnside to Knoxville, arriving September 1. The battery helped to defend Knoxville against the attack and siege of James Longstreet in the fall of 1863. During the winter of 1863–1864, it faced Longstreet's corps in upper East Tennessee.[20]

Thus Franklin and Robert Fisher and James G. Helm of both Illinois batteries fought more than once on the same fields of battle against their nephews and cousins from Marshall County, Tennessee, birthplace of them all, Union and Confederate.

Chapter 1

The Beginning, Secession through 1862

Two of John and Mildred Stratton Fisher's sons, Tom's half-brothers Elisha Monroe, 25, and James Wesley, 23, enlisted in the service of the Southern Confederacy on November 16, 1861, almost a year before their brothers Frank, Will, and Tom volunteered, but over five months after the people of Tennessee voted by referendum on June 8 to dissolve their connection with the Federal government and to seek to join the Southern Confederacy.[1]

The vote in Marshall County where the Fishers lived was about sixteen to one for secession, a near unanimity of opinion which spared the majority the fierce and sometimes violent and murderous dissents which wracked many counties and communities more evenly divided on the issue.

Statewide the vote was a bit over two to one, or about seven to three, with Middle Tennessee counties voting thirty to four for secession and West Tennessee counties favoring secession by fourteen to four. Among the counties of East Tennessee, however, twenty-three opposed secession while only six favored it.[2]

There is irony in the sectional votes. Middle Tennessee, whose voters were most overwhelmingly in favor of secession, has been a rather consistently liberal-voting subregion for the better part of the twentieth century. East and West Tennessee have been comparatively conservative.

Prior to the fall of Fort Sumter and the call of President Lincoln for 75,000 military volunteers in April 1861, a clear majority of Tennesseans was opposed to withdrawing from the Union. In the presidential election on November 6, 1860, Tennessee voters gave to their native son, John Bell, candidate of the Constitutional Union Party, 69,710 votes, a plurality of 4,657 votes against a split Democratic Party with two sectional candidates, Stephen A. Douglas of Illinois with 11,394 votes, and John C. Breckenridge of Kentucky with 65,053 votes.

It may be conjectured as to how John Fisher and his sons voted in the presidential race that year, if they voted at all. Of John's sons, only Frank, Jim, and Monroe were old enough to vote. Their choices were between Bell, a Whig, and the two Democratic candidates. That none of John Fisher's sons

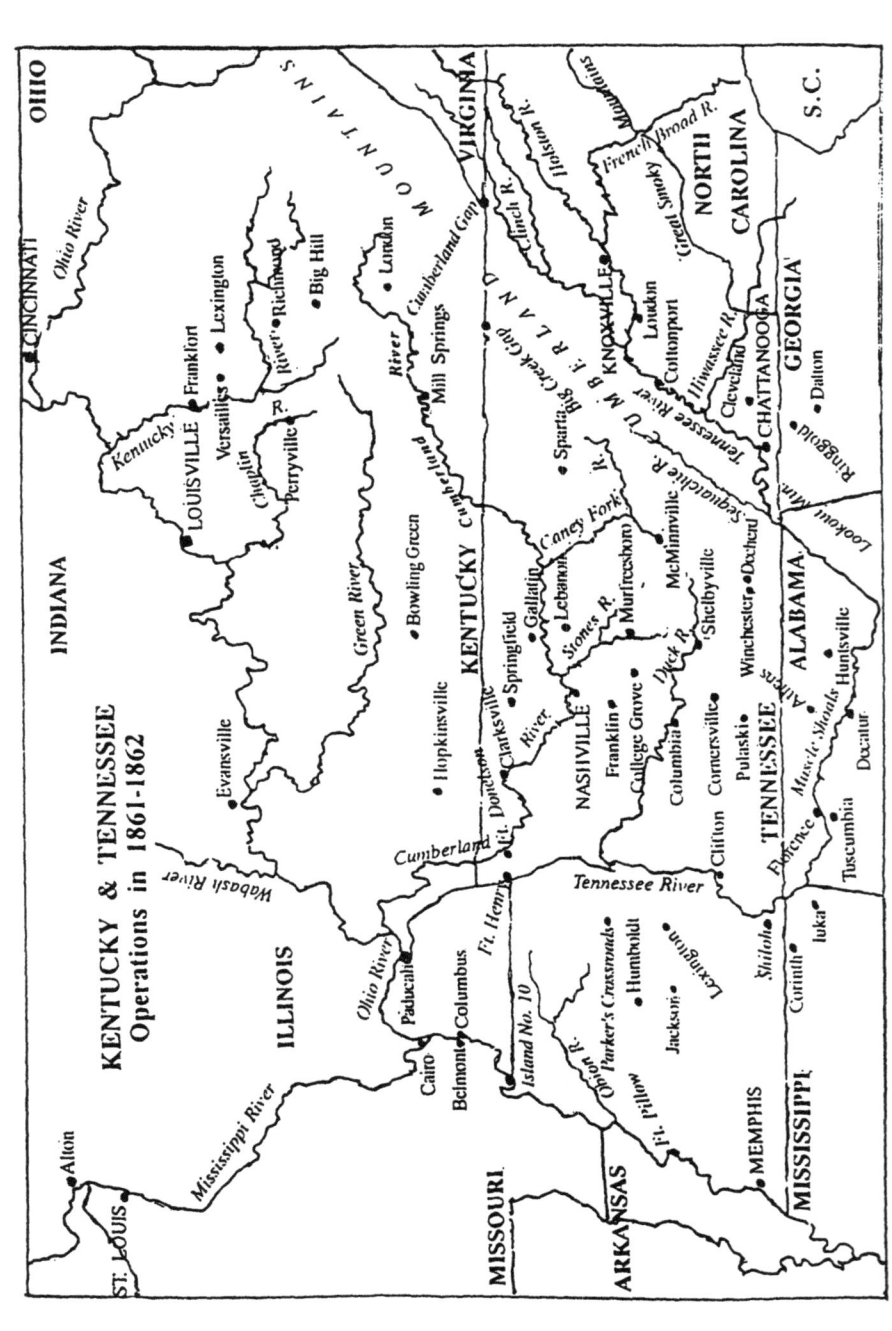

rushed pellmell to join the Confederate army suggests that they were Unionists, perhaps Jacksonian Democrats, who might have voted for Bell, who seemed the best choice for preserving the federal Union, a Jacksonian desideratum.

The Republican Party candidate, Abraham Lincoln of Illinois, was not on the ballot in Tennessee. Nevertheless, the vote may be seen as an indication of the strength of Union sentiment in the state since Bell, who consolidated the Whig vote, has been regarded as the only truly national candidate running.

Despite Tennessee's plurality vote in Bell's favor in 1860, Marshall County voted by about two to one in favor of the Democrat Breckenridge (1,326 votes) over Bell (662 votes) in 1860, about the same proportional majority vote that the county's voters had given Democratic Party presidential candidates over their Whig opponents in every election since 1840 when the county first recorded a presidential vote. Accordingly, it may be argued that, despite the Fisher's apparent Unionism, if they (those of voting age) had been voting Democratic for the past twenty years, as most voters in Marshall County had, they likely followed their established bent in 1860 and were a part of the county electorate that rejected Bell and voted for Breckenridge. Stephen A. Douglas, the other Democratic candidate, received only 43 votes, or 2.1 percent of Marshall County's presidential vote, in 1860.[3]

After the election of Lincoln, by a sectional and minority vote over a badly divided opposition, the states of South Carolina, Mississippi, Alabama, Florida, Georgia, Louisiana, and Texas seceded from the Federal Union and organized the Confederate States of America at Montgomery, Alabama, February 4, 1861, exactly one month before Lincoln took office.

On February 9, the people of Tennessee voted by a majority of almost four to one *against* calling a state convention to consider the secession question. The plebiscite was held pursuant to a resolution of the state legislature which Governor Isham G. Harris had called into special session and which met on January 7, 1861.[4]

Tennesseans were quite willing for sister states to leave the Union in peace if they so desired. But they implicitly opposed the use of the military to force states to remain in the Union against their will. And it was their own desire to remain in the Union.

But the situation changed in April. On the twelfth, South Carolina troops attacked and forced the surrender of the U.S. Army garrison at Fort Sumter in Charleston Harbor. Three days later, President Lincoln issued a call for 75,000 military volunteers, and the Secretary of War, Simon Cameron, requested of Governor Harris of Tennessee two regiments of militia for immediate Federal service. Harris rejected the request and pressed preparations for the state to arm itself in the event a general conflict ensued.[5]

It had been a widely held hope that Tennessee might remain neutral in a conflict between the Federal and Confederate governments. Correspondence with that object in view was exchanged between Governor Harris and Beriah Magoffin, the pro-slavery governor of Kentucky.[6]

But preparations for war in both the North and South, beginning in April, convinced Harris that his state would likely be overrun by the contending armies and become a battleground, making it unlikely that Tennessee could remain neutral. In addition, as early as January 1861, Governor Harris and a majority of members of the state legislature revealed a bias against the Federal government coercing the seceding states back into the Union. As events continued to gather momentum, this bias grew stronger.

The special session of the state legislature in January had passed an act to reorganize the state militia, which had previously been permitted to languish into a state of decay. Repeal of a law requiring drills and public parades had left the state without military organization and equipment except for a few volunteer companies in a few of the larger cities and towns.

On April 18, Harris called for another special session of the legislature to convene on the twenty-fifth. When the assembly met, the governor recommended that it pass an ordinance formally declaring the independence of the state from the federal Union, an action which would then be submitted as soon as possible to the voters of the state to ratify or reject. Harris also recommended that the state be put on a wartime footing with the raising of volunteers for immediate duty and a further strengthening of the organization and equipment of the militia.

The legislature acceded to the governor's recommendations and further passed a joint resolution authorizing the governor to appoint three commissioners who were to meet with representatives of the Confederate government in Nashville on May 7 to enter into a league with said government. When a military league was agreed to at the meeting on the seventh, the legislature added to the referendum to be decided by the voters on June 8 the question of the state joining the Southern Confederacy.[7]

As the time for the referendum approached, more and more Tennessee Unionists, particularly in Middle Tennessee, became outspoken for secession. All five Nashville newspaper editors abandoned their Unionism because they said they came to believe that the people of the North had abandoned their love of constitutional government and were ready to run roughshod over the interests of the people of the slave states.

In early March, John Bell, who had been mentioned as a leading candidate for a cabinet post and who was the most logical politician to dispense patronage in Tennessee for the new administration, attended Lincoln's inauguration in Washington and urged on the new president a policy of conciliation toward the seceded states. Subsequently, when Lincoln, an ex–Whig, chose a lifelong Democrat, Andrew Johnson, to dispense presidential patronage in Tennessee and left Bell and other political conservatives with nothing, Bell changed his mind about Lincoln and the Republicans. As April wore on, he became less resolutely Unionist.[8]

This time, June 8, most Tennessee voters were ready to dissolve their relationship with the Federal government and to enter into league with the Confederate states. But there was a small minority in the state which continued to oppose the breakup of the Union. Resistant Whigs and Jacksonian Democrats voted no to the proposal for Tennessee's secession and, of course, no to that of the state's joining the Confederacy.

Notwithstanding the Unionists' vote, a majority of Tennessee's voters finally favored secession. Tennessee became the last state to leave the Union and, as events transpired, the first state to reenter after the war. The Confederate Congress in Montgomery, in anticipation of the voters' action, had already provisionally admitted Tennessee to their confederacy by act of May 17.[9]

Preparations for invasion from the north were of high priority in the days and weeks after Tennessee's secession. The state's military organization was staffed, and arms were gathered from public and private sources. Enlistees initially furnished their own arms. State bonds were issued to support the war effort. Women organized into societies to collect and distribute supplies needed by soldiers in camp, field, and hospital. By July 31, transfer of the Provisional Army of Tennessee to the service, command, and care of the Confederate states had begun.

During the summer, factories in Nashville were manufacturing 100,000 percussion caps daily. Two Memphis foundries were manufacturing cannons, as were smaller operations in Clarksville, Murfreesboro, Lebanon, Pulaski, Shelbyville, and Franklin. Soon muskets and cannon, shot and shell, saddles, harness, knapsacks, and military drill manuals were produced in Nashville.

On October 7, 1861, the governor reported to the state legislature on progress made in arming the state. In the first two months, 30,000 volunteers had been placed in the field; the official transfer to the Confederate Army of the state's provisional army began on July 31; a total of thirty-eight regiments of infantry, seven battalions of cavalry, and sixteen artillery companies had been raised, and progress had been made toward equipping the military forces at a cost exceeding $5 million. Property taxes had been raised while the value of real property had declined.[10]

Just to the north of the state border, Tennessee troops under Brigadier General Gideon J. Pillow, pursuant to an order of Major General Leonidas Polk, commanding the Western Department of the Southern Confederacy, occupied Columbus, Kentucky, on the banks of the Mississippi, on September 3.[11] The move violated Kentucky's avowed neutrality, undercut pro–Southern sentiment in the state, and opened up Tennessee to attack from across the Kentucky border.

Federal troops under Brigadier General U.S. Grant occupied Paducah two days later. But not until November 7 did Tennessee troops become involved in actual fighting near their northern border. On that day, troops under Polk and Pillow fought to a standstill, both sides claiming victory, an attack by Federal forces under Grant on Belmont, Missouri, just across the river from Columbus, Kentucky.[12]

Tennessee troops were in Missouri because Tennessee's governor, Isham G. Harris, prior to Polk's violation of Kentucky's neutrality, believed that Kentucky was a buffer to Federal invasion of his state from the north and that his best strategic gambit was to conduct a military campaign into Missouri and Illinois.[13]

Ten days later, in the face of repeated requests for more armed Tennessee men by General Albert Sidney Johnston, the Confederacy's first permanent Western commander, and believing the war was indeed coming near enough to threaten their home, James Wesley and Elisha Monroe Fisher left the family hearth to volunteer in the fight for state and homeland.

Their actions suggest that they were Unionists who rejected the early enthusiasm for war and glory which infected so many of the early enlistees. But as the months went by, there seemed to be a solidification of community sentiment around a rallying cry of "all for one and one for all." It became increasingly rare to talk to people within the community who were willing to run against the tide and stand up for Unionism as they once had.

Throughout much of Middle Tennessee, people seemed to unite on the mores of a slaveholding society without regard to class interests after Ft. Sumter was attacked. Strict conformity was sought, and a crusade to crush dissenters was launched against locals opposed to secession. Nonconforming Northerners were no longer welcome. They found it prudent to go back north.

Monroe and Jim rode to Camp Cheatham, near Springfield, Robertson County, Tennessee, near the Kentucky border, a distance of 84 miles. The camp was commanded by Brigadier General Robert C. Foster III, a political appointee and a Whig, late of the Provisional Army of Tennessee.

As expert and avid horsemen who were used to riding high-spirited saddle horses, Jim and Monroe, together with a cousin, Jacob C. Fisher, and a number of other volunteers from Marshall County, enlisted in Company D of what became James W. Starnes' Eighth Tennessee Cavalry Battalion on December 11, 1861. Two other cousins, Michael R. and Turner M. Fisher, their father's first cousins, and other Marshall County recruits, enlisted in Company A of the same battalion on the same day.[14]

When the battalion was organized, one of the Fishers' most prosperous and prominent neighbors, Ewing A. Wilson of Chapel Hill, was elected major and second in command. He reportedly owned 2,000 acres of land near Chapel Hill, had been a brigadier general in the state militia prior to the war, and wanted to serve in 1861.

As it turned out, despite his having reported to Camp Cheatham along with the Fisher brothers, cousins, and other neighbors, Wilson, 43, was in poor health and unable to perform in camp or on the field of battle. He rode home with a heavy heart but was well enough to serve Bedford and Marshall counties in the 34th (Confederate) State Senate during 1861–1863.

After the war, Thomas Fisher married Wilson's niece and heir, Sallie Roberts, in 1872. During 1877–1881 and again during 1882–1883, Tom and Sallie shared Wilson's capacious home with him until his death at age 65 from pneumonia in 1883.[15]

Monroe was elected lieutenant by his fellow volunteers, but became ill with measles after the battalion was sent to Chattanooga in February 1862. His health was so impaired that he resigned and came home to convalesce, only to take up arms again when his other brothers enlisted in September.

But James Wesley, along with his cousins, remained in Starnes' Eighth Battalion. The battalion, with the addition of four companies, was reorganized on May 26, 1862, in Bledsoe County and became Starnes' Fourth Tennessee Cavalry Regiment.

The regiment Jim Fisher served in may be confused with Murray's Fourth Tennessee Cavalry, which was disbanded in January 1863, several companies of which thereupon went into Baxter Smith's Eighth Tennessee Cavalry Regiment, usually referred to as the Fourth Tennessee because of its connection with Murray's Fourth.

The three "Fourth" regiments are usually distinguished by adding their commanders' names to their numerical designations. Murray's Fourth was so called for Colonel John P. Murray, the regiment's only commanding officer. After Starnes' death on June 30, 1863, in action against Rosecrans' advance toward Chattanooga, his regiment was referred to as McLemore's Fourth after Major, then Colonel, W.S. McLemore, who succeeded Starnes. After Baxter Smith's capture on May 9, 1863, while on patrol on the Caney Fork River in Tennessee, Colonel Paul F. Anderson assumed command of the third "Fourth" regiment and gave his name to its designation.

Another complication in identifying Starnes' Fourth arises because the regiment was originally and mistakenly called the Third Tennessee Cavalry Regiment, although the designation had already been given to a regiment organized in Memphis in January 1862 and commanded by then Colonel Nathan Bedford Forrest. Some military records contain this mistaken designation.[16]

In the current narrative, the regiment in which Jim Fisher served will be understood to be Starnes' or McLemore's Fourth Tennessee Cavalry.

James Wesley was often on the same field of battle with his brothers after the latter volunteered as members of a partisan ranger company which became part of Nathan Bedford Forrest's "Old Brigade," the veterans and recruits that Forrest fashioned into an effective fighting force after his return from Bragg's Kentucky campaign in late October 1862.

Starnes' Fourth Tennessee Cavalry was one of the seasoned regiments composing the original "Old Brigade." It had marched to Chattanooga in late February 1862, after forts Henry and Donelson were lost, Bowling Green was abandoned, and Nashville was occupied by Union forces. At Chattanooga, the regiment was placed in the new Department of East Tennessee under the command of Major General Edmund Kirby Smith. Its first duty was to help protect the East Tennessee & Virginia and the East Tennessee & Georgia railroads, vital links in the Confederacy's east-west transportation chain.

Against Major General Don Carlos Buell's menacing Union army, the Fourth skirmished at Wartrace in Bedford County and at Readyville in Rutherford County in April and June respectively. On May 18 in a skirmish at Paint Rock in Roane County, John L. Houston, 21, of Company D was wounded and presumed to be dead by his comrades. Houston apparently joined four of his company comrades in death, the others, Warren Swiney, 38; Thomas Hunter, 27; Willis Collins, 23; and David Jones, 25, having died in Chattanooga and Franklin County, May 3–18, from unreported causes.

On June 24, six days after Smith ordered Brigadier General Carter L. Stevenson to abandon Cumberland Gap and to fall back to Morristown to avoid being outflanked, the Fourth was directed to join Stevenson's division at Rogersville. There they were to act as scouts in upper East Tennessee beyond Cumberland Gap, prevent the enemy from foraging in Clinch Valley in sparsely populated but strongly Unionist Hawkins and Hancock counties, subdue the local Unionists, and defend the East Tennessee & Virginia Railroad from attack.

On July 3, 1862, Smith joined Starnes' Fourth Cavalry Regiment to Colonel Benjamin Allston's First Cavalry Brigade of Brigadier General Henry Heth's division in the Department of East Tennessee.[17]

But before the men of the Fourth left for the east, they had already suffered a defection. On May 26, it was reported that forty-four-year-old Turner M. Fisher of Company A had been left near Winchester, Tennessee, on the eighteenth to hunt a stray horse and had not been heard from since. Turner was the son of George H. Fisher, 72, a farmer of Marshall County, Tennessee. George was a brother of Jacob Fisher, grandfather of the five brothers Fisher.[18]

The unhappy termination of Turner Fisher's volunteer enlistment was not at all unusual for a private soldier of his age. Experience proved time and again that older men were less likely to be able to adjust to and endure the rigors of field and camp life in the army. A rigorously applied system of medical examinations should have winnowed him out and saved him and the army a lot of grief. But many volunteers early in the war were not examined to see if they were fit to serve, although army medical regulations in 1861 provided for examinations of all soldiers.[19] Before an effective screening system was established, many volunteers were accepted who were ill-prepared to endure life in camp and on the field.

Despite defections such as that of Turner Fisher, members of the volunteer Tennessee units that went off to war in 1861 and 1862 were most often organized on a community or county basis pursuant to the state's militia law. They usually felt they were a team as a company or regiment, electing

Lieutenant General Nathan Bedford Forrest

their own officers, both commissioned and non-commissioned. Troops and units became objects of community pride and members felt a strong bonding which saw many of them through the cruelest experiences on the field and kept others together through disappointment and disaster.

The Confederate army, however, faced some peculiarly difficult problems which eventually overcame much of the bonding of the soldiery and produced widespread and fatal disaffections. Records of the personnel of the two companies in which the five Fisher brothers served make clear the extent of the problems faced.

Before the ultimate failure of Southern arms became widely apparent, however, members of volunteer units endured army commanders whom they neither liked nor respected. Some soldiers concluded that the election of officers by their peers in volunteer units produced, on balance, a better product than did the appointment of senior staff by senior officers.

Edmund Kirby Smith, heading the Department of East Tennessee in a strongly Unionist area, first moved his headquarters from Chattanooga to Knoxville and then took his army north, on August 14, 1862, bypassing Cumberland Gap, into Kentucky, hoping to encourage latent support for the Southern Confederacy in the Bluegrass State.

With no chief of cavalry in Smith's department, the cavalry brigade of Colonel John S. Scott of Louisiana filed out of Kingston, Tennessee, on the night of August 13 and traversed 160 miles north in seventy hours over the rugged Cumberland Mountains in close support of Smith's infantry. On the seventeenth, at London, Kentucky, Scott's brigade fell upon a battalion of the Third Tennessee Volunteer Infantry Regiment, U.S.A., under Colonel Leonidas C. Houk, and drove Houk's battalion out of town.

On August 23, Scott's brigade again encountered the Third Tennessee Volunteer Infantry, U.S.A., this time at Big Hill on the road to Lexington. Scott ordered an attack and his brigade drove the East Tennessee Unionists back to Richmond, Kentucky.[20]

Starnes' Fourth Tennessee Cavalry Regiment reinforced Scott's brigade on August 27, having crossed the mountains into Kentucky via Big Creek Gap. On the thirtieth, after an infantry engagement at Richmond ended in a precipitous retreat of Union forces toward Lexington, Scott's reinforced cavalry, sent to the rear of the enemy to cut off a retreat, forced the surrender of half the Union troops on the ground.

On September 3, 1862, Scott's brigade captured Frankfort, the Kentucky capital. Then on September 6, Smith reported that Scott's cavalry had gone well beyond Frankfort to within twelve miles of Louisville.[21]

Smith's Confederate forces were joined by those of General Braxton Bragg, and Bragg assumed command of Smith's forces on October 2, 1862, this after Bragg's army had begun marching to Kentucky from Chattanooga on August 28.

Bragg witnessed the inauguration of Richard Hawes in Frankfort on

October 4 as governor of a provisional Confederate State of Kentucky just prior to the retaking of the state's capital by Union forces. Scott's cavalry continued to picket about Frankfort and reported on October 6 and 7, first, that the Yankees were shelling the town, and second, that 20,000 Union infantry were crossing the Kentucky River at Frankfort.[22]

The combined Confederate army, under Bragg, fought a battle at Perryville on the eighth against a superior Union army under Major General Don Carlos Buell and drove the latter back from the Chaplin River. The river's water was the principal objective of the contending armies owing to a seasonal drought.[23] But the Confederate forces were not equal to the task of remaining in their advanced position in Kentucky owing to insufficient support of Kentuckians for the Southern cause.

Company D, Jim Fisher's company in the Fourth Tennessee Cavalry, managed to enlist nine recruits in the Kentucky campaign from September 6 to October 5. Thomas J. Bryant, J.H. Redman, John Slucer, H.B. Tinsley, Thaddeus Yunt, Daniel Monnigan, and R.H. Bryant enlisted at Frankfort in September. J.T. Cowper and J.W. Sutt joined at Versailles on October 5. The company's only casualty in Kentucky was Henry C. Call, captured in September but exchanged on January 11, 1863, and returned to duty.[24]

Bragg's and Smith's combined forces began their retreat from Kentucky back to East Tennessee on October 10 with the army in poor condition but intact and claiming a vast amount of captured supplies.

At that time, Jim Fisher and the other men of the Fourth were a part of Brigadier General John Pegram's cavalry brigade, assigned to Brigadier General Henry Heth's infantry division. On October 31, they were at Cumberland and Big Creek gaps in East Tennessee.

They moved to Middle Tennessee with other Bragg forces for a major invasion and became a part of a cavalry force of about 3,000 under Brigadier General Nathan Bedford Forrest on November 5 in a demonstration in Nashville's southern and eastern suburbs against a Federal force of over 12,000 which was defending Nashville under Brigadier General James S. Negley.

Starnes' Fourth, together with the battalion of D.C. Douglass, soon to be a part of the Eleventh Tennessee Cavalry, proceeding north on the Nolensville Road, attacked Union troops within three miles of the city and were engaged in the city's suburbs on the Nolensville, Mill Creek, and Franklin pikes leading into Nashville before they retired.[25]

The Fourth accompanied Forrest in his expedition into West Tennessee beginning December 15, 1862, via a Tennessee River crossing near Clifton in which the regiment attacked Humboldt, Tennessee, on the nineteenth, took 100 prisoners, destroyed the stockade and the railroad depot, and burned a nearby railroad trestle.

Forrest's raid ended with a narrow escape from entrapment in the Battle of Parker's Crossroads on December 31, 1862, a battle in which the Fourth was heavily engaged in cutting off the retreat of a Federal brigade under Colonel Cyrus L. Dunham, capturing its supply train, and warmly attacking Dunham's troops so as to prevent the springing of a trap when Forrest was caught between Dunham and fresh troops under Brigadier General Jeremiah C. Sullivan.[26]

At the end of 1862, Jim Fisher's Company D had suffered no reported casualties in West Tennessee but had lost eight discharged soldiers, according to their service records. Discharges were issued beginning with W. Pinckney Ledford, 25, discharged on July 23 after having been left sick at Chattanooga on May 6. Ledford was followed by Littlebury J. Swiney, 29, discharged on September 26. The reason for these two discharges was not given in the soldiers' service records.

Milton C. Stegall was discharged on November 13 after complaining of being under age. The statement regarding Stegall on the Company D muster roll dated May 26, 1862, states: "Claims to be only sixteen and I suppose correctly." A similar claim was made by William D. Swiney, who enlisted in November 1861 claiming to be old enough for military service. "Claims to be under 18," however, is noted on the company's muster roll in May. Swiney was discharged on November 13, 1862, as was Woodson C. Gates, 42, who had *understated* his age when he enlisted in 1861.

Two more soldiers were discharged on December 11 because they were over age 35. They were William Crabtree and Alexander M. Endsley.

The greatest single source of loss in 1862 in Company D derived from fourteen soldiers who were reported absent without leave and for whom there are no subsequent military records. They were: Allen Darnell, 18; William Baldin, 25; Elisha P. Harrison, 26; William R. Smith, 39; Henry Lawwell, 27; Melchisedec B. Muse, 20; Benjamin F. Lents, 22; George Smith, 31; Samuel J. Sutton, 30; John H. White, 30; Richard A. Harrison, 23; William W. McCullough; Samuel C. Brown; and Henry H. Glasscock, 19.

Note that ages of soldiers, where recorded in their service records and shown herein, are virtually all the ages reported by each soldier at his enlistment. They are not necessarily the true age of each soldier. "Service Records" does not record the ages of all soldiers in Company D of the Fourth or Company C of the Eleventh. Hence the omission of ages of some soldiers.

The 14 soldiers listed above, together with another, John L. Houston, 21, reported "wounded and presumed dead" at Paint Rock on May 18, and yet another, William W. Walker, 20, absent, no reason given, for whom there are no subsequent service records, are the missing soldiers of Company D in 1862, a total of sixteen.

Company D recorded a deserter in 1862, William M. Meadows, 32, one of the company's original enlistees. Meadows was reported a deserter on December 8 and afterward resisted arrest when troops were sent after him. At Cornersville in Giles County, Meadows shot and wounded one arresting soldier and mortally wounded another. He continued to resist until the house from which he was shooting was set afire.

Meadows' court-martial was held February 8, 1863. The accused was found guilty of three of five charges and was sentenced to death by firing squad in the presence of the troops of his brigade. The sentence was scheduled to be executed on Thursday, February 26, 1863. Meadows being ill, execution of his sentence was postponed until Friday, March 13.[27]

On September 30, 1862, when he was 18, Thomas Fisher joined a company of partisan rangers organized by Captain T.C.H. Miller, 54, a well-to-do farmer of Chapel Hill, Marshall County, Tennessee. Fisher enlisted for three years. His horse was valued at $200 and his equipment $12 when he volunteered.[28]

His company's recruitment was timely. It occurred a few days after the issuance of an order on September 25 by General Braxton Bragg to Brigadier General Nathan Bedford Forrest to return to Middle Tennessee from Kentucky, there to raise four regiments of infantry and two of cavalry, muster them into the Confederate service and operate with them on partisan service against the enemy in all practicable ways, cutting off supplies, capturing trains, continually harassing and intimidating the Federals and giving them no rest.[29] The new company of partisans was ready-made, after training, field experience, and seasoning, to implement Bragg's order.

Tom volunteered along with a number of other local men and boys including his brothers John Franklin, 31; William Stratton, 20; and Elisha Monroe, 26, the last enlisting for the second time. Each of them was an accomplished horseman with access to good riding animals from their father's pastures. They had not been swept away by the war hysteria which had emotionally moved so many young men to join the colors in the spring and summer of 1861, believing that the fight would be a short, painless, and glorious one. On the contrary, they ostensibly were still Unionists then.

The Confederate government had enacted a conscription act, "An Act to further provide for the public defense," on April 16, 1862, America's first conscription law, which conscripted white male citizens aged 18 to 35.[30] The Fishers may have been subject thereto morally but not actually since they lived in an area which was not then under the control of the Confederate government.

By the time they joined, they must have known that the conflict was already painful and destructive and likely to be protracted. From the beginning, the war in the central South had not gone well for the Confederacy. And the policy of the Richmond authorities in giving priority in men, animals, forage, materiel, and strategic importance to the Army of Northern Virginia made the Southern war effort outside Virginia's borders more difficult to wage than it should have been.[31]

On January 19–20, 1862, a Confederate invasion force under Brigadier General George B. Crittenden was decisively defeated and turned back by a Union army under Brigadier General George H. Thomas of Virginia at the Battle of Fishing Creek, Mill Springs, Somerset, or Logan's Crossroads (the same battle) in Kentucky.[32] This battle opened up East Tennessee, with its large Unionist population, to occupation by Federal forces.

Owing to the influence of a Mississippi River bloc of constituents who primarily feared a Yankee invasion down the Mississippi River which, members of the bloc believed, would likely foment a slave insurrection, most Tennessee troops under General Albert Sidney Johnston were placed in a position to defend West Tennessee rather than Nashville or East Tennessee, which were key to the defense of the Confederacy.[33]

Accordingly, Federal troops captured forts Henry and Donelson and occupied Nashville in February 1862. Nashville soon would become the principal Union command and supply center in the West. Generals Grant and Sherman, successively commanding the Military District of the Mississippi, made the city their headquarters.

On April 6–7, Union troops under Grant and Major General Don Carlos Buell defeated a Confederate army under generals Albert Sidney Johnston and Pierre G.T. Beauregard at Shiloh, Tennessee, in the first great battle of the war. Total casualties were almost 24,000, including almost 3,500 known killed. Almost 22 percent of close to 110,000 combatants were casualties, with over 16,000 wounded and almost 4,000 missing.[34]

The next day, a great Federal push began down the Mississippi to sever in twain the Confederate States. A Confederate garrison of 7,000 and the river fortifications on Island No. 10 in the Mississippi River at the Kentucky-Tennessee border were surrendered to a Union force of close to 20,000 under Major General John Pope. This surrender opened up the Mississippi to Union forces south to Ft. Pillow, fifty miles above Memphis.

On April 11, a Federal force of about 5,000 under Major General Ormsby M. Mitchell proceeded from Murfreesboro, Tennessee, south via Shelbyville (only seventeen miles from the Fishers' home) and Fayetteville, to capture Huntsville, Alabama.[35] The war was getting very close indeed to those of the Fishers who were still at home.

Then on April 24, a U.S. naval fleet under the command of David Glasgow Farragut of Tennessee passed up the Mississippi River beyond the protecting forts and captured New Orleans.[36]

Ft. Pillow's Confederate garrison vacated its position and surrendered on June 3, and Memphis fell to Union forces three days later after a brief bombardment and the destruction of a vaunted but quite vulnerable Confederate river fleet. By June 18, Cumberland Gap, the defensive position on a major passage at the juncture of the Kentucky-Tennessee-Virginia state lines, was in Union hands. And on August 28, Braxton Bragg began his march from Chattanooga north on his Kentucky Campaign, described above, from which he began his retreat back to Tennessee on October 10.[37]

All these Confederate reverses in and around Tennessee formed the backdrop for the decision of the brothers Fisher to actively join the struggle of the Confederacy.

Thomas Fisher, late in his life, wrote that he volunteered for army service because he came to believe that the rights of the Southern people were being overridden and their institutions imperiled. Of course, it is quite possible that he believed as he did because he accepted what his role models, local and state politicians, newspaper editors, and leading planters, business, and professional men, led him to believe. But he also would have wanted to serve because he had a brother, cousins, and neighbors who were already in the struggle, and he would not have wished to turn his back on them.

Fisher wrote that he never believed it was right to hold people as slaves. But he said that he never agreed with the way slavery was abolished.[38] Although he did not specify the source of his disagreement, one might believe that he disapproved of abolition by force of arms and with no recompense to slaveholders for their loss of property.

While slavery was within the mores of the Southern culture and regarded as essential to group welfare, Thomas Fisher indicated by his disapproval of slavery that he was at odds with one of the critical folkways of the time and place. If indeed he was, he was not unlike some men of classical Greece who, in the time of Aristotle, said that "slavery was an injustice due to violence and established by law."[39]

But his decision to defend home and country must have been both painful and thoughtful rather than exuberantly euphoric, as he waited until the initial secession hysteria had subsided and a succession of Union successes had placed his county, state, and region well within Union lines and given him little reason or evidence to be optimistic about the ultimate success of Confederate arms.

Despite the overwhelming evidence that they were championing a lost cause, the Fisher brothers made their decisions and obviously meant to adhere to them to the end. Each of them enlisted for three years as required by law. They became members of T.C.H. Miller's company of partisan rangers and remained in the same company throughout the war.

Their company was reported to Forrest and sworn into the service of the Confederate States in October at Murfreesboro, Rutherford County, Tennessee, a town which was only temporarily occupied by Bragg's army.

But Forrest did not immediately attach their company to a command. The company had been organized pursuant to an authorization to Alexander Winn,[30] a schoolmaster of College Grove, Williamson County, to raise a battalion. Winn, who joined the army early in 1861 along with a number of his students, became adjutant of the Twentieth Tennessee Infantry Regiment, then sought to raise his own company of cavalry.

But Winn could not give bond, in consequence of the enemy having possession of his home and property in Williamson County. After it was ascertained that Winn would not get his cavalry command, the company acted with a battalion commanded by Major D.C. Douglass beginning in late October 1862.[40]

While his fresh new company served with the Douglass battalion, Thomas Fisher met for the first time the man whose surname he had been given at birth by his parents. On an October day when Fisher, freshly sworn into military service, was standing picket on the Nashville turnpike seven miles north of Murfreesboro, William Burr, along with a colleague, Larry Bryant, came through the military lines north to south on their way to the Tennessee Annual Conference, held that year in the village of Cornersville in Giles County. Fisher chatted with the two clergymen and, one hopes, found Burr to be everything his admiring parents said he was.

Methodist clerics were required to be hardy men in those days. They must have slept out on the ground while attending the annual conference that year, a conference which lasted six days, October 15–20, the last Tennessee Annual Conference held for the balance of the war.[41] Cornersville's amenities were severely limited then as now and taxed and tested the vigor, resolve, and affability of conference attendees.

As members of the Douglass battalion, two of the enlistees in T.C.H. Miller's new partisan ranger company saw action near Nashville in November 1862 and were captured. The fate of J.M. Aldridge, 24, following his capture is unknown. But J.T. Davis, 24, captured on November 20, 1862, near Nashville, was sent to and arrived at the military prison at Alton, Illinois, on January 10, 1863. He was exchanged at City Point, Virginia, on April 1, 1863, and returned to his company. He would be captured again later in 1863 but would not be so fortunate in being able to return to his comrades in arms in his second encounter with prison life.

Jesse N. Bryan of Company C of the Eleventh Tennessee Cavalry, for whatever reason, accompanied Nathan Bedford Forrest in West Tennessee in December 1862. He was captured at Lexington on the way in and admitted to the U.S. Army General Hospital in Jackson, Tennessee, on January 6, 1863. Discharged from the hospital on January 10, he was received at the military prison in Alton, Illinois, on February 2 and died therein of variola on February 22, 1863.[42]

When Forrest was ordered by General Braxton Bragg to break up the enemy's communications and to demonstrate in the rear of Major General Ulysses S. Grant's forces in West Tennessee, Bragg appointed West Point-trained, twenty-six-year-old Brigadier General Joseph Wheeler to relieve Forrest as commander of cavalry in his department.[43]

Bragg believed that the self-taught Forrest was best suited to recruitment, arming recruits with enemy captures, and applied training of recruits in small-scale partisan warfare rather than to command of permanent large-scale military forces. Bragg, of course, might be excused for his assessment of Forrest's capabilities at this point in the conflict (late 1862). In time other contemporaries, American generals Sherman, Lee, and J.E. Johnston, British

Major General Joseph Wheeler

Field Marshal Viscount Wolseley, Commander-in-Chief of Her Majesty's Forces, and Confederate President Jefferson Davis, however, saw Forrest quite differently.[44]

Forrest was born and reared in the village of Chapel Hill in Bedford (later Marshall) County, Tennessee, only ten miles north of the birthplace of the Fisher brothers between Farmington and Verona in the same county. His superior, Bragg, continued to be shortsighted in his evaluation of Forrest's successes, a purblindness which led to a bitter confrontation between the two in October 1863 in which Forrest, with the greatest candor, refused to serve under Bragg in the future and threatened his life should he thereafter cross his path.

Bragg was having difficulty with other senior officers, for which seemingly he was not altogether blameworthy. Shortly after the Forrest confrontation, Bragg approved Forrest's transfer to Mississippi and the department commanded by General Joseph E. Johnston.[45]

Some students of the military have come to believe that Forrest, the subject of eight major biographies to date, was the most striking military leader produced in the Civil War and that the South might have had a better chance to win its fight for independence had its leaders given Forrest the larger role that his successes insistently indicated he could have handled.

But Forrest was not a member of the tightly-knit elitist club which controlled the destiny of the Confederacy. Thus the opportunity to use his skills effectively on a grander scale was lost.

Soldiers who served under Forrest were devoted to him even though they might not approve of everything he did in his interpersonal relations. Forrest sometimes was violent and out of control in one-on-one encounters. But in combat he was consistently resourceful and firmly in command.

Some volunteer soldiers might not have wanted to work for him in peacetime. But most apparently believed he was, in wartime, the best, most decisive, most often right battle leader that one could hope to follow. He understood the goals to be sought in battle and motivated by his own example, his courage, attention to detail, professional bearing, and tactical brilliance.

William Shakespeare described King Henry V, leading his troops at the Battle of Agincourt, in words that are as apt for Forrest:

> In peace there's nothing so becomes a man
> As modest stillness and humility;
> But when the blast of war blows in our ears,
> Then imitate the action of the tiger:
> Stiffen the sinews, summon up the blood,
> Disguise fair nature with hard-favour's rage;
> Then lend the eye a terrible aspect.[46]

T.C.H. Miller's company did not go with Forrest to West Tennessee in December 1862, but instead operated under Wheeler's command out of northwest Rutherford County in the vicinity of LaVergne, near where members of the company subsequently participated in their first ordeal by fire at the Battle of Murfreesboro, or Stones River, from December 31, 1862, to January 2, 1863.

Wheeler's cavalry held a position fifteen miles in advance of Bragg's main force, which numbered almost 38,000, including close to 4,000 cavalry in three brigades. The cavalry under Wheeler's direct command was based just south of the town of LaVergne on the turnpike between Murfreesboro and Nashville. It had engaged in a number of sharp skirmishes with the enemy during the two weeks before Christmas.[47]

There was other cavalry attached to Bragg's army, two brigades which operated under two subordinates to Wheeler, brigadier generals John Pegram and John A. Wharton. But they were not usually under Wheeler's immediate command in the operations leading up to and including the battle along Stones River just northwest of Murfreesboro.

Wheeler pushed forward to within sight of Nashville on the twenty-second and noted that the activity he observed indicated that Major General William S. Rosecrans was getting ready to move out. Rosecrans' actual advance on Murfreesboro began the day after Christmas.[48]

Wheeler's forces began engaging the advancing Union army, numbering close to 60,000 in three corps, on December 27, having been ordered to impede the advance for four days in order to give Bragg the time he needed to concentrate his army in line of battle just to the north of Stones River outside Murfreesboro. For three days, the cavalry made repeated stands against the advancing army, breaking off whenever the weight of numbers dictated the advisability of a discretionary retreat.

On the night of December 29, Wheeler took a position on the right flank of Bragg's army at Stones River while Rosecrans' army arrived in the vicinity of the battleground on the afternoon of the thirtieth. As soon as Wheeler, after three days of riding and dogged fighting, joined Bragg's army at Stones River, he was ordered at midnight on the twenty-ninth to take his exhausted troops on a circuit of the federal army.

In company with Wharton's brigade now, Wheeler's cavalry passed between the Federal army and Nashville in a wide sweeping arc from east to west. Returning to the vicinity of their old base near LaVergne and sweeping west to the Nolensville road, they captured hundreds of troops and enough rifles and ammunition to arm a brigade.

Wheeler remounted a portion of his troops and destroyed hundreds of wagons loaded with over a million dollars' worth of commissary stores. And this was accomplished without the loss of a single soldier killed. Then Wheeler rejoined the main army, this time occupying a position on the left flank of Bragg's army, next to Lieutenant General William J. Hardee's corps and opposite Major General Alexander M. McCook's corps, on the morning of December 31, with fighting at Stones River already underway.[49]

On the field at Stones River, the battle on the first day resulted in a turning of the Union right and an apparently decisive Confederate victory, but with heavy losses. Wheeler was then ordered out the next morning to hit the Union army in retreat.

But he found it was not in retreat. He found only hospital trains returning to Nashville with the wounded. Wheeler rode on as far north as La-Vergne, over half the 32-mile distance to Nashville, where he fell upon wagons and stores on their way to the front. Upon retiring to his own lines, Wheeler reported that the Federals were digging in and bringing up fresh supplies.[50]

The second day, January 1, 1863, was given over by both armies to retrieving the dead and wounded on the battlefield rather than, as expected, to Rosecrans retreating or Bragg initiating an attack.

The third and last day was mostly quiet except for efforts to gain information about what the other army was doing, plus a disastrous assault on a ridge on the Confederate right by Bragg's Kentucky infantry under Major General John C. Breckenridge which began at four in the afternoon. The ridge was taken, then lost, at a cost of over 1,300 casualties.[51]

The next morning, Bragg decided to withdraw his army from Murfreesboro in the direction of Chattanooga owing to heavy casualties, the realization that Rosecrans' army was much larger than his, and the real possibility that he would lose his army if he stayed and Rosecrans attacked. The Army of Tennessee withdrew to a portion of the Highland Rim which surrounds the Nashville Basin around the towns of Shelbyville, Wartrace, and Winchester in the direction of Chattanooga.[52]

Wheeler's corps, full of raw recruits who still were learning to fight, scout, and destroy by fighting, scouting, and destroying, formed an unsteady but largely resilient buffer for the main army as it retreated southeastward from Stones River and Murfreesboro.

Chapter 2

The Year 1863 through Streight's Raid, January 3–May 3, 1863

Immediately after the Battle of Stones River or Murfreesboro, Holman's and Douglass's battalions, as parts of Wheeler's cavalry, remained in Murfreesboro after Bragg's army retired to the southeast. The troops skirmished with the enemy on the evening of Sunday, January 4, 1863.[1]

At 3 P.M. on Monday the fifth, Wheeler's corps warmly opposed a strong enemy advance on Murfreesboro and halted it. Then on January 8, the cavalry moved north on a raid to the Cumberland River and destroyed a railroad bridge over Mill Creek near Nashville and a Union construction train nearby.[2]

On January 12, Wheeler's raiders drove a Union foraging train into Nashville. On the thirteenth and fourteenth, they captured a gunboat and two transports and destroyed military stores at Ashland City, west of Nashville.

On January 25, they captured a construction train near Antioch, southeast of Nashville in Davidson County. On the seventeenth, a detachment under Major Daniel W. Holman had captured another Union transport on the Cumberland River.

Wheeler attacked a Federal force defending Fort Donelson with the intention of taking and holding the fort and thereby being in a position to interdict Federal waterborne shipping from the north into Nashville. For the attack, Wheeler was reinforced by a cavalry force commanded by Nathan Bedford Forrest which Wheeler had ordered from Columbia, Tennessee, to the vicinity of Dover, below Nashville on the Cumberland River.

The attack failed. Forrest had two horses shot out from under him and suffered what he regarded as insupportable losses to his command. After the battle, Forrest, with characteristic candor, reminded Wheeler that he had advised against the attack and requested that Wheeler say in his report to Braxton Bragg that he (Forrest) "will be in my coffin before I will fight again under your command."

Wheeler, apparently without animosity toward Forrest, took the respon-

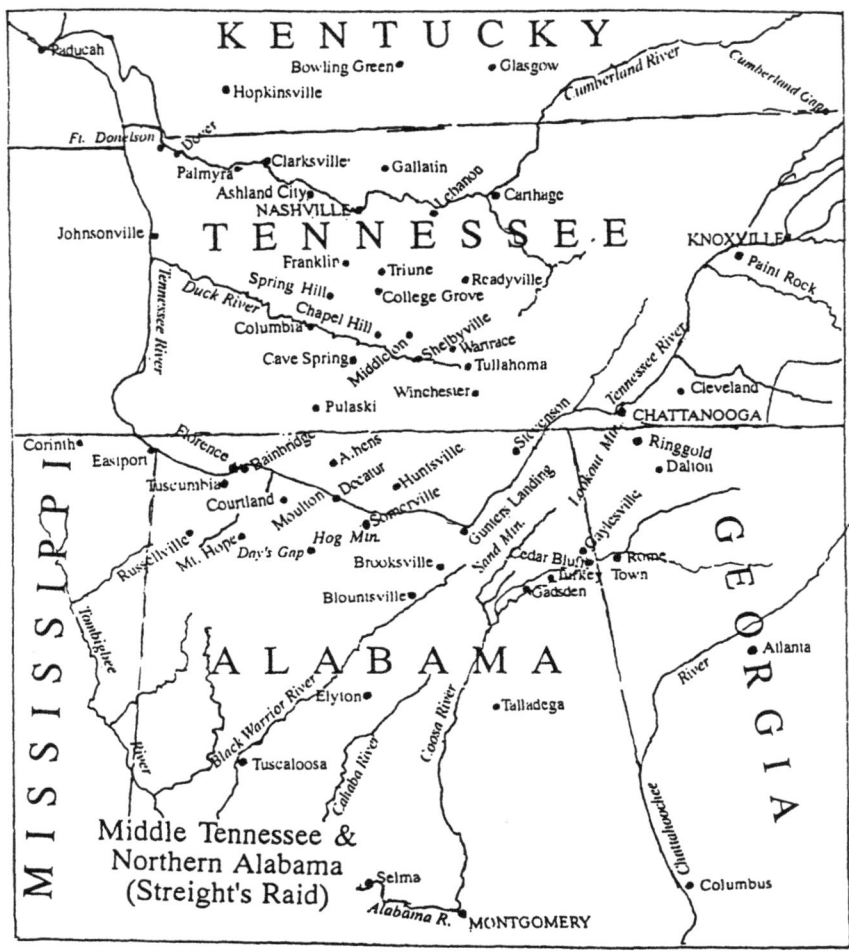

Middle Tennessee & Northern Alabama (Streight's Raid)

sibility for the failure of the attack. He and Forrest went their separate ways and saw little of each other for the balance of the war.[3]

In the Confederate cavalry's actions after the fall of Murfreesboro and ending with the aborted action against the garrison at Fort Donelson, Company D of the Fourth Tennessee, in which Jim Fisher served, lost only one soldier, John Anderson, missing after the battle at Dover on February 3. Company C of the Eleventh, in which Jim's brothers served, lost John Carter, captured at Murfreesboro on January 5, 1863. But the company, on January 31, suffered the capture and loss of twelve private soldiers and two sergeants, a not inconsequential loss to the company's strength. The loss, however, proved to be temporary. All captives were held briefly then exchanged within a period of a few weeks or months.

For Captain T.C.H. Miller's company, the suffered loss was in connection with the capture of Major D.C. Douglass, battalion commander, one captain, a lieutenant, and forty-one men on January 31, 1863, near Middleton, four miles east of Unionville in Bedford County.

Captured soldiers from Company C were sergeants Joseph A. Billington and Peter M.W. McConnell, plus Theodore Riggs Adams, John H. Bruce, W.D. Chrisman, W.S. Fisher, J.Z.B. Hunter, J.W. Little, Benjamin C. Primrose, W.G. Reynolds, Edward D. Royster, Samuel A. Smith, James Chesley Williams, and W.H. Williamson.[4]

Officers and men were surprised and overrun by the Second and Third Tennessee cavalry regiments, U.S.A., each recruited in East Tennessee in the summer and fall of 1862.[5] The Second and Third Tennessee were units of the U.S. First Division, XX Army Corps, Army of the Cumberland, under the command of Brigadier General Jefferson C. Davis, U.S.A., of Indiana, an officer who, on September 29, 1862, allegedly shot and killed his superior, Major General William Nelson, while Nelson, commanding the Army of Kentucky, Department of the Ohio, was organizing the defense of Louisville against Kirby Smith's Kentucky invaders. Although Davis was arrested and confined, he was soon released and returned to his command reportedly because there were insufficient officers available to convene a court-martial.[6]

One of the captives near Middleton was William Stratton Fisher of T.C.H. Miller's company. Will and the other enlisted prisoners were sent by rail to Fort McHenry, Baltimore, Maryland, for incarceration, arriving on February 15. Will was a prisoner almost four months.

He was exchanged at Fortress Monroe, Hampton, Virginia, in June, with permission to go home for a brief rest and to get more adequate clothing. At Shelbyville, Tennessee, however, with only a few more miles to go, Will broke out with measles, a major source of death in the army, and was sent to a hospital at Ringgold, Georgia.

A fellow prisoner and neighbor, Wesley Williamson, who was returning home in Will's company, brought the news of Will's illness to his parents, John and Mildred Fisher. Wesley Williamson, after the war, would marry one of Will's cousins, Elizabeth Fisher, on December 9, 1866. Upon hearing the news of his son's illness, John Fisher, justifiably fearing the worst about conditions in field hospitals, went at once to Ringgold, found Will and stayed to nurse him back to health, thus insuring that his son did not die from neglect.

When he was well enough to travel, Will was granted leave to return to his home for further convalescence. On June 29, 1863, when he had regained sufficient strength, Will came back to his company and served, with two more brief furloughs for health reasons in 1864, to the end of the war. His health, however, continued to decline even as he remained in the field and jeopardized his hopes for longevity in the years after the war.[7]

In the absence of Major Douglass, T.C.H. Miller, by common consent, commanded the Douglass battalion until the component companies were ordered to report to Nathan Bedford Forrest at Columbia, seat of Maury County, at the end of February. Forrest then merged the Douglass and Holman battalions with two other companies, Charles McDonald's (originally Company K of the Third, Forrest's "Old Regiment") and Phil T. Allin's (a consolidation of two companies commanded by Captain W.H. Forrest and Captain James H. Edmundson) to form the Eleventh Tennessee Cavalry. The new regiment then became a part of Forrest's "Old Brigade."

Other original elements of Forrest's "Old Brigade" included George G. Dibrell's Eighth Tennessee, J.B. Biffle's Ninth Tennessee, and A.A. Russell's Fourth Alabama, along with Forrest's staff and artillery, the latter under the command of Samuel L. Freeman until his death in battle in April 1863, then by John W. Morton.[8] When the Eleventh Tennessee was formed and joined the brigade in late February, Russell's Fourth Alabama was transferred to one of Joe Wheeler's Alabama brigades.[9]

Colonel James H. Edmundson of Memphis was the Eleventh's first commanding officer. But Edmundson's selection was unpopular and he resigned later in the year, but only after the regiment had performed well under his leadership. Thereupon Colonel D.W. Holman of Fayetteville, after recovering from wounds he had received at Fort Donelson, assumed command.[10]

Thus the company of partisan rangers which four of the Fisher brothers joined in the fall of 1862 ceased to some extent to have the mark of its original wild and untamed character. It was incorporated into a regiment and made a part of a brigade which was making a name for itself under the command of Nathan Bedford Forrest.

But Douglass's battalion was partially made up, characteristically for partisan companies, of a group of nonconformists who were particularly insistent that Tennessee volunteers had the right and privilege of electing their own officers rather than having them assigned by corps commanders. And they were not mollified by the dubious honor of becoming a cog in a larger military body.

Some of the battalion's officers, namely, captains Nathan W. Carter, Richard McCann, and Felix H. Blackman, objected so strenuously to their consolidation into a regiment and their loss of volunteer partisan status that Forrest felt constrained to clap them in jail in Columbia to cool them off. When Major General Earl Van Dorn arrived from Mississippi to take command of the cavalry in late February, he had them released, and they rejoined their respective companies.[11]

But the dissension in the small world of Forrest's, then Van Dorn's, cavalry apparently was nothing contrasted to what was going on in the early months of 1863 in and about Tullahoma involving Bragg's differences with his top generals. Bragg's competence to lead the army was candidly questioned by members of his top staff and the names of possible successors were broached. Subsequently Bragg moved against some of his subordinates and placed the blame on them for his army's lack of success.

Bragg first filed a charge against Major General John Porter McCown of Tennessee who was court-martialed, convicted of ordering unauthorized details of officers and men to Charleston and other places, and suspended from his command for six months.

After prolonged acrimony between Bragg and Major General John C. Breckenridge of Kentucky, Breckenridge, alleged to be a heavy drinker, was transferred out of the army to Mississippi. And Bragg, in his official report on the Battle of Murfreesboro, failed to include the name of a citizen-soldier, Major General Frank Cheatham of Tennessee, an omission which almost caused Cheatham to resign and provoked continuing and strong enmity between Bragg and Cheatham. Further, there was open hostility between Bragg and two of his corps commanders, Leonidas Polk and William J. Hardee.[12]

Army politics fed by personal prejudices was rife in the upper echelons of the Army of Tennessee. And its prevalence tended to weaken efforts to get the army ready for the next challenge it faced from the enemy.

Graduating from raids and running skirmishes, the men of the Fourth and Eleventh Tennessee cavalry regiments saw action in early March 1863 against a substantial force of infantry and cavalry at Thompson's Station. Van Dorn's Confederate cavalry was quartered near Spring Hill when a large forage train of wagons was sent out south from Franklin, guarded by a strong force of Union cavalry and infantry under Colonel John Coburn of Indiana, a force which was to juncture at Spring Hill with another column sent out from Murfreesboro to the east under Brigadier General Philip H. Sheridan.

Coburn's force began to encounter reconnoitering Confederates only four miles south of its base at Franklin. But Coburn pushed on to just north of Thompson's Station, where he encountered the Confederate cavalry in force under Major General Earl Van Dorn on the morning of March 5.

Coburn commanded a force of four infantry regiments, a battery, and cavalry, numbering about 2,800 men in all. He was opposed by Confederate cavalry, no infantry, drawn up across the highway, dismounted, with Forrest's brigade, including Freeman's battery, posted well out to the right, a force of about 7,000.

Coburn's artillery opened fire. Then the Federal infantry on the right charged a Confederate battery. A countercharge by a superior Confederate force of dismounted cavalry followed, and fighting continued briskly with charge and countercharge ensuing for several hours.

The Confederate right, made up primarily of men of the Fourth and Eleventh Tennessee cavalry regiments, bore the brunt of the fighting amongst the units of Forrest's brigade. The tide finally turned for the larger force when Forrest ordered in Cox's Tenth and Biffle's Nineteenth Tennessee regiments late in the afternoon. The latter units, held in reserve, provided the leverage needed to win the battle.

With Forrest personally leading the assault on the right flank, the movement caved in the enemy's left flank, turning them back toward the Franklin Road, at the juncture of which, the infantry threw down their arms and surrendered.

Fighting ceased at about four o'clock in the afternoon, six hours after the two forces first faced each other across the gently undulating land of Thompson's Station. Over 1,200 captives were taken by Van Dorn, including Colonel Coburn and a total of seventy-eight officers. Most of the Federal cavalry and artillery was able to return to Franklin.[13]

Thomas Fisher fired twenty-three rounds in the engagement and, while firing from the protection of a rock wall, was struck by an almost-spent Minié ball which had force enough to cut through the cape of his overcoat but not enough to pass through his body. He experienced considerable pain from the shot, so much that he handed his gun to Lieutenant Frank Rainey of Chapel Hill and walked back some distance, taking hold of his right arm with his left hand, turning and twisting the arm to see if it were broken. Although the pain persisted, he became satisfied that he was not seriously wounded, returned to his place in line, reloaded his gun and resumed firing.

Not so lucky as Fisher was Alfred A. Dysart, 29, Captain of Company D of Starnes' Fourth Tennessee Cavalry in which Jim Fisher served. Dysart was a neighbor of the Fishers in Marshall County's Sixth Civil District who lived alone and described his occupation to his census taker in 1860 as simply "gentleman." He had gone to Camp Cheatham and enlisted in Company D on November 16, 1861, along with Jim and Monroe Fisher and other neighbors. He, along with Monroe, was elected first lieutenant by his comrades. He became company captain in June 1862.

At Thompson's Station, he was mortally wounded by a shot through his head. He died on March 8, 1863.

Other Company D casualties at Thompson's Station included James M. Bartlett, severely wounded in both legs, Corporal William R. Horton, wounded slightly in the shoulder, J.H. Pyland with a leg wound, Isaac A. Thomas, 27, with a gunshot wound in a hand, and A. Franklin Sumey, 38, with a wound in each hand. Sumey died six weeks later on May 18, 1863, in Franklin County, Tennessee, but his military record is silent on the cause of his death. J.W. Sutt of Company D was reportedly captured in the engagement and sent to Louisville, then to Baltimore, and finally to City Point, Virginia, for exchange. But there is no subsequent service record of Sutt.

John Bailey, 23, wounded, was the only casualty of record of Company C of the Eleventh at Thompson's Station.[14]

After the fight at Thompson's Station, the Confederate cavalry under Van Dorn, including both Starnes' Fourth and Edmundson's Eleventh, continued to operate from its base at Spring Hill. The ensuing weeks were spent in running fights and skirmishes in the vicinity of College Grove, Triune, Franklin, and Brentwood, the latter only twelve miles south of Nashville.

At Brentwood on March 25, Forrest captured an infantry garrison of over 750. The Fourth acted independently of the main attacking force, skirmished with Union cavalry on the Hillsboro Road west of Brentwood, but sustained no casualties in the action. Forrest intimidated the garrison's commander with a show of force and won a capitulation with virtually no casualties. The Eleventh Tennessee Cavalry was given charge of the prisoners and wagons and escorted them south to Columbia.[15]

On April 10, 1863, Forrest's brigade was proceeding north on the Lewisburg Pike about two miles from Franklin, a redoubtable Union base, when it was ambushed by the Fourth U.S. Cavalry at Douglas Church. Captain Samuel L. Freeman and a number of officers and men of his battery, as well as several field pieces, were captured. Members of the Confederate cavalry regiments present proceeded to exchange shots with the U.S. regulars, charged and recaptured the guns and most of the officers and men — all but Freeman and about thirty men. A member of the Fourth U.S., being anxious to disengage, and seeing that he could not get away with his captive, shot and killed Freeman.

This skirmish created great bitterness in the minds and hearts of troops of Forrest's "Old Brigade" toward soldiers of the Fourth U.S., a veritable "Foreign Legion" of immigrants, as were many U.S. regular units.

Members of these two enemy contingents met again late in the war on April 2, 1865, almost two years later, near Selma, Alabama, in what Federal authorities claimed was a wantonly murderous attack by Forrest's troops against defenseless, i.e., sleeping men. The Federal claim was denied by members of the attacking force.[16]

None of the Fisher brothers was a part of the latter attack. Frank, Monroe, Tom, and Will of the Eleventh were about thirty miles away to the north trying vainly to cross the flooded Cahaba River in order to join Forrest. Jim of the Fourth is believed to have been 600 miles away in North Carolina picketing and scouting between Sherman's and Johnston's armies in the area between Goldsboro and Raleigh.

Starnes' Fourth Tennessee Cavalry was just in the rear of Freeman's Battery when the engagement at Douglas Church commenced. H.B. Tinsley of Company D of the Fourth was captured in the action and reportedly forwarded to Nashville before the paper trail on him disappeared. Jim Fisher was among the wounded, the only member of Company D reported wounded in the action. He received a gunshot wound in the right thigh which entered near the groin. Being about twenty-five miles from home, he sought leave to receive treatment there. Upon receiving permission, he left at once, after getting word to Monroe, now in the Eleventh, that he was wounded and was going home.

At Bethesda, a village in Williamson County, a surgeon probed for the ball, but could not locate it. At Cave Spring, Francis Rice, whom Jim knew as a family physician, examined the patient, also could not locate the ball, but stated his belief that the projectile would become encysted and give Jim no trouble in the future. Within a month, Jim was back with his company and, it is believed, remained with it until its survivors surrendered near Washington, Georgia, on May 5, 1865.[17]

Cave Spring so far, and indeed throughout the war, was largely spared the worst of the wartime destruction which abounded in the state owing to its geographical location, which lacked strategic importance. Rather than being a center of production for strategic war materiel or on a major railroad, turnpike or river where it surely would have been occupied and reoccupied by contending armies during 1861–1865, it was part of an agricultural county which occupied a neutral eminence almost equidistant by close to twenty miles between two strategic rail lines, the Nashville & Decatur and the Nashville & Chattanooga.

John Fisher's farm was on Rock Creek, a tributary of Duck River, the latter flowing westward into the Tennessee. But the creek is well above the navigable portion of the Duck and therefore out of harm's way in terms of strategic wartime importance. Nor was the farm on a major turnpike which might have attracted contending armies to join battle on either side of the main house.

Several times during the war, of course, there were troop movements back across the pasture to the rear of the property as well as on the Verona to Farmington road, which ran east-west in front of the family residence's southern exposure.

Members of the Fisher family, and their servants, who remained at home, doubtless did not soon forget the urgent pounding of the hoofs of a thousand horses as they approached no one knew how close to the house and then retreated in the dark on an otherwise still morning before there was a hint of light or life stirring in man, beast, or fowl in the vicinity. John and Mildred Fisher could not have been unaware of policies promulgated by Major General David S. Stanley, chief of cavalry of the Army of the Cumberland during 1862 and 1863, which not only authorized but encouraged destruction of houses and other real and personal property of families with sons or near relatives in the Confederate service.

Brigadier James B. Steedman, commanding the Third Cavalry Division under Stanley, reported carrying out the policy relative to a skirmish near Chapel Hill, less than a dozen miles from Cave Spring, on April 13, 1863. In the instant action, hay and oats were mistakenly burned and lost in the destruction of a large barn on the property of a family with a son in the Confederate army. Of course, the preferred action was to take the forage for one's own use, then burn the barn.[18]

James Wesley's wounding and convalescence prevented his participating with his regiment, the Fourth Tennessee Cavalry, in one of the most unusual military actions of the war, i.e., the pursuit and capture of Colonel Abel D. Streight of the Fifty-First Indiana Volunteers and his picked raiders.

But Jim's four brothers of the Eleventh Tennessee, together with other elements of Forrest's brigade, joined in the pursuit of Streight's bold command in a wild ride and running fight of five days' and nights' duration across much of the width of Alabama and ending just short of the Georgia border near Cedar Bluff on May 3, 1863.

The raid was conceived by Streight as a means of destroying rail connections to Chattanooga from Atlanta and Knoxville, an eventuality that Streight believed would force the Confederates to abandon Chattanooga to Rosecrans' advancing armies as the latter pushed Bragg's forces south of Tullahoma. Bragg might opt to retreat to Dalton or Atlanta if he found that Chattanooga was untenable by virtue of its isolation from supplies and reinforcements from the south or east.

But if Bragg remained in and about Chattanooga, he likely could be dislodged only by the expenditure of numerous casualties owing to the difficulties posed by the geography and topography of the Chattanooga area as well as the defensive capability of Bragg's army.

A year earlier, Captain James J. Andrews, a Kentucky Unionist spy, had led a group of twenty-one soldiers, out of uniform, stolen the locomotive *General*, and attempted to destroy the bridges of the railroad between Chattanooga and Atlanta in a daring raid that sought the isolation of Chattanooga from support from the south. The venture failed, but its purpose was quite similar to that of Streight.

Streight submitted his plan to Brigadier General Thomas J. Wood who, in turn referred it to Rosecran's chief of staff, Brigadier General James A. Garfield. The plan was warmly approved and its details worked out meticulously.

The body of officers and men involved was specially selected, armed, and equipped according to the nature of the expedition, and designated an "independent provisional brigade designed for special secret service." It was made up of four regiments of mounted infantry, the Eighteenth Illinois, the Fifty-First and Seventy-Third Indiana, and the Third Ohio, together with two companies raised in northern Alabama and designated as the First Middle Tennessee Cavalry U.S.A., about 1,700 officers and men in all, according to Streight.[19]

The expedition left Nashville by steamboat on April 11 intending to travel via the Cumberland River as far as Palmyra, Tennessee. Thence it marched overland forty miles to Fort Henry where it took transports via the Tennessee River to Eastport, Mississippi, near the Alabama line. Thus the expedition was saved from unnecessary exertions and hardships until it was within 25 miles of the beginning of its overland raid.

At Eastport, where it arrived on April 20, Streight's force was met by a Union force of 8,000 men, under the command of Brigadier General Grenville M. Dodge, who had come east from Corinth, Mississippi, to form a screen for the raiders up the valley of the Tennessee River until Streight's provisional brigade could break free on its way to its first objective, Rome, Georgia. Dodge's cavalry could cover Streight's expedition in the event the latter was discovered by the enemy and thus prevent Streight from being pursued.

The combined Union force of about 9,700 infantry and cavalry beginning this invasion of northern Alabama was faced by a force of only 1,200 Confederate cavalry under Colonel Philip D. Roddey at Tuscumbia. Roddey and Dodge's forces had skirmished as early as April 17. But the combined Union advance up the river in the direction of Tuscumbia did not begin until April 22.[20]

Tuscumbia was reached on April 24. The next two days were passed in the town where army surgeons checked all of Streight's troops for their fitness to undertake their arduous independent expedition. The number selected out reduced Streight's command to only 1,500 men, according to Streight, whose report of his raid was made on August 22, 1864, after his escape from Libby Prison in Richmond.

Meanwhile, Roddey reported the Union advance to General Joseph E. Johnston, who supervised Confederate western operations from his headquarters in Chattanooga. On the night of April 23, Forrest received orders at Spring Hill, Tennessee, to make a forced march with his brigade to Decatur on the south side of the Tennessee River in Alabama, join Roddey, who would come under Forrest's command, and take action to oppose Dodge's invasion.[21]

Among the Confederates, there was still no inkling of the plan to spring Streight loose on his secret expedition to cut rail lines to Chattanooga.

Forrest immediately dispatched the Eleventh Tennessee Cavalry under Colonel Edmundson to a point across the river from Bainbridge, Alabama, east of Florence and Tuscumbia, where there was a ferry across the Tennessee River, to cross there and effect a juncture with Colonel Roddey.[22]

Following with other components of his brigade, Forrest hastened south, crossed the Tennessee River on April 26 at Brown's Ferry near Courtland, Alabama, 14 miles west of Decatur and about 17 miles upstream from where Edmundson's regiment crossed the river.[23]

Forrest's calculations were excellent. Troops of the Eleventh Tennessee Cavalry arrived at the right place and the right time to support Roddey's badly outnumbered cavalry in opposing Dodge's drive to the east, now past Tuscumbia, and by the twenty-eighth they had crossed Town Creek, eight miles east of Tuscumbia. Forrest's main force crossed the Tennessee River upstream on the twenty-sixth and was in a position to block Dodge's advance.

On the evening of the very day Forrest came into position to confront Dodge's forces, Colonel Streight's "lightning brigade" rode out of Tuscumbia, cutting loose from all support in pursuit of its mission. Streight moved south to Russellville, then east to Mt. Hope, then to Moulton on the 28th.

During the evening of April 28, James Moon, one of Roddey's scouts, informed Forrest of Streight's line of march, a march which put Streight into the rear of Forrest's left flank and a day's march away.[24]

The events of the last several days posed a question as to whether the main threat against Forrest came from Dodge with Streight's march simply a flanking movement, or whether the main threat came from Streight as a raiding force.

Forrest did not linger long with indecision. Reviewing all the information at hand regarding the disposition of the enemy, Forrest first gave orders to hold Dodge where he was or force him back to Tuscumbia. In order to accomplish this end, a courier was sent to George Dibrell, who had stayed just north of the river, to attack Dodge's outposts in the vicinity of Florence, to use his artillery freely, and generally to give Dodge the impression that he was threatened with a large force in his rear.[25]

Forrest then directed Roddey to take his command, together with the Eleventh Tennessee Cavalry Regiment, and W.R. Julian's Georgia battalion, and interpose them between Dodge's and Streight's forces to insure that one did not go forward to reinforce the other.[26]

Starnes' Fourth and Biffle's Ninth Tennessee regiments, together with two pieces of John W. Morton, Jr.'s Tennessee battery and C.B. Ferrell's six-piece Georgia battery were quickly prepared for the pursuit of Streight under Forrest's personal command. The officers and men of these organizations had already marched from Spring Hill and fought at Town Creek over a period of five days and nights. But by one o'clock on the morning of the twenty-ninth, they rode out of Courtland in a rain, over miserable roads, to begin a pursuit and running fight lasting another five days and nights, virtually without rest, against a cavalry force three times their size, and over the most difficult mountain terrain.[27]

By the twenty-ninth, Dodge, sure that he had accomplished his goal of providing a cover for Streight, began his withdrawal west to Mississippi whence he had come. Accordingly, Roddey's command, including the Eleventh Tennessee Cavalry Regiment and Julian's battalion, turned and joined in the pursuit of Streight, scarcely twenty-four hours behind Forrest and his original pursuit force.[28]

By sunrise on April 30, troops of the Eleventh were in a sharp attack at Day's Gap, Streight's first ambuscade at the crest of Sand Mountain, where Whitman Ransom of Company C of the Eleventh was captured, and where Captain William Forrest, the general's brother, who was in charge of a group of scouts, suffered a shattered femur. The four Fisher brothers of the Eleventh were among the attackers thrown into line, advancing within about a hundred yards of Streight's troops.[29]

Following a temporary reversal against withering fire, in which two artillery pieces were lost to the enemy, Forrest came among his troops at the forefront with saber drawn and, lecturing them in the strongest possible language, directed an attack to regain lost ground and, more importantly, to recapture the artillery pieces. As the troops advanced and again came upon the strong ground from which they had been so recently dislodged, they were hit by rifle fire but without artillery. At this point Forrest ordered them to charge. They swept all before them as Streight's troops began a general withdrawal from Sand Mountain on their way east.[30]

Streight's purpose, of course, was to continue his eastward march to reach the rail spur of the Western & Atlantic Railroad at Rome, Georgia, *not* to fight battles along the way. His path to Rome was through difficult mountain terrain, lightly populated, but with a fair number of Union sympathizers, many of whom had sons and fathers who were among Streight's troops.

Streight would have preferred proceeding without the hindrance of Forrest's horsemen who, once they caught up with him on April 29, pressed him continually, causing Streight to pause and improvise rearguard actions to keep them from overrunning his command.

Forrest's tactic was not only to continually press the rear of Streight's command, but to send regiments round the flanks of the Union force and to press home his attacks continually so as to give Streight, his officers and men no rest, no possibility of resuscitation, no sleep, no opportunity to halt and chow down, no possibility of reorganizing their resources, of feeding or watering horses and mules, of caring for the dead or the wounded or their animals.

On the other hand, Streight, although he complained that his mules, which he had chosen as mounts because of the difficult mountain terrain, were deficient, diseased and broken-down, had the advantage of a larger force, and an ability to scour the country to secure replacement mounts leaving the broken-down animals in their wake as replacements for Forrest's horses which dropped out of the race. Furthermore, by setting ambushes for their pursuers at natural defensive positions of their own choosing, Streight's forces were able to induce a degree of caution in Forrest's horsemen. They also took advantage of the presence of friendly local Unionists who were willing to direct and sustain them.

Forrest, moreover, divided and thus weakened his attack force in order to guard against perceived unwanted eventualities including Streight's escape. During his pursuit of the enemy just after the ambuscade at Day's Gap, Forrest sent Roddey's regiment and Julian's battalion back to observe Dodge's forces, not knowing what Dodge was doing or if Streight might attempt a reunion with Dodge's command.[31]

Next, to preclude the possibility of Streight attempting an escape via Guntersville on the Tennessee River, Forrest sent the Eleventh Tennessee Cavalry on a left flanking movement to a route through Somerville and Brooksville that was parallel with the route which Streight seemed to be pursuing. Thus Forrest placed his newest regiment between Streight and the river to insure that Streight had no escape in that direction.[32]

With the Fourth and Ninth Tennessee regiments, his artillery and scouts, Forrest personally pressed on in his dogged pursuit. Nine miles east of Day's Gap, a running skirmish commenced which led to a night fight on a ridge called Hog Mountain. Streight reported that here he inflicted heavy casualties on his pursuers.[33]

The next morning, May Day, Streight's command reached Blountsville at ten o'clock, forty-three miles and forty-eight hours from Day's Gap. Here men, with their beasts, had a rare but brief two-hour respite, were fed, got new mounts, and abandoned their wagons in the interest of making better speed, transferring the wagons' contents to pack mules.[34]

The wagons were bunched and set afire by the rear guard. But before the burning had proceeded far, Forrest and the Fourth Tennessee Cavalry came charging into Blountsville, driving off the rear guard and extinguishing the wagon fires.[35]

The pursuit was unrelenting. Ten miles east of Blountsville, Streight had to effect a crossing of a swift and dangerous stream, the Black Warrior River, at a ford while fending off a charge from Forrest's attackers. The crossing was completed by about five o'clock in the afternoon of May 1.[36]

After the crossing, Forrest gave his main body of troops a three-hour respite while two companies pressed on the attack.[37] At about nine o'clock the next morning, with Forrest in the forefront, the main body of Confederate troops bore down on the bridge over Black Creek, a difficult mountain stream near Gadsden. Streight meant to cross the creek, then burn the bridge and give his men the rest that they needed. Streight's intelligence indicated that the stream was a formidable barrier and that, save for the bridge, there was no other convenient or accessible means of crossing it available to Forrest.

But the general, in the forefront of the Confederate advance, came across a sixteen-year-old girl, Emma Sanson, who lived with her mother and two sisters on a farm abutting Black Creek and the bridge that crossed it. Emma's father had died in 1859, and she had a brother absent from home in the Nineteenth Alabama Infantry, C.S.A. She was eager to be of service in the pursuit and capture of Streight's raiders.

In the urgency of the moment and with the utmost calm, she mounted Forrest's horse behind the general and directed him in reconnoitering a ford of Black Creek on her family's property which she said she had seen cattle use in crossing the stream. The ford, unknown to others, was found to be usable.[38]

So Forrest's command relentlessly continued their pursuit eastward toward and beyond Gadsden. Streight could not rest in Gadsden even though some of his animals and men were so worn out that they could not keep up. They were captured.

Streight's scouts reported to him that a column of the enemy, the Eleventh Tennessee Cavalry, was moving on his left parallel to his own route and might overtake him and block his progress if he did not advance rapidly enough. Streight recognized now that his only hope lay in getting to Rome, crossing the river there and destroying the bridge. This would delay Forrest a day or two and give his command a while to sleep, without which it would be impossible for them to proceed further.

But Forrest's command was even more in extremis in two respects. Officers and men had had little opportunity to obtain fresh mounts in their pursuit because Streight's command had corralled virtually all the fit riding stock as they advanced to the east. Furthermore, the pursuers had been subjected to far greater rigors of marching and fighting than had Streight's troops, having endured a forced march from Spring Hill, Tennessee, of almost 200 miles beginning April 23 and continuing till noon of May 2 with almost continuous fighting for the last four days.

Forrest marched east of Gadsden with at best between five and six hundred troops, no more than a third of Streight's command. Fifteen miles from Gadsden, Streight halted at Blount's Plantation to procure forage for the animals. The balance of the command was formed in line of battle while the rear guard, severely engaged, was driven in.

Streight reported a year and a quarter later that the engagement at Blount's Plantation revealed to him that nearly all of his remaining ammunition was worthless, having become wet.[39]

Forrest, not overlooking anything of importance, dispatched couriers to Rome to advise its citizens to either guard or burn the bridge leading into their town in order to stop Streight's raiders from entering Rome.

Yet it was reported that a rural mail carrier, J.H. Wisdom, upon finding Gadsden in the hands of the enemy, on his own volition headed east toward Rome, sixty-seven miles distant. Changing mounts frequently, he was the first to warn the citizens of Rome that the Yankees were coming.[40]

The resultant local preparations frustrated an attempt to take Rome by an advance contingent, under Captain Milton Russell, of two hundred of the best-mounted men in Streight's force, who approached Rome on May 3 and, seeing the bridge defended by a fair number of home guards, decided not to attack.[41]

Still bound for Rome, Streight again sought to do in his pursuers with ambuscades. But Forrest was too wary and sent flanking movements about his antagonist to force withdrawal. Streight crossed the Chattooga River on a bridge which he subsequently burned, hoping thereby to gain time to stop, feed the animals and men, and give all a chance to sleep.

But Forrest was not delayed long by the bridge-burning. Once again he forded the stream, and his advance units were once again on the heels of the desperately fatigued Federals. Furthermore, Forrest had managed to provide most of his command ten hours of sleep and rest while Streight's forces were searching in the dark for the bridge across the Chattooga River. Yet Forrest consistently used a part of his command to engage Streight's forces almost continually during his pursuit.[42]

At last Forrest caught up with Streight at the Lawrence Farm, near Cedar Bluff, Alabama, thirty-one miles east of Gadsden, on the morning of May 3. So exhausted were Streight's officers and men that, when halted and dismounted, they dropped to the ground and fell asleep. Even when aroused and thrown in line of battle against Forrest's encircling troops, they closed their eyes and slept when prone on the ground facing the enemy. Indeed, in his official report, Streight wrote that "nature was exhausted. A large portion of my best troops actually went to sleep while lying in line of battle under a severe skirmish fire."[43]

Forrest sent in Captain Henry Pointer under a flag of truce to demand the surrender of Streight and his command in order to avoid "the further effusion of blood." Colonel Streight replied that he would parley with General Forrest.

Forrest used bluff to get his way, telling Streight of nonexistent forces under his command nearer Rome and force enough on the ground to run over him, including fresh troops. Streight believed he was outnumbered by about three to one. Forrest let him see two pieces of Ferrell's battery appearing and reappearing at so many points as to convince Streight that he had seen at least fifteen pieces.

Astonished, Streight asked, "How many guns have you got? There's fifteen I've counted already!"

Straight-faced, Forrest answered, "I reckon that's all that has kept up."

Other portions of Forrest's command marched round and round the surrounding hills and convinced Streight and his staff that further resistance was useless against such observed overwhelming odds.

Streight's officers wanted to give up the fight, hopeless, as they saw it. And they at length convinced their leader of the futility of further fighting. Streight told Forrest that he wished officers and men to be treated as prisoners of war, and officers to retain their sidearms and personal baggage.

Forrest assented and accepted Streight's surrender.[44]

Military prisoners surrendered at the Lawrence Farm totaled 1,466. The addition of Captain Russell's force, taken as it returned from Rome, raised the total to about 1,670, or about three times the strength of Forrest's command on the field at the surrender. The prisoners were taken to Rome under guard of Forrest's men. The latter were feted and celebrated lavishly by the Romans.[45]

In addition, Forrest captured about 150 blacks who had joined Streight's raiders as they swept across Alabama. With respect to the blacks, the Confederacy's Adjutant and Inspector General and senior officer in Richmond, General Samuel Cooper, 65, advised Braxton Bragg to send them to "the nearest camp of instruction pursuant to General Orders, No. 25."[46]

General order No. 25, pursuant to law, established at military camps of instruction depots for slaves arrested by capture from the enemy. Commanding officers were to send slaves to camps where they were advertised and subsisted until claimed by their owners. The order stated that such captives might be put to work on public works. The closest such depot in Alabama was at Talladega.[47]

Most of Streight's captured officers and enlisted men were imprisoned briefly and exchanged. But Streight and four senior officers were sent to Libby Prison in Richmond, from which they escaped on the night of February 9, 1864. Streight returned to active duty on June 1 and made a report of his raid on August 22, 1864.[48]

In his report, Streight stated that a total of 15 officers and 130 men of his command were killed and wounded in his campaign and estimated that his enemy's losses were higher, while giving no numbers. Streight complained of the barbarous treatment accorded his wounded who had to be left along the way. The enemy stole their blankets, clothing, rations, money, medical stores and equipment and left his wounded in the most pitiable condition, he said. Streight reported that he had left two physicians to attend the wounded.[49]

Forrest's battle plan and its execution remain models for professional soldiers. Forrest left no detail dangling. He was thorough, demonstrated the finest leadership, and knew when and where to attack as well as when to desist. And he inspired his staff and men to the most extraordinary feats of physical and moral endurance. He and his command were splendid, measured by the strictest criteria of military excellence.

Whitman Ransom, 39, captured on April 30, was the only casualty of Company C of the Eleventh in the Streight campaign. Company D of the Fourth reported no casualties. But Forrest's contingent of Fishers from Cave Spring was being beaten up and put out of action when Streight's campaign was frustrated. Will Fisher was still in prison in Ft. McHenry, Maryland. Jim was continuing his convalescence from his thigh wound and the Minié ball he still carried. And Tom developed an uneasy stomach and an intestinal infection which virtually rendered him hors de combat. There was an epidemic of sickness in early 1863, and desertions, many temporary, became rife in May and June 1863 in Company C of the Eleventh. Men of Company D of the Fourth also showed the results of stress and apprehension during this period.[50]

Chapter 3

Through the Chickamauga Holocaust, May 4–October 29, 1863

In the long march in pursuit of Streight, Thomas Fisher suffered much with a sore arm caused by a vaccination. A cake had formed under his left arm which was several inches square. The shaking induced by the movement of his horse caused constant pain. Then he had to hold his arm aloof from his body to prevent chafing and further painful irritation to and about the scab. This became exceedingly tiresome mile after mile.

But he boasted that he never lost an hour of duty on the Streight expedition, which covered a distance of about 200 miles and returned without rest save briefly right after the capture, when Forrest's troops took their prisoners to Rome and found themselves feted as heroes. When Tom was back in camp at Spring Hill, Tennessee, his infection had to be relieved of a massive accumulation of pus by lancing. The infection healed slowly over a period of weeks.

His vaccination problem appears to have been a case of "spurious vaccinia" caused by being vaccinated by an impure vaccine virus. This usually produced large, repulsive-appearing ulcers either at the point of vaccination or elsewhere on the body, a common problem in the army when vaccines were made from vaccination scabs purchased or taken from anybody.[1]

The records of Company C of the Eleventh Tennessee Cavalry indicate that Fisher was not the only member of the company with something about him that produced dissatisfaction. James Hill, 18, had been dissatisfied sufficiently to desert the company in February 1863. He was the first soldier in Company C to desert. His military service record reveals nothing of what happened to him thereafter. He may have simply gone home, or hid out, or gone West.

The March–April 1863 muster roll for Company C recorded many soldiers "absent, sick." J.E. Crockett, 39; W.G. Davis, 24; J.H. Holt, 34; J.M. Lamb, D.V. Putman, N.R. Taylor, and Joseph Wilson, 32, were so recorded. R.T. Holland was recorded as "absent, one-armed and absent." M.V. Rambo,

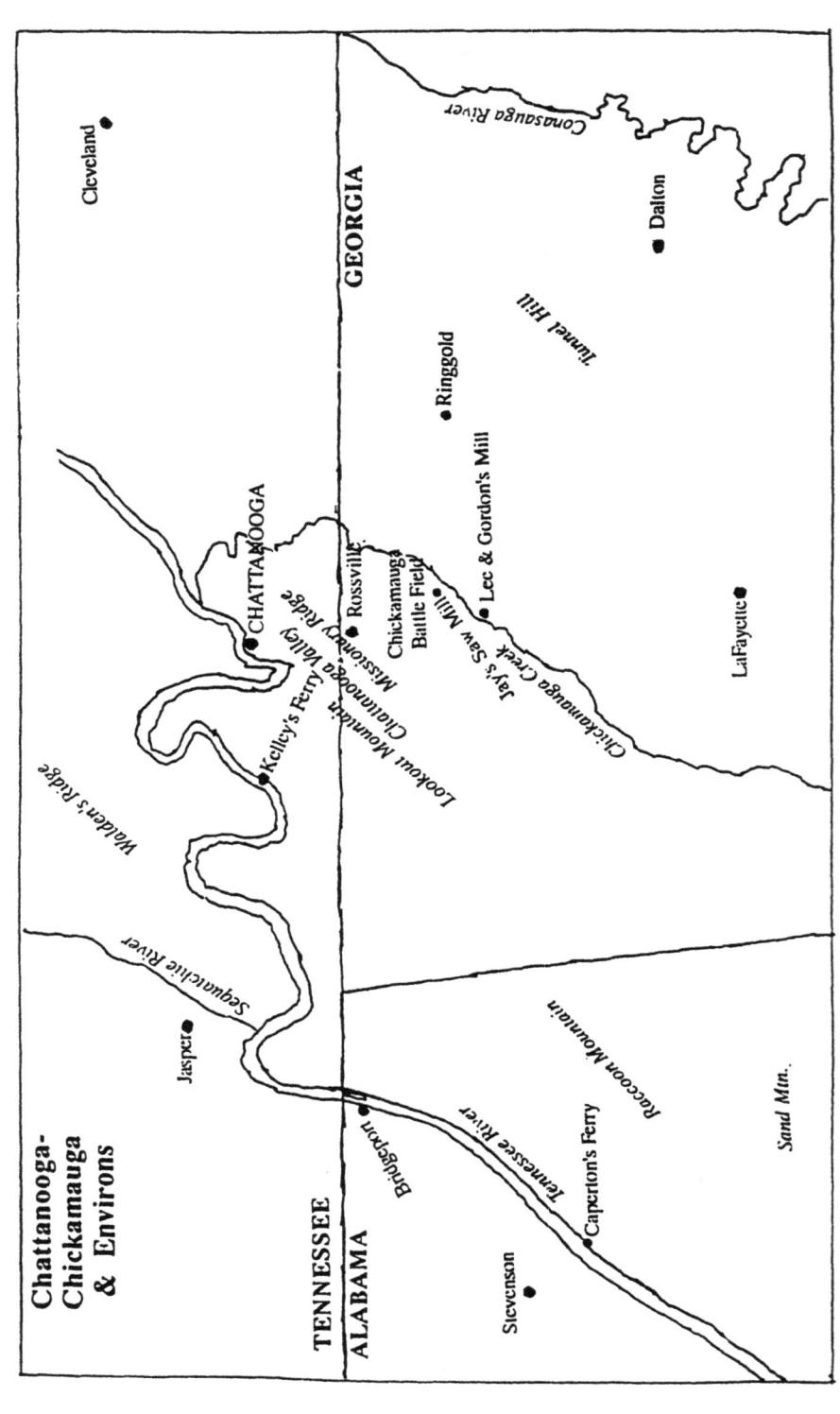

29, was absent with "sore eyes." D.W. Devan and J.B. Jones were present but dismounted.

The May-June 1863 muster roll for Company C was prepared in Sulphur Springs, Rhea County, Tennessee, where Forrest's cavalry had moved from Spring Hill after covering Bragg's retreat to Chattanooga. The record showed that W.G. Reynolds was absent. He had been "left in Middle Tennessee sick, a weak man hardly able for duty at any time." J.E. Crockett, W.G. Davis, J.M. Lamb, D.V. Putman, M.V. Rambo, N.R. Taylor, and Joseph Wilson continued absent, sick, as they had been on the previous muster roll two months earlier.

Desertions from Company C became rife in June 1863 during the retreat from Middle Tennessee. Reported as deserted were J.G. Allen, 21; John H. Bruce; J.W. Bruce, 18; W.H. Davis, 19; John H. Hay, 30; George W. Joice, 33; T.J. Ramsey, 31; Edward D. Royster; J.W. Royster; W.C. Taylor, 24; and J.C. Turner, 17.

Of those reported as having deserted in June, however, six returned to serve again. Likely they should have been reported as absent without leave rather than deserted. They were J.G. Allen, John H. Bruce, J.W. Bruce, W.H. Davis, John H. Hay, and Edward D. Royster.

Virtually all of the soldiers in Company C of the Eleventh were from Bedford, Marshall, Maury, and Rutherford counties in the heart of Middle Tennessee. In June 1863 they retreated from the familiar scenes of home for the first time and probably had little expectation of an early return thereto. This may account for the number of soldiers reported as deserted or absent without leave when the army moved out.

The soldiers of Company D of the Fourth, virtually all of whom were residents of Bedford and Marshall counties, began to experience a desertion problem on May 10, 1863, when W.M. Cunningham left. But leaving the scenes of home in June was not so traumatic for the men of Company D. They had been in the service for ten months longer than had the troops of the Eleventh and had seen more widespread duty. They had been in Kentucky and East and West Tennessee, hundreds of miles from home to the north, east, and west. Being away from home was not a new experience for them.

Nevertheless James F. Cook of Company D deserted on June 15, perhaps because he was overage and found the life of an enlisted man too demanding both physically and emotionally. When he enlisted in November 1861, Cook gave his age as 28. Later he insisted he was over 35.

William R. Horton also deserted on June 15. He surrendered to Federal troops at Shelbyville, Tennessee, on August 8, 1863, took the oath of allegiance to the United States, and was released. Horton had been wounded slightly in the fight at Thompson's Station.

On June 30, Nathan Glasscock deserted. And the following day, Christopher C. Thomas, 26, followed suit. Thomas surrendered to Federal troops at Shelbyville on August 8 and took the oath of allegiance.

On the May–June, 1863, Company D muster roll, Sergeant Benton W. Long was reported absent, sick in Marshall County with "chronic sore eyes." He was left at home when the army moved out toward Chattanooga.[2]

In the weeks following the Alabama campaign, after first returning to Spring Hill, then covering Bragg's latest retreat, Thomas Fisher contracted dysentery as a result of, or so he was led to believe, eating lean beef and unbolted meal and being continually assailed by rainy weather.

Confederate medical officers generally ascribed the causes of diarrhea and dysentery, terms used almost interchangeably in the army, to inadequate rations, poor preparation of food, and impure water, aggravated by fatigue and exposure. Dysentery is no friend of soldiers, being a very common incapacitating illness and one of the leading causes of death in the army. After walking perhaps a hundred yards, Thomas would become so weak that he would have to stop and rest.

While picketing in the Sequatchie Valley and feeling unwell, he noticed that there was an apple orchard at hand in which the fruit was just ripening. The sight of the ripened fruit was inviting. Tom craved an apple yet feared to touch one because of the possibility that it might induce diarrhea, a malady with which he was already painfully familiar.

Finally throwing caution to the wind, he gave way to his craving, climbed the fence between him and the trees, and plucked an acidulous green crab apple, a variety which is native to the southern Appalachians. As it turned out, the apple proved to be exactly what his digestive tract needed. The first few bites were almost exhilarating in their effect on him. Completing his consumption of the fruit, he went back for another until his delicate appetite was less fragile and sufficiently satiated.[3]

While Forrest had been away in pursuit of Colonel Streight in Alabama, Earl Van Dorn had been fatally shot on May 7 by a resident of the vicinity of Spring Hill, George B. Peters, 45, a farmer and physician, who fled to the enemy's lines after claiming that he acted because Van Dorn had violated the sanctity of his home by his attentions to Peters' wife, Jessie, 25, while Peters was away attending to his farming interests in Mississippi. Van Dorn was believed to have a special fondness for attractive women, but his friends claimed a treacherous and disloyal political motive for the doctor's foul deed.[4]

Prior to the war Peters owned real property which he valued at $132,000 and personal property aggregating $80,000 in 1860. These values represented a substantial individual fortune in the rural economy of Hardeman County, where he lived in West Tennessee just before the war. Jessie Helen McKissack, a native of Spring Hill, was then Peters' third wife.

But his hot temper in the matter which resulted in Van Dorn's untimely death cost him dearly in the short term in his ownership of property. Ten years later, while living again in the 22nd Civil District of Maury County, Tennessee, Peters reported owning no property, either real or personal, while his wife, Jessie, reportedly owned $6,000 in real estate and $700 in personal property. She reportedly had owned no property in 1860. The reduction in family worth in the ten-year period is not altogether explicable by the deflation of property values wrought by the economically ruinous war of 1861–1865.

But Robert G. Hartje, Van Dorn's biographer, wrote that Peters first divorced, then remarried Jessie after the war, then recouped his fortune and became well-established in Memphis and Arkansas. He owned land in Phillips County, Arkansas, and served a term in the Arkansas State Senate. He died in 1889 at age 74 while still living with Jessie. His widow survived him until 1921 when she died at age 83.[5]

From May 16 to July 6, 1863, Forrest's cavalry covered the retreat of the Army of Tennessee under Braxton Bragg out of Middle Tennessee in the direction of Chattanooga. Major General William S. Rosecrans adroitly maneuvered his Union Army of the Cumberland southeast from its forward base in Murfreesboro against Bragg's poorly-led army quartered in Shelbyville, Manchester, Tullahoma, and beyond.

Forrest's cavalry moved east from Spring Hill on the Confederate left to help cover the withdrawal which was accomplished without a major battle but with a number of sharp cavalry skirmishes, including one at Franklin on June 7 and another at Triune on June 20. Yet another, on the Tullahoma-Manchester Road, resulted in the death of Colonel James W. Starnes, commander of the Fourth Tennessee Cavalry, in which James Wesley Fisher served.

Forrest had chosen Starnes to be commander of his "Old Brigade" in May 1863 when Forrest himself had been chosen by Bragg to succeed to Earl Van Dorn's command.[6] Starnes, born in North Carolina, was a well-to-do 45-year-old landholder from the eastern subdivision of Williamson County, Tennessee, one of the state's wealthier rural counties. His death on June 30 was a significant loss of leadership for the Western Cavalry. He was survived by a young widow and two children.

The day after Starnes' death, the Fourth, less dramatically lost yet another soldier, 33-year-old Michael R. Fisher, a younger brother of Turner M. Fisher who had deserted on May 26, 1862. Michael was reported absent from Company A as of July 1.[7] He had given up the fight.

Earlier in the retreat from Middle Tennessee, A. Franklin Sumey, 38, of the Fourth's Company D, died in Franklin County, Tennessee, on May 18. He had been severely wounded at Thompson's Station on March 5, 1863. But the cause of his death was not stated in his company's records.

Five days later Second Lieutenant Francis M. Webb, 32, of Company D, resigned because of a disability. He suffered "chronic rheumatic pains in the knee." His resignation was approved on July 18, 1863. Webb was captured by Federal troops at Shelbyville on August 8, 1863. His captors mistook him for a deserter. He took the oath of allegiance and was released.

On June 25, Reuben S. Price of Company D was captured in Coffee County between Pelham and Hillsborough, Tennessee. Price arrived at Camp Chase, Columbus, Ohio, on July 8 but was transferred to Fort Delaware, an island in the Delaware River, six days later. He languished there for almost 20 months until he was exchanged on February 27, 1865.

On June 28, William M. Boyce of the Eleventh's Company C was captured at Shelbyville. Boyce reportedly suffered from rheumatism and indeed spent time in a hospital in Nashville following his capture, according to a roll of prisoners of war dated July 18, 1863. Boyce was sent to Camp Chase on July 27, 1863, and was transferred on March 3, 1864, to Fort Delaware, where he stayed until the end of hostilities. Lucky indeed to have survived both Camp Chase and Fort Delaware for over 21 months, he took the oath of allegiance and was released on May 7, 1865.[8]

Bragg's army continued its retreat, covered by the cavalry under Wheeler and Forrest, until it reached Chattanooga on July 6. During the last days of the retreat, Colonel George G. Dibrell's brigade, including the Fourth and Eleventh regiments, was ordered to remain for thirty-six hours at the site designated University Place of the recently chartered (1857) but still unopened University of the South at Sewanee. Then the brigade followed on across the Cumberland Mountains in the direction of Jasper, covering the withdrawal of Lieutenant General William J. Hardee's corps. Dibrell's brigade crossed the Tennessee River at Kelly's Ferry and moved to the vicinity of Chattanooga.[9]

Company D of the Fourth continued to suffer losses in July 1863. Jasper Pendergrass, 24, was captured on July 3 at Tullahoma, Tennessee, during the retreat. On July 9, Pendergrass took the oath of allegiance at Tullahoma and was released to go home. On July 22, Hiram W. Burrow, 19, deserted. The next day Ethan Lawwell, 26, also deserted. On July 21, three soldiers for whom there are no records of subsequent service were reported absent without leave. They were Second Sergeant John A. Duling, 19, John W. Peyton, and Robert Reese. Peyton and Reese had enlisted at Nolensville, Tennessee, in November 1862.

And the Eleventh's Company C lost three men by capture in July 1863. They were J.G. Smith, captured at Tullahoma on July 1, A.W. Cartwright at Pulaski on July 13, and William B. Reese at Spring Hill on July 25. One can only conjecture why Cartwright was at Pulaski or Reese at Spring Hill when Forrest's cavalry had fallen back to Chattanooga. Both soldiers were sent to Camp Chase, Ohio, from which point Cartwright was transferred to Fort Delaware, March 4, 1864, thence to City Point, Virginia, for exchange on February 27, 1865. Reese was not so fortunate. He died of diarrhea July 25, 1864, at Camp Chase and was interred in grave #191 in the prison yard.

Also in July, Corporal T.M. Chapman, 34, deserted from Company C. He was captured by Federal troops in Giles County, October 27, 1863. While being transferred to Camp Morton, Indianapolis, Indiana, for incarceration,

Chapman reportedly escaped from his guards somewhere between Nashville and Louisville. Military service records reveal nothing about his subsequent fate nor that of W.C. Harper, 28, who also deserted from Company C in July.[10]

Forrest's command remained in Chattanooga and rested until July 24, when it moved out in the direction of Kingston, Tennessee, where the Fourth and Eleventh Tennessee cavalry regiments were primarily occupied in scouting and vidette duty in East Tennessee on the right flank of the Confederate Army of Tennessee until shortly before the Battle of Chickamauga was fought on September 19–20, 1863.[11]

During this period of desultory fighting, night marches, and boredom interspersed with real danger from enemy patrols, Thomas Fisher experienced and retained in memory to the end of his life the entrancing beauty of the mountains at dawn and dusk. After an all-night scouting expedition, he returned in the company of his comrades in the direction of sanctuary—hungry, weary, and sleepy. The scouts reached the summit of Walden's Ridge riding eastward out of the Sequatchie Valley at dawn when Tom saw a vision of beauty that he remembered three thousand years before he was born had been described aptly in the line from Homer's *Odyssey*: "Soon as the early, rosy-fingered Aurora appeared."

The head of the column had halted. But as others rode up, they turned their horses to the right and rode in a column silently facing the east. The beauty of the scene was entrancing. Spread out before the intrepid horse soldiers was a succession of parallel ridges, each rising higher than the nearer one. Along each intervening valley stretched a line of iridescent fog growing faintly more brilliant by degrees as the solar light increased. Finally the sun rose to a degree that it flooded the scene with its dazzling nuclear brilliance. The beauty of the vision was such as to make the soldiers forget their physical exhaustion and to indelibly mark Tom's memory.[12]

Forrest was headquartered at Kingston, seventy miles northeast of Chattanooga, where the Clinch River flows into the Tennessee. The Army of Tennessee was spread along the south bank of the Tennessee River from northern Alabama, where Wheeler's cavalry marked the Confederate left flank, to Kingston, where Forrest's cavalry guarded the right flank.

Both the Fourth and the Eleventh Tennessee cavalry regiments were in Dibrell's brigade of Forrest's corps. The Eleventh was at Post Oak Springs near Kingston on August 27 and had been under the command of Colonel Daniel W. Holman for a month. Holman had succeeded Colonel James H. Edmundson after Holman had recovered from wounds suffered at Dover, Tennessee, on February 3, 1863. When relieved, Edmundson sought a leave of absence and shortly after resigned.

Following the death of Starnes on June 30, the Fourth had been under the command of Major W.S. McLemore, 33, who, before and after the war, was a prosperous attorney, husband, and father in Williamson County,

Tennessee. McLemore had attended Transylvania College in Lexington, Kentucky, and Cumberland Law School in Lebanon, Tennessee. He began his military service in 1861 and was elected captain of Company F of the Fourth at the reorganization of Starnes' command in the Sequatchie Valley on May 26, 1862. He was promoted to major in March 1863. His colonelcy dated from February 25, 1864.[13]

On August 17, 1863, the day after the Army of the Cumberland began another general advance, Rosecrans sent Colonel Robert H.G. Minty's cavalry east from McMinnville to Sparta where it engaged portions of the Fourth and Eighth Tennessee regiments under George G. Dibrell in several running fights along Wild Cat Creek and Calfkiller River.

Dibrell and the Eighth had been sent by Forrest to Sparta, whence they had been recruited, to keep an eye on Rosecrans' movements and to recruit, get supplies, and remount, the last being a luxury few members of the cavalry were in a position to enjoy. They had been joined at Bon Air, seven miles east on the brow of Cumberland Mountain, by reinforcements, including the Fourth, sent by Forrest, and together they returned to Sparta.

H.B. Davidson of the Fourth's Company D was killed in action on August 18, 1863, in one of the running fights on Wild Cat Creek. Davidson had enlisted in the company at Murfreesboro on October 10, 1862.[14]

In his new general advance, begun on August 16, Rosecrans' objective was to flush Bragg out of Chattanooga. His troops began crossing the Tennessee River below Chattanooga in Alabama at Caperton's Ferry on August 27. His corps, however, became badly fragmented and, against an adversary capable of getting his subordinates to follow orders to advance and attack, Rosecrans might have suffered as many as three stinging defeats resulting in the virtual destruction of his entire command.

Instead, he and Bragg blundered on for a month, the latter not knowing where the bulk of Rosecrans' army was, but mistakenly believing it was to the north of Chattanooga where only one of Rosecrans' three corps was located.

By August 30, Forrest was ordered to picket the south bank of the Tennessee from Chattanooga north to the Hiwassee River. On September 10 and 11, Forrest's command was committed to slowing the progress of Major General T.L. Crittenden's corps which had crossed Walden's Ridge in the direction of the Tennessee River at the mouth of the Hiwassee and proceeded south in the direction of Chattanooga and Chickamauga.[15]

The activity of Bragg's and Rosecrans' armies was leading to a denouement in North Georgia by the west fork of Chickamauga Creek, the Indian name of which, it is said, means "river of death." And the battle of Chickamauga, one of the great battles of the war, true to its namesake, would prove to be the costliest two days of the American Civil War. It was so because of the failure of military leadership on both sides. There were over 34,000 casualties including almost 4,000 killed. Twenty-eight percent of approximately 124,000 combatants ended as casualties, with over 24,000 wounded and over 6,000 missing.[16]

In the jockeying for position leading up to the start of the battle, Company C of the Eleventh lost J.G. Allen, 21, captured near Chattanooga on September 16. Allen reportedly took the oath of allegiance at Louisville on September 30, 1863, but was not released. He was sent through Kemper Barracks, Cincinnati, on October 1 on his way to Camp Chase, Ohio, where he died of typhoid fever on December 15, 1863.

On September 17 and 18, Company D of the Fourth lost William H. Reeder, 17, and Marshall V. Kerr both captured near Chickamauga. Reeder was sent first to Camp Chase on September 30, then to the Rock Island Prison Barracks in Illinois on January 14, 1864. He was permitted to take the oath of allegiance on October 25, 1864, and returned to his home at New Hope in Marion County, Tennessee.

Marshall Kerr arrived at Camp Douglas on the south side of Chicago on October 4, 1863. He applied to take the oath of allegiance in February 1865 claiming "to be loyal, enlisted through false representation.... Desires to take the oath of allegiance to the United States and become a loyal citizen." But his captors did not release him until May 4, 1865. He signed his oath with his mark.[17]

Fighting at Chickamauga began near Jay's Saw Mill about 7:30 on the morning of Saturday, September 19, between members of Brigadier General John Pegram's brigade of Forrest's corps and Colonel John Croxton's brigade of Brigadier General John M. Brannan's division. As the battle opened, Forrest's men, as was their practice, dismounted and fought as infantry.

Manning the Confederates' right flank, Forrest's cavalry was outnumbered and in desperate need of help during the morning hours. Forrest requested Armstrong's division to come up but only got Forrest's "Old Brigade" under Dibrell.[18]

Both the Fourth and Eleventh Tennessee cavalry regiments were under Dibrell in the "Old Brigade," a part of Frank Armstrong's division. They became engaged before noon on the first day. At 6 P.M., they were engaged on the right flank of Major General Patrick Cleburne's infantry division, one of the best in either army, when the latter successfully charged the enemy at their front.[19]

While engaged and pending help on Saturday morning, close to one-fourth of Brigadier General John Pegram's division of Forrest's command was lost as casualties, according to Pegram.[20] But Forrest's dismounted troops managed to hold on as help belatedly came forward after Forrest personally went back to secure infantry reinforcements. He first secured, from the reserve corps, Major General W.H.T. Walker's division under the command of Brigadier General States Rights Gist, the First Brigade of which was thrown into line to the left of his dismounted cavalry.[21]

Charge and counter-charge ensued with Forrest in personal command of his and Gist's combined force. Seeing the need for additional help, Forrest again went back and commandeered Colonel Matthew D. Ector's brigade of infantry which he placed in line squarely in the middle between Gist's infantry and his own dismounted cavalry.[22]

With the help of reinforcements, the enemy was again driven back at great cost to both sides only to rally again. Then, just after midday, the help that Forrest had asked for arrived, infantry from the reserve corps commanded by Major General W.H.T. Walker, consisting of two brigades of Brigadier General St. John R. Liddell's division, Brigadier General Edward C. Walthall's Mississippians and Colonel Daniel C. Govan's Arkansans. Walker, the senior officer present, now took command from Forrest of the Confederate right flank.[23]

Heavy fighting continued up and down the line until nightfall, by which time the Confederate line had advanced, but only incrementally. During the night that followed, Union strongpoints were fortified by the felling of trees. The Confederate right flank was strengthened by the arrival of Brigadier General Frank C. Armstrong and a brigade commanded by Colonel James T. Wheeler. Both armies anticipated a resumption of the costly killing that had marked the first day's fight.[24]

And so it was on Sunday, September 20, after a late and confused start owing to Leonidas Polk's failure to open the attack as directed. The Eleventh had been sent forward at daybreak on a reconnaissance that lasted two to three hours. It returned with prisoners and reports of a demoralized enemy.[25]

Forrest, still in command of the cavalry on the right flank, moved up in line with Major General John C. Breckenridge's infantry division and continued to press the Union left flank up to the Lafayette-Chattanooga road using mounted cavalry of the First Confederate Regiment and the Eighteenth Tennessee Battalion under Major Charles McDonald.[26]

But the Union line held very well from flank to flank until late in the afternoon when Rosecrans ordered the withdrawal of the First Division of the XXI Army Corps under Brigadier General Thomas J. Wood without replacing it. At this point, the Confederate left wing under Lieutenant General James Longstreet effected a breakthrough. The division of Major General Alexander P. Stewart broke the Union line and proceeded to pour through the breach followed by troops under brigadier generals William Preston and Bushrod Johnson as well as Major General T.C. Hindman's division.[27]

Then on the right wing troops under major generals Patrick Cleburne and John C. Breckinridge advanced in a heavy assault which broke the lines of the XIV Army Corps, commanded by Major General George H. Thomas. The day's fighting ended with a general Union withdrawal all along the line at nightfall.[28]

Forrest's command was kept on the field all through the night of the twentieth, and suffered from want of water and food. The horses also suffered having had only a partial feed in two days. But Forrest paid tribute to the conduct of the officers and men of Armstrong's division, fighting mostly on foot, keeping up with, and frequently in advance of, the infantry.[29]

On Monday morning the twenty-first, Forrest's cavalry started in hot pursuit of Rosecrans' retreating army on the LaFayette Road in the direction of Chattanooga. On Tuesday, Forrest moved into Chattanooga's southern suburbs and fought to take and hold the most strategic positions from Missionary Ridge westward athwart the Chattanooga Valley to Point Lookout on the northern end of Lookout Mountain, which dominates both the river and the railroad which Rosecrans needed for his supply.[30]

The Eleventh, proceeding north up Missionary Ridge, was ordered, in tandem with the Tenth, to descend into the Chattanooga Valley on the Rossville Road and go as far as possible toward the city. Under the command of Colonel Daniel W. Holman, the two regiments proceeded to within a half mile of Chattanooga where they were stopped by strongly entrenched infantry, supported by artillery, which poured a galling fire on the horsemen and inflicted a number of casualties. Holman ordered a battery of artillery to open up on the enemy and dismounted his troops to fight as infantry.

But it soon became obvious that the infantry and artillery between Holman's two regiments and the city were not to be moved from their entrenchments.[31]

All of Dibrell's brigade, including the Fourth, Eighth, and Ninth regiments, and Hamilton's battalion, with Major Jo Shaw commanding, were ordered to approach Chattanooga from the foot of Lookout Mountain. But they found Federal infantry and artillery strongly entrenched which denied them access to the city from the west.[32]

It was past noon on Wednesday the twenty-third before the infantry of the Army of Tennessee began to arrive to man the positions about Chattanooga which Forrest's horsemen occupied. Forrest had reported promptly to Bragg that the Union army in Chattanooga was demoralized and could be easily captured. Bragg, skeptical of the ability of his army to launch a successful assault, reportedly asked Forrest how he could move his army without supplies. To which Forrest replied: "We can get all the supplies our army needs in Chattanooga." But all Bragg would do was to send infantry to relieve the cavalry belatedly while Forrest, thoroughly and wearily displeased with Bragg, was ordered to march east of Chattanooga where he went into camp at Bird's Mill.[33]

Dibrell's command maintained its position until noon of the twenty-third, when it was ordered to withdraw to Tyner's Station to feed both man and beast, quite close to exhaustion and starvation from their relentless fighting and riding for a week.[34]

On Friday the twenty-fifth, Forrest was ordered to move up the valley of the Tennessee to meet Burnside's army, thought to be approaching from

Knoxville. On his way, Forrest was ordered to go to Charleston and disperse the enemy there. At Charleston he crossed the Hiwassee River and pursued the Union cavalry under Kentucky Colonel Frank Wolford to Philadelphia in Loudon County within thirty-five miles of Knoxville.[35]

Despite Forrest's heavy losses at Chickamauga and a shortage of ammunition, that part of his command in which the five brothers Fisher served, i.e., Armstrong's division under George Dibrell, badly beat Wolford's troops, driving them in full flight from the field and taking one hundred twenty prisoners.[36]

John Allen Wyeth reported that Forrest's soldiers became aware that their brilliant but costly performance at Chickamauga, fighting shoulder to shoulder with the infantry, greatly increased Forrest's popularity both in the army and among the Southern population at large.[37]

What Forrest's troops experienced at Chickamauga was hardly the traditional manner of cavalry operations. But it represented a portion of Forrest's style and was eventually adopted by other cavalry commanders, although by no means all, and not without opposition.

In the fight at Chickamauga, Dibrell's brigade, consisting of the Eleventh Tennessee Cavalry, along with the Fourth, Eighth, Ninth, and Tenth Tennessee regiments, had been joined by Jo Shaw's and O.P. Hamilton's battalions and R.D. Allison's squadron, consolidated and commanded by Major Shaw, and Captain John W. Morton's and Captain Amariah L. Huggin's Tennessee batteries.[38]

In the thick of the fight, Thomas Fisher was impressed that the incessant roar of musketry he heard at Chickamauga was so deafening in his sector that he was scarcely able to hear the boom of the field pieces which were heavily used by both sides. But despite being in the thick of the fight, Fisher's company and that of his brother, Jim, in the Fourth, continued to be unusually fortunate in combat. The two companies reported no killed, wounded, captured, or missing in the great battle.[39]

On September 28, Major General Joseph Wheeler was given command of all the cavalry of the Army of Tennessee, with which he was ordered to cross the Tennessee River and the intervening mountains and valleys into Middle Tennessee where he was to break up Rosecrans' communications.

When he received orders to turn over his command to Wheeler, Forrest wrote to Wheeler that he was sending him Davidson's and Armstrong's brigades while retaining Dibrell's and Pegram's. Citing his command's fatigue, lack of rations and ammunition, and an inability to shoe the horses, Forrest candidly assured Wheeler that his command was in no condition to mount an expedition to Middle Tennessee.[40]

When Armstrong's and Davidson's brigades reported to him on the thirtieth, Wheeler found that they were a skeleton force of scarcely 500 men each, short of ammunition, poorly mounted, worn out, and short of rations. Allowing the horses in the worst condition to remain behind, Wheeler took the remainder and, on October 1, 1863, with a force of about 1,500 men, crossed the Tennessee River at Cottonport, about 38 miles above Chattanooga in Meigs County, on a raid that began successfully enough in the course of covering about 140 miles while lasting only eight days.[41]

After crossing Walden's Ridge and marching down the Sequatchie Valley, Wheeler's command looted and destroyed a Union wagon train of 32 six-mule wagons. Then a few miles south, near Jasper, Wheeler's force overtook a much larger train consisting of 800 six-mule wagons and others bringing the total number of wagons to perhaps 1,500. The wagons were loaded with millions of dollars' worth of enemy supplies, including ordnance, quartermaster's and commissary stores. Wheeler beat off the train's infantry escort in a sharp fight with few losses to his command.[42]

Wheeler's poorly clothed soldiers outfitted themselves in Yankee uniforms, then set fire to over three hundred wagons of ordnance. The earsplitting noise rent the air all the way to Chattanooga, where both Union and Confederate troops thought another battle had commenced.[43]

Finally, Wheeler's soldiers destroyed up to 4,000 of the train's mules, as many as they could not use, either sabering or shooting them. Until scavengers did their work, this created a devastating environmental pollution problem. Then they moved on across the mountains to the northwest and the town of McMinnville, where they captured a Union garrison of 587 men, a wagon train, 200 horses, and a railroad train. The stores which could not be carried off were destroyed, as were the railroad locomotive and cars, and a bridge over Hickory Creek. Then they rode to Murfreesboro, where the rail line was their primary target.[44]

Moving south, Wheeler's force destroyed all railroad bridges and trestles between Murfreesboro and Wartrace on the Nashville & Chattanooga Railroad while on their way to Shelbyville, located on a spur line. They looted and destroyed a large amount of sutler's stores of all kinds and many shops at Shelbyville. The latter town was sacked and thoroughly plundered in what was described as a shameful display of ill discipline.[45]

By now, however, the Federals were on Wheeler's trail, and they attacked him when he was at Farmington, fifteen miles west of Shelbyville, on his way to Lewisburg. In the fight at Farmington, Wheeler incurred substantial losses in a shattering rout of his troops and, for the raid overall, indifferent results in terms of hurting Rosecrans strategically.

His ranking antagonist at Farmington, Brigadier General Robert B. Mitchell, reported that Wheeler had lost six artillery pieces and between 2,000 and 3,000 men killed, wounded, and lost as prisoners and deserters during his eight-day raid.[46] Mitchell's figures relative to troop losses were an exaggeration, exceeding the total number of men in Wheeler's raiding force.

Wheeler's raid resulted in military action closer to the Fishers' home, two miles, than any other during the war. But none of the five brothers saw action so near their home. They had remained in Forrest's "Old Brigade," now commanded by George G. Dibrell, in East Tennessee and did not participate in Wheeler's raid in Middle Tennessee.

The action at Farmington was a running cavalry fight two miles east of John Fisher's farm on October 7, 1863. News of the fight must have been disquieting to members of the family on the home front. Wheeler's command was badly mauled after a third of it, a brigade under Brigadier General Henry B. Davidson, was permitted to stray and was almost trapped. Union cavalry brigades in the fight were commanded by brigadier generals Robert B. Mitchell and George H. Crook.

George Guild, of Baxter Smith's Fourth Tennessee Cavalry, was with Wheeler on the raid. Guild wrote that at Farmington Wheeler's men "were so full of plunder that fighting had gone out of their minds, and they were anxious to get to a safe place where they could make an inventory of their property."[47]

The Confederate defeat at Farmington marked the beginning of a precipitous cavalry flight south to the Tennessee River by pursued and pursuers alike. Wheeler managed to put his troops across to sanctuary and rest near the head of Muscle Shoals during the evening of October 9.

John J. McAdams, of Company D of McLemore's Fourth, was captured at Sugar Tree in Giles County, Tennessee, on October 9, barely missing a successful exit from the raid. McAdams was sent to Camp Morton, Indianapolis, Indiana, where he languished in prison for the balance of the war. He took the oath of allegiance and was released on May 1, 1865.

For all his trouble, McAdams apparently was the lone member of his regiment on this abortive raid.[48] The remainder stayed in East Tennessee with Forrest.

In October, Forrest was virtually stripped of his command again when he was detached from the Army of Tennessee and assigned to northern Mississippi and West Tennessee where he was to raise, train, and equip from enemy captures what was to become another superb fighting force. The regiments of his "Old Brigade," which he had raised in Middle Tennessee the year before, remained with the Army of Tennessee as a part of Wheeler's cavalry corps. Some of the troops thereof were on picket duty in the vicinity of Knoxville when Forrest left to go west. Forrest took with him only his staff and escort, Captain John W. Morton, Jr.'s Tennessee Battery and the late Major Charles McDonald's Eighteenth Tennessee Battalion, fewer than 300 men.[49]

But Forrest's "Old Brigade" was far from the unit it had been prior to Forrest's promotion to divisional commander after the death of Van Dorn in May 1863. In a reorganization of Bragg's army on November 20, 1863, after Wheeler's Middle Tennessee raid, the Fourth and Eleventh Tennessee cavalry regiments along with the First, Second, and Sixth, were reunited in Brigadier General Henry B. Davidson's brigade of Major General John A. Wharton's division. The Eighth and Ninth were in Brigadier General William Y.C. Humes' brigade of Brigadier General Frank Armstrong's division.

But there were other units which had more recently served in Forrest's brigade. Colonel Thomas G. Woodward's Second Kentucky was now in the Second Brigade of Brigadier General John H. Kelly's division. Cox's Tenth Tennessee, McKenzie's Fifth Tennessee, and Baxter Smith's, later Paul Anderson's, Fourth Tennessee, were in the First Brigade of Brigadier General Frank Armstrong's division.[50]

Forrest would not rejoin the Army of Tennessee for a year, long after Bragg had been replaced and sent to Richmond as military advisor to President Jefferson Davis.

But Forrest's and Bragg's farewell scene, played about this time, is well worth the retelling and reveals something of why Forrest had such a hold on everyone who served under him. The narrative was supplied by J.B. Cowan, a surgeon and cousin of Mary Ann Montgomery Forrest, the general's wife, who accompanied Forrest to see Bragg in the latter's field tent on Missionary Ridge, just east of Chattanooga.

As Forrest and he rapidly strode along, Cowan was aware that his companion was greatly agitated. He knew that Forrest had recently sent Bragg a letter just after he had been relieved of his command for the third time. But Cowan could only speculate about what Forrest had said in his letter. There was talk that Forrest might simply resign and go home.

Forrest uncharacteristically did not return the salute of the sentry in front of Bragg's tent. Inside, Bragg rose, greeted Forrest, and offered him his hand. Forrest refused it, saying he was "not here to pass civilities or compliments with you."

Standing stiff and erect before Bragg, Forrest delivered an angry indictment of what he perceived to be his superior's "cowardly and contemptible persecution" of him. Bragg's actions had begun soon after the Battle of Shiloh in April 1862. First Forrest accused Bragg of robbing him of his command in Kentucky and giving it to one of his favorites, Wheeler. Forrest had raised, trained, armed and equipped these fighting men through his own efforts against the enemy. Next, Bragg had sent him into West Tennessee in the fall and winter of 1862 with another brigade with improper arms and insufficient ammunition. Forrest accused Bragg of doing this "to ruin me and my career." But Forrest returned with his second brigade, having equipped it with enemy captures in the process of which he developed it into a superb fighting machine. And now, "in order to further humiliate me," Forrest said, Bragg had removed him from command of these troops. He also accused Bragg of fawning on the authorities in Richmond by reporting "damned lies" while he (Forrest) told the truth. If that were not enough, Forrest said that Bragg was revengeful and spiteful toward him because he (again Forrest) would not toady to him as others did.

Forrest was belligerent and threatening. He called Bragg "a damned scoundrel." Then, accusing him of cowardice, he ranted: "If you were any part of a man I would slap your jaws and force you to resent it!"

Indicating that he had stood Bragg's pettiness for as long as he intended, Forrest said that "you need not issue any more orders to me, for I will not obey them! And I will hold you personally responsible for any further indignities which you may try to inflict on me."

Referring to an alleged threat by Bragg to arrest him for not obeying orders, Forrest dared him to do it and asserted: "If you ever again try to interfere with me or cross my path, it will be at the peril of your life!"[51]

Fortunately Bragg, the army's commander, sat passively through the whole tirade.

Shortly thereafter, Forrest considered sending his resignation to Bragg. But President Davis, then visiting the Army of Tennessee and recognizing Forrest's value, intervened to keep Forrest in the army and have him transferred. On October 29, 1863, Bragg approved Forrest's transfer out of his department.[52]

The parting of Forrest with members of his "Old Brigade" was particularly and mutually regretted. The men of Starnes' Fourth, Biffle's Fifth, Dibrell's Eighth, Cox's Tenth, and Holman's Eleventh Tennessee cavalry regiments, together with Freeman's battery, bore something of the image of their mentor and leader. They were saddened at his removal.

Virtually all of the soldiers who served under Forrest agreed that his departure for duty in Mississippi was another blow to the effectiveness of their army, one that portended further problems for them in the weeks and months ahead.[53]

Chapter 4

Chattanooga, Knoxville, and into the Atlanta Campaign, October 30, 1863–July 22, 1864

Of course, the results of the Confederate victory at Chickamauga were disappointing to the victors because Bragg did not follow up his victory to pursue and annihilate or force the withdrawal of Rosecrans' forces north of the Tennessee River. Accordingly, only two months later, with U.S. Grant now in command of a magnificently reinforced Union Army of the Cumberland, the badly outnumbered Confederate Army of Tennessee, still weakened by acrimonious defections and professional ineptitude among its leaders, was stunningly defeated at the Battle of Chattanooga (November 23–25, 1863), thus vitiating the effects of its victory at Chickamauga.[1]

By the end of October, Bragg, at Jefferson Davis's suggestion, had further weakened his command by sending Longstreet to Knoxville to seek to dislodge Ambrose Burnside, commanding the Federal Army of the Ohio, who had taken the town on September 1. Longstreet had only recently come from Virginia and joined the Army of Tennessee for the Battle of Chickamauga. But in a short period of time, Bragg and his willfully ambitious subordinate found that they did not get along any better than did Bragg with other of his senior staff officers.[2]

Longstreet took with him to Knoxville the two divisions of his own corps which he had brought with him from the Army of Northern Virginia, McLaws' division under Major General Lafayette McLaws and John B. Hood's division under Brigadier General Micah Jenkins.

Longstreet's command also included his corps artillery under Colonel E. Porter Alexander as well as Major A. Leydon's artillery and Major General Robert Ransom, Jr.'s, cavalry division from Virginia and a part of Joseph Wheeler's cavalry corps. The latter included five brigades of horsemen, two under the command of Brigadier General William T. Martin and two under Brigadier General Frank C. Armstrong, plus John A. Wharton's First Brigade under Colonel Thomas Harrison. Altogether Longstreet's force consisted of about 14,000 effectives or about one third of the Army of Tennessee.[3]

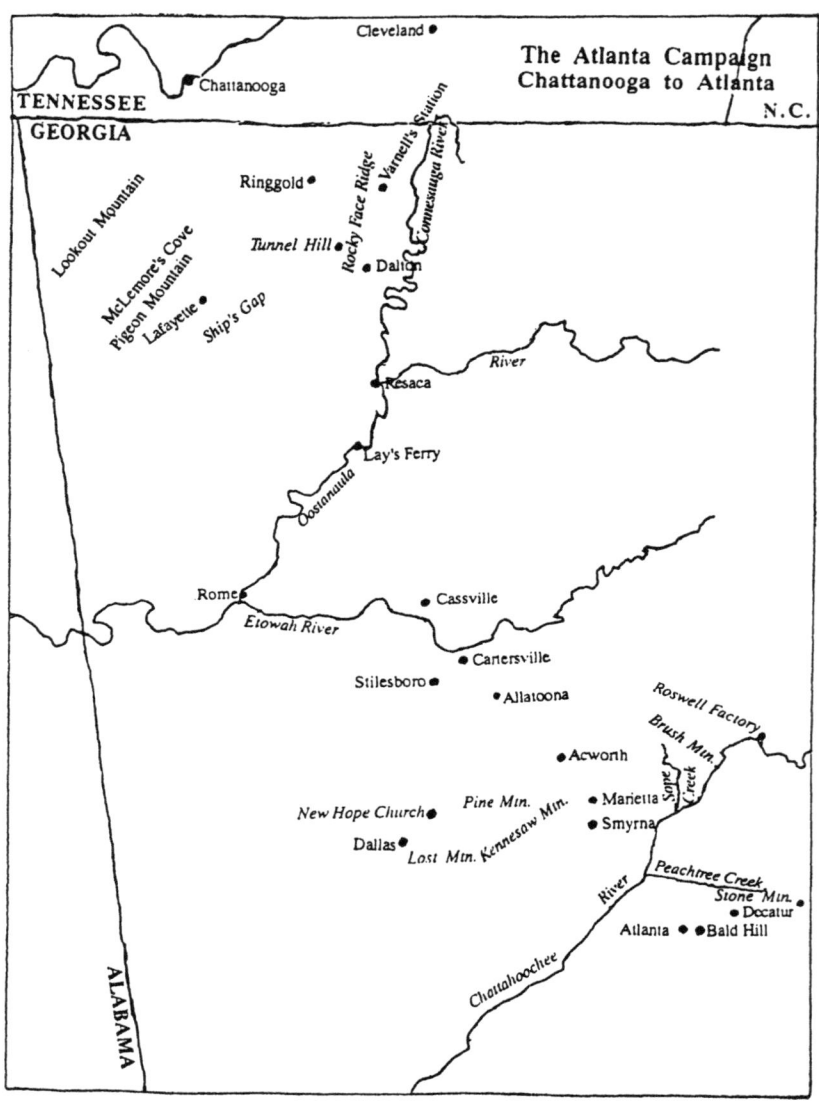

Both the Fourth and Eleventh Tennessee cavalry regiments were assigned to Wharton's Second Brigade, headed by Brigadier General Henry B. Davidson, as a result of a reorganization of Bragg's army on November 20, 1863.[4]

McLemore's Fourth and Holman's Eleventh remained with the main part of Bragg's Army of Tennessee around Chattanooga, then Dalton, along with the First, Second, and Sixth Tennessee cavalry regiments as a part of the Second Brigade of John A. Wharton's division. The brigade, reinforced by the Fifth Tennessee Cavalry and a Tennessee artillery battery, the latter under Captain Gustave A. Huwald, made up Bragg's cavalry arm through the late fall of 1863.[5]

The few cavalry regiments retained by Bragg when he sent Longstreet's corps and most of Bragg's cavalry in late October to besiege Burnside at Knoxville were used primarily for reconnoitering and vidette duty on the various approaches to Chattanooga which Bragg thought might be used by attacking armies.

Sometimes Bragg's cavalry units skirmished with the enemy's infantry or cavalry. As late as November 20, the Fourth Tennessee Cavalry was reported by the enemy in action in McLemore's Cove between Pigeon and Lookout Mountain in Georgia in a minor engagement which presaged Grant's attack on Chattanooga three days later.[6] But scant use was made of cavalry in the decisive Battle of Chattanooga.

On December 10, McLemore's Fourth was reported officially as having replaced Baxter Smith's Fourth Tennessee Cavalry in Frank Armstrong's division in upper East Tennessee. George Guild, however, in his regimental history of Baxter Smith's Fourth, indicates that the regiment did not go with Longstreet to Knoxville, but remained about Chattanooga.

Holman's Eleventh was first reported with Longstreet on December 31, 1863. Both McLemore's Fourth and the Eleventh remained in upper East Tennessee until March 29, 1864. But Daniel Holman's history of the Eleventh and references to the Fourth from other sources indicate that both regiments were with Longstreet in upper East Tennessee before they were officially reported there in the manning tables of the Army of Tennessee.[7]

Indeed on Sunday, November 1, 1863, Daniel Holman's Eleventh Tennessee Cavalry was reported with a detachment of Dibrell's brigade which was ordered to report to Brigadier General John C. Vaughn at Morganton in Loudon County on the east bank of the Little Tennessee River. Fording and swimming the river, the command was all night making the crossing. Vaughn then moved the detachment north to Unitia just south of the Tennessee River.

Federal troops were on the north shore of the river in force. A brisk duel across the river was joined with scant casualties to either side. Vaughn's detachment then retraced its steps and, marching all night, began to recross the Little Tennessee at Morganton. Before the command had crossed, however, it was attacked by a force of Federal cavalry.

Several men of Miller's Company C and Captain Chatham Coffee's Company H of the Eleventh were captured in the attack. Holman reported that several of the captured men escaped and crossed the river upstream at Niles Ferry.

At least six captured Company C men did not escape and were sent north to prisoner of war camps, where two died. The captured men included

Corporal Thomas A. Boyd, 19, of Marshall County, who was sent to Camp Chase, Ohio, on November 11, 1863. Boyd was transferred to Ft. Delaware on February 29, 1864, where he stayed until paroled and exchanged at City Point, Virginia, on February 27, 1865. At the end of the war, Boyd surrendered and was paroled at Nashville upon taking the oath of allegiance on May 10, 1865.

Other captives, James T. Drumwright, 32; Thomas J. Epperson, 18; W.T.C. King, Samuel Warner, and Joseph B. Wynn, 30, were similarly incarcerated at Camp Chase and Ft. Delaware.

Epperson and King died at Ft. Delaware, Epperson of scurvy on August 5, and King of chronic diarrhea almost two weeks later, August 18, 1864. The remains of both were "buried on the Jersey shore." They were interred in trenches, a mass grave in which the remains rather quickly became unidentifiable.

The burial ground is marked by tiny Finn's Point National Cemetery, Salem, New Jersey, where the remains of almost 2,500 POWs from Ft. Delaware were interred. Finn's Point was designated a national cemetery in 1875. An eighty-five-foot memorial obelisk, with bronze tablets surrounding its base, was erected by the United States in 1910.[8] The bronze tablets record the names of prisoners who died at Ft. Delaware and whose remains are in the cemetery.

At Sweetwater in Monroe County on the morning of November 12, Longstreet revealed to his staff his plan for approaching Burnside's army in Knoxville. His infantry corps, together with his corps artillery, would cross the Tennessee River at Huff's Ferry and advance on Knoxville from the west. Wheeler was to furnish sufficient cavalry to picket the river from the mouth of the Hiwassee River east to Loudon, the area where the army crossed, to insure the main force's continued access to the river.

With the balance of his command, Wheeler was to advance on the Federal garrison at Maryville, some twenty miles south of Knoxville, disperse it, then march in the direction of Knoxville and try to take possession of the southeastern approaches to the town and hold the heights on the south bank of the Tennessee River which overlook the town.[9]

At dark on November 13, Wheeler began a night march to Maryville, where his precipitous and unexpected appearance on the scene just at daybreak caused the Union regiment there, the Eleventh Kentucky Cavalry, to decamp as rapidly as possible. Wheeler stated that he captured 151 of the Kentuckians before they could make good their escape.[10]

But before the engagement was completed, Wheeler's force was struck by Colonel Frank Wolford's cavalry brigade in an attack which was repulsed and which resulted in the capture of 85 prisoners, again according to Wheeler.

At dawn on the fourteenth, Wheeler undertook to carry out his other orders relative to approaching Knoxville from the southeast quarter. This resulted in a day of sharp fighting across Little River and Stock Creek as Wheeler's horsemen pushed the Union forces right up to the Cherokee Heights on the south bank of the Tennessee River at the city limits.[11]

Meanwhile, Thomas Fisher had been detached from his company and regiment and detailed as a courier on Longstreet's staff. He was sent on the morning of the fourteenth by Longstreet with a message to Wheeler whom he was told he would find somewhere south and east of Knoxville. He rode all day, much of the time with his thumb on the hammer of his gun. He was aware that he was riding alone through country populated by Unionists whose capacity, thirst, and inclination to kill Confederates had been well established from the beginning of the war.

Fisher found Wheeler after dark and delivered his message. The message indicated that Longstreet would like Wheeler to send him a division of cavalry to join his force. With the remainder of his cavalry "on your present line," he wanted Wheeler to "[threaten] Knoxville as far as in your power." He also wanted Wheeler to "have all the beef-cattle that may be found collected for us, and as much flour collected as you may spare from your own command." As an afterthought, Longstreet told Wheeler that if he could get across the Holston River, he would like him "to cross your whole command and operate with us."[12]

Wheeler told Fisher to turn in with his escort, feed his mount, and get something to eat. He said that there was a citizen with Southern sympathies who lived on the Holston River who was with him who would leave for home about ten o'clock and direct Fisher and three other soldiers who were going back to Longstreet's corps to a safe means of crossing the river and rejoining Longstreet west of Knoxville.

Before leaving, Fisher was given a message by Wheeler to be carried to Longstreet informing the latter of Wheeler's plan to return to the army's main force. Riding back in the company of three comrades, Tom crossed the river about daybreak and reached Longstreet on the morning of the fifteenth with the desired reply. Two days later on November 17, crossing the Holston at Louisville, Wheeler's cavalry rejoined Longstreet west of Knoxville.[13]

Confederate investment of Knoxville began on the eighteenth. Wheeler's cavalry extended the infantry line on the left flank from the Knoxville & Clinton Railroad east to the Holston River, a distance of about four miles. For six days the line was kept almost continuously skirmishing with the enemy.[14]

The Eleventh occupied the Cumberland Gap Road in full view of the city and got little rest throughout the siege.[15] On November 23, Wheeler withdrew a portion of his cavalry, including the Eleventh, and went west to Kingston to ascertain the strength of Federal forces there. The next day Wheeler attacked the Federal forces at Kingston but could not dislodge them. Then Wheeler withdrew to Knoxville where the Eleventh resumed its position on the Cumberland Gap Road on the twenty-sixth.[16]

Two days later, November 28, 1863, Company D of the Fourth Tennessee Cavalry lost three men who deserted. They were John A. Bills and Richard T. Long, 24, and Sergeant William W. Wiggs, 20, who surrendered to Federal troops, possibly in Campbell County, north of Knoxville.[17]

The siege of Knoxville continued for two more weeks until finally an early morning assault was launched, without artillery preparation, against Fort Sanders, a site that is now a part of the campus of the University of Tennessee.[18] The attack came on Sunday, November 29, at the northwest angle of the fortified lines. The fort's defenses used staked-down telegraph wire as an obstruction, there being no barbed wire then, in advance of a deep ditch and the parapet of the fort. The attackers found that the steep and icy slopes of the ditch could not be climbed. They were slaughtered by time-fuse shells used as hand grenades and thrown into their midst. Burnside wrote that the attackers losses totaled over 1,000 killed, wounded, and captured, while he lost 13.

Colonel George G. Dibrell of the Tennessee Eighth Cavalry reported that Longstreet's attack was ill-advised. A few nights before the attack, the cavalry made a demonstration in front of the enemy to test the strength of their lines. The reaction indicated a very weak line in front of the cavalry. Although this was reported to Longstreet, Dibrell reported that the general ordered the attack to be made on the Federals' strongest fortified position.[19]

Following the unsuccessful assault, Longstreet received a telegram from President Jefferson Davis ordering him to come to Bragg's assistance at Chattanooga. Then word came via a captured letter from Grant to Burnside that a force under Major General William T. Sherman was coming from Chattanooga to Burnside's relief, another from Decherd, Tennessee, under Brigadier General Washington Lafayette Elliott, and yet another from Cumberland Gap under Brigadier General John Gray Foster.

Longstreet decided to remain in front of Knoxville to hold down for as long as possible the Federal forces which he faced. But on December 2, 1863, Longstreet issued orders to his corps to lift their siege of Knoxville and march up the valley and into winter quarters in the town of Russellville, about forty-nine miles east northeast of Knoxville in Hamblen County. Martin's cavalry remained about Knoxville to cover the withdrawal of the infantry.[20]

Early in the morning of the first, however, Frank Armstrong's cavalry division, which included both the Fourth and Eleventh, had been ordered north out the Cumberland Gap Road to meet Foster's troops bent upon relieving Burnside of his siege. Near Maynardville, Dibrell's advance cavalry met the advance cavalry of Foster's force and skirmished with them near nightfall.

The next day, while in pursuit of Foster's troops a few miles northeast of Maynardville, Dibrell's Eighth Regiment ran into an ambuscade on Lone Mountain while following a narrow wagon trail covered with ice. Near the foot of the mountain, the cavalry met Foster's infantry in force. In a sharp skirmish, Foster's Indiana troops began to withdraw when they were hit by a mounted charge by the Fourth Tennessee supported on the left by the Eleventh. Foster's troops retired to the protection of rail works and fought off the cavalry charge. Thereupon, the Fourth, Eighth, and Tenth Tennessee cavalry regiments dismounted and drove the enemy back across the Clinch River.

The brigade commander, Colonel George G. Dibrell, was wounded in the action on the second and was subsequently replaced by Brigadier William Y.C. Humes, then by Colonel Jacob Biffle, then by Colonel Daniel W. Holman before Dibrell returned to duty about two months later, in late January 1864.[21]

While Company C of the Eleventh recorded no men killed or wounded on December 2 in the fight at Lone Mountain, the company lost four men captured, Thomas P. Giles, William J. Pate, Benjamin C. Primrose, and Sergeant J.G. Owen, on December 2 and 3. They were captured some 25 miles to the west at Jacksboro, seat of Campbell County. Each captive was sent to the Rock Island (Illinois) Prison Barracks for incarceration, arriving on December 23, 1863, where each subsequently expressed a desire to take the oath of allegiance, a desire recorded on a muster roll of POWs dated March 18, 1864.

Primrose was recorded on his prison record as having "deserted" because he was "always opposed to the rebellion." A prewar resident of Unionville in Bedford County, Tennessee, Primrose was permitted to take the oath and was released on January 30, 1865.

Owen, a resident of Williamson County, Tennessee, expressed a desire to sign the oath, to be released, and to go to Nashville. But he was not released from Rock Island until the war was over, May 18, 1865.

Pate, like Owen, a resident of Reed's Crossroads in southeastern Williamson County, wished to take the oath and go to Nashville. He was released just before the war ended on April 3, 1865.

Giles was recorded as wanting to take the oath and go home, which was reportedly "near Nashville." But his military record is incomplete and does not reveal his post-prison fate.

On December 3, Company D of the Fourth lost Corporal James M. Bartlett, 24, captured by men of the Ninth Illinois Infantry Regiment at Athens, Alabama. What he was doing in Alabama is unclear. Bartlett was sent to the Rock Island Prison Barracks, arriving January 5, 1864. He died there three weeks later of variola on January 28. His remains were interred in grave #306, south of the prison barracks. Bartlett prior to the war was a farmer of Marshall County, Tennessee.[22]

The weather continued to be unusually cold and the roads frozen. On the night of December 2, word reached Armstrong that the siege of Knoxville had been lifted and Longstreet's army was moving back in the direction of Virginia. After burying its dead, the cavalry followed the main army to the east, remaining on the north side of the Holston River for about three weeks. Most of their forage was obtained on the Holston River and Buffalo Creek in Grainger County. The cavalry was kept active through the cold winter months.[23]

The same day the siege of Knoxville was lifted, Wheeler wrote to Longstreet that Bragg wished his cavalry returned to the main army at Dalton. Longstreet, however, declined to do so, believing that his own position was precarious in the extreme and that the enemy's cavalry facing him was numerically superior to his own.

For four months through the winter, the bitterest winter of the war, and into the spring of 1864, Longstreet's corps lived off the country and held the last remaining area of Tennessee in the hands of the Confederacy, ironically, the First Congressional District of the state, of which it is said that it furnished more volunteer soldiers to the United States Army during the rebellion than any other district in the country.[24]

The cavalry which went into winter quarters with Longstreet in early December was no longer personally commanded by Joe Wheeler, who had received orders on November 24, during the Battle of Chattanooga, to rejoin Bragg at Missionary Ridge. Wheeler returned south following the Army of Tennessee's latest debacle, being run out of the environs of Chattanooga by vastly superior forces under Grant's command. Wheeler left William T. Martin, now a major general, in charge of Longstreet's cavalry while he and his escort crossed the mountains to arrive in Dalton, Georgia, and report to Bragg.[25]

In the reorganization of December 10, McLemore's Fourth Tennessee Cavalry was reported in Longstreet's command in Brigadier General William Y.C. Humes' brigade of Frank Armstrong's division. Humes' brigade, formerly Dibrell's, prior to the latter's wounding on December 2, was now composed of the Fourth, Fifth, Eighth, Ninth, and Tenth Tennessee cavalry regiments. By December 31, Humes had been relieved by Jacob Biffle and the Fifth Regiment had been replaced by the Eleventh, placing all five of the brothers Fisher once again in the same brigade.[26]

The Eleventh was kept quite busy through December. It sought out Federal forces by moving about to Blaine's Crossroads, Rutledge, Bean's Station, and Bull's Gap. On the sixteenth, it captured 16 prisoners at Massengill's Mills in Grainger County. On the twenty-third it was active in a fight involving Dibrell's brigade near Mossy Creek after crossing the Holston River at Thompson Ford. Again, on the twenty-ninth, the Eleventh fought in the vicinity of Mossy Creek, a place both armies sought because it was agriculturally rich and productive.[27]

Company C continued to suffer attrition of its manpower. T.J. Ashworth deserted in Campbell County on December 11. On the eighteenth, R.M. Higginbottom was captured near Knoxville and arrived at the Rock Island Prison Barracks on January 23, 1864. T.R. King was captured on December 20 and was sent to Camp Chase at Columbus, Ohio, on January 1, 1864.[28]

The severity of the winter of 1863–1864 in the uplands of East Tennessee served to emphasize the deplorable state of the cavalry of the Army of Tennessee. Company complements reportedly were far below their original strengths owing to a variety of casualties, including captures and desertions. Some of the men were without horses or had horses which were without saddles or bridles and in need of shoeing, and the men themselves were poorly supplied with clothing, blankets, tents, overcoats, and shoes. They frequently lacked food and ammunition. When they became ill, as often happened because of poor diet and physical hardship, they had scant recourse to medical attention or care. And now the severe winter weather took an additional toll in sickness and death and tested the resolve of the most committed soldiers.

The cavalry had not been paid for several months, nor had the troops had systematic furloughs. Badly needed supplies for Biffle's Tennessee brigade had been sent to the main Army of Tennessee, now in Georgia, and were not received by the brigade until March 1864.

Morale was understandably low and discipline likewise suffered. Shoes, clothing, and forage were in short supply. There were incidents of marauding and depredations against the military as well as the civilian population, friend and foe. The infantry of Longstreet's corps was in a similar, if not sorrier, state.[29]

And still the enemy tested them through the winter months, the cavalry bearing the brunt of enemy contacts, protecting the front and flanks of Longstreet's corps. There was either skirmishing or pitched battles at Bean's Station, Russellville, Strawberry Plains, Mossy Creek, Maryville, Shook's Gap, Bull's Gap, and Dandridge.

Company C of the Eleventh lost Joseph Bugg, 17, and Elias King, captured on January 10–11, 1864, at Morristown, Tennessee. They were both sent, via Knoxville and Louisville, to Rock Island Prison Barracks for incarceration, arriving on January 29, 1864. King died at Rock Island of chronic diarrhea on March 17, 1864. His remains were interred in grave #838, south of the prison barracks.

On a muster roll of prisoners dated March 18, 1864, Bugg reportedly desired to take the oath of allegiance. He was quoted as being "tired of C.S.A., will be loyal." But there are no subsequent military service records for Bugg, and we are left to conjecture what became of his efforts to be released.[30]

Dibrell's brigade, in defense of the corps' supply train, beat off the enemy strongly entrenched at Dandridge on January 20 and drove the Federals west past Strawberry Plains toward Knoxville. The Eleventh dismounted and fought with the infantry in the engagement at Dandridge.

On the twenty-sixth, after crossing the French Broad River and moving in the direction of Sevierville, Dibrell's brigade met Colonel Frank Wolford's cavalry brigade near Grassy Valley and the Pigeon River and drove them three to four miles. Two days later a sharp morning engagement with the enemy near the Blant residence at Blant's Hill on the road from Sevierville to Newport resulted in the withdrawal of the enemy.

The next day, the brigade moved down the French Broad River and went into camp on January 30 on the Pigeon River, about three miles below Sevierville where the brigade remained encamped until February 22.

The Fourth was reported in a skirmish near Knoxville on the Sevierville Road on February 20, 1864.[31] And there was incessant picket duty in bitter cold, sleet, and snow against the north wind, which cut through the soldiers' inadequate clothing to the very marrow, rendering each mount a shivering piece of frozen sculpture.

On January 29, 1864, Longstreet wrote General Samuel Cooper, Adjutant and Inspector General of the army in Richmond, that Major General William T. Martin lacked experience to command his cavalry and should be replaced. He suggested Major General Wade Hampton as Martin's replacement.

Cooper sent along Longstreet's message to the Secretary of War, James A. Seddon, with an indorsement that he believed Longstreet had not established the need for the recommended change and that he further believed that Hampton could not be spared from the army in Virginia.

Unsurprisingly, Seddon concurred with Cooper. The following summer, on August 15, Martin would be relieved of duty by Wheeler near Dalton, Georgia, when Martin, following execution of a demarche, was derelict in informing Wheeler of his whereabouts.

On January 30, 1864, Longstreet reported to Samuel Cooper in Richmond that, according to William T. Martin, about a hundred Alabama cavalry officers and men had left for home on the night of the twenty-seventh. Longstreet blamed Wheeler for this turn of events because Wheeler, he said, had withheld wagons and supplies and kept back officers and men in Georgia and even put them in a camp to rest. Word of this had reached Wheeler's troops under Longstreet who were facing the worst sort of discomfort and privation. Many of them were growing restless and felt put upon. Longstreet requested that Cooper use his good offices to remedy the situation.

And again on February 6, Longstreet complained to Cooper that there was an insufficient number of general officers for the cavalry attached to his corps. He had only two, Major General William T. Martin and Brigadier General John T. Morgan. But he had six brigades. Longstreet said he thought he had good material, but he needed leaders. Also forage was running low, he said, which seriously interfered with the cavalry's capacity to perform efficiently.[32]

Those troops who were veterans of Forrest's command, in their arctic isolation were oblivious to thanks tendered them in a resolution passed by the Confederate States Congress in Richmond on February 17, 1864. The Congress thanked Forrest and the officers and men of his command for meritorious service in the field, specifically naming their capture of Streight's raiders, their service in the Battle of Chickamauga, and their recent "brilliant" service in West Tennessee.

The last reference was to Forrest's latest visit to Jackson, Tennessee, in December, 1863, where he raised and extricated a largely unarmed force of about 3,500 men which was threatened by three vastly superior enemy forces, each of which was larger, and most certainly better trained and armed, than Forrest's inchoate body of recruits.[33]

But most of Forrest's veterans who had been with him in the capture of Streight and at the Battle of Chickamauga now were under Wheeler or in Longstreet's command. Those operating with Longstreet's corps, however, gained some satisfaction in knowing that the Confederate Congress on the very same day had passed a joint resolution of thanks to Longstreet and his command for their gallant services and brilliant achievements in the war.[34]

There was good news for most of Wheeler's cavalry operating with Longstreet on February 25, 1864. Longstreet ordered Martin with his division of two cavalry brigades to rejoin the Army of Tennessee, now under Joseph E. Johnston, at Dalton, Georgia.[35] This meant that, of Wheeler's cavalry, only Biffle's (once again Dibrell's) brigade, which included the Fourth and Eleventh Tennessee, and Harrison's brigade, the latter consisting only of the Third Arkansas and the Eighth and Eleventh Texas regiments, continued to serve with Longstreet.

Dibrell's brigade continued to bear its share of fighting in the coldest winter of the war. On February 20, Longstreet directed the cavalry to go to Knoxville, where the Federals seemed to be holed up, to make a reconnaisance in force and develop the Federals. Going to the hills overlooking the city, the Tennessee brigade was attacked by Burnside's cavalry and forced to fight to avoid capture. Colonel Holman of the Eleventh, acting brigade commander, came near being captured.

On its return, the brigade crossed the French Broad River at Evan's Ford and, moving by way of Dandridge, camped for several days near the mouth of the Chucky River before moving to Newport in Cocke County where it remained until March 15. It was here in March that the brigade belatedly received its winter clothing.[36]

The unspeakable hardships endured by Confederate soldiers in Longstreet's army in icy upper East Tennessee led to many desertions by cold, sick, bored, and lonely soldiers. Such was the case of F.M. Williamson, a neighbor of the Fishers at Cave Spring who had enlisted in Company C of the Eleventh on September 30, 1862, when four Fisher brothers and their friend, Wesley Williamson, volunteered in the same company. F.M. rode away one day in January and was not seen again by his comrades. He took the oath of allegiance to the United States on January 22, 1864, at the Office of the Provost Marshal General in Knoxville, thus ending his fight for Southern independence.[37]

And from Company D of the Fourth in February, Jacob C. Fisher, a first cousin of the five brothers and son of their uncle, George W. Fisher, took leave of his comrades and took the oath of allegiance. He had ridden with Jim and Monroe to Camp Cheatham and joined the Fourth with his cousins on November 16, 1861.

Jacob C. Fisher was 24 years of age when he took up arms. He had been a farmer and had clerked for W.S. Hurt, a relative of his Aunt Sarah Hurt Fisher, at Hurt's Crossroads in Maury County, Tennessee. He had a history of poor health during his army service. On May 6, 1862, he was sick and had been left at Chattanooga to recover while his regiment moved on to action against the enemy in both Middle and East Tennessee.

On December 6, 1862, Jacob C. Fisher received a Certificate of Disability for Discharge from Edward Swanson, regimental surgeon. Swanson had found him incapable of performing the duties of a soldier because of a "predisposition of scrofula of the lungs," a diagnosis which perhaps suggested a case of pulmonary tuberculosis.

Despite his exemption from combat, Jacob remained with his regiment and served in the debilitating winter of 1863–1864 in upper East Tennessee. This time, however, the condition of his health evidently was jaded and painful enough for him to determine that the prognosis was so unpromising that he had had enough fighting.

In order for him to resume living back home in federally-controlled Marshall or Maury County, Tennessee, without being a fugitive, he may have felt it was necessary for him to take the oath of allegiance to the United States and renounce any intention thereafter of giving support to the Southern Confederacy or any of its adherents.

He took the oath in Knoxville in February 1864 and returned to his home. In the postwar years, he became a merchant successively in Verona, Fayetteville, and Shelbyville, all in Tennessee, before returning to farming in 1885. He married Mattie Bell in Fayetteville in 1872, and they raised a family of six children.[38]

Company D of the Fourth lost two other soldiers to desertion. William H. Collins signed with his mark the oath of allegiance in Nashville on January 4, 1864. He had been left sick in Loudon, Tennessee, in late November 1863, just prior to Longstreet's siege of Knoxville. A prewar resident of Marshall County, it appears that he may have tried to make his way home when he was captured. When he enlisted in the company as one of the original recruits in November 1861, he gave his age as 28. He later claimed to be over 35.

On February 29, 1864, another Company D soldier, Sergeant Gashan A. Bills, 25, took the oath of allegiance, after deserting, at the Office of the Provost Marshall General of East Tennessee in Knoxville, and was released.[39]

The unrelentingly hostile winter weather claimed yet another victim. On March 8 William Stratton Fisher temporarily defected from Company C of the Eleventh at Newport owing to ill health, a respiratory problem which might have been pulmonary tuberculosis, catarrh, or acute bronchitis, exacerbated by the chilling weather, lack of proper food and medical attention, and his lack of suitable arctic-type clothing and shelter. He got a forty-day furlough and, spurning convalescence in a military hospital in Atlanta, made his way stealthily through territory that was almost entirely enemy-held. After a brief convalescence, he rejoined the army in North Georgia on April 18, 1864, in time for the start of Sherman's Atlanta campaign.[40]

With the coming of spring 1864, Longstreet and his corps started back to Virginia, whence they had come in September, six months earlier. And the surviving members of Wheeler's cavalry marched south to North Georgia to rejoin the Army of Tennessee, which, since December 27, 1863, had been under the command of General Joseph Eggleston Johnston.

The Army of Tennessee remnant was within about three miles of Warrensburg, in Greene County, Tennessee, where, on March 22, 1864, snow had fallen to a depth of ten inches. On the twenty-fifth, the brigade moved up to Cedar Creek and camped. Four days later, the command crossed Paint Mountain at Paint Rock and camped near Hot Springs, just across the border in North Carolina. Then it marched up the French Broad River across the Unaka Mountains and through Asheville on March 31, thence south through Saluda Gap into South Carolina.

It arrived in Greenville on April 3, where it rested for a day, reached Anderson on April 6 and rested three days, moved to the Seneca River on April 9 and camped one day, crossed the Tugaloo River on the tenth and was back in Georgia, reached Athens on the thirteenth and Marietta on the eighteenth, left Marietta to go up to the front on April 19, reached Resaca on the twenty-third and remained in camp there until May 4, when it marched back north to Dalton, just below Chattanooga.[41]

Veterans of Longstreet's campaign were glad to leave behind the winter weather they had recently endured and looked forward hopefully to being a part of the command of Joe Johnston rather than his predecessor, Braxton Bragg.

In transit in South Carolina on April 8, 1864, Lieutenant E.G. Hamilton of Company C of the Eleventh was "dropped" from the company's roll. The company's January–June 1864 muster roll reported Hamilton absent on June 29, 1864, and recorded that Hamilton had been "arrested April 19, 1863, came out [from Middle Tennessee] with the army, sent or admitted to go to Tenn. by Gen. Forrest. No knowledge of his being notified of his release."

Subsequently Hamilton, a prewar farmer of Marshall County, Tennessee, was apparently reinstated to his company's rolls because he was reported a deserter on February 15, 1865, and took the oath of allegiance in Nashville on March 9, 1865. On April 24, 1865, depositions regarding Hamilton's alleged activities as a guerrilla and bushwhacker during the war would be taken by the United States Provost Marshal at Shelbyville, Tennessee. But the depositions seem to have been insufficiently conclusive regarding Hamilton's alleged illegal activities during the war. His service record reports no subsequent legal action against Hamilton by the army.[42]

The last detached elements of Wheeler's cavalry rejoined other units of the cavalry of the Army of Tennessee which had stayed with the main force about Chattanooga throughout the winter of 1863–1864 or had been ordered back from upper East Tennessee earlier. The brigade of which the Fourth and Eleventh were a part remained under the command of Colonel George G. Dibrell and was placed in Brigadier General John H. Kelly's division of Major General Joseph Wheeler's cavalry corps of the Army of Tennessee, now under the command of General Joseph E. Johnston.[43]

These last returning veterans of Longstreet's winter stand in East Tennessee arrived just in time to become involved in opposing Sherman's Atlanta Campaign, which commenced on May 7 with just over 100,000 Union troops opposed by not more than half as many Confederates. The arrival a week later of the Army of Mississippi under Leonidas Polk brought the Confederate total up to about 63,000.[44]

Wheeler's cavalry, picketing the front and flank of the army extending from Ship's Gap on the left flank to the Connesauga River on the right, received the first impact of Sherman's advance north of Tunnel Hill on May 6 where the Western & Atlantic Railroad tunnels through Rocky Face Ridge between Chattanooga and Dalton.[45] Pushing ahead, Sherman, from a slight elevation, surveyed the situation around Dalton and decided against launching a frontal assault on Johnston's army. Instead he opted for Major General James B. McPherson capturing and holding the railroad to the south in the rear of Johnston's army at Dalton.[46]

Wheeler's cavalry moved north of Dalton on the road which led to Cleveland, Tennessee. Near Varnell's Station on May 7, the Eighth Tennessee Cavalry was on picket duty when they were attacked and driven in by a portion of Sherman's cavalry under Major General Alexander M. McCook, who had been sent to create a diversion on the Confederate right flank. Two days later, Dibrell's brigade, including the Fourth and Eleventh Tennessee cavalry regiments, and a part of Allen's brigade, dismounted, all under Colonel George G. Dibrell, met a charge by McCook's troops. Aided by a mounted counter charge of the Eighth Confederate and Eighth Texas regiments, they drove McCook's horsemen from the field, taking about a hundred prisoners.[47]

On May 11, 1864, Wheeler was ordered by Johnston to determine what the Union forces were doing on the west side of Rocky Face Ridge, a question of utmost importance to the Confederate Army of Tennessee in anticipating where to expect the next blow from the Union Army of the Tennessee.[48]

Wheeler took all his cavalry and moved, with men of Dibrell's brigade in the van, through Varnell's Station westward against Brigadier General George Stoneman's cavalry. Dibrell's troops drove back the enemy, took prisoners, and destroyed a large number of wagons and supplies.[49] But more importantly, Wheeler confirmed what the Confederate command should have suspected all along: that the main Union force, all but two divisions, was moving south behind Rocky Face Ridge and would likely entrap Johnston's army if its leaders chose to remain at Dalton.[50]

The Army of Tennessee at this time consisted of two corps under the command of lieutenant generals John B. Hood and William J. Hardee. Leonidas Polk's Army of Mississippi, marching from Mississippi, was approaching Dalton by rail from Atlanta and had detrained south of Dalton at Resaca. Polk brought with him about 10,000 infantry and 4,000 cavalry. Polk's cavalry division was under the command of Brigadier General William H. Jackson and consisted of three brigades plus three artillery batteries.[51] By July 31, 1864, Jackson's cavalry had been removed from Polk's command and placed in Wheeler's corps.[52]

On the morning of May 13, Johnston abandoned Dalton and, covered by Wheeler's cavalry, fell back south, with Hood's and Hardee's corps, to join with Polk at Resaca.

Fighting began at Resaca on the thirteenth between Polk's troops and those of Major General James B. McPherson. Early the next day, Kelly's cavalry division went out ahead of the infantry to ascertain the position and strength of the enemy. Kelly's cavalry was driven back in a severe fight just preceding a heavy Union attack against Hood's infantry corps on the Confederate right.[53] Wheeler's cavalry corps dismounted and went into trenches all across the Confederate front from left to right.[54] The Eleventh was on the extreme right of the Confederate line, with the regiment's left resting on the adjacent infantry and its right on the river. The regiment participated in the fighting against repeated Federal attacks.[55]

Trench warfare characterized the war from this period to the end.

Later on the fourteenth, Johnston directed Wheeler to go forward and ascertain the strength of the left flank of the Union force facing Hood. Wheeler's subsequent report indicated that the force might be vulnerable to a Confederate attack. Johnston ordered an assault, and Hood's troops drove the Federals back from the vicinity of the railroad late on the fourteenth. The next day, fighting was resumed amidst reports that Union forces were crossing the Oostanaula River below Resaca at Lay's Ferry in the rear of the Confederate left flank.

Hugh Frank Ezell, 18, of Company C of the Eleventh, was captured in the fighting at Resaca on May 14. He was sent to the military prison at Alton, Illinois, arriving on May 23, then was transferred to Camp Douglas in Chicago, Illinois, on August 23, 1864. On March 31, 1865, Ezell arrived at Point Lookout, Maryland, where he stayed until he took the oath and was released on June 11, 1865. He arrived on June 22 in Washington, D.C., where transportation for him to Shelbyville, Tennessee, was ordered by the Provost Marshal General. His residence was in nearby Marshall County, Tennessee.[56]

On the fifteenth, the Eleventh, on the Confederate right, initiated a mounted charge against a strong infantry skirmish line, one of the few such charges that occurred during the war, according to Daniel Holman, who led the attack. The charge was made across a level field nearly two miles long, a half-mile wide, and bounded by woods on the left and the river on the right.

The horsemen charged, broke through the infantry line, and proceeded close to a mile beyond where they re-formed and were about to charge the Federal batteries which were only lightly protected in the rear. But they noticed, between them and their own lines, that a strong column of Federal infantry was moving across the field they had just crossed which would have cut off their egress back to their own lines.

Further, three batteries of the artillery recovered sufficiently to begin pouring a lethal fire on them now drawn up in plain view on the field. Officers and men of the Eleventh began a precipitous charge in the direction of the infantry column, then changed their course at the last possible moment, veered to the left and made a mad dash to the river bank which lay below the level of vision of the infantry. Darting down a narrow and slippery pathway, they managed to exit precariously in single file and made good their escape with the loss of five men.

Colonel Holman of the Eleventh congratulated himself and his regiment by writing that the charge broke the advance of the left wing of Sherman's army and relieved mounting pressure on the Confederate right.[57]

On May 18, Dibrell's Eighth Tennessee Cavalry Regiment held the Copper Mine Road out of Resaca against a general Union advance. The next day, Wheeler's corps formed a line a mile in advance of the infantry against an enemy that continued to advance. Toward the end of the day, Kelly's division close in to Resaca took a cavalry charge. But it responded with a successful counter charge.[58]

Although his forces inflicted heavy losses on Sherman's command in three days of fighting before Resaca, Johnston decided that his position was untenable against so large a force as Sherman's. So he fell back and, true to his stated tactical plan, left nothing behind of use to the enemy and kept on the alert for an opportunity to strike back when the enemy was divided or unguarded.[59]

By nightfall Johnston's forces, covered by Wheeler's cavalry, withdrew behind the Oostenaula River to cross a wide valley south to the Etowah River. During May 21 and 22, the cavalry rested in camp near the Alabama Road.[60]

Johnston wished to take a stand along the Etowah. But both Hood and Polk advised against it. Hardee favored the stand. But Johnston decided to abandon his plan believing that if two out of three corps commanders thought their position untenable, it would be fruitless to attempt a fight. But his decision to retreat was one he bitterly regretted thereafter.[61]

And so the Confederate retreat upon the northern approaches to Atlanta continued as Johnston's army fell back from the Etowah on May 20 and moved into the Allatoona heights to the south of the stream.[62]

On May 23, Johnston directed Wheeler to recross the Etowah and proceed in the direction of Cassville to ascertain the location and troop movements of the enemy and to interrupt their communications and supplies.[63]

Wheeler briefly rested his command, then set out just after midnight on the twenty-fourth, crossed the river, attacked Stoneman's cavalry and some infantry at Cassville with Kelly's division, captured a train of over a hundred wagons, horses and mules, and returned, with a quantity of commissary and sutler's stores, on the twenty-fifth to Johnston's army, which by then had fallen back to Acworth. Wheeler had interrogated prisoners and private citizens, and made personal observations which provided him a good estimate of the strength, location, and movement of the enemy in pursuit of the Army of Tennessee.[64]

Wheeler reported to Johnston information which indicated that Sherman was abandoning his southeasterly course along the Western & Atlantic Railroad. Instead, Sherman was proceeding directly south, crossing the Etowah at Stilesboro, west of the rail line, and proceeding in the direction of New Hope Church and Dallas.[65]

Sherman's movement was promptly met by countermovements of Confederate troops. Dibrell's cavalry brigade, as well as a large number of other cavalry under Kelley, moved to the point of attack. In some of the hardest fighting of the war, the Eleventh participated in holding back Sherman's assaults on the Confederate left.[66]

Sherman's movement had begun on May 23. Two days later, he arrived at New Hope Church only to find Johnston facing him in full force. The Union army attacked in three days of battle in which Sherman's forward progress was thwarted. On the night of the twenty-seventh, Pat Cleburne's infantry division, supported by the cavalry, charged the enemy, and Cleburne claimed the enemy lost no less than 3,000 killed and wounded as well as upward of 1,200 small arms.[67]

When Wheeler's cavalry returned from its reconnaissance near Cassville, it moved from Acworth on May 26 and took positions on the army's right on the Acworth and Dallas Road. Portions of the brigades of Brigadier General William Wirt Allen and Colonel Moses W. Hannon of Kelly's division, dismounted, were placed close in on the right flank of Major General Patrick Cleburne's division. They threw up entrenchments and extended the flanks of Johnston's army by some 800 yards as it took Sherman's attack.[68]

Additional cavalry under Major General William T. Martin was placed even farther out on the Confederate right where it formed a line of skirmishers and provoked attacks from the enemy. Wheeler reported that only 822 of his men were engaged in the battle at Dallas. The remainder were primarily held in reserve to move to any part of the extended right flank where they might be needed.[69]

In Wheeler's efforts to oppose Sherman's advance from Tunnel Hill on May 6, 1864, through the battle at Dallas and subsequent skirmishing up to the end of May, Kelly's division of Tennessee troops, including the Fourth and Eleventh, bore the brunt of casualties in Wheeler's corps. Kelly's division lost 39 killed, 154 wounded, 16 captured, and 23 missing.[70] But the two companies in which the five Fisher brothers served suffered no losses.

After a fruitless fight in which each army suffered about 3,000 casualties, Sherman decided to return eastward to the rail line and proceed toward Atlanta via the rail route. On June 4, he began his movement back to the railroad about Acworth. Johnston reacted to Sherman's move by also returning to the railroad, establishing himself on the slopes of Kennesaw Mountain, his center about Gilgal Church, his right flank on Brush Mountain, his left flank on Lost Mountain, and a forward position to the north on Pine Mountain.[71]

Dibrell's cavalry had covered Federal assaults on the Confederate left until June 4 when they were ordered to the vicinity of Kennesaw. Nearby some of the men of the Fourth and Eleventh Tennessee regiments, including the five Fisher brothers and many of their comrades, found and visited friends from Marshall County in the Fifty-Third Tennessee Infantry Regiment on Wednesday, June 8. The visit marked a final farewell for them and many of their friends.

The Fifty-Third had arrived from Mississippi in the brigade of Brigadier General W.A. Quarles on May 27 at New Hope Church. Fighting in Lieutenant General A.P. Stewart's corps, the brigade was to suffer heavily in its engagement on Lick Skillet Road west of Atlanta on July 28, 1864, losing 514 killed and wounded.[72]

For the greater part of the month of June, Johnston and Sherman fought each other from their opposing positions athwart the Western & Atlantic Railroad thirty miles out of Atlanta.

On June 13, Colonel Holman was ordered to report with the Eleventh to General Joseph E. Johnston in Atlanta for whatever service the commanding general of the Army of Tennessee might have for him and his regiment. The men of the Eleventh were exhausted from the strain of fighting daily for over a month. The change of service, although not without onerous duty, did provide the troops more opportunity for rest and sleep than they previously had.[73]

On the fourteenth Monroe Fisher went to an Army hospital in Atlanta. His medical complaint is unknown. He was hospitalized for about nine days and may have been treated for a wound or for one of the more prevalent diseases that afflicted Confederate soldiers: diarrhea, dysentery, camp itch (a nonparasitic skin irritation), mental depression, scurvy, or night blindness. The latter two were related, both resulting from dietary deficiencies owing to deprivation of fresh food, especially vegetables, over a period of four to six months, which results in a want of vitamins C (causing scurvy) and A (causing night blindness). Late in the war, dietary deficiencies assumed epidemic proportions in the army.[74]

There were four Confederate Army hospitals in Atlanta then in charge of Surgeon Joseph P. Logan. While Monroe was hospitalized, his brothers, Frank and Jim Fisher, were sent from the front south of Atlanta to pasture cavalry horses.[75]

Also on June 14, Bishop-General Leonidas Polk, one of Johnston's corps commanders, was killed by a shell from a Union Parrott rifled gun which hit him in his left arm, passed laterally through his body, tore through his right arm, and exploded only when it struck a tree. His death occurred on Pine Mountain, interrupting a consultation between generals Johnston, Hardee, and Polk.[76]

Polk, whose family's home was in Maury County, Tennessee, had served with the Army of Tennessee since the army's inception, with the exception of a few months in Mississippi just prior to the beginning of the Atlanta campaign. At one time or another, he had commanded most of the troops in the army. Polk, a man who possessed a great deal of charm, was a favorite officer among the men of the Army of Tennessee. But his colleagues generally believed that his military knowledge and experience were so limited that he should not have been entrusted with the important commands that were given to him. His military conduct had been subject to charges of insubordination, hasty and ill-advised decision-making, and inflexibility once he was committed to a course of action. And his personal vendetta against Braxton Bragg undermined the latter's relations with his senior staff and the effectiveness of the Army of Tennessee.

Immediately after graduation from West Point, Polk had resigned his commission to study for the priesthood of the Protestant Episcopal Church. After twenty years as a priest and bishop in Louisiana, Polk entered the military service of the Confederacy in June 1861, shortly after Tennessee seceded, at the behest of his friend and West Point classmate, Jefferson Davis.[77]

At his death, Polk, whose remains were interred in Augusta, Georgia, was succeeded as corps commander by Major General William W. Loring for a few days. Then his corps was given to Major General Alexander P. Stewart of Tennessee.[78]

During their special duty operating out of the commander's headquarters, details of men of the Eleventh policed the city of Atlanta. In addition, details were made for couriers, scouts, pickets, and almost any duty conceivable incident to the army. And they still experienced conflict. Whenever emergencies required, details were sent to the front to repel assaults or to strengthen a line.

On June 20, the men of the Eleventh Tennessee Cavalry Regiment were assigned to seek and round up stragglers from the Army of Tennessee in the area about Marietta south to the Chattahoochee River. Regimental troops then returned to their camp on the right flank of Johnston's army.

On June 21, 1864, Colonel Robert H.G. Minty, commanding the First Brigade, Second Cavalry Division, Department of the Cumberland, reported a sharp cavalry engagement at Noonday Creek, north of Marietta. The Confederates, who reportedly gave the better in the action, included Martin's, Kelley's, and Humes' divisions as well as two independent brigades, Dibrell's Tennessee and Williams' Kentucky, according to Minty, whose Union force was outnumbered.[79]

On June 21, 1864, a Medical Examining Board recommended a leave of absence of sixty days at Oliver Hospital in Tuscaloosa, Alabama, for Second Lieutenant N.E. Frank Rainey, 28, of Company C of the Eleventh. Rainey's complaint was "phthisis pulmonalis with general debility & extreme emaciation." And on the twenty-third Monroe Fisher was released from a hospital in Atlanta and was met by his brother, Will, who returned with him to camp for three more days of rest.[80]

After nearly three weeks of a face-off, Sherman made a strong frontal attack on Confederate positions on and about Kennesaw Mountain on June 27. The attack was repulsed in about three quarters of an hour with light casualties among the defenders fighting behind well-manned entrenchments.

The attacking forces were needlessly slaughtered, according to Sherman's critics, and suffered about 3,000 casualties. Wheeler's cavalry fought dismounted on the flanks.[81]

On the twenty-eighth, some men of the Eleventh Tennessee Cavalry escorted prisoners to Atlanta for temporary incarceration and subsequent transfer to prisons farther south. During July 2–5, twenty members of the Eleventh Tennessee Cavalry were detailed to a commissary officer in Atlanta, Captain James F. Cummings, acting quartermaster, for the purpose of driving cattle to pasture near the city, then driving others to the front.

While in Atlanta Will Fisher took the opportunity to attend services at the Central Presbyterian Church on Washington Street on the evening of Sunday, July 3, 1864.[82]

The muster roll for January–June 1864 of Company C of the Eleventh Tennessee Cavalry showed 21 absentees when it was reported on June 30, or about 21 percent of the company's original complement. At least nine had not been seen since the army left Middle Tennessee a year earlier. They included John H. Bruce (sick); J.W. Bruce (sick); J.E. Crockett (left in Tennessee with leave [no subsequent record]); J.M. Johnson, 42 (left sick, "the Yankees got between him and his command, fate uncertain"); George W. Joice (absent, "remained in Tennessee when the army came out June 25, 1863"); M.V. Rambo ("unfit for duty with sore eyes when the army left Tenn."); R.L. Shepherd ("absent, sick in Middle Tenn. not fit for duty and not fit for service last time out" [no subsequent records]), J.W. Stilwell, 18; ("absent in Tenn. severely wounded, do not know whether well or not"); and Joseph Wilson ("remained in Tenn. when the army fell back" [no subsequent records]).

Ten more absentees included Lieutenant William W. Braden, 30 (absent, no reason); Corporal T.J. Cathey ("has leave of absence, sick, from Lt. Braden"); T.R. King (absent with leave [actually captured on December 20, 1863]); J.W. Little (absent without leave [no subsequent records]); J.W. Poindexter, 23 ("absent, detailed as teamster for Capt. White, QM" [no subsequent record]); Aaron B. Robinson (absent with leave); W.D. Shelton, 18 (transferred into company, then detailed as scout [no subsequent records]); Samuel A. Smith ("absent with Gen. Forrest"); W.R. Taylor (absent with leave); and John H. Wilson (absent with leave [no subsequent records]). Other absentees included W.G. Davis (deserter [no subsequent records]) and F.M. Williamson (deserted and took oath of allegiance).

And the Eleventh's Company C lost another soldier soon thereafter from desertion. Edward D. Royster of Marshall County, Tennessee, took the oath of allegiance on July 8, 1864, at Louisville after he had deserted for the second time. He first deserted in June 1863. After taking the oath of allegiance on July 8, Royster was released north of the Ohio River.[83]

Again Sherman determined on a flanking movement against the Confederate left to force Johnston's army closer to Atlanta. On July 2 McPherson's corps marched from Sherman's left to his right to begin the flanking movement. Johnston retreated eight miles along the railroad to a fortified defensive position at Smyrna.

Pressed closely by troops under Major General George H. Thomas, Johnston's retreating forces kept up a lively skirmish line with the enemy south from Kennesaw Mountain and Marietta. So closely and lethally were the Confederates followed that they had to continue their withdrawal beyond Smyrna to a second line on the banks of the Chattahoochee River which consisted of five to six miles of entrenchments.

On July 8, Federal troops under Thomas and McPherson attacked the Confederate entrenchments while Major General John M. Schofield marched to Sherman's rear and left to cross the Chattahoochee at Sope Creek, near Roswell factory, ten miles above the center of the Confederate battle line. As the Union troops crossed the river, they encountered elements of Wheeler's cavalry, including the Fourth and the balance of Dibrell's Tennessee brigade, out in front of the Confederate infantry from down below the Western & Atlantic Railroad bridge northeast to the fords and ferries which led to Decatur.[84]

On July 15, the Fourth lost six soldiers of Company D who were captured by troops of Schofield's corps. They were George D. Dysart, Simm Fonville, James K. Polk Graves, James M. Killough, R.S. Rankin, and Hiram Tennison, 18. They were all reportedly captured after a hard skirmish at

Lawrenceville, Georgia, and all sent to Camp Chase, Ohio, arriving on August 8, 1864. It is likely that none of the six ever returned to serve again in the Fourth. Fonville and Graves, both residents of Marshall County, took the oath of allegiance on March 14, 1865, at Camp Chase and were released the same day. The others, Dysart, Killough, Rankin, and Tennison, had been transferred to Point Lookout, Maryland, on February 12, 1865, for exchange.

Dysart's service record terminates at Point Lookout. Killough, after exchange, was admitted to "Receiving and Wayside Hospital or General Hospital No. 9, Richmond, Virginia," on February 23, 1865. Here his service record terminates.

Rankin, a resident of Marshall County, apparently was exchanged, then made his way to Nashville where he took the oath of allegiance on March 31, 1865. On May 3, 1865, his name appeared on a list of rebel deserters who failed to report monthly as directed to the United States Provost Marshal at Shelbyville.

Tennison, of Marshall County, when exchanged was "received at Boulwares & Cox Wharf, James River, Virginia," on February 20, 1865. He reportedly deserted on March 10 and took the oath of allegiance at Nashville on April 5, 1865. On May 1, 1865, he was ordered to report monthly to the United States Provost Marshal in Shelbyville until further orders.

Killough wrote from Waco, Texas, in a letter to the *Confederate Veteran* in 1904 of the skirmish in which the six soldiers were captured. Acknowledging that the "day's fighting may never be mentioned in history, although it was about the hardest fight I was in during the years that I followed the immortal Forrest, lasting from early in the morning till late in the afternoon, when we were offered the alternative of surrendering or being killed, and some of the boys already had more Yankee lead in their bodies than they could carry comfortably." Killough wrote that, in deference to the wounded, they opted for surrender.[85]

Meanwhile, duty was discharged continuously by those soldiers who were free to do so. For several days, the Fourth made its camp at Poplar Springs on the Peachtree Road, facing Schofield's corps, until ordered back across Peachtree Creek on the fateful day, the seventeenth, when Hood superseded Johnston as army chief.

When he was apprised that Schofield had crossed the river, Johnston withdrew his infantry south of the river on the night of July 9 and placed them near the mouth of Peachtree Creek. As Sherman gradually effected the transfer of his army south of the Chattahoochee, not completed for eight days, and began his approach to the city of Atlanta, Johnston again moved his forces south of Peachtree and Peavine creeks to entrenchments situated on a gentle rise of ground where he again waited.[86]

The Eleventh Tennessee Cavalry Regiment was on picket duty on Peachtree Creek on July 10. Its camp was only a mile from Atlanta on the Old

Peachtree Road. From July 12 to July 17, the regiment was on provost guard duty in and about Atlanta.

The provost duty provided the Fisher brothers and their regimental comrades the opportunity to attend services on Sunday, July 17, at Trinity Methodist Episcopal Church, South, on Mitchell Street in Atlanta, across from the city hall and Fulton County Courthouse, where they heard John B. McFerrin of the Tennessee Conference preach. McFerrin had come south after Nashville fell on February 23, 1862. He had served as agent of the church's publishing house in Nashville, the property of which was then in the hands of Federal authorities.[87]

The soldiers' church attendance coincided with their hearing earlier in the day of the relief from command of the Army of Tennessee of the beloved and trusted Joe Johnston, who had dramatically reversed the downward trend of morale of the soldiers of the army, and his replacement by a very junior officer, thirty-four-year-old Lieutenant General John B. Hood of Kentucky.

The authorities in Richmond had come to believe that Johnston could not bring himself to attack Sherman's army in a decisive offensive battle and that he likely would give up Atlanta without fighting to defend the city. It was said that they believed Hood, perceived as a bold, brash, and combative fighter, would turn the Army of Tennessee into an unstoppable war machine capable of inflicting a terminal blow on Sherman's three-corps army.[88]

Those who believed that all that was needed to win against Sherman was a bold leader also believed that troops of the Army of Tennessee had lost the will to fight and that Sherman's army was much smaller than it actually was. But troops of Hood's army were grieved to learn of Johnston's removal. They had learned to respect and trust Johnston for his competence and leadership. They believed that he had kept most of them alive and together and had skillfully kept them from desperate, ill-advised, sanguinary battles against Sherman's more numerous and better equipped army. They had confidence that Johnston was always alert to an opportunity to fight from a position of advantage, as he said he was. This seemed the only prudent course to follow under the circumstances. And they felt that eventually Johnston would attack when and if the opportunity were present.

They also remembered Braxton Bragg who sometimes seemed to them to have gone out of his way to alienate his troops. Sam Watkins of Feild's First Tennessee Infantry Regiment blamed Bragg for scrimping on rations for the troops which resulted in widespread hunger and the development of a black market in food which enriched personnel with commissary duties. Bragg was charged with neglecting pay and furloughs for the troops. He tended to be distant and authoritarian and was not loved by his officers and men. His attempts at disciplining troops were seen to be punitive and intended to intimidate. They were not well received. Morale was low and desertion was rife under Bragg.[89]

Johnston changed all this, according to Sam Watkins. He came among his troops, developed rapport with them, increased their rations, paid them when pay was due, began furloughing them systematically, and seemed to know how to discipline them without rancor, for their own good, and for that of the army. He showed that he knew the difference between the trivialities and the essential burdens of a soldier's life. And in battle, he had a due regard for the lives of his soldiers and a professionalism which earned him the love and respect of those he led.

Under Johnston, morale soared. Soldiers had a renewed sense of self-esteem and patriotism. Discipline was restored, and the troops fought better. Johnston knew how to motivate an army and make it a more effective fighting force. And when he fought, Sam Watkins wrote, "he fought for victory, not for glory." He never needlessly sacrificed his men.[90]

In Hood, Johnston's successor, the troops of the Army of Tennessee had little confidence. Hood had made a reputation for himself as a division commander in the Army of Northern Virginia before he suffered two traumatic wounds, the first at Gettysburg when his arm was shattered and rendered useless. Then, on the battlefield at Chickamauga, his leg was amputated. Thereafter Hood had to be assisted into his saddle and strapped to his horse. There were those who regarded Hood as clearly unfit, both mentally and physically, for military duty as a result of his wounds.

While convalescing in Richmond in the fall and winter of 1863-1864, however, Hood ingratiated himself with President Jefferson Davis and told the president what he wanted to hear, that Sherman's army could be successfully attacked and defeated by the Army of Tennessee. All that was needed was a bold and aggressive commander.

Davis sent Hood to Georgia as a corps commander under Johnston early in 1864. Hood thereupon began a correspondence with Davis which strongly supported Davis's views of Johnston which were that Johnston was an incompetent army commander who was unwilling to fight Sherman.[91]

At a most critical juncture of events, when the battle for Atlanta was about to commence, Johnston was relieved of command and succeeded by Hood. Conscious of the criticality of the moment, Hood importuned Johnston to ignore his orders for the time being and continue as the head of the army. But Johnston would not.

Corps commander A.P. Stewart wrote that the removal of Johnston was the final coup de grace to the Confederate cause. And Hardee believed that Hood was incompetent to command. He applied to be relieved of duty, but later relented at Jefferson Davis's request. His relations with Hood, however, were openly hostile, and the reaction to the change of command of thousands of private soldiers in the Army of Tennessee was expressed in manifestations of deep frustration and sorrow. Seasoned soldiers wept openly. They were deeply disappointed at the turn of events.[92]

But the most highly motivated soldiers in the Army of Tennessee doggedly continued to perform in battle with the same fearless disregard of their own lives as before. They fought for family and homeland regardless of whom the authorities in Richmond chose to place in command.

Johnston had left the Army of Tennessee in rather a good defensive position to the north of Atlanta and behind Peachtree and Peavine creeks, with his army's left flank on the Western & Atlantic Railroad, about two miles south of the Chattahoochee, and its right flank extending east to the Georgia railroad track between Atlanta and Decatur.

Stewart's corps was on the left, nearest the Chattahoochee. Hardee held the center. And Major General Benjamin Franklin Cheatham, now temporarily in charge of Hood's old corps, was on the right. Some five thousand Georgia militia under Major General Gustavus W. Smith were also on the right.[93]

Wheeler's cavalry was divided. Wheeler had lost Humes' division from his command. Kelly's division, from which the officers and men of the Eleventh were detached, had been detached from Wheeler's immediate command to guard the Augusta Railroad to the east of Atlanta. Brigadier General John Stuart Williams had been detached to report to Cheatham, an infantry corps commander, although Williams' division remained with Wheeler.

Wheeler had only about 2,500 soldiers left in the divisions of Williams and Brigadier General Alfred Iverson, Jr., and in Brigadier General Samuel W. Ferguson's brigade. The latter was from the cavalry corps of the Army of Mississippi, which the late Leonidas Polk had led into North Georgia in May.[94]

Wheeler's command resisted the advance of Thomas's corps in front of Peachtree Creek on July 17 and 18. On the nineteenth and twentieth, Wheeler and his 2,500 troops joined Kelly's division of about 750 on the Confederate right just in time to receive McPherson's advance westward along the Georgia Railroad.

Kelly's division, undermanned and consisting of little more than George G. Dibrell's Tennessee brigade, warmly engaged McPherson's advancing cavalry near Stone Mountain on July 19 and 20 before being ordered to fall back to Conyers owing to McPherson's infantry moving west toward Atlanta, which would have cut off the division. The latter was reduced to vidette and scouting duties on Hood's extreme right for about three weeks until assigned to participate in Wheeler's next Tennessee raid.[95]

The Union army approached Atlanta in this wise: Major General John M. Schofield's corps of 25,000 marched straight from their upstream crossing of the Chattahoochee in the direction of Decatur. Major General James B. McPherson's corps of 25,000 crossed to the east of Schofield's corps, and his cavalry began the destruction of the Georgia Railroad between Decatur and Stone Mountain to the east. Major General George H. Thomas, whose corps numbered 50,000, crossed the Chattahoochee near the mouth of Peachtree Creek.[96]

Sherman's wide separation of his armies might have subjected him to a charge of negligence but for the fact that his forces were so superior to the enemy's that there was little likelihood that any one of his armies could be successfully challenged by the Confederates at Atlanta.

On July 19, Hood found that Thomas's corps was proceeding to cross Peachtree Creek. A formidable portion was already on the south side. Hood determined that the time to attack Thomas was the next day, utilizing Stewart's and Hardee's corps in the assault, while leaving Cheatham's corps to fend off McPherson and Schofield, separated from Thomas by two and more miles to the east.

But about the time, one in the afternoon on the twentieth, when the attack on Thomas was to have commenced, a defensive adjustment had to be made owing to McPherson's push along the Georgia rail line from the east toward Atlanta. McPherson's corps of 25,000 troops was opposed only by Wheeler's 2,500 horse soldiers.

Of course, Wheeler's badly outnumbered defenders were no match for McPherson's corps. In order to contain McPherson's thrust, the entire Confederate front had to be adjusted to the right so that Patrick Cleburne's division of infantry might assist Wheeler's cavalry and immediately become engaged with McPherson. But still McPherson's assault on Wheeler's troops continued on Cleburne's right flank on the twenty-first.

The adjustment ordered by Hood delayed his assault on Thomas's corps, known as the Battle of Peachtree Creek, until about four in the afternoon, by which time, Thomas had completed his crossing of the creek and had at least partially dug in.

The attack was initiated with abandon by Stewart's and Hardee's corps, although the results of the fighting were not as favorable as Hood had wished. The attacks were renewed repeatedly until it was determined to be too dark to continue effectively. Confederate losses, including prisoners, were as high as 5,000. Union losses were about half those of the Confederates.[97] The heavy Confederate losses were a portent of future losses caused by Hood's recklessly aggressive tactical style.

Fighting was resumed on the morning of July 21 on the Federal left along the Georgia Railroad when troops from McPherson's corps renewed their attack against Wheeler's command which had been reinforced the previous day by reserve infantry from Pat Cleburne's division, a part of Hardee's corps, the absence of which in the Confederate assault on Thomas's position the previous day had considerably weakened the attack.

And the diversion to the right of Cleburne's division was insufficient to turn the tide against McPherson's assault on the Confederate right. Bald Hill, in bitter combat, was wrested from the hands of the Confederates in a move which made Hood's right flank quite vulnerable.[98]

Hood reacted with alacrity to the threat on his right. He ordered Hardee to withdraw four divisions from the Confederate center, to march them through and south of Atlanta, thence east in the dark of night, to be ready to fall upon McPherson's corps to the rear of McPherson's left flank in a surprise attack on the morning of the twenty-second.[99]

Wheeler, with Brigadier General Samuel W. Ferguson's brigade out of Jackson's cavalry corps of the Army of Mississippi, had just been ordered to go directly to Decatur, where he was to hit McPherson's supply train guarded by two regiments of infantry.

Wheeler's raid on Decatur on the twenty-second was successful, but not without a severe fight in which the Union troops were supported by artillery. Wheeler took away about 225 prisoners, a cache of small arms, a 12-pound gun, a forge, a battery wagon and caisson, six wagons with teams, camp equipage, stores, and hospitals. Wheeler drove off the Union infantry and began pursuit of them.

But now Hardee, in personal command of his four divisions diverted to the right, sent a courier to Wheeler requesting his assistance in fighting the main body of McPherson's corps, which had just been reinforced by a fresh division, that of Brigadier General Grenville M. Dodge, the position of which, quite by accident, was critical in saving McPherson's command from what might well have become a general rout. Dodge's troops, upon arrival in line, had simply extended McPherson's left flank farther south and prevented Hardee from getting to the rear of McPherson's left flank for his attack.

Wheeler rushed to Hardee's assistance. But his comparatively small force, together with a sharp attack on the Union lines by Cheatham's corps, positioned on Hardee's left, in the afternoon, was unable to turn the tide of battle and produce a Confederate victory rather than the standoff that ensued.[100]

The next day at noon, Wheeler's cavalry was directed to pursue a Union raiding force advancing on Covington. Wheeler rode forty miles until midnight only to discover that the Union cavalry had returned to its main army even before Wheeler had received his orders to pursue. Wheeler returned to the right flank of Cleburne's division where he continued to skirmish with the enemy until the twenty-seventh.[101]

Hood's hopes of smashing McPherson's corps through a bold and imaginative surprise attack, vigorously pressed, were disappointed. The numerical superiority of the Union forces was a decisive factor in virtually all the military encounters in the vicinity of Atlanta. Still the Confederates had a military raison d'etre which seemed to have a momentum of its own. They continued the struggle with passionate vigor and reckless abandon in the face of daunting odds.

The battle on the twenty-second, known as the Battle of Atlanta, resulted in losses to the Confederates which the South could ill afford to bear. They suffered 10,000 casualties, including 2,500 dead. Hardee dealt McPherson's corps a heavy blow—3,521 dead and wounded plus 2,000 prisoners, eight guns, and thirteen battle flags.[102]

Among the Union casualties was the corps commander, Major General James B. McPherson of Ohio, thirty-six years old, an engineering officer of great promise, who was meeting with Sherman at the latter's headquarters when the sound of musketry and cannon made clear to him that his corps was under attack. He immediately mounted and made a dash cross-country to lead his command. In his haste, he mistakenly rushed headlong into Hardee's spearhead, which had penetrated well behind his lines. Suddenly he came upon enemy troops and was ordered to surrender. Preferring instead to try to ride and fight his way out of his tragic predicament, he reportedly touched the brim of his hat in salute and wheeled his horse to gallop away in the opposite direction.

McPherson was shot through the head. Corporal R.H. "Bob" Coleman of Company A of the Twenty-First Tennessee Infantry Regiment from Memphis is said to have been the sharpshooter who brought down the general. The first his troops knew that there was something amiss with McPherson was when his riderless horse emerged from the woods near where the general had been shot and where he died instantly.

McPherson was a member of the class of 1853 at West Point, as were several of his colleagues in the Atlanta campaign, generals Sherman and Schofield of the Union army and Hood of the Confederate army. McPherson had many friends on both sides of the civil conflict. A popular soldier, he was sincerely mourned by his officers and men as well as by the patriotic public in the North and his friends in the South.[103] He is remembered today in the nation's capital with an equestrian statue erected in 1876 in McPherson Square at 15th Street between K and I streets, Northwest.

Chapter 5

The Siege of Atlanta and Wheeler's Tennessee Raid, July 23–September 2, 1864

After the Battle of Atlanta on July 22, the siege of Atlanta began. Sherman consolidated his lines to the north and east of the city and began to extend his lines westward hoping thereby to get control of the railroads leading from Atlanta to the south to Macon and to the west to Montgomery, Alabama. When his lines were close enough, Sherman began shelling nonmilitary targets in the city. Atlantans who had not already left the city took refuge in underground shelters amidst large-scale destruction of homes and businesses. The night sky was regularly illuminated with the light of fires set by the bombardment.[1]

The Eleventh Tennessee Cavalry Regiment had missed both the Battle of Peachtree Creek on the twentieth and the Battle of Atlanta on the twenty-second owing to its special duty out of Hood's headquarters. On July 20, its camp had been moved within the inner Confederate fortifications of Atlanta. The next day, men of Company C of the Eleventh reported to Hood's headquarters for duty. Their duty, July 22–26, was to drive beef cattle to Jonesboro, thence to Atlanta for slaughter to feed the army.

On the twenty-seventh, the men of Company C briefly returned to their regiment, which was then at East Point guarding the railroad to Montgomery just south of the site of the next battle of Sherman's campaign, fought at Ezra Church just to the west of Atlanta on July 28.[2]

Major General Oliver O. Howard had taken command of McPherson's corps with orders from Sherman to move it around from east of the city to the west, forming a line which faced east with its right flank extending near the railroad junction at East Point.

Hood took note of Howard's march, which started on the morning of the twenty-seventh. He began attacking the Federal column before it was in place, being determined to prevent Sherman from establishing himself to the west of Atlanta where Hood's rail supply lines to the south and southwest might be threatened. He sent Lieutenant General Stephen D. Lee, now

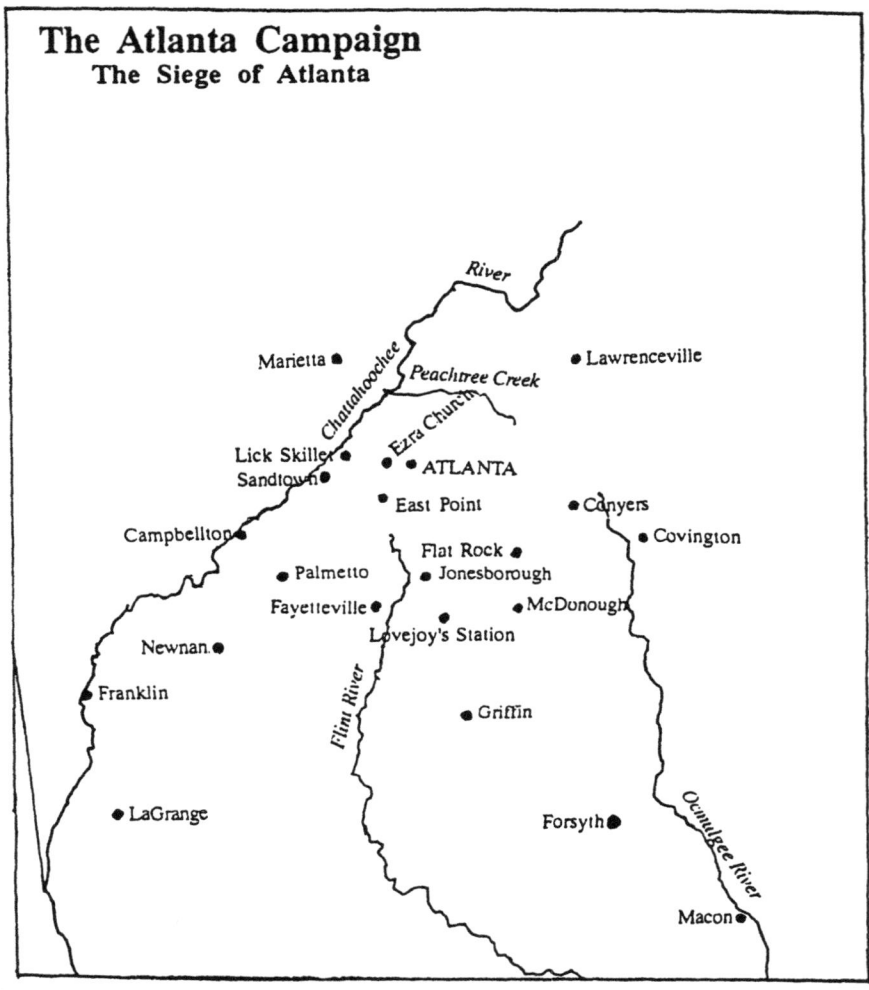

commanding Polk's corps, directly west through Atlanta, out Sandtown and Lick Skillet roads, to confront Howard's command. Hood also planned for Stewart's corps to take a wide sweep to the south and west and to hit Howard from the rear on the twenty-ninth.[3]

Lee's command, however, became so heavily engaged on the afternoon of the twenty-eighth that Stewart aborted the plan to attack Howard from the rear. He sent his troops directly in to reinforce Lee. The Confederates made repeated attacks against the Federals, the latter fighting from behind newly constructed breastworks. As the fighting wore on, each attack became less vigorously pursued and had less chance of success than the preceding attack. The battle ended with the onset of night. The Confederate soldiers engaged were quite demoralized and disheartened by heavy losses and their failure to move the enemy from his position.[4]

Under cover of Howard's march to the west of Atlanta, Sherman ordered, on July 27, a cavalry pincer movement in an effort to disrupt Hood's railway supply route from Macon via the Macon & Western Railroad. The left arm of the pincer consisted of a combined force of 6,885 men under the command of Major General George Stoneman. It was to move via the east of Atlanta to McDonough, located nearly thirty miles southeast of the city.[5]

Brigadier General Edward M. McCook with 2,330 horsemen formed the right arm of the pincer. It was to swing west of Atlanta and proceed to Fayetteville, some thirty miles south of the city. Acting in concert, the two cavalry forces were to come together on the night of July 28 at Lovejoy's Station, located about equidistant between McDonough and Fayetteville. There they were to proceed to tear up the Macon & Western Railroad.[6]

Stoneman was so ebulliently confident of success that he asked Sherman's permission to proceed farther south to Macon and even Andersonville, both sites of Confederate prisons, where he proposed to free prisoners of war. Sherman agreed but stipulated that Stoneman had leave to pursue his extended plan *only* after Wheeler's cavalry had been whipped and then only with a part of his command, 2,658 cavalrymen of the Army of the Ohio. Troops under Brigadier General Kenner Garrard, who accompanied Stoneman and numbered 4,227, were to return to their position on the main army's left flank after their original mission had been accomplished and *not* go to Macon.[7]

Stoneman divided his cavalry, sending Garrard's force as a decoy to Flat Rock while the cavalry under his personal command proceeded to Covington, some forty miles to the east of Atlanta, before turning south.[8]

Wheeler, whose cavalry had replaced Hardee's infantry to the east of Atlanta on the morning of July 27, 1864, discovered Garrard moving across Flat Creek on the morning of the twenty-eighth. In twenty-four hours, Wheeler had positioned his cavalry in front of Garrard and was skirmishing with him. Garrard had expected to meet Stoneman somewhere along the way to McDonough. Being pressed hard by Wheeler and with Stoneman nowhere to be found, Garrard decided to withdraw from Wheeler's assaults and rejoin, via Conyers, the left flank of the Union army east of Atlanta and north of the Augusta Railroad. Garrard's command sustained few losses in its encounter with Wheeler's cavalry.[9]

Stoneman had *not* joined Garrard on his way to McDonough because he had abandoned the plan originally agreed upon, which was to go to McDonough, then join McCook, tear up the railroad around Lovejoy's Station, and whip Wheeler's cavalry. Instead, upon reaching Covington, Stoneman, with his 2,658 men, struck out south along the east side of the Ocmulgee River for Macon and Andersonville, leaving Garrard and McCook to fend for themselves.[10]

When Wheeler became apprised of Stoneman's daring solo move in the direction of Macon, he sent a portion of his command under Brigadier General Alfred Iverson, Jr., three brigades including Iverson's, Brigadier General William W. Allen's, and a third commanded by Colonel William C.P. Breckinridge, to intercept, engage, and destroy Stoneman's cavalry.[11] Iverson's Brigade was comprised of Georgians, Allen's of Alabamians, and Breckenridge's of Kentuckians.

Stoneman, who undertook to damage and destroy rails and rolling stock along his way, reached Macon on July 29, and shelled the city from across the river.[12] He was confronted at Macon only by an ill-equipped body of hastily rounded-up old men, rejects, and youngsters led by Howell Cobb, too old to serve in the army, who had served as first President of the Provisional Congress of the Confederate States in Montgomery in February 1861, and whose plantation near Milledgeville, by Sherman's explicit orders, would be thoroughly looted and left in ruins after Sherman spent the night in it on November 22, 1864, in the course of Sherman's renowned march of destruction from Atlanta to the sea.[13]

But hard on Stoneman's heels appeared Iverson's three undersized brigades, a force of little more than 1,600. In a swift and decisive cavalry operation, Stoneman's force was cut up and run over by Wheeler's horse soldiers. Stoneman and five hundred of his officers and men rallied and tried to ride through Wheeler's troops and escape to Atlanta. But the entire force was cut off and captured as were several hundred more, in particular Colonel Horace Capron's brigade made up of soldiers of the Fourteenth Illinois, the Eighth Michigan, and William McLaughlin's Ohio squadron, many of whom, while hastily on their way back to their army north of Atlanta, broke ranks and fled. Stoneman later wrote, ironically from prison in Macon, describing his losses in killed and wounded as unspecified but quite large.[14]

Wheeler reported that out of Stoneman's force of 2,200 (Wheeler's estimate) only a handful was able to escape capture and straggle back to union lines. On the other hand, Sherman reported that Adams' brigade came back intact along with many stragglers. The brigade referred to by Sherman was Colonel Alexander W. Holeman's independent brigade, consisting of the First and Eleventh Kentucky Cavalry regiments with Lieutenant Colonel Silas Adams of the First Kentucky in command.[15]

On September 14, 1864, Colonel Israel Garrard, commanding Stoneman's cavalry division in Stoneman's absence, reported casualties of 10 killed, 26 wounded, and 1,229 missing from the division's expedition to Macon. Garrard said his report, however, was incomplete since he had received no report from Holeman's independent brigade, which Sherman said had returned intact.[16]

But what of McCook and his command, which formed the right arm of the Federal cavalry pincer? McCook had proceeded down the west side of the Chattahoochee River to Campbellton, where he crossed the river by means of a pontoon bridge. Then he proceeded in a southeasterly direction through Palmetto to Fayetteville, where he captured 300 quartermaster personnel and destroyed a quantity of Confederate stores before proceeding on to Lovejoy's Station late on July 28 according to plan.

Although Stoneman was not there to help, McCook did not hesitate to have the station burned and several hundred feet of track ripped up before turning back westward through Fayetteville in the direction of Newnan, some forty miles southwest of Atlanta. His cavalry was intact, and he was bringing out captures.[17]

On the twenty-eighth, Wheeler had been apprised of McCook's crossing of the Chattahoochee. He immediately ordered Colonel Henry M. Ashby's brigade of Brigadier General William Y.C. Humes' division to move to Jonesborough on the railroad to Macon.

He ordered Kelly to hold Garrard's division in check with Dibrell's brigade and to send Brigadier General Samuel R. Anderson's brigade after Wheeler south on the road to Jonesborough. Anderson's brigade consisted of the Third, Eighth, Tenth, and Twelfth Confederate cavalry regiments plus the Fifth Georgia Cavalry.

Wheeler, with only his escort, rode south on the Jonesborough Road, overtook Ashby's brigade, and arrived at Jonesborough at 4 P.M. Here he learned that McCook had struck the railroad six miles south at Lovejoy's Station. When Wheeler arrived at Lovejoy's, he found that McCook had gone off on the road to Fayetteville.

About this time, a courier from Brigadier General William H. Jackson arrived with a proposal that Wheeler might pursue McCook while Jackson would try to head him off. Wheeler agreed to the plan. But as it turned out, McCook's progress and Wheeler's pursuit were too rapid to permit Jackson to gain McCook's front.

When McCook encamped at Skagerag for a brief rest, he was surprised and routed when Wheeler attacked at five in the morning with only 400 men. McCook suffered forty killed and wounded and two hundred captured. He pushed on toward Newnan where he expected to gain some surcease from his pursuers.

Upon approaching Newnan, however, McCook was surprised to find the town filled with a few hundred Confederate cavalry commanded by Phillip D. Roddey, a colonel when, in April and May of 1863, he had joined Forrest's command in North Alabama in the pursuit and capture of Colonel Streight. Now Roddey was a brigadier who was moving his cavalry, a force of only 600, from Alabama to join the Army of Tennessee at Atlanta.

Roddey was passing through Newnan quite by happenstance at the moment when he might join Wheeler's chase of McCook's cavalry. As it turned out, however, his troops and mounts were so exhausted by their long journey from Opelika, Alabama, that they took only a brief part in the pursuit of McCook down the road to LaGrange before Wheeler ordered them to return to Newnan to rest. Four days later, they were ordered to return to Opelika. They had made their long and exhausting journey for nothing.

Two miles east of Newnan, Wheeler was joined by Lieutenant Colonel Gustave Cook and the Eighth Texas Cavalry Regiment of Colonel Thomas Harrison's brigade of Brigadier General William Y.C. Humes' division, and by Brigadier General Lawrence S. Ross of Jackson's corps with two regiments.[18]

McCook darted to the south of Newnan, still headed west, then circled partway around and got on the road to LaGrange toward the southwest. Attacked on all sides by Wheeler's cavalry when he stopped to make a stand, McCook, who was losing more troops by capture than by gunshot, was finally hemmed in and forced to find a means of escape as evening fell.

McCook lost all his captures in his final efforts to wrench himself free of his attackers and find his way back to his own lines. Just west of Newnan he broke through the surrounding Confederates by taking Colonel Fielder A. Jones and his brigade and moving off at a fast trot in a column in the direction of the Chattahoochee. He ordered colonels John T. Croxton and William H. Torrey to do the same with what remained of their brigades in separate actions.[19]

On the night of July 30, McCook recrossed the Chattahoochee River below Franklin, some sixty miles southwest of Atlanta, with what remained of Jones' Brigade, then made his way back to Sherman's army in siege of Atlanta. Wheeler reported that he pursued McCook north of the river before turning back.[20]

Sherman reported that McCook lost 500 officers and men and that McCook destroyed most of his artillery to keep it from falling into enemy hands. Wheeler, on the other hand, reported that McCook returned with a remnant of less than 400 out of picked force of 3,200, most of whom had thrown away their arms in their haste to escape.[21]

Sherman was deeply disappointed that his cavalry had performed so poorly in its pincer movement against the Macon & Western Railroad.[22] The break in the rail line at Lovejoy's Station was quickly repaired and Hood's supply route to Macon and the south was virtually uninterrupted by the cavalry strike. His cavalry commanders had not yet learned the lessons they might have learned from the examples of Forrest's brilliantly conceived and executed exploits, now well executed by Wheeler and his cavalry. But other Northern cavalry commanders were learning, and they would, in a few months, with superior numbers, equipment, and training, learn to dominate the once indomitable Western cavalry of the Confederacy.

From the Battle of Ezra Church on July 28, 1864, the siege of Atlanta settled down for about a month with occasional brisk fighting but only a modicum of lateral movement by the infantry or by the cavalry on the periphery of the siege. From July 31 to August 13, the Eleventh Tennessee Cavalry Regiment was scouting and picketing beyond the periphery of Confederate defensive lines around Atlanta.

The regiment was back in Atlanta by the fourteenth for a week during which Will Fisher heard Richard P. Ransom, a member of the Tennessee Conference of the Methodist Episcopal Church, South, preach on Sunday morning of the fourteenth as well as on Tuesday evening of the sixteenth at Trinity Church. On the following Sunday, Will's regiment began picketing out the McDonough Road to the south southeast of Atlanta.[23]

Wheeler quartered the bulk of his cavalry at Covington, forty miles east of Atlanta, following his defeats of Stoneman and McCook on July 29 and 30, 1864. There his troops rested until August 10, 1864.

On the eighth of August, H.C. Dwiggins of the Fourth Tennessee Cavalry's Company D deserted.[24] Dwiggins was never reported captured or sent to a prison in the North or reported as having taken the oath of allegiance. Of course, he may have been killed. On the other hand, perhaps he went home and hid out for the balance of the war.

Hood planned that Wheeler would ride north with 4,000 men, destroying Sherman's communications along the way. He was to cross the Tennessee River above Chattanooga, then proceed northwestward toward Nashville and destroy the Nashville & Chattanooga Railroad as he went, then the Nashville & Decatur Railroad before he came out.

The plan had Wheeler leaving 1,200 of his men along the way to keep the rail lines cut, a portion of the plan which Wheeler did *not* carry out, and returning with the remainder of his cavalry, cutting the Western & Atlantic Railroad from Chattanooga to Atlanta again as he returned.

It was believed that Wheeler's raid might force Sherman's retreat from Georgia. Instead the plan played right into Sherman's hands in two ways. It substantially deprived Hood of his eyes around Atlanta. And it gave Sherman superiority over Hood's cavalry, again in the vicinity of Atlanta. Hood thought so little of Sherman's cavalry that he felt no threat from them even with Wheeler, commanding Hood's cavalry corps, dispatched hundreds of miles away from Atlanta.

The plan for the cavalry raid was similar to one that Joseph E. Johnston had proposed to President Jefferson Davis shortly before Johnston had been relieved of command of the Army of Tennessee on July 17 last but with one decisive difference: The raid planned by Johnston was to be carried out by Nathan Bedford Forrest, sent from Mississippi, while Wheeler was to continue to give close support to the army defending Atlanta.[25]

So Hood's plan proceeded to execution when Wheeler and his cavalry, worn down with rapid marching and a serious scarcity of forage for their horses, rode out of Covington on August 10, circling around the left flank of Sherman's army besieging Atlanta on the north, and turning west toward Marietta on the Western & Atlantic Railroad.

The ten companies of the Fourth Tennessee Cavalry Regiment went with Wheeler in George Dibrell's brigade. But the soldiers of the Eleventh still were detached from the brigade for special service in and about Atlanta as couriers, cowboys, guards, police, pilots, and scouts.

About the time when, on August 10, Wheeler left Covington to raid Tennessee, Monroe resigned as Orderly (First) Sergeant of Company C of the Eleventh Tennessee Cavalry. One may only conjecture as to why he resigned. The impetus might have arisen from differences with his superiors, his company commander, Captain T.C.H. Miller, or perhaps Lieutenant Frank Rainey, or because of his dissatisfaction with the nature of his duties while his regiment operated out of Hood's headquarters. Perhaps it was something in his current state of mind. There are no records which reveal the circumstances of how or why the matter came to pass. His demotion cost him nothing since he had not been paid for over a year and doubtless expected no pay in the future. He had volunteered his services to the Confederate army to repel invaders of his country. And this purpose alone would keep him fighting in the field.

Quite surprisingly, the company's first sergeantcy thereupon came to Thomas Fisher. Tom was Monroe's youngest brother in the service of the Southern Confederacy and one of the youngest men in the company. It is not recorded whether he was the choice of his comrades in Company C or simply that of his company commander.[26] He and Monroe were the most articulate of John Fisher's sons. This characteristic alone set them apart and assured that they would be considered by their associates for positions of leadership throughout their lives.

A few miles above Marietta, Wheeler's cavalry tore up the railroad and then did the same above Cassville and Calhoun. At the latter town, Colonel Moses W. Hannon's small Alabama brigade of only three regiments captured 1,700 head of beef cattle consigned to Sherman's army. The cattle were herded back south by Hannon's men to feed Hood's army instead. Hannon's brigade did not rejoin Wheeler for the balance of the latter's raid but, once back in the vicinity of Atlanta, stayed with Hood's main force.

Pushing on north on the rail line from Marietta to Dalton, Wheeler destroyed about 35 miles of track and burned the railroad bridge over the Etowah River south of Cassville. Prior to striking the Federal force at Dalton, Wheeler detached Major General William T. Martin with a body of troops to hit the Federals at Tilton. Martin had orders to complete his strike, then rejoin the main body of troops before they struck the Dalton garrison.

Wheeler proceeded to Dalton in the company of divisions commanded by brigadier generals William Y.C. Humes and John H. Kelly. At Dalton, Wheeler demanded the surrender of the garrison commanded by Colonel Bernard Laiboldt. While declining Wheeler's demand, Laiboldt immediately requested reinforcements of Major General James B. Steedman in Chattanooga.[27]

Before reinforcements could arrive, Humes' and Kelly's commands drove the town's defenders out of Dalton and into their fort, a very strong position, on a nearby hill on the afternoon of August 14. Dibrell's Tennessee brigade charged the fort, but was ordered to stop and retire by its division commander, John H. Kelly.

After the war, Dibrell wrote bitterly of Kelly's order. He believed that if his troops had been permitted to continue their attack, they would have taken the fort and captured the entire garrison.

Steedman with reinforcements, both cavalry and infantry, arrived by eight in the evening, and Wheeler withdrew to await the detached Martin. Wheeler discovered at dawn on the fifteenth that Martin had come up within seven miles of him at Dalton and had put his troops into camp for the night without making any effort to apprise him of his whereabouts and availability to help deal with Steedman. Wheeler summarily relieved Martin of duty. Martin was arrested, sent back to the army in Atlanta, then transferred to Mississippi when Wheeler returned from his raid.[28]

In order to insure that the railroad tracks which his men had torn up would not be repaired immediately, Wheeler commenced a series of marches and countermarches between Dalton and Chattanooga, hitting the railroad at various points in an effort to enlist pursuit by Steedman and his troops and their subsequent neglect of the needed repairs to the rail line for as long as possible.

Wheeler's ploy worked for three days, after which Steedman divined his purpose, remitted his pursuit and, after August 20, proceeded to have the railroad repaired. But Wheeler left two hundred men in the hills in the area with orders to keep the rail service disrupted with nighttime strikes while he continued with his raid north into Tennessee.[29]

Cutting the railroad had been made difficult by continuing rains, which made burning ties almost impossible. But Wheeler had to leave the railroad and proceed north into Tennessee because of a chronic lack of forage for horses in North Georgia. He anticipated that forage would be abundant farther north in Tennessee in the Ocoee and Hiwassee river valleys, east of Chattanooga where the country had not been so well burned over.

It had been Wheeler's intention to cross the Tennessee River almost forty miles above Chattanooga at Cottonport in Meigs County, then swing northwestward around Chattanooga in the direction of the Nashville & Chattanooga Railroad upon which he hoped to wreak destruction. But heavy rains had raised the level of water ten feet in the Tennessee River.[30]

Wheeler sent scouts to report on the advisability of fording the Tennessee at Cottonport. Captain James W. McReynolds of Company I of the Eighth Tennessee Cavalry reported that the river could be crossed. But other scouts reported just the opposite. Wheeler made a decision on the basis of the latter opinion. He found it inadvisable to attempt to ford the river below Kingston in the vicinity of Knoxville.[31]

Wheeler changed his plans again, concluding that he would have to remain south and east of the river temporarily while he marched northeast through the Great Valley of the Tennessee until he reached a point just beyond the headwaters of the Tennessee River above the confluences of the Clinch, the Little Tennessee, the Holston, and the French Broad rivers with the Tennessee a few miles east of Knoxville. He hoped to cross these smaller rivers one by one before riding southwest to hit the Nashville & Chattanooga Railroad.[32] Thus Wheeler purposed to make an almost two-hundred-mile detour to cross the Tennessee River, a demarche which eventuated in one of even greater length than he had planned owing to the high waters.

There is irony in excessive rainfall in the midsummer in East Tennessee, a time when the earth normally is parched and streams run low and clear from insufficient precipitation. But such were the incongruities of war and weather which overtook and taxed Wheeler and his freewheeling cavalry in August 1864.

From just east of Chattanooga, Wheeler advanced further east to Cleveland, thence northeast to Charleston, Athens, and Loudon, destroying miles of railroad track as he went. He crossed the Little Tennessee a few miles east of Loudon with scant difficulty. But a few miles further, Wheeler found that the Tennessee, near Lenoir Station, was too deep and treacherous to be crossed. His intelligence told him that he would have to proceed to just east of Knoxville to find a fordable point on both the Holston and French Broad rivers. This he did with as much speed as possible, but only after capturing the garrison at Stewart's Landing.[33]

Wheeler and his officers and men were passing through country that many of them remembered from the previous fall and winter when they accompanied Longstreet to Knoxville to dislodge from the town forces under the command of Ambrose Everett Burnside, after which they (minus Wheeler and his staff who were called back to Chattanooga) wintered in the country east of Knoxville with Longstreet's headquarters in Russellville.

The previous winter, the cavalry had fought a battle at Strawberry Plains, a village about 24 miles east-northeast of Knoxville where a small college had operated from 1848 until interrupted by the war and the destruction of its buildings. Since they were in the neighborhood, Brigadier General John Stuart Williams requested Wheeler's permission to take his brigade with one other, along with half the artillery, so that they might hit the bridge and garrison at Strawberry Plains.

At first Wheeler was opposed, believing that already too much time had been spent in moving about on the raid owing to the eccentricities of the weather. But Wheeler finally relented, instructing Williams to make haste, march at night and rendezvous with him before dawn north of the Holston River.

So Williams and Wheeler went their separate ways. Wheeler crossed the river, not without a fight with the enemy who guarded the crossings, and camped through the night to await Williams' arrival. But when dawn arrived and Williams was nowhere to be found, Wheeler set out without him. In doing so, he lost the use of over a third of his command, about 1,500 officers and men.[34]

Williams indeed had marched to Strawberry Plains by moonlight and found the garrison there to be stronger than he had anticipated. He declined to attack, believing his chances of success to be unpromising. He tried to rejoin Wheeler but failed to catch up with his fast-paced commanding general. Williams unsuccessfully pursued Wheeler's main body of troops into Middle Tennessee as far as Shelbyville, Farmington, and Cornersville in Bedford and Marshall counties before turning back toward East Tennessee, where he operated with other departmental Confederate forces until he led his troops across the state line into Virginia and participated in the Battle of Saltville on October 2, 1864. By November 1, 1864, he and his troops had rejoined Wheeler's command for the Savannah, Georgia, campaign.[35]

Wheeler made almost a complete circuit of Knoxville, now circling north of the city and heading west across the Black Oak Ridge, which eighty years later would provide the name for the new atomic city of Oak Ridge. Once clear of Knoxville and the Federal garrison there, to which he gave a wide berth, Wheeler headed west by southwest travelling sometimes by the old Walton Road which, almost since the beginning of the nineteenth century, had been the most direct route west of Nashville from Kingston (forty miles west of Knoxville) and points east.

After crossing the Clinch River and Crab Orchard Mountain beyond and penetrating the wild, primitive, sparsely populated, and forbidding Cumberland Plateau, Wheeler, near Standing Stone, now the town of Monterey, turned left on another ancient road which took a more southerly route to Nashville via Sparta, McMinnville, and Murfreesboro.

Dibrell's brigade of Wheeler's cavalry rode through Sparta and struck a small Federal detachment of three companies under the command of Major Shelah Waters at McMinnville on August 29. Waters' command decamped just in the nick of time, leaving behind their camp equipage, ten wagons, an ambulance, and three teams of horses.[36]

Because Wheeler's command had been inadvertently divided into three detachments, Wheeler's main force, Dibrell's brigade, and Williams' division, the three spread destruction across a swath of fifty miles or more as Wheeler approached Nashville. Railroads and telegraph lines, blockhouses and their defenders at bridges, as well as railway supplies were waylaid at Bell Buckle, Lebanon, and Smyrna.[37]

George G. Dibrell, who had been promoted to the rank of Brigadier General on July 26, 1864, now commanded a small brigade with six companies (companies A, B, C, D, E, and G) of the Fourth Tennessee (four other companies of the Fourth stayed with Wheeler's main force) as well as his own Eighth Regiment. He had been left in the vicinity of Sparta on September 2 to rest and recruit more troops. When he attempted to rejoin Wheeler's command, he was attacked in camp on the seventh by a Union force under the command of Colonel Thomas J. Jordan of the Ninth Pennsylvania Cavalry Regiment. The Union force consisted of Jordan's Ninth plus over 600 officers and men of the Fourteenth U.S. Colored Infantry Regiment, which had been organized at Gallatin, Tennessee, in November 1863. The attack took place between Readyville and Woodbury in Cannon County.

Surprised and outnumbered, and with few of Dibrell's men having arms, most being recent unarmed recruits, Dibrell's brigade was lucky to have escaped capture or destruction. Unable to break through the Union troops to the west, Dibrell and his troops joined at Sparta with the fragment of Wheeler's raiders under Brigadier General John S. Williams which had been lost to Wheeler east of Knoxville in late August.

Two days before Dibrell was turned back at Woodbury, James O. Nowlin of Company D of the Fourth was captured near Woodbury. His fighting days were over. He was incarcerated at Camp Chase (Ohio) on September 17. He took the oath of allegiance on March 31, 1865, at Camp Chase and was released to go home to Marshall County.

Dibrell and Williams held a counsel of war in Sparta and agreed upon a course to pursue in returning to the main Confederate army. The troops initially moved north as if going into Kentucky. At Sinking Cane, where they stopped for two days to forage and shoe horses, they turned eastward and marched across the Cumberland Mountains via Wartburg, Robertsville, Sneedville, and Rogersville, to Bristol.[38]

As previously noted, together they continued east to Saltville in Southwest Virginia where, on October 2, they helped beat off a Federal attack on the South's principal wartime source of salt. Later in October, they rejoined Wheeler in Georgia and, because of the small size of their force, dogged Sherman's progress to the sea ineffectually in November and December 1864.

Concluding his Tennessee raid, Wheeler rode up the Nashville & Chattanooga Railroad from the vicinity of Murfreesboro to within eight miles of Nashville, an area readily recognized by Wheeler's seasoned veterans who had fought there one and two years before. Some of his officers importuned him to attempt the capture of Tennessee's capital city in order to enhance his reputation and put to rest forever criticism of Wheeler's performance as a long-distance cavalry raider.

But Wheeler was keenly aware that Nashville was too heavily fortified to succumb to a cavalry raid of less than 3,000 attackers with fewer than ten field pieces. Wheeler responded to his importuning officers that the good of their common cause, that of the Southern Confederacy, was more important than his reputation as a cavalry commander.

Prior to returning south, Wheeler issued a proclamation to the people of Tennessee on August 30 urging them to join his command and come south with him to Atlanta where so many chivalrous sons of Tennessee were then fighting. He promised that the state eventually would be redeemed, with their help.

Although Wheeler reported success in reinstating some 800 absentees from the army and in recruiting 2,000 new recruits, few of the absentees and recruits ever actually materialized to do battle.[39]

On September 1, 1864, William A. Dysart, being sick, was left to convalesce in Middle Tennessee, probably at his home in Marshall County. On the same day, five new recruits were enlisted in Company D of the Fourth Tennessee Cavalry Regiment at Shelbyville, Tennessee. Their enlistments were made by Captain William M. Robinson who then commanded Company D of the Fourth. The recruits were John Barnes, George Brotherton, W.A. Hunter, William R. Loving, and Jeremiah Yopp.

It is possible that recruitment of the five new enlistees was facilitated by Lieutenant N.C. Davis or Corporal James Wesley Fisher, who were shown on Company D's muster roll dated June 30 to December 31, 1864, as absent with leave to go to Middle Tennessee to get recruits. It is not known whether the two soldiers were absent for the entire six-month period covered by the muster roll or for only part of the period.

Such recruiting duty behind the Federal lines was encouraged by the Confederate high command as a means of shoring up their hard-pressed armies, depleted by casualties and indifferent support on the home front. The two leading cavalry commanders in the West, Forrest and Wheeler, clearly had opposite views of the duty. Forrest saw it as fit primarily for malingerers and jayhawkers and ineffective in its results. But Wheeler credited the recruiters with maintaining and even increasing the strength of his command.

Military service records, however, fail to indicate any other enlistments in Tennessee of soldiers in Company D of the Fourth during the last six months of 1864. If the five enlistees recruited on September 1 at Shelbyville were the only recruits that Davis and Fisher managed to find, their mission seems hardly to have been worth the effort.

It is possible, of course, that Davis and Fisher made contact with some of Wheeler's raiders in late August within days before Wheeler began his withdrawal from the state. They might then have referred new unarmed local mounted recruits to Captain Francisco Rice, commanding Company K of the Fourth Tennessee Cavalry, or to any other of Wheeler's officers, who would take the recruits or stragglers with him south to where they were needed by the army.

George Dibrell reported gathering up several hundred raw recruits and army dropouts in and around Sparta in September 1864. Many of the absentees, he said, "had been hunted for like wild beasts" while at home. "Some had been killed, the houses of some had been burned and their families insulted and abused...." They were glad to get back in the army "to avenge their wrongs," according to Dibrell. Davis and Fisher may have had a hand in recruiting some of the men Dibrell gathered up around Sparta, although it is impossible to know in the absence of records.

Of course, Wheeler claimed to have brought out from Tennessee in his August–September 1864 raid some 800 absentees and 2,000 recruits. But skeptics doubted the figures. The claimed numbers reportedly did not materialize.[40]

The lives of Davis and Fisher as Confederate soldiers behind enemy lines likely were precarious daily. They were in uniform and in hiding from occupying forces and indigenous armed Unionists. To be found *out* of uniform would subject them immediately to a court-martial or a summary extralegal judgment, either of which would surely result in death. Indeed their chances of *not* being summarily dispatched by a Union soldier or an indigenous civilian Unionist who might apprehend them *in* uniform would seem to have been unpromising.

The example of Sam Davis, a Confederate scout who engaged in military intelligence, and who in later years was given the heroic epithet, "Boy Hero of the Confederacy," by neo–Confederate admirers in the 1890s, may have been known to Davis and Fisher when they undertook their mission behind Federal lines in Middle Tennessee.

Just prior to the war, Davis had been a student at the Western Military Institute in Nashville where he studied under the disciplined tutelage of Bushrod Johnson, headmaster, later in Confederate service. On November 19, 1863, late in the afternoon, Davis, a just-turned-twenty-one-year-old soldier from Smyrna, was captured by troops of the Seventh Kansas Cavalry of the XVI Army Corps while riding alone in Giles County near Pulaski, Tennessee. He was wearing a gray military jacket and a captured Union army overcoat which had been dyed butternut, a coat which was similar to those commonly worn by Confederate soldiers who could not procure a regulation Confederate overcoat, which was either in short supply or simply unavailable.

In Davis's boot was a pass signed by one E. Coleman, a pseudonym for Captain Henry B. Shaw of Nashville, who was in charge of scouts engaged in military intelligence in Middle Tennessee in the service of the Army of Tennessee. In addition, Davis carried a Confederate soldier's innocent personal letter home, from Dan to Nannie (Dan's spouse), written from Chattanooga on November 11, which chattily revealed information of personal interest. He also had a personally incriminating letter written in Giles County earlier on the day Davis was captured, November 19, by Coleman to Colonel Alexander McKinstry, provost marshal general of the Army of Tennessee in Chattanooga, accurately detailing the location of Federal troops in Middle Tennessee. McKinstry headed the army's intelligence service.

This second letter was said to have been given Davis by Shaw, who also had been captured and incarcerated in the jail in Pulaski while Davis was held there pending his court-martial. Davis also had maps and descriptions of Federal fortifications at Nashville. Davis had been in Middle Tennessee, within Federal lines, for ten days.

Davis was remanded to Pulaski and brought before Brigadier General Grenville M. Dodge, commander of the left wing of the XVI Army Corps. Dodge told Davis he regarded him as one of Bragg's spies and that he (Dodge) must know who furnished Davis the information found on him.

Dodge divined that the informant must be someone close to headquarters of his own staff. He was, it seems, as close to Dodge as the Pulaski lockup. Although Dodge insisted that Davis reveal the name of his informant, Davis respectfully declined.

Dodge, a civil engineer who was active in railroading for half a century, told Davis that he would have to convene a court-martial the verdict of which likely would be a sentence of death, considering the compelling evidence of spying found on Davis. Even when faced with the weight of Dodge's logic, Davis firmly declined to reveal the source of his information.

"I know that I will have to die but I will not tell where I got the information, and there is no power on earth that can make me tell. You are doing your duty as a soldier and I am doing mine. If I have to die I will do so feeling that I am doing my duty to God and my country." This according to Dodge.

The court-martial convened on November 22 found Davis guilty of two charges: one, "being a spy," although he was not, since he was captured in uniform, that of a Confederate soldier; and two, "being a carrier of mails, communications, and information from within the lines of the U.S. Army to persons in arms against the Government," a charge which simply was extralegal, not a violation of any law.

Davis, who had refused counsel, apparently was the victim of a legal farce when the court sentenced him to death by hanging rather than simply remanding him to the Pulaski jail as a prisoner of war, as it should have.

That night, Davis wrote sorrowfully to his mother in Smyrna that he must bid her goodbye forever: "Mother, I do not fear to die. . . . Do not forget me. . . . But do not grieve for me; it will do no good. Father, you can send after my remains if you want to do so. . . ."

Execution was set for Friday, November 27, the day after Thanksgiving. That morning, after Davis had said his farewells to his fellow prisoners in the county lockup on the public square in Pulaski, he rode in a wagon seated on his coffin to a grove of trees at the eastern edge of the town where scaffolding had been erected.

After Davis had mounted the scaffold, Captain L.A. Naron, an Alabamian who was Dodge's chief of scouts, arrived and made one last effort to get the name of Davis's informant, offering Davis his life and safe conduct to Confederate lines if he would name him.

To this final offer, Davis is reported to have responded: "Do you suppose were I your friend that I would betray you? . . . If I had a thousand lives I would lose them all here before I would betray my friends."

Among the witnesses to the hanging was Second Lieutenant Henry I. Smith of the Seventh Iowa Infantry Regiment, who made his home in Mason

City, Iowa. Smith was close enough to see Davis's features and countenance when he was executed. He recorded that "there were few dry eyes among those who were the sorrowful witnesses. And when the drop fell, there was such a pall of sadness and silence that the air was oppressive."[41]

The example of Sam Davis's honesty, courage, devotion to duty, fidelity to the confidant with whom he worked and to the cause he served manifestly serves to set a lofty professional and patriotic standard of excellence for all who work in the military intelligence trade. Although the intelligence service of the Army of Tennessee was sometimes criticized as being amateurish and ineffectual, Davis's conduct sets him apart and marks him as an extraordinary and eminently emulative operative as well as a man of unshakable principle.

Within a few miles of Nashville, Wheeler finally became the object of a chase. Major General Lovell H. Rousseau, with cavalry and infantry, set out in pursuit from Nashville, and Steedman was ordered out from Chattanooga. Wheeler sought to avoid capture by withdrawing south along the Nashville & Decatur Railroad from the vicinity of Nashville, through Franklin and Columbia.

In a minor action near Franklin, Brigadier General John H. Kelly, a promising West Point cadet from Alabama when he resigned from the academy on December 29, 1860, expecting Alabama to secede, was mortally wounded in an action against Federal cavalry under Brigadier General James D. Brownlow. Kelly's death a few days later, while in the care of the family of William H. Harrison at Harrison House, about five miles south of Franklin, was, to Wheeler, a poignant and tragic personal as well as collegial loss.

At Columbia, Wheeler left the rail line and rode south-southwest toward Florence, Alabama, where he planned to cross the Tennessee River to find sanctuary. His march became a running fight of feints and small skirmishes but no pitched battles. On September 1 David R. Corlett, 32, was captured in Williamson County. Corlett, a member of Company C of the Eleventh Tennessee Cavalry, apparently was on detail to Wheeler's command, although his military service record does not record the detail. Following his capture, he was transferred to Camp Chase (Ohio) on September 10, 1864, where he took the oath of allegiance and was released on April 8, 1865.

By September 2, Wheeler had placed his command south of the Tennessee at Tuscumbia, Alabama. But he felt little satisfaction in the results of his raid despite filing a brave and self-justifying report to headquarters.[42] He had accomplished little in terms of interfering with Sherman's lifeline, while he had suffered substantial losses to his command.

Counting his troops under John Stuart Williams, who had gone astray at Strawberry Plains and never caught up, and George G. Dibrell's brigade, which had been turned back east in Cannon County, Wheeler had lost more than half his cavalry on the raid, including William T. Martin, arrested and relieved of his command, and John H. Kelly, dead.[43]

Wheeler seemingly had demonstrated for the second time that he was not adept at commanding large-scale cavalry operations independent of the main army. He had first failed in his raid of Middle Tennessee in September and October 1863, and again almost a year later.

On the other hand, in close support of the Army of Tennessee during 1862 and 1863, as well as in the Army's retreat from Chattanooga to Atlanta, and in its subsequent operations in the vicinity of Atlanta in 1864, Wheeler had performed very well indeed.

Back in Georgia, Sherman was brewing more trouble for the Confederates.

Chapter 6

The Fall of Atlanta, Sherman's March, and Surrender in the East, August 25, 1864–May 19, 1865

While Wheeler was away on his raid through North Georgia and Tennessee, Sherman set in motion his infantry to cut Atlanta's rail communications and drive Hood out of the city. On August 25, 1864, Sherman desisted from his intermittent shelling of Atlanta and evacuated his army's entrenchments to the north of the city, leaving only one corps across the Western & Atlantic Railroad. With the bulk of his formidable force, Sherman swung west of Atlanta, then south, and finally east, to strike first at the Atlanta & West Point Railroad to Montgomery, Alabama, destroying track, then to hit the Macon & Western Railroad around Jonesboro, twenty-two miles south of Atlanta.[1]

Hardee's corps went south from Atlanta, followed by Hood's old corps, now commanded by Stephen D. Lee, to meet the new Federal challenge. Hood's plan was to have Hardee's corps in place at Jonesboro, facing west. From its position, the corps would drive the approaching Federal army back into the Flint River at its rear.

In the event that Hardee's thrust succeeded, Lee's and Stewart's corps, together with some state troops, beginning at Rough and Ready, halfway back to Atlanta, were to march south down the valley of the Flint River to strike the Federal forces on their left flank while the latter were engaged frontally by Hardee.[2]

Hardee made his attack on the afternoon of August 31 in what is known as the Battle of Jonesboro. He attacked the enemy lodged behind breastworks and failed to move him.

The next day, the Federals launched their own attack against Hardee's corps. Fighting this time behind their own entrenchments, Hardee's troops repulsed the assault. But since Hood's army had been unsuccessful in driving the attacking forces back in retreat to the west across the Flint River, Hood deemed it essential to evacuate Atlanta and seek to re-form his divided army to the south of the city. He believed that, had he tried to hold Atlanta, he would have invited entrapment by clearly superior forces whose noose about the city was being drawn ever more tightly.[3]

So Hood ordered a pullback to the south, taking everything possible of use to him but destroying six railroad locomotives and two large trains of ordnance and ammunition which should have been sent south earlier but which now could not be carried away. It was reported that Sherman heard explosions from the city at about two in the morning of September 2. Later that morning, Federal forces under Major General Henry W. Slocum marched into Atlanta. Mayor James M. Calhoun rode out to meet Colonel John Coburn of the Thirty-Third Indiana Infantry Regiment at 11 A.M., parleyed, and surrendered the city.[4]

The previous day and into the early morning hours of the next, members of the Eleventh Tennessee Cavalry acted as a provost guard. It was necessary to clear the vicinity of the rail yard in Atlanta of civilians and stragglers as six engines and two large trains of ordnance stores were destroyed. And someone had to clear stragglers from the bars, bedrooms, and bordellos of Atlanta, sending them south. Finally the men of the Eleventh joined the rear guard in covering the retreat down the road to McDonough on the third, thence to Lovejoy's Station on the fourth.[5]

With Lee's corps and its attached cavalry guarding the rear, Hood's last two corps, those of A.P. Stewart and Gustavus W. Smith, marched south from Atlanta to rendezvous with Hardee's corps, which by now had withdrawn about seven miles south of Jonesboro to Lovejoy's Station on the Macon & Western Railroad.[6]

The capture of Atlanta gave strong impetus to the war party in the North, which had been hard pressed to exhibit compelling evidence that the days left to the Southern Confederacy were indeed numbered. Continued pursuit of war objectives now seemed more prudent, reasonable, and attainable. Men and women in the North who wished the Federal Union to be restored now could more clearly see the light at the end of the tunnel.

But the Northern victory at Atlanta, alas for the victors, did not involve the destruction of the Army of Tennessee. On the second of September, Hood clearly believed that Sherman would continue his offensive begun on August 25 when he put in motion the movement of his corps to the south of Atlanta. But Sherman surprised Hood and his army. He retired his forces north to Atlanta on September 6 for rest while he attempted to rethink his most appropriate next move.

When Sherman began his drive from the Tennessee border toward Atlanta on May 7, 1864, he believed that the destruction of the opposing army was his objective. Now it seemed enough for him simply to celebrate his capture of Atlanta while leaving Hood's army to pursue its own plans and purposes.[7]

The fighting about Atlanta had been costly to both sides. From July 28, after Hood took command of the Army of Tennessee, until September 20,

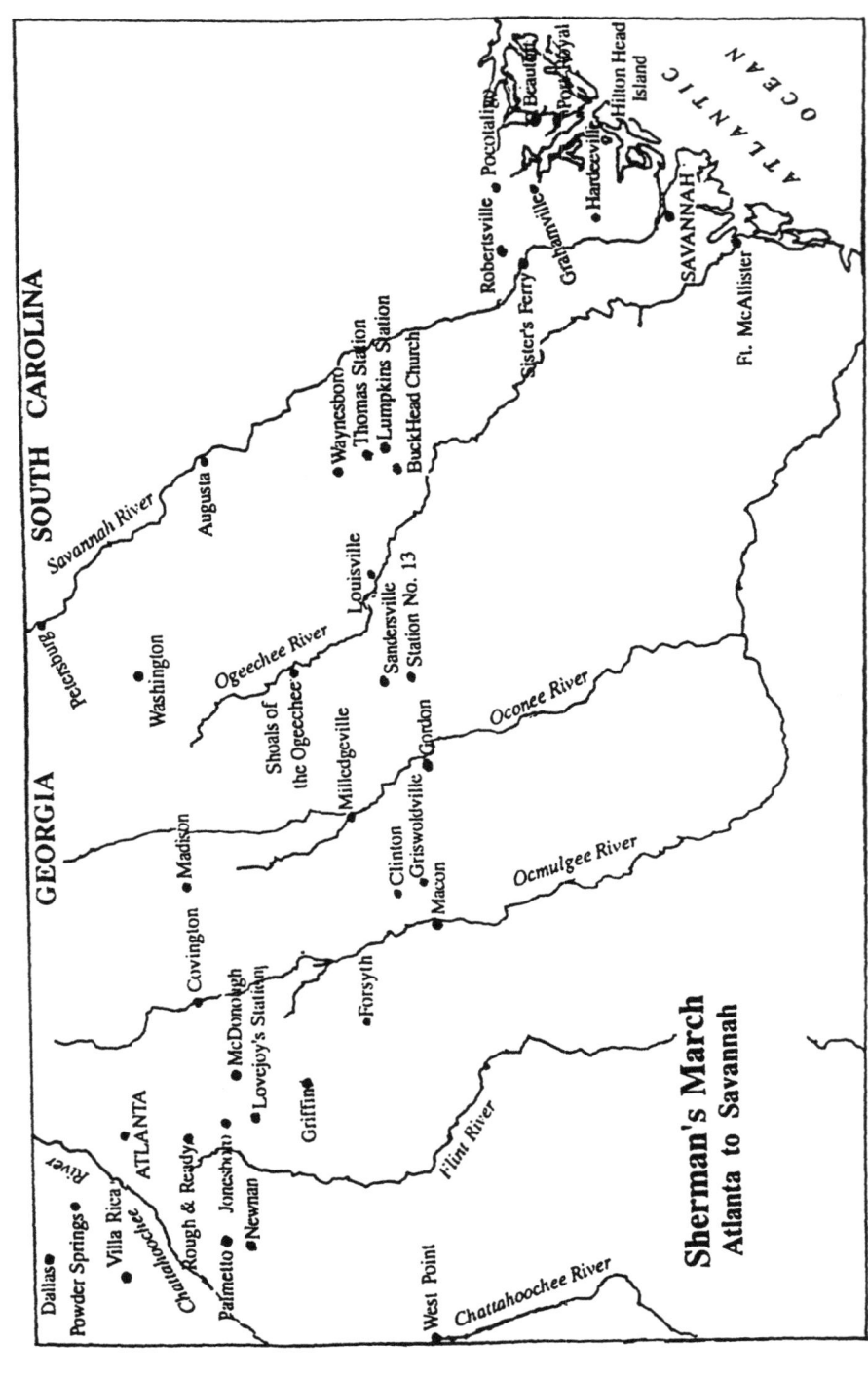

1864, Hood reported that he suffered total losses from all causes of 9,124 out of a force which originally numbered from 48,000 to 50,000.[8] Sherman reported Union losses from May to September, inclusive, of 4,423 killed, 22,822 wounded, and 4,442 missing, an aggregate loss of 31,687.

Sherman claimed that Hood underreported all his losses, but especially his missing. Sherman claimed prisoners taken by his army totalled 12,983, a figure which included over 2,400 deserters. He claimed that Southern losses totalled 34,979, exceeding his own losses by 3,292.[9]

The two armies had been through particularly grueling combat for forty-five days from July 20 to September 6, with heavy losses inflicted on both sides. Soldiers in each army had a healthy respect for each other. Sherman complained in a dispatch that he could not get his soldiers to move a hundred yards without their digging in to protect themselves behind entrenchments.[10]

Leaders of the two armies came under criticism for the ways in which their armies were handled in the campaign. Hood was bewildered by the movement of Sherman's forces in the latter stages and lost one chance after another to hit Sherman's columns in the flanks or rear.[11]

Hood's bewilderment resulted primarily from his failure or inability to use his cavalry as his eyes while his army's cavalry corps commander, Joe Wheeler, was away. Hood had Brigadier General William H. Jackson, who commanded a cavalry division of about 4,000 effectives. In addition, he had four brigade commanders, brigadier generals Alfred C. Iverson, Jr., who had close to 1,000 Georgia horsemen under his command during August and September, John T. Morgan, with almost 1,000 Alabama horsemen, Samuel W. Ferguson, with a small brigade of perhaps 600 effectives, plus Colonel Moses W. Hannon with another small brigade of 500 to 600 Alabamians.[12] Hood manifested a degree of ineptitude with respect to the use of cavalry. In Georgia, Hood primarily used the cavalry for close support of his infantry, for a raid to threaten the enemy's lifeline, and to intercept threatening attacks by the enemy's mounted troops. But not so much as his eyes and ears.

Further, Hood permitted his corps to become scattered and thus subject to being hit and destroyed separately by Sherman's larger and better equipped corps. Fortunately for Hood, his opponent's strategic shortcomings obviated the possibility of this decisive denouement actually coming to pass.

Sherman, on the other hand, failed to make the most effective use of his awesome military superiority throughout the campaign. And at the end, he failed to deliver the coup de grace that might have destroyed Hood's tough but dispirited and badly mauled army. Instead, he turned away from the enemy back to Atlanta and left the Army of Tennessee a destructive force still in being with the capability yet of causing extensive effusion of blood in the powerful Union army.

In Sherman's view, the people of Atlanta constituted an element with potential for interfering substantially with Union military operations. After setting up his headquarters in Atlanta, Sherman lost little time in decreeing that civilians in the city were not welcome and were to be driven out. They would not be suffered because their houses were needed to house soldiers and for storage of military materiel. Their supply and maintenance by itinerant and local subtlers would be an additional care and encumbrance for the army. And their mere presence would impede and interfere with the taking of essential military measures by needlessly expanding the garrison needed and by thrusting additional police duties on the occupying army.

With respect to those civilians who might wish to depart south within the Confederate lines, Sherman announced to Hood on September 7 that under an armistice he would provide transport as far as Rough and Ready. He invited Hood to meet the civilian refugees there and help them to get as far as Lovejoy's Station. There trains might transport them farther south to wherever they might wish to go.

Hood, with an army vastly and obviously inferior to Sherman's army, felt that he had no option but to cooperate in the expulsion, which was carried out during a ten-day truce commencing on September 12 and ending on the twenty-first. Hood protested to Sherman that his plan transcended in cruelty anything else of which he was aware in the long and dark annals of war. Sherman, however, was unmoved by Hood's protest. The two carried on a brief but wordy self-justifying correspondence regarding the matter.

The number of Atlantans going south pursuant to Sherman's expulsion apparently represented a mere remnant. By July 13, 1864, when Joe Johnston retreated into Atlanta's fortifications, it was reported that most Atlantans had already left the city. Yet most of the exiles had no place to go. They suffered most desperately, having few independent resources for sustaining themselves, but they were hardly the first of the war's refugees.

There had been refugees, primarily Southerners, from the first few months of the war in 1861 as contending armies swept north and south dislodging civilian populations wherever their weight was felt. There were additional refugees in every year of the war. In the South, they swelled the populations of towns and cities in the cotton states and added to shortages of food, water, and consumer goods as well as services already in short supply.

Hood dealt with the refugees from Atlanta as best he could, providing army wagons to help haul some of the exiles and their possessions while his troops lent assistance to children, the aged and infirmed, and those who were totally bereft of resources sufficient to keep body and soul together.[13]

But Hood desperately wanted to make plans for moving his army out in order to attack Sherman's communications. Unfortunately for him, however, he was not operating from a position of strength. His mobility was frozen by the felt necessity of keeping his army between Sherman's forces and the military prison at Andersonville, Georgia. He wished to have the prisoners moved to Florida to free him to maneuver.

His badly outnumbered army had not been paid in ten months or longer, and its morale was sagging. Further, its strength was reduced somewhat on September 10 when the Georgia State Militia was furloughed by Governor Joseph E. Brown to harvest corn and sorghum following the fall of Atlanta.[14]

There were even rumors of the possibility of Georgia making a separate peace with the Federal government. Sherman reported to President Lincoln on September 17 that he was seeking, through mediators, to negotiate with Governor Brown the permanent withdrawal of the state's militia from the Confederate army and help in expelling Hood from the borders of the state in return for Sherman's pledge to forgo the worst depredations and destruction of property in Georgia by confining his troops to the main roads and paying the locals for his army's subsistence.[15]

While Governor Brown's support of the Confederate cause may have grown more tepid with each successive failure of Confederate arms, the governor could not bring himself to go quite as far as Sherman would have wished. Thus Sherman's diplomatic initiatives went for naught. And the greatest suffering of Georgians was yet to be.

On September 16, a few days before the evacuation of Federal prisoners from Andersonville to Florida began, Hood commenced moving his army westward to Palmetto, via Rough and Ready, on the rail line to Montgomery, about twenty-five miles southwest of Atlanta. The Eleventh Tennessee Cavalry arrived at Palmetto on the twentieth and camped at Jones' Camp Ground, a scene of bygone religious ecstasy experienced by the faithful in camp meetings and revivals.

Hood left only a cavalry brigade under Alfred Iverson to watch Sherman's army in Atlanta while he prepared to move his army around Atlanta to the west, then to the north.[16]

Meanwhile, the Confederate high command in Richmond was bestirring itself uneasily about plans for the army's reaction to Sherman's ensconcement in Atlanta. President Jefferson Davis arrived in Palmetto on September 25 to discuss the military situation facing Hood and to deliver a speech to the troops of the beleaguered Army of Tennessee.[17]

Following his talks with Davis and the president's departure, Hood undertook to place his army north of the Chattahoochee River and to interfere with Sherman's communications through North Georgia. On the twenty-ninth, Sherman wired General Henry W. Halleck, army chief of staff in Washington, of his confidence that he could whip Hood's infantry.

"But his cavalry is to be feared."[18]

After moving through Powder Springs, on October 2 Hood notified Braxton Bragg in Richmond that he was in line of battle a few miles west of Marietta with his left at Lost Mountain where it threatened the Western & Atlantic Railroad.[19]

Prior to crossing the Chattahoochee on October 1, a detail of ten enlisted men from Company C of the Eleventh, which included Will Fisher, drove a large herd of sheep from Palmetto to Newnan to insure that the animals did not fall into the hands of the invaders.[20]

On the fourth, Stewart's corps attacked and captured garrisons at Acworth and Big Shanty and tore up fifteen miles of rails. On October 5, Major General Samuel G. French went with his division to the next town north, Allatoona, where he barely missed an opportunity to capture or destroy a large store of strongly guarded Union supplies.[21]

Captain Jacob T. Martin of Company G of the Eleventh Tennessee Cavalry was given charge of 280 prisoners on October 5 who had been captured while the latter were tearing up the railroad between Big Shanty and Allatoona. Martin and his guard detail set out to deliver the prisoners to West Point, Georgia, travelling via Villa Rica and Newnan.

The guard detail included William Stratton Fisher of Company C, who did not go all the way but cast off from the detail when the prisoners were put safely across the Chattahoochee River on the eighth. He and a companion from the Eleventh named Swanson, either Ira or John J. Swanson, from Captain Martin's Company G, started back to rejoin their regiment with Wheeler.

The Swansons of Company G were two of three Swansons, perhaps brothers, who were recruited by Daniel W. Holman at Thompson's Station in Williamson County, Tennessee, on September 22, 1862. Felix Z. Swanson was killed near Brentwood in the same county on March 25, 1863, when Forrest, with light casualties, captured an infantry garrison of 750. Subsequently Ira and John J. Swanson deserted their company on January 15, 1865, pursuant to Forrest directing Chalmers to grant a twenty-day furlough to troops of their brigade, then in Mississippi, until January 20. They returned to Tennessee, surrendered, then took the oath of allegiance to the United States in the headquarters of the Provost Marshal General, Department of the Cumberland, in Nashville, on February 28, 1865.

On October 10, 1864, Fisher and Swanson met Captain T.C.H. Miller of Company C near Carrollton. Miller was escorting 750 captured troops, mostly colored, from Dalton to West Point. Fisher went with Miller's guard to West Point, arriving on the thirteenth. Fisher and the guard returned north to rejoin Hood's army after the latter had gone into Alabama. Their detail camped at Jacksonville, Alabama, October 18–20, and rejoined the main army at Gadsden on the twenty-first.[22]

Sherman meanwhile, on October 3, went in pursuit of Hood with five corps, about 65,000 men, leaving Major General Henry W. Slocum to hold the city of Atlanta with the XX Corps. After Hood had attacked Federal garrisons at Acworth, Big Shanty, and Allatoona, Sherman discovered from Allatoona on the ninth that Hood was proceeding north above Dallas and New Hope Church, where heavy fighting had occurred in June.

About this time, Sherman first suggested to Grant the possibility of cutting loose from Atlanta and his supply line to the north (which he confided he could not effectively protect against Hood, Forrest, and Wheeler). He wanted to cut his lines, destroy the railroad south of Chattanooga and begin a march in the direction of Milledgeville and Savannah. "I can make this march and make Georgia howl!" he boasted.[23]

Meanwhile, back within Confederate lines in Tuscumbia, Alabama, on September 20, 1864, Joe Wheeler had conferred with Forrest who was himself preparing a cavalry raid into Middle Tennessee. Forrest was now under the command of Lieutenant General Richard Taylor, the new commander of the Department of Alabama, Mississippi, and East Louisiana.

Although Taylor bore the burden of being Jefferson Davis's brother-in-law, he had other useful connections. He was credited with having a brilliant mind for public affairs and a fine grasp of the strategic realities of the war following publication of his reminiscences in 1877 under the title *Destruction and Reconstruction*.

Taylor, who reputedly had few peers in the art of swearing, was a Yale graduate, a Louisiana plantation owner, and son of the Mexican War hero and U.S. President, Zachary Taylor. He, Forrest, and Wade Hampton of South Carolina were the only Confederate officers *not* West Point graduates who rose as high as the rank of lieutenant general.[24]

Belatedly, it was planned that Forrest would do what Wheeler had failed to do to Sherman's lifeline. But by now, when the opposing armies were so unequal in strength and Sherman's progress so close to the full realization of his plans (Atlanta had fallen on September 2) it was too late.

Wheeler, who was the senior officer (although fifteen years the younger) of the two, called upon Forrest and suggested that they might join forces in the latter's raid. Wheeler pointed out that some of his troops were still in Tennessee, that by joining Forrest's raid he might be able to find and lead his lost troops out. The latter reference was primarily to troops under Williams and Dibrell from whom nothing had been heard for the better part of a month.

Wheeler was discouraged and on the point of resigning, as Forrest reported in a letter to Taylor on September 20 detailing the meeting he had had with Wheeler. He also reported that Wheeler's command was demoralized, Wheeler had lost the confidence of his officers, and despite Wheeler claiming to have brought out 2,000 troops from his raid, his adjutant general thought that, so unfit were his troops and mounts, he would not be able to contribute more than a thousand at best, but more likely not over 500 to Forrest's command in its planned campaign in Middle Tennessee.

Among the personnel Wheeler brought back from his raid was a remnant of Forrest's "Old Brigade," which Wheeler relinquished to Forrest on September 20. The remnant included only what remained of four companies of the Fourth Tennessee Cavalry, Starnes' old regiment, now under Colonel W.S. McLemore, and the remains of a brigade commanded by Jacob Biffle. In addition, Wheeler relinquished to Forrest all that remained of Colonel George H. Nixon's Twenty-Second Tennessee Cavalry Regiment.

Forrest ruefully reported to Taylor that all that was left of two of his regiments numbered 60 men, whereas ten months ago when he left his old brigade with Wheeler, the brigade had numbered no fewer than 2,300 men. Of course, Forrest's reference to missing troops, except for those lost as casualties, was to those under Dibrell and Williams who had been separated from Wheeler's main force and left behind in Tennessee when Wheeler came south to Tuscumbia.

With respect to the troops Wheeler reported as absent, Forrest wrote to Taylor that he hoped "to be instrumental in gathering them up" on his raid, a hope that he failed to bring to fruition.[25] Forrest's abbreviated two-week-long raid beginning September 21 lacked efficacy, was thwarted by threatened confrontations with repositioned Union troops of overwhelmingly superior numbers, and came too late to be of any help in turning Sherman back in Georgia.

Since the "lost troops" under Dibrell and Williams, with six companies of the Fourth Tennessee, had turned back to East Tennessee whence they had come in late August 1864, they were nowhere near Forrest and his raiders in Middle Tennessee. As indicated earlier, Williams' and Dibrell's commands in early October went to Saltville in southwest Virginia to defend against a Union attempt to take and destroy the salt works there.

George Guild of Paul Anderson's (formerly Baxter Smith's) Fourth Tennessee Cavalry wrote that Williams' command was repeatedly set upon by bushwhackers while marching through upper East Tennessee. Williams' troops were angry and inclined to answer their attackers in kind. Guild related that Williams had three privates and a lieutenant court-martialed and executed for excessive retaliation against local Unionists.

Nearby on September 2, 1864, Major General John Hunt Morgan, C.S.A., had been killed, "murdered" according to Guild, by ambush, and his lifeless body lifted to the back of his horse and paraded triumphantly through the streets of Greeneville.

Williams reported on October 1 from Clinch Mountain and on October 5 from Saltville describing the poor condition of his command and requesting help. He reported that his horses were entirely broken down and in need of rest and reshoeing. He had a fighting force of only 1,000 effectives. Many of his men were barefooted and almost naked and in need of arms. And in September the desertion of W.H. Blanton of Company D of the Fourth Tennessee incrementally depleted Dibrell's brigade which accompanied Williams' division. Blanton apparently escaped captured by the enemy, and may have gone home.[26]

The troops of McLemore's Fourth who went to Saltville may or may not have counted among their number Jim Fisher of Company D, who had leave to recruit troops in Middle Tennessee sometime during the last six months of 1864. Some of them who went, however, were witnesses to the brutal murder of up to 51 wounded and captured black soldiers, twelve white soldiers, and at least one white officer following the battle at Saltville, the details of which, and a subsequent court-martial, shed an oblique light on the many-sided duties and activities of the Western and partisan cavalry in which the brothers Fisher served.

The Union troops engaged at Saltville had marched from Lexington, Kentucky, and consisted primarily of Kentucky troops augmented by other infantry from Michigan and cavalry from Ohio. Official reports filed by two Union officers, Colonel James S. Brisbin, commander of the Fifth U.S. Colored Cavalry Regiment, and Surgeon William H. Gardner of the Thirtieth Kentucky Infantry, related either rumors or eyewitness accounts of the murder of captured black troops.[27]

George Guild of Paul Anderson's Fourth Tennessee Cavalry Regiment wrote that the action at Saltville was the first time members of his regiment had fought black troops, in this instance a detachment of about 400 men of the Fifth Regular U.S. Colored Cavalry.[28]

According to the report of their commanding officer, Colonel Brisbin, the latter were recruits then organizing at Camp Nelson, Kentucky. They joined the main body of troops at Prestonburg and were assigned to the brigade of Colonel R.W. Ratliff of the Twelfth Ohio Volunteer Cavalry.

Although openly despised, ridiculed, and mocked by their white comrades in blue who tormented them, stealing their caps and even their horses, the men of the Fifth fought well, according to their commanding officer, Brisbin, inflicting heavy casualties but suffering the highest casualties of any of the Federal forces participating. Four officers and 114 men were either killed or wounded. Fifty-one were reported missing.[29]

Brigadier General George G. Dibrell, commanding the dismounted Eighth Tennessee Cavalry on a line high up on a hillside covered with a thick coat of briers, reported that "the negroes were put in front, and driven [up] through the briers." Dibrell also observed that, "As the enemy began to emerge from the brier-thicket, some of the Eighth became exasperated when they saw it was negroes in front."[30]

A report was filed by a Union surgeon, William H. Gardner, of the Thirtieth Kentucky Infantry, U.S.A., stating that on Monday morning, October 3, several armed men came to his field hospital — he believed they were Confederate soldiers — took five black wounded prisoners and shot them. Again on Friday, October 7, at 10 P.M. in the Emory and Henry College hospital, several armed men shot and killed two black soldiers in their beds.

Gardner also told of a white officer being killed after the fighting by the guerrilla Champ Ferguson, who reportedly commanded an independent cavalry company. Gardner wrote that about seventy wounded Union soldiers had been moved by Confederate surgeons to nearby Emory and Henry College, where the main hall was converted to a hospital. They were attended by Union surgeons who had remained with the wounded on the field, as well as by Confederate surgeons, one of the latter, James B. Murfree of Tennessee, serving as surgeon-in-chief.

On Saturday afternoon, October 8, 1864, several armed men wearing Confederate uniforms arrived at the college hospital and, after overpowering the guards, went upstairs, found and shot dead First Lieutenant Ezra C. Smith, 28, of Company F, the Thirteenth Regiment of Kentucky Cavalry, U.S.A. They then called out for two other officers, Colonel Charles S. Hanson, commanding the Thirty-Seventh Kentucky Volunteer Infantry, and Captain Charles M. Degenfeld of Company I, the Twelfth Ohio Cavalry.

They were, however, prevented from killing them by the courageous intervention of the surgeon-in-chief, James B. Murfree. Gardner related that Murfree confronted Ferguson and defended the intended victims, and after a life-threatening standoff, when Ferguson and his men left, Murfree helped them, as well as Gardner, to leave and go to a place of safety.

Gardner said that, since leaving the hospital at Emory and Henry, he had been informed that the 70 wounded prisoners left behind had been killed. Gardner reported this after he returned to Lexington, Kentucky, and filed a report on October 26, 1864.[31]

Gardner's information relative to the deaths of the prisoners who remained appears, however, to have been incorrect. Apparently most if not all of the prisoners, wounded and otherwise, were sent to Lynchburg, Virginia. Colonel Hanson and Captain Degenfeld were hospitalized at Lynchburg, then imprisoned in Richmond. They were exchanged in February 1865.[32]

Apparently having no knowledge of the murders alleged by Surgeon Gardner, Will Jennings, surgeon and medical director in the field, C.S.A., reported from Abingdon, ten miles away, on the very same day, Saturday, October 8, that Ezra Smith was killed, and that there were 98 wounded, both Union and Confederate, then in the Emory and Henry Hospital, including all who had been found upon the field of battle up to Wednesday, October 5, at 4 P.M.

Jennings also reported that seven more wounded Union soldiers had been apprehended by Brigadier General Alfred E. Jackson, soldiers who, Jennings said, were to be sent by Jackson to the hospital at Emory and Henry.

But on the same day, October 8, that Jennings wrote, Jackson reported that he had sent to Lynchburg 61 prisoners, including the surgeon and attendants at Emory and Henry Hospital, sending five wounded Federals to the hospital in Lynchburg and two captives to Abingdon to be tried for desertion.[33]

Ferguson was tried after the war by a military court in Nashville for being a guerrilla and for the murders of Smith, two black soldiers (names unknown) shot while lying wounded in prison in Saltville, twelve other soldiers (believed to be white, names unknown) shot and killed while lying wounded on the battlefield at Saltville, and others. The trial began on July 11, 1865.

Ferguson was charged with the murder of fifty-three persons during the course of his career as a guerrilla from 1861 to 1865. The army, however, built its case upon the death of Lieutenant Ezra Smith almost exclusively and presented scant or, in most instances, no evidence relative to the deaths of the other fifty-two.

Former Confederate Major General Joseph Wheeler testified for the defense, stating that he considered Ferguson to be a regular member of the Army of the Confederate States since he had served in his command more than once, and that he was entitled to treatment as a prisoner of war.

But a part of the problem of his defense at the trial was Ferguson's inability to produce evidence that he had ever had a commission in the Confederate army or that he had been paroled as a regular Southern soldier at the end of the war.[34] And although the lack of records is not conclusive, military records of Civil War soldiers being fragmentary, there appear to be no military records of Champ Ferguson among those of other Confederate soldiers in the National Archives today.

Ferguson came from a sparsely populated mountain area, Clinton County, Kentucky, where wartime passions seem to have run high. In 1860, Champion Ferguson, 38, a farmer of modest means, lived in Clinton County with his wife, Martha, 34, and daughter, Ann, 9, as well as a live-in male farm worker, Marion Cowan, 21.

With the onset of hostilities in 1861 and reported humiliating abuses against his wife and daughter by local Unionists, Ferguson moved his family for safety across the border some fifty miles south to near Sparta, seat of White County, Tennessee.[35]

After organizing his military company early in 1862, Ferguson alternated operating independently in several mountain counties around the Tennessee-Kentucky border including Clinton County, Kentucky, and Scott, Morgan, Fentress, and Clay counties, Tennessee, and operating with organized Confederate forces during 1862 and 1863.

During this period, Ferguson seems to have operated in conjunction with Lieutenant Colonel Oliver P. Hamilton's Tennessee cavalry battalion. Then on July 9, 1862, Ferguson was reported by Union sources as being a part of forces under Colonel John Hunt Morgan in an action at Celina, Tennessee. And Colonel George G. Dibrell reported that he was reinforced by Ferguson and a part of his company in an action at Calfkiller River in White County, Tennessee, on August 9, 1863. Ferguson and his company joined with Dibrell's brigade in Sparta in September 1864 and went east with it to Saltville.[36]

In 1860 Ezra Smith lived in Cumberland County, Kentucky, adjoining Clinton County, with his bride, Sarah Ann, 18. Three years later, he joined for one year the Thirteenth Kentucky Cavalry Regiment, U.S.A., on October 28, 1863, and was mustered into service on December 23, 1863. The 1860 census record shows Smith's age as 20, but he gave his age as 28 when he enlisted in the army in 1863.[37] Perhaps he inflated his age by eight years to indicate greater maturity and to merit a commission.

With respect to the Champ Ferguson-Ezra Sith antagonism, it may be noted that Colonel Hamilton, with whom Ferguson had operated, had been captured at Celina, Tennessee, on March 4, 1864. Hamilton was charged by Federal officials with being a guerrilla. While being taken to Lexington, Kentucky, to stand trial, he was killed by a member or members of his guard.[38]

Ferguson must have believed that Smith was responsible for Hamilton's death. Indeed, James B. Murfree, surgeon in charge of the hospital at Emory and Henry College, after the war wrote an account of the murder of Smith and stated that Ferguson and his companions shouted, upon leaving the hospital just after Smith's death, that they had thus avenged the murder of Colonel Hamilton.

George B. Guild, a kinsman of Jo Conn Guild, defense attorney for Ferguson, repeated an account alleging that Ferguson murdered Smith because the latter was responsible for the murder of Hamilton. Guild also asserted a widely held belief that Ferguson was deceived into surrendering himself after the war with promises of a parole by army authorities.[39]

Ferguson's trial had begun on July 11, 1865. The predictable guilty verdict of the military commission which heard the evidence was made public on October 10.

After his trial, Ferguson reportedly acknowledged in an interview that he had killed Smith because the latter had captured a number of his men on different occasions and added that Smith "always killed the last one of them."

Ferguson's execution by hanging took place at the state penitentiary in Nashville, October 20, 1865. The place of execution was heavily guarded by troops of the Fifteenth U.S. Colored Infantry, a regiment organized at Shelbyville, Tennessee, in late September 1864. It had performed guard duty on the Edgefield & Kentucky Railroad, and in Springfield, Tennessee, as well as guard and fatigue duty in Nashville during virtually all of its organized history.[40]

Ferguson's widow and daughter took his remains to White County, Tennessee, for burial at his wartime home near the Calfkiller River. They reportedly went west and lived in the Indian Territory, now Oklahoma.[41]

It is said that Champ Ferguson was one of only two men tried, convicted, and executed by the United States Army for war crimes following the war. The commander of the prison at Andersonville, Georgia, Captain Henri Wirz, was the other.

Wheeler wrote to Hood on September 20, 1864, of his meeting with Forrest and pressed his argument for returning to Tennessee on Forrest's projected raid. But Hood would have none of it. On September 15, he had wired Wheeler to rejoin the left of his army near Atlanta. He was needed and would be most useful in close support of the main army. Hood reiterated his order to Wheeler on the twenty-first from Palmetto, Georgia.[42]

But Wheeler did not repair to Georgia immediately. He felt the need to rest and refurbish his badly mauled command at Tuscumbia. Then, with his request to join forces with Forrest rejected, he and his command made their way across North Alabama at a leisurely pace, recrossing the Tennessee River at Decatur and marching through Huntsville, thence east, destroying rails and whatever else might be of use to the Federal army, crossing the Tennessee again before arriving in Georgia and threatening the Federal garrison at Dalton on October 2, 1864, for the second time in about six weeks.[43]

But Wheeler did little more than make an appearance before the Dalton garrison. Camping nearby at Snake Creek Gap, Wheeler rested through the night, then tore up some recently-mended railroad track which he had destroyed in August. At dawn, he headed south in the direction of the Connesauga River.

The Connesauga was awash with high water. Wheeler set his men to work felling trees and building rafts. But the rafts were not to be used by his army for crossing or rafting. They were set adrift in the river to be carried downstream by the swift current to lodge against the supporting pillars of the railroad bridge at Resaca. The rafts were too bulky to float between the piers. Their weight, plus the force of the raging water against the piles, caused the bridge to be swept away.[44]

On October 4, Wheeler turned west in the direction of Rome, where a Federal army detachment was garrisoned. But he decided not to become engaged there. On the eighth, he met and rejoined Hood's army on its way north from the environs of Atlanta. Thus the troops of the Eleventh Tennessee, who stayed with Hood in Georgia while Wheeler raided Tennessee, once again came under Wheeler's command.

Hood continued his northward march, crossing the Coosa River near Rome on October 10. Flanking Rome, Hood swung east toward the railroad and captured the garrison of 750 men, primarily the Forty-Fourth U.S. Colored Infantry Regiment, blacks commanded by white officers, Colonel Lewis Johnson, commanding, at Dalton on the thirteenth.

Colonel Daniel W. Holman, whose regiment, the Eleventh Tennessee Cavalry, was charged with guarding the prisoners, wrote that the black enlisted men, together with other prisoners, were marched to West Point, Georgia.

The white officers, according to Holman, were at first greatly alarmed for their personal safety, knowing the feeling of Southern troops relative to fighting black troops. They soon, however, were reassured and, when exchanged under a flag of truce on October 15, "expressed their gratitude for the kind treatment they had received, each warmly shaking the hands of the officers of the regiment, and pronouncing, as they took their departure, benedictions on its officers and men."[45]

Subsequently it was reported that many of the troops of the Forty-Fourth were returned as runaway slaves to those who had been, or claimed to have been, their former owners, in accordance with Confederate army policy for dealing with blacks captured in the field.

The colored regiment had been organized at Chattanooga in March and April 1864 and recruited up to strength after being moved to Rome, Georgia, about the middle of July.[46] Thus its recruits were quite new to warfare.

Hood now headed west and encamped in a valley a few miles south of Lafayette before proceeding southwest to Gadsden, Alabama, which he reached on the twentieth and where he parleyed with his superior, Pierre G.T. Beauregard. The latter had been transferred from Virginia on October 3 and placed in charge of a new Military Division of the West which embraced the departments headed by Hood and Taylor. In Gadsden on the twentieth, Hood discussed with Beauregard his plans to march north through Middle Tennessee, and thence into Kentucky, hard by Cincinnati. Beauregard, according to Jefferson Davis, had already committed himself to Hood's plan in conversations with the president in Augusta, Georgia, the day he accepted his new command.[47]

On October 16, while still in Georgia, Hood had learned that Sherman's pursuing army had come as far north as Snake Creek Gap on the thirteenth. Hood's diminished cavalry was now at the front of Sherman's army, attempting to slow its advance. Hood wrote that he decided to select an advantageous position, turn his army about, and fight Sherman's advance.

But the big fight was not to be. Hood's officers were opposed. Sherman's forces were too numerous, well-trained and led, and menacingly equipped. Accordingly, Hood would hereafter content himself with his plan to march into Middle Tennessee "with the hope of eventually establishing our line in Kentucky."[48] Besides, Sherman had already communicated to Grant on October 9 his plan to cut his line of communication, turn his back on Hood's army, and set out for Savannah and the sea.[49]

A part of Sherman's plan was to leave Atlanta undefended and send George H. Thomas back north to Nashville to face Hood's advance in that quarter. Sherman left Atlanta on November 16, having burned the city the previous night, riding east on the Decatur Road in company with his staff and escort and the XIV Corps. Most of his army had left the day before.[50]

On October 22, Hood notified Wheeler of his plan to switch cavalry commanders for his march to Tennessee. He left Wheeler in North Georgia with 4,500 horsemen and instructions to follow Sherman wherever he might go. Wheeler had close to 2,000 horsemen brought back from his Tennessee raid. He was given Martin's division consisting of Iverson's and Morgan's brigades. And before November 1, Wheeler would be rejoined by Williams' division and Dibrell's brigade, the latter under strength, both of which had failed to return with him from Tennessee in early September.[51]

With the main strength of the badly battered Army of Tennessee going back north, Hood would look to Forrest to lead the army's cavalry and be his eyes and ears in his advance into Middle Tennessee.

Hood marched his army from Gadsden to Decatur, Alabama, where there was an enemy presence which produced skirmishing by Hood's infantry on October 27-28. Thence Hood continued to Tuscumbia which was reached on October 30. This move gave Hood's army access to a damaged rail line which went west to Corinth, Mississippi, where it intersected the Mobile & Ohio Railroad, the latter going south to Mobile Bay.

Hood arrived at Tuscumbia with approximately 27,000 infantry and artillery as well as 2,000 cavalry, the latter under the command of Brigadier General William H. Jackson.[52] But before pursuing the matter of Hood's return to Tennessee, there is the matter of what transpired between Sherman and his pursuers to the east, a dramatic story of the last days of the war.

The cavalry which Hood brought out of Georgia with him included the Eleventh Tennessee Cavalry, but not the Fourth. The latter, divided in early September on Wheeler's last Middle Tennessee raid, remained so. Wheeler relinquished four companies of the Fourth to Forrest for his last raids of Middle and West Tennessee, in October-November 1864. The remaining six companies were en route in late October from the vicinity of Saltville in southwest Virginia to Georgia in George Dibrell's brigade. In Georgia they would rejoin Wheeler at Griffin.

Wheeler's cavalry would attempt to block and interrupt the progress of Sherman's march from Atlanta all the way to the city of Savannah near where the Savannah River empties into the North Atlantic Ocean. They would spar with Sherman's cavalry, under the command of Brigadier General Judson Kilpatrick, one of Wheeler's West Point classmates, and would provide the only regular Confederate force to contest Sherman's famous destructive march through Georgia.

During the first week of Sherman's campaign, there were about 3,000 Georgia militia and some 12,000 Confederate infantry from scattered points within the department which were sent to Macon when it was thought that Sherman was rushing to capture the city. But when the Union army failed to attack Macon and, instead marched toward the state capital, Milledgeville, Hardee, the departmental commander, on November 21, sent all his disposable forces at Macon, with the exception of Wheeler's cavalry, to Savannah.

Braxton Bragg, once again out of Richmond and in the field, arrived in Augusta with 10,000 troops from North Carolina for the defense of that city.[53] As it happened, Sherman tactically deceived his enemies again and bypassed Augusta in his drive to the Atlantic Ocean.

But too much credit should not accrue to Sherman's military genius in tactically deceiving Hardee, whose defensive forces were vastly inferior to Sherman's offensive juggernaut. Hardee justifiably felt the need to do the best he could to defend population centers such as Macon and Savannah. These necessities played into the hands of Sherman's army, which marched in four columns practically unimpeded through the central Georgia countryside of farms and small towns.

Sherman's army of 62,000 picked men was delayed hardly at all by Wheeler's undermanned cavalry force of, at best, 4,500. Nevertheless, Wheeler's resistance, however ineffectual, formed a pretext, pursuant to Sherman's Special Field Order No. 120 of November 9, 1864, for the invading army to inflict ever more severe depredations, such as destruction of mills, houses, cotton gins, etc., upon people and property found in the path of its march.[54]

When Sherman's army began its march to the sea, and beyond to Richmond, on November 15–16, leaving Atlanta a ruined city, Wheeler had been keeping an eye on Union army operations in Atlanta from the vantage point of Jonesboro, 22 miles south.[55]

Sherman's army started east toward the sea, the left wing passing through Covington the second day out to give the impression of marching to Augusta. The left wing, comprised of the XIV and XX corps, was commanded by Major General Henry W. Slocum. The right wing, comprised of the XV and XVII corps and threatening Macon, was commanded by Major General Oliver O. Howard. Judson Kilpatrick, Sherman's cavalry commander, started out through Jonesboro and McDonough on the army's right flank and feinted in the direction of Forsyth to further lead the Southerners to believe Sherman was headed for Macon.[56]

Indeed Wheeler arrived in Macon at 11 P.M. on November 19, 1864, where he found Lieutenant General William J. Hardee, new commander of the Department of South Carolina, Georgia, and Florida. Wheeler began skirmishing with Kilpatrick's forces near Clinton, after which he moved to block Kilpatrick going down the road from Milledgeville to Macon. He subsequently fought and drove the enemy out of Griswoldville, but not before the town had been burned.[57]

It now became apparent that the enemy did not intend making any further demonstrations against Macon. Meanwhile, to the north, Slocum's left wing changed directions at Madison on the Augusta Road and started south-southeast for Milledgeville which it reached on November 22, putting the torch to the arsenal and other public buildings there. Howard's right wing reached Gordon, only ten miles away, on the same day.[58]

On the twenty-fourth and twenty-fifth, Wheeler's troops rode east and swam the Oconee River near Milledgeville and occupied Sandersville, 28 miles to the east after spending the night of the twenty-fifth nearby at Station No. 13 on the Macon & Western Central Railroad.

The next day, Wheeler engaged troops of the XIV and XX corps on their way to Sandersville. But he had not the force to arrest their advance. His troops burned forage in fields near the town to keep it from falling into the hands of Sherman's army.[59]

Upon leaving Milledgeville on November 24, Sherman directed Kilpatrick to shift from his right flank to his left in the direction of Augusta to convey the impression to the enemy that he meant to attack and take the city.

On November 27, Wheeler's pickets at the Shoals of the Ogeechee River discovered that Kilpatrick had crossed the river going in the direction of Augusta.

Leaving Iverson's Georgia brigade to observe the enemy, Wheeler went in hot pursuit, overtook Kilpatrick about midnight, promptly attacked, led by a mounted charge by men of the Fourth and Eighth Tennessee regiments, drove Kilpatrick's cavalry out of their camps, and made some captures.

Kilpatrick's force reorganized and continued on its way in the direction of Augusta, leaving rear guards at frequent intervals along the way to slow Wheeler's pursuit. As he pursued Kilpatrick's force, Wheeler noted that the enemy was setting fire to everything that was flammable both on farms and in towns. He reported that he frequently slowed his own progress by stopping to put out fires.[60]

Kilpatrick now turned off toward Waynesboro and proceeded to put the town to the torch and to begin destruction of the Augusta & Savannah Railroad when Wheeler entered the town just as Kilpatrick was leaving in the evening hours of November 28. Wheeler assailed Kilpatrick's cavalry south of Waynesboro as they continued to damage the railroad.

Wheeler's attack continued the morning of the twenty-ninth, and his troops drove Kilpatrick south past Thomas and Lumpkins stations to the vicinity of Buck Head Creek, some twenty miles below Waynesboro, capturing, killing, and wounding nearly 200 troops along the way.

What was left of Dibrell's Tennessee brigade overtook Kilpatrick's cavalry at the Buck Head Creek bridge, which had been destroyed. Dibrell reported that his men repaired the bridge to make it usable by using the seats which they took from nearby Buck Head Church.

Wheeler's attack continued until dusk, with Kilpatrick's cavalry going off in disarray to the west on the road to Louisville.[61] One of the results of this lengthy chase and series of fierce attacks, according to Wheeler, was that Kilpatrick thereafter sought the protection of Sherman's infantry and worked in close support with them during the remainder of the campaign.

Indeed Sherman paid tribute to Wheeler's "hard and persistent fighting" from the beginning of his Atlanta campaign but claimed that Wheeler's cavalry division had been reduced to the size of a brigade because of it. Dibrell confirmed that the Eighth Tennessee Cavalry suffered severe losses in their running attacks on Kilpatrick's force, but Wheeler did not acknowledge such losses to his command as a whole.[62]

On December 2, Kilpatrick's cavalry, reinforced by Brigadier General Absalom Baird's division of infantry from the XIV Corps, advanced upon Waynesboro via the road from Louisville. Wheeler met them at Rocky Creek and a warm fight ensued. The Union forces, however, outflanked Wheeler's force by crossing open fields in the direction of Thomas Station.

On the third, Wheeler fell back on Waynesboro and was driven out to the north when repeatedly charged by massed infantry. Sherman's soldiers remained in Waynesboro only about three hours, then moved south down the Savannah Road.

Wheeler, with most of his force, temporarily remained in position to protect Augusta against an expected attack that never came. But he had Brigadier General Joseph H. Lewis's brigade and the six companies of the Fourth Tennessee Cavalry Regiment fall back before Kilpatrick and the XIV Corps infantry in the direction of Savannah. Then when Wheeler was convinced that the force he faced was not bound for Augusta, he followed behind and attacked the rear of the Federal infantry.[63]

On the night of December 8, Wheeler fell upon a camp of the XIV Corps, shelling it and causing the infantry to decamp in some confusion. Wheeler reported that here a great many blacks who had joined and followed Sherman's victorious army across Georgia were captured and sent back to their former owners, doubtless via the depot for recaptured slaves at Macon. He estimated that his cavalry captured from the enemy as many as 2,000 blacks during the Savannah campaign.[64]

As the operation proceeded, however, Wheeler's cavalry, living off the land as was the Yankee invader, and destroying property usable by Sherman's army, reportedly became almost as dreaded by members of the indigenous population for its theft and destruction of private property as was Sherman's force.[65]

Still following in the wake of Sherman's army, Wheeler rode until he was within ten miles of Savannah. Then, believing there was no way he could do further damage to the enemy, Wheeler crossed the Savannah River to South Carolina. Only Iverson's Georgia brigade was left south of the river to watch Sherman's army.[66]

Dibrell reported that the last significant fight in Georgia in which his brigade was engaged was below Sister's Ferry on the Savannah River when his men came upon the enemy, both infantry and cavalry, after they had gone into camp. Upon seeing the Southerners at the crest of a prominence, Kilpatrick's cavalry began a mounted charge up a gentle slope. But before they could reach the top, a countercharge was made down the slope by the Fourth, the Eighth, and Major Joseph Shaw's Tennessee Cavalry battalion in which the Union charge was broken up and scattered and Shaw was mortally wounded.[67]

In the wake of Sherman's destruction, Dibrell's truncated command, when it left Georgia, had not had an issue of meal or flour for ten days and subsisted on potatoes and such rations as they might pick up. They crossed the Savannah River into South Carolina at Hendron's Ferry in a steamer, then moved via Robertsville down to Chevis's rice plantation, six miles above and opposite Savannah, where they foraged their horses on rice.[68]

Wheeler moved down the river to hold a line of communications from Huger's Landing to the town of Hardeeville to facilitate the evacuation of Confederate forces in and about Savannah.[69]

On December 9 and 10, Sherman and his army approached and carefully surveyed Savannah's well planned and well constructed defenses, watery parapets of deep ditches, canals, and bayous. After investing Savannah's outer defenses, taking Fort McAllister on the thirteenth, and opening communications with the fleet offshore (which delivered mail to the army), Sherman demanded the city's surrender on December 17. Hardee rejected the demand but, anticipating a lethal assault by heavy naval ordnance brought from nearby Hilton Head Island as well as troop assaults by land, he immediately made preparations to leave Savannah and to get what he could of its defensive forces across to South Carolina.[70]

Hardee's evacuation of the city was completed successfully enough on December 20, although he was forced to leave valuable quantities of heavy guns and ordnance, small arms and ammunition, stores, cotton, as well as railroad locomotives and rolling stock after he blew up the navy yard and ironclads.

Sherman's troops occupied the city of Savannah on December 21. Sherman rested his army and waited to take on supplies, reinforcements, and arms, the latter provided by the fleet, for the next phase of his operation.[71]

But what was to be the next phase? A march north through the Carolinas to join Grant's army in Virginia? Or sea transport from a coastal port direct to Virginia to join Grant's army in its siege of Richmond?

On December 6, Grant had revealed to Sherman a plan to establish a base on the sea coast, leave there a force of artillery, cavalry , and enough infantry to protect it, then to leave, with the balance of his force, by sea, and come directly to Virginia so that their combined armies might face Lee with overwhelming force.

But in a letter to Sherman on December 18, Grant wrote that events had changed his mind. He had been informed that the sea transport of Sherman's army would take two months, and he felt now that Sherman could do more good by advancing north on land through the Carolinas than he could by being brought to Virginia by naval forces.[72]

In Savannah, Sherman proceeded to dismantle the city's sea defenses, shipped captured heavy ordnance to Hilton Head Island and Fort Pulaski for safe keeping, and waited for the navy to clear the Savannah River of submerged obstructions. He reported that the civil and commercial affairs of Savannah during his sojourn there were conducted on a basis of mutual restraint, and that care was taken by the army to gratuitously distribute flour, hams, sugar, coffee, etc. to the people until the resumption of normal trade enabled people to provide for themselves, and that the civil authorities there were cooperating.

As commanding general of the Military Division of the Mississippi, Sherman had reason to celebrate both the successful transfer of his army from Atlanta to Savannah and, also within his command, the recent successful work of troops under George H. Thomas at Nashville. Sherman stated his aggregate losses in his Georgia campaign (November–December 1864) at 764 killed, wounded, and missing. At the same time, he claimed to have captured 1,888 of the enemy.[73]

In a letter to Sherman dated December 27, 1864, Grant definitely opted for Sherman to march north from Savannah and eventually to join Grant and his army in Virginia. He believed that the effect of such a campaign would be to disorganize the South and prevent the recruitment of new rebel forces from the broken fragments of the South's states and armies.[74]

On January 2, 1865, Sherman expressed to Grant a need for larger supplies of stores, especially grains, in order to undertake his campaign in the Carolinas. The same day, he concluded that he would secure a foothold on the South Carolina side of the Savannah River. Howard was to move his right wing by transports to the head of Broad River and Beaufort, to reestablish the Port Royal Ferry, and to mass the wing in the neighborhood of Pocotaligo at the Charleston Railroad.

His left wing was to move across the causeway to Hardeeville and to open a road by which wagons could reach their corps about Broad River, and it was to secure Sister's Ferry across the Savannah River as well as the Augusta Road out of Robertsville. Then all ordnance, ammunition, and stores were to move up by January 15 for the use of the army in a new advance. The advance was to be in the direction of Columbia, South Carolina, a route which afforded the best chance of finding forage and provisions. Quite deceptively, Sherman hinted broadly that he was going to Augusta or Charleston. In this way he kept the slim enemy forces at the ready to defend those cities and away from concentrating in front of his army.[75]

Heavy winter rains, beginning in early January, produced very high waters on the Savannah River and delayed the army's departure for two weeks. Sherman's left wing under Slocum had to cross at Sister's Ferry, some forty miles above the city of Savannah. It was ordered to rendezvous at Robertsville with Kilpatrick's cavalry. Owing to flooding conditions, the rendezvous was delayed until the first of February. Sherman and his headquarters staff had crossed the Savannah River to South Carolina on January 21. On the twenty-fifth, the weather turned clear and bright, an indication that the army would soon be able to march north in earnest. It did so on February 1.[76]

The last muster roll of Company D of the Fourth Tennessee Cavalry was prepared in Robertsville, South Carolina, at the end of 1864 for the period June 30 to December 31, 1864. The only records of military service available for soldiers of the company in 1865, the last year of the war, are from enemy sources. The last muster roll recorded nine soldiers of the company who deserted in December 1864. On December 25, William C. Rambo, 19, of Marshall County, Tennessee, deserted. He took an oath of anmesty on January 19, 1865.

On the last day of the year, seven soldiers of Company D deserted and appear to have escaped capture, that is, none was reported captured by a U.S. provost marshal general. They were Sergeant James M. Dysart, Robert A. Dysart, Farrier Thomas J. Dysart, Sergeant William A. McCurdy, 20; Benjamin A. Smith, George C. Thomas, 18; and William W. Walker. R.C. Hobbs also deserted from the company at some time from June 30 to the end of 1864, but the day and month are not stated in the record.

Thomas Burr Fisher related in his post-war memoir (written in 1921) that George C. Thomas and he were lifelong friends. George Thomas was one of the seven soldiers of Company D who deserted December 31, 1864. Fisher and Thomas grew up in the same community, and their birthdays were only 38 days apart.

The two recently had spent a week together as Fisher was writing his memoir in 1921. After the war, George Thomas became a lumber dealer in Winchester, Tennessee, according to Fisher. Their lifetime friendship attests that Thomas's desertion from the army and Fisher's remaining in the army were not obstacles to a warm interpersonal relationship between them. Indeed, all desertions were not considered heinous during the war. Men who went home to help their families seemed to be welcomed back into the army without the exaction of penalties. And desertions toward the end of the war were not consistently regarded as dishonorable.[77]

As Sherman's juggernaut made progress north of Savannah, Wheeler reported almost daily his efforts to block the progress of the Union army across the Palmetto State with his meager cavalry. He also reported in some detail the location and direction of march of Union army units. He interrogated prisoners, who often gave conflicting conjectures about plans of Sherman's army to go either to Augusta or Charleston. As it turned out, the army went to neither place.

When Sherman's army crossed into South Carolina in force, a portion of Wheeler's cavalry, consisting of a fragment of the Fourth Tennessee Regiment, the Eighth, and Shaw's Tennessee battalion, all under George G. Dibrell, plus Colonel William C.P. Breckenridge's Kentucky brigade, together with Captain J.H. Wiggins' Arkansas battery, temporarily commanded by Lieutenant Thomas M. Ellis, was ordered back to Sumterville where it spent about a week needlessly blockading roads with felled trees.

Moving south to meet Sherman's advance, Dibrell's force made a determined stand for five hours against the XV Corps, losing about 50 men killed and wounded, before falling back in the direction of Barnwell.

Wheeler briefly checked the advance of Sherman's right wing at Loper's Crossroads, the juncture of the Augusta and Pocotaligo roads with the Hardeeville and Orangeburg roads, then won a skirmish in the town of Aiken against Kilpatrick's cavalry on February 11 which temporarily raised the hopes of the locals.[78]

But Sherman's northward march was irresistible against sporadic and weak opposition. Indeed, as in Sherman's march from Atlanta to the sea,

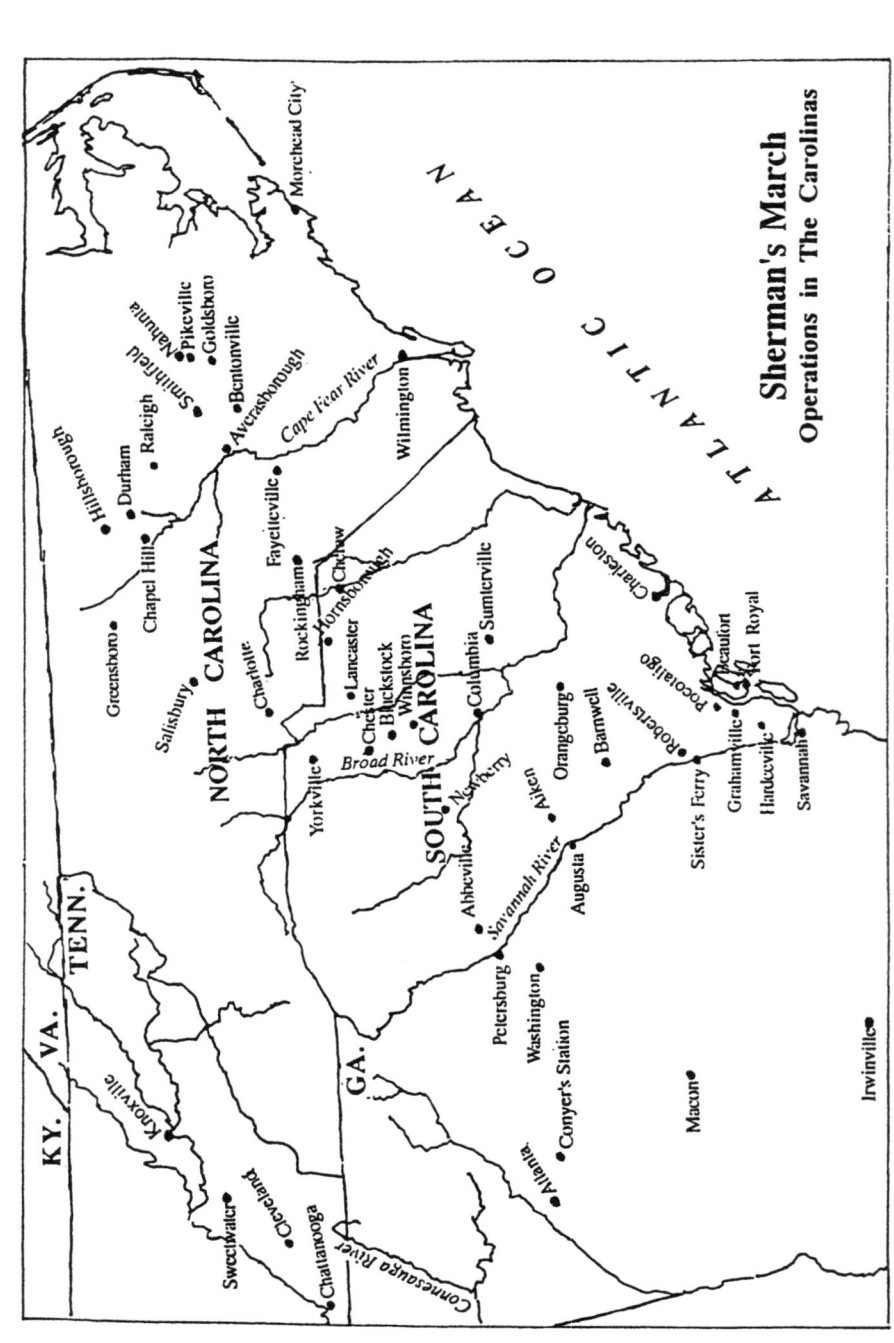

there was little, indeed, no resistance that held the slightest chance of seriously interfering with the fulfillment of Sherman's strategic plans. But there continued to be casualties on both sides, and physical destruction was caused by pursuer and pursued alike.

Sherman's left wing took Orangeburg on February 12. The next day Sherman ordered all columns to make for Columbia, where it was supposed the enemy had concentrated all possible forces from Augusta, Charleston, and even from Virginia. But that night, the interrogation of a Rebel officer revealed that the only Confederate presence in Columbia was a small cavalry force under Wade Hampton.[79]

Sherman led the XV Corps, under Major General John A. Logan of Illinois, into Columbia, the state capital, on February 17, 1865. The city was pillaged and burned despite Sherman's protestations that he had expressly forbidden any destruction in the city other than that of government and other strategically significant property which might be of use to the enemy.[80]

Sherman's right wing and cavalry departed Columbia on the twentieth and marched north to Winnsboro, reaching the town on February 21. The left wing met them there having come by way of Alston to the northwest of Columbia. The next day, the XX Corps of the right wing reached Rocky Mount, and Kilpatrick moved further north to Chester, where he turned east toward Rocky Mount. When he arrived in Rocky Mount, he was directed to move north again to Lancaster to deceive the enemy into believing the army was heading for Charlotte, North Carolina.[81]

Wheeler's small cavalry command was now under South Carolina Lieutenant General Wade Hampton, who came south from Virginia with Joe Johnston in the middle of February and commanded all Confederate cavalry in the state. Hampton brought with him from Virginia only Brigadier General T.M. Logan's cavalry brigade under Major General M.C. Butler with 1,019 effectives. When added to Wheeler's 3,074 effectives, Hampton had a cavalry force of 4,093, as reported on March 27, 1865.

But it was the only hostile force in the state that had position to attempt to retard Sherman's progress. Hampton's combined cavalry compared favorably with Kilpatrick's, which numbered 4,229 on March 31. But it was powerless to protect the state against the combined strength of Sherman's four massive corps.[82]

There had been contingents of Southern troops, infantry and artillery, at Augusta as well as at Charleston. They were in place to defend those cities which were never attacked. In the end, they were drawn off to North Carolina and were engaged at Bentonville on March 19–21 in the last, indeed the only, real battle of the campaign.

The city of Charleston was evacuated without a fight by Confederate forces under Hardee on February 17, the same day that Columbia fell, and was surrendered by the mayor, Charles Macbeth, to Lieutenant Colonel Augustus G. Bennett, commanding the Twenty-First U.S. Colored Infantry from Morris Island at the mouth of Charleston Harbor. Officers and men of the Twenty-First now took up the occupation of Charleston.[83]

Hardee's defensive force withdrew to Cheraw, near the North Carolina border, bringing with them a cache of arms which fell into Union hands when Sherman's army swept eastward toward the North Carolina border in the direction of Fayetteville.[84]

General Joseph E. Johnston received orders on February 22, 1865, to assume command of all the troops of the Department of South Carolina, Georgia, and Florida and to relieve General P.G.T. Beauregard of the command of the luckless but indefatigable Army of Tennessee.[85] The major remnant of the latter had been sent from Tupelo, Mississippi, where it had gone for rest and resupply after the painful disasters which overtook it at Franklin and Nashville in November and December. Then it came east, travelling by rail, steamboat, and foot via Augusta, Georgia, to oppose Sherman's northward advance through the Carolinas and his probable linkup with Grant in Virginia.

Crossing the Savannah River at Augusta, the depleted army marched through upcountry South Carolina, through the towns of Newberry and Chester, to Charlotte, North Carolina, where it entrained for Smithfield via Salisbury, Greensboro, Durham, and Raleigh, to join in late February other depleted commands under Hardee and Bragg, the latter a full general now in charge of the Department of North Carolina.[86]

Although there is no substantiating record, one may presume on the basis of probable evidence and a lack of proof to the contrary that the four companies of McLemore's Fourth Tennessee Cavalry relinquished by Wheeler to Forrest in September 1864 were among the Army of Tennessee troops that made the arduous trek from Mississippi to North Carolina.

After serving with Forrest in raids in Middle Tennessee and West Tennessee as well as in Hood's campaign that got as far as Nashville before retreating south to the Tennessee River, the four companies were ordered by Forrest, on January 20, 1865, to rejoin the other six companies of their regiment then serving in South Carolina under Wheeler and Dibrell.[87]

If James Wesley Fisher of Company D of the Fourth had terminated his recruiting efforts in Middle Tennessee prior to January 20, one may further presume that he made the winter journey east from Tupelo to rejoin his company comrades in the Carolinas. There is an absence of evidence that Jim Fisher did anything but rejoin his regimental comrades in the East.

There appear to be no surviving company records relative to the whereabouts of *any* of the officers and men of Jim Fisher's company after December 31, 1864. Only Dibrell's reports that troops of the Fourth were with him in the Carolinas and Forrest's order on January 20, 1865, that separated troops under his command were to rejoin their regiments in South Carolina indicate where the officers and men of the Fourth were or were supposed to be.

On January 6, Dibrell was at Grahamville, South Carolina, 35 miles above the city of Savannah, and reported fifty soldiers of the Fourth Tennessee at Dawson's Bluff nearby.[88] By the time the regiment was reunited, as it almost surely was, the six companies thereof then serving under Dibrell had been pushed northward about 250 miles into North Carolina by Sherman's army.

In his actions against Sherman's army, George Dibrell believed that his brigade's efforts to discipline Sherman's troops who engaged in the destruction of private property along the path of the army were salutary indeed. He acknowledged that against Sherman's immense army the cavalry could do little to impede the invaders. But "we did what we could, and kept his stragglers up pretty well, and prevented much destruction of property."

Although Sherman, according to Dibrell, "'smashed things,' as he, in his letter to Gen. Grant, said he would do," Dibrell stated ominously that "many of his men, captured in their acts of vandalism, *met their fate* [italics added], and ceased to depredate upon defenseless women and children."[89]

From Waynesboro, Georgia, to near Savannah, Dibrell reported that his brigade was "almost daily in a skirmish with some of Gen. Sherman's army. Sometimes we were in his advance, blockading roads; then in his rear picking up his stragglers; then upon his flanks, driving his marauders into line." He reported that at the town of Blackstock, South Carolina, while operating in the rear of Sherman's army, the Tennessee and Kentucky brigades "found thirty-five or forty Federals amusing themselves at Stroud's mills burning houses, cotton-gins, etc.; and our boys charged and captured the entire command."

Dibrell reported that the next morning, his horsemen crossed Rock Creek and surprised the enemy who were out foraging the country in large numbers. Dibrell's troops captured 150 prisoners and 14 wagons "loaded principally with forage taken from our citizens. Our presence in that locality was a Godsend to the citizens, and they appreciated it greatly."[90]

Wheeler struck the enemy's flank at Hornsborough, South Carolina, on March 4, then attacked Kilpatrick's cavalry near Rockingham, North Carolina, on March 7, as Sherman swept into the Old North State. The following day, Wheeler moved toward Fayetteville.

On March 10, Wheeler's cavalry again attacked Kilpatrick's cavalry at daylight while the latter was in camp. In a fierce fight lasting two hours, Wheeler took 365 prisoners, routed Kilpatrick out of his tent in his bed clothes, and claimed an undetermined number of dead and wounded while sustaining heavy damage to his field officer corps. Three brigade commanders, Brigadier General William Y.C. Humes, colonels Moses W. Hannon and James Hagan, plus every field officer in Hagan's brigade, were wounded. Brigadier General William Wirt Allen and Colonel Henry M. Ashby had horses shot and killed under them.

The Kentucky and Tennessee brigades were held in reserve in the action on the tenth. They had just caught up with Wheeler and Hampton after having spent a week in the rear of Sherman's army and reportedly had marched sixty-five miles uninterrupted on the ninth to overtake the remainder of their cavalry command.[91]

On March 11, the XIV and XVII corps reached Fayetteville, North Carolina. Wheeler's cavalry, including the Fourth Tennessee, engaged in heavy skirmishing near the town. Brigadier General J. Patton Anderson, who commanded an Army of Tennessee infantry brigade, was wounded in the fighting.

Sherman's troops destroyed the old U.S. arsenal at Fayetteville as well as machinery which had been moved there from the arsenal at Harper's Ferry, Virginia, with which the Confederates, according to Sherman, had vastly improved the facility.[92]

Wheeler crossed the Cape Fear River near Fayetteville and burned the bridge. Two days later, Wheeler's cavalry again engaged in heavy skirmishing eight to ten miles from Fayetteville. On March 16, Wheeler went to the assistance of Hardee's infantry when it was attacked at Averasborough. Wheeler's cavalry, including the Tennessee brigade, effectively covered Hardee's retreat therefrom, although it was pushed out of Averasborough on the seventeenth and skirmished hard most of the day with the enemy.[93]

Athwart the Fayetteville-Goldsboro road on March 19–21, 1865, the Army of Tennessee, with only 22,000 survivors, made one last gallant stand at Bentonville, North Carolina, for three days, attacking the left wing of Sherman's reinforced 86,000-man army on the first day, withstanding attacks from both Sherman's left and right wings on the second day, barely escaping being cut off and surrounded, and making an orderly withdrawal on the third day.

Preliminary to the Battle of Bentonville, Wheeler's cavalry reached the town on March 18 and occupied a position on the Confederate army's right. The next day, in heavy skirmishing, Wheeler's men took about 40 prisoners. On March 20, they moved around to the army's left and engaged a large force of infantry which was moving up toward Goldsboro on the Bentonville Road. In a severe fight, they checked the enemy's advance.

During the evening of the twentieth, Wheeler's cavalry was replaced on the army's left by a division of infantry under Major General Robert Frederick Hoke, a North Carolinian. Wheeler's command once again was placed on the army's right where, during the night, the cavalrymen constructed breastworks.

On March 21, in all-day fighting, Wheeler saw the infantry on his left giving way at about 4 P.M., while XX Corps troops under Major General Joseph Anthony Mower poured into the breach, moved toward the Confederate rear, and occupied the only line of retreat of the Confederate forces.

Wheeler ordered an immediate attack against the enemy's left flank by his dismounted cavalry, Hagan's brigade of Alabama troops under Brigadier

General William Wirt Allen, and by the Eighth Texas Cavalry Regiment, which made a mounted charge. Although outnumbered and with inferior fire power, Wheeler's cavalry charged with such determination and ferocity that they ran over Mower's infantry and threw the latter into a rapid withdrawal, thus saving the Rebel army from almost certain disaster.

General Hardee's sixteen-year-old son, William J. Hardee, Jr., in the Eighth Texas Cavalry, saw his first and last action of the war and died on the field in this last charge of the Army of Tennessee.[94]

Leaving many of their dead and wounded on the field, the army withdrew toward Smithfield at midnight on the twenty-first in a cold rain. Wheeler remained to check the enemy's advance which began before daylight the next morning. Then he withdrew to the crossing of Black Creek on the Smithfield Road and checked the Federal advance for the day at that point.

The next day, Wheeler moved through Smithfield, retreating toward Raleigh, then stopped when his pursuers rested. Sherman's army was resting, reorganizing, and replenishing their stocks at Goldsboro. Until Sherman's next advance on April 10, Wheeler's cavalry picketed the front of the Confederate army and skirmished daily with scouting and foraging parties of the enemy. The Tennessee brigade was camped at Nahunta, near Pikeville, for close to three weeks.[95]

In the fighting at Bentonville, Joe Johnston believed that Sherman's veterans were reminded again of the punishment that the soldiers of the Army of Tennessee were capable of delivering, especially in the vigor and ferocity of the attacks on the field by the terminally outnumbered men of Cheatham's and Stewart's corps. And Johnston had only the highest praise for his troops who he said "have fully disproved slanders that have been published against them." He was referring to fresh evidence of the reckless gallantry of the soldiers of the Army of Tennessee which their former commander, John B. Hood, had called into question.[96]

Sherman's army moved to Goldsboro on March 23 and united their forces with Schofield's Army of the Ohio, which had come out of Tennessee by rail through Virginia and by sea transport to Wilmington, North Carolina, thence to Goldsboro by rail, arriving on the twenty-first. Now Sherman had an army of over 100,000 against a force of a little over 21,000. He had marched 425 miles in fifty days since leaving Savannah, averaging almost ten miles per day.[97]

On March 25, Sherman, leaving Schofield in command of his army, left Goldsboro by rail, then proceeded by steamer from Morehead City, North Carolina, via Fortress Monroe, Virginia, up the James River to City Point where he conferred with Grant on March 27. The same day, he and Grant together went to see President Lincoln, who was nearby on the James River aboard the steamer *River Queen*. They saw the president again on the twenty-eighth. Then Sherman began his return trip to Goldsboro.

In his *Memoirs*, Sherman recorded a tribute to Lincoln which was based upon their two meetings at City Point. He wrote: "Of all the men I ever met, he seemed to possess more of the elements of greatness, combined with goodness, than any other."[98]

Returning to North Carolina, Sherman reached Goldsboro from the James on the evening of March 30. He began reorganizing his command and replenishing stores so as to be ready to launch a new offensive by April 10. Meanwhile news of the fall of Richmond and Petersburg reached Goldsboro on the sixth. Sherman began driving the Confederates, encamped at Smithfield, back toward Raleigh on the tenth.[99] Wheeler's cavalry was on the Army of Tennessee's right front and took the first blow of the advance, giving way before superior numbers and firepower.

The last two casualties of the war in Dibrell's Tennessee brigade, both from the Fourth Tennessee Cavalry, were suffered in the hard skirmishing on April 10. They were Thomas Bass, Company C, and James A. Short, Company A, killed in action as Sherman's army moved out.[100]

During the night of the eleventh, Sherman was informed by Grant of Lee's surrender of his army at Appomattox Court House on April 9. Sherman announced the news to his troops on the twelfth, and wholesale rejoicing exploded within the army which entered and occupied the state capital on the thirteenth without resistance. Kilpatrick's advance cavalry engaged Wheeler's retreating cavalry covering the army's front west of Raleigh in the direction of Chapel Hill.[101]

Meanwhile, in Raleigh on the evening of the twelfth, Brigadier General George G. Dibrell received orders to proceed as rapidly as possible to Greensboro, eighty-five miles distant, there to report to President Davis. Dibrell took with him Colonel William C.P. Breckenridge's Kentucky brigade, together with Captain J.H. Wiggins' Arkansas battery, as well as his own Tennessee brigade, which was composed of McLemore's Fourth and Dibrell's Eighth regiments of Tennessee cavalry as well as Major Jo Shaw's battalion under Captain R.V. Wright, altogether a force of about 1,300 soldiers. The command rode hard to arrive in Greensboro about midnight on April 14, leaving behind their comrades still withdrawing before Sherman's army.[102]

Johnston retreated through Chapel Hill in the direction of Greensboro with Wheeler covering the rear, burning bridges behind him but with orders to avoid further contact with the enemy unless attacked. Wheeler's depleted troops were the last to leave Chapel Hill, evacuating the town on Easter Sunday, April 16.[103]

Lee had surrendered the Army of Northern Virginia on April 9. The Confederate President Jefferson Davis, fleeing via the Richmond & Danville Railroad, arrived in Greensboro on the twelfth with three members of his cabinet. In a conference with Johnston and Beauregard, Davis opposed Johnston's projected plan to surrender his army. Davis affected to believe that they could still stay out of the hands of Federal authorities and raise large numbers of volunteer soldiers to pursue the aims of Southern independence.

Only the Secretary of the Treasury, Judah P. Benjamin, agreed with Davis. Johnston insisted on the hopelessness of the situation as well as the cruelty and moral recklessness of trying to oppose Sherman's massive army, which soon would be reinforced with Grant's 180,000-strong Army of the Potomac now that the latter was free of fighting Lee's army.[104]

Finally Davis yielded the point, and on April 14 Johnston requested of Sherman a truce for the purpose of negotiating a surrender. The two army commanders met, along with Lieutenant General Wade Hampton, C.S.A., at the Bennett farmhouse just west of Durham Station.[105]

Then a second meeting, this time with John C. Breckinridge present, not acting as Confederate secretary of war but as a major general in the Confederate army, produced a surrender document on April 18, written by Sherman, that was considered too political and too generous in the bitter days of recrimination following the assassination of President Lincoln on the fourteenth. Sherman was denounced at home for his leniency toward the rebels.[106]

When word was received on the twenty-fourth that the terms of the surrender had been disapproved in Washington, there was anxiety that Sherman's and Johnston's armies might have at it again.

The surrender document was a far-reaching political accord the terms of which provided for an orderly disbandment of the Confederate army with freedom from molestation for former members thereof due to their participation in the war following their laying down their arms and agreeing to cease from acts of war, recognition of existing state governments, reestablishment of Federal courts, a Constitutional guarantee of civil rights, and a general amnesty.

The document represented a wise and generous attempt to stop the bloodletting and to heal the wounds of the war, and its terms were in keeping with the late President Lincoln's liberal policy toward the South, the details of which the president had discussed with Sherman in their last meeting on March 28. Rear Admiral David D. Porter, U.S.N., was present at the meeting with Lincoln on the twenty-eighth and made notes of the conversations.[107]

But on April 26 terms of a surrender similar to those offered to Lee at Appomattox Court House were agreed to by the two army commanders. The Confederates would cease their acts of war, their arms and public property were to be given up and deposited at Greensboro, combatants were to agree in writing not to take up arms against the U.S. government, officers were to retain their sidearms, private horses and baggage, and muster rolls of officers and men were to be furnished to an officer designated by Sherman.[108]

A subsequent military convention provided supplemental terms to facilitate the return of Confederate soldiers to their homes. Field transportation, including artillery horses, might be loaned to troops on their march home.

Each military unit could retain a number of arms equal to one-seventh of its effective strength until they arrived at their respective state capitals. Horses and other private property were to be retained by officers and men. Naval forces were included in the terms of the convention.[109]

Most of the Southern soldiers were ready to give up their fight, and while they grieved over the failure of the cause for which they had fought so well, they experienced a measure of relief that the war was over. But not quite all members of the army were willing to let go.

After the surrender agreement had been reached, Wheeler, at the urging of President Davis, asked for volunteers from his cavalry, encamped at Company's Shops, a village just east of Greensboro, to supplement the president's escort and accompany Davis on a "desperate enterprise."

His solicitation brought forth a force of 600 volunteers, men who were to supplement those of Dibrell's command who had already been called to join the presidential party in its flight south.[110]

But there were few soldiers who wished to carry on the fight at that point. Earlier at Greensboro, on the night of the fifteenth, thousands of demoralized Confederate troops from Lee's army, as well as stragglers, state troops, and others were found who could easily have constituted an unruly mob, and indeed were treated as such by some North Carolina state troops who fired on them in the evening to disperse them.

James Brown of Company D, the Eighth Tennessee Cavalry, was killed in the crowd that was fired upon. Brown was a popular soldier, according to Dibrell, and his death created indignation among his comrades who felt that the action by the state troops was unnecessary and ill-advised.

Because of the threat of further violence from unattached soldiers on the run, the command, together with President Davis and his staff, moved out six to eight miles from Greensboro and camped for the night.[111]

Wheeler wrote to Hampton from Holtsburg, North Carolina, on April 26 advising him that he should bring with him all the Enfield rifles and ammunition practicable, as the arms in his men's hands could not be supplied with ammunition.[112]

Hampton wrote to Johnston the same day that Secretary of War John C. Breckenridge had ordered him to South Carolina. The next day Johnston replied to Hampton that he should return to Hillsborough, North Carolina, with Butler's division. Johnston also wrote to Wheeler on the twenty-seventh that he should obey his (Johnston's) orders to remain, surrender, and receive his parole *unless he had contrary orders from a superior authority.*

Hampton replied to Johnston that henceforth he should consider him a straggler, one who chose not to receive his parole pursuant to the convention entered into by Johnston with Sherman. And he would take only stragglers with him as he rode south to join Davis.[113]

But when Hampton, the Army of Tennessee's senior cavalry commander, made an appeal to Butler's division, which he had brought out of

Virginia in February, he realized very poor results indeed. He marched south from Greensboro accompanied only by his escort of thirty men.[114]

President Davis believed that, despite the surrender of both the Army of Northern Virginia and the Army of Tennessee, there was still hope of carrying on the conflict in the Transmississippi to establish the independence of the Confederate States. The troops recruited by Hampton and Wheeler, and Davis with his staff and escort, were to travel separately and rendezvous at Washington, Georgia. But the hopes of the desperate Davis and colleagues were dashed before the rendezvous took place.

Wheeler travelled south via Yorkville, South Carolina. Here he stopped to visit Wade Hampton and Mrs. Hampton in their home on Monday, May 2. He reported that he found Hampton, promoted to lieutenant general on February 15, 1865, to be a broken man, unfit to go forward to his planned rendezvous with President Davis. Even Hampton's small escort had deserted him one by one on the way south, until he arrived home alone.[115]

On their way south from Greensboro, Dibrell's troops, augmented at Charlotte by a small contingent of cavalry out of the Department of East Tennessee under the command of Brigadier General John C. Vaughn and a handful of veterans of Morgan's raiders, under Brigadier General Basil W. Duke, arriving after duty in Southwest Virginia,[116] found themselves in a sea of paroled, demoralized, or relieved prisoners of war going home. Although Dibrell complimented his troops for maintaining their discipline on their way south, the troops were obviously influenced by the troops they passed for whom the war was over. Many of the latter were enjoying a growing sense of relief and anticipation.

In the late afternoon of May 2 in a meeting called by Davis in the Armistead Burt home in Abbeville, South Carolina, near the Savannah River, with hopes steadily sagging, Vaughn, Dibrell, Duke, and other cavalry officers present, including Brigadier General Samuel W. Ferguson and Colonel W.C.P. Breckenridge, as well as the president's confidant, General Braxton Bragg, and Secretary of War John C. Breckenridge, the latter commanding the escort, were astounded that Davis still insisted that the fight might yet be carried on. They unanimously agreed that any plan for continuing the fight was so illusory and unpopular that the men of their commands, some of whom had grown openly rebellious, should be permitted the choice of giving up the fight, receiving paroles, and going to their homes. After the president left the meeting, it was agreed to put to a vote of the men of their commands the question of staying or disbanding.[117]

That night the president with his staff and escort left Abbeville in the direction of the Savannah River, which they crossed into Georgia at dawn on Wednesday, May 3, and stopped to eat and rest. Here the restive escort was paid a portion of a sum totalling $108,000 in silver coin from the funds of the Confederate treasury, which had been brought south from Richmond.[118] The disbursement had been agreed to by Davis and the officers at the war council convened the afternoon of the previous day. George Dibrell remembered the sum as $26.25 each. Basil Duke remembered it as $32.00 each, regardless of rank or rate.[119]

The remainder of the funds, including a quantity of gold was disposed of on May 4. Richmond bank funds were deposited in the Washington, Georgia, bank. Specie in the amount of $86,000 was delivered to James A. Semple, Confederate States Navy Paymaster in charge, who was to see that the funds were shipped to agents abroad and placed in bank accounts of the Confederate states for payment of the government's debts to foreign suppliers. Funds reportedly were also given over to Braxton Bragg and John C. Breckinridge, ostensibly to support future Confederate operations in the Transmississippi, and a portion reportedly remained with the president and his escort.[120]

Jefferson Davis had entered the idyllic town of Washington, Georgia, at noon on the third and gone to the home of J.J. Robertson, bank clerk, who lived in the Georgia Bank Building.[121]

A remnant of the evaporating Confederate cabinet met for the last time at Washington on May 4, 1865, at which time the president dissolved his government and concluded to continue south only with an escort of ten men.[122] He hoped to go to the south of Georgia, then turn west in anticipation of joining with his brother-in-law, Lieutenant General Richard Taylor, in Alabama, and thence across the Mississippi.

Davis was assigned the company of Captain Given Campbell of the Ninth Kentucky Cavalry Regiment, reduced to ten men at Davis's insistence, from Colonel W.C.P. Breckenridge's Kentucky brigade, to serve as the president's escort. The Davis entourage started south from Washington before noon on the fourth.[123]

Wheeler and his cavalry force of volunteers arrived in Washington twelve hours after the Davis party dispersed. Upon learning that Davis and members of his cabinet had abandoned the fight, Wheeler cut loose from his reluctant force of 600 and, together with a small party of likeminded officers and men, three officers and eleven privates, took to the woods, bypasses, and thickets in hopes of reaching their homes before being captured.

But they did not.

On the morning of May 9, they were made prisoners by a detachment of the Twelfth Ohio Cavalry as they slept on the ground near Conyer's Station, Georgia, just west of the Yellow River near Atlanta.[124]

Davis was captured in Irwinville, in the south of Georgia, on May 10, 1865, by a detachment of the Fourth Regiment of Michigan Cavalry under Captain John C. Hathaway. Davis, his family, and members of his cabinet were taken to Macon, then Atlanta, and then by train to Augusta, where they were joined by Wheeler, and transferred to a tugboat, the *Standish*, for the trip down the Savannah River to the city of Savannah. Here the party was transferred to a steamer, the *William P. Clyde*, for the ocean voyage north and

Davis's imprisonment at Fortress Monroe, Hampton Roads, Virginia, which they reached on the nineteenth. Wheeler was sent north to Ft. Delaware for imprisonment.[125]

Although the men of the Fourth Tennessee Cavalry Regiment were included in the surrender instrument signed at Greensboro, North Carolina, on April 26 and were to have been paroled at Charlotte May 3, 1865, they were still armed and at large on May 5, though not for long.

Dibrell and his troops surrendered that day at the Petersburg pontoon bridge on the Savannah River near Washington to troops under Brigadier General William J. Palmer who were thick in the area in search of Jefferson Davis and the treasures of gold and silver which he carried.

The war-weary volunteers under Dibrell's command were paroled on May 11 by Captain Lot Abrahams of the Fourth Iowa Cavalry Regiment, an officer sent for the purpose from Macon by the scourge of Alabama, Major General James H. Wilson.[126] Indeed they, Wheeler, and Jefferson Davis all were captured by units of Wilson's corps, which only a month earlier had been in Selma, Alabama, which they had taken and destroyed after encountering units of Forrest's cavalry in Forrest's last combat of the war.

Two days before paroling the officers and men of Dibrell's command, Abrahams reported to Wilson that he had no instructions relative to receiving property. As a result, he was permitting all parolees to keep their private property.

The same day, however, in response to an inquiry from Emory Upton, who commanded the Third Cavalry Division of the Military Division of the Mississippi, Wilson stated that paroled officers were to retain their sidearms and private horses, but the men were to be dismounted and disarmed.

Wilson, headquartered in Macon, Georgia, and seemingly playing his surrender and parole roles by guess, temporarily established a more severe term for private soldiers than that under which they thought they had been surrendered. But later, on May 9, Wilson reversed himself after receiving another inquiry from Upton, who related a plea from Brigadier General John C. Vaughn, who told him that all the cavalry surrendered in North Carolina had been permitted to retain their horses. Vaughn requested the same privilege for his command. Wilson relented, saying that all of Vaughn's men who could not go home by train would be permitted to retain their horses.[127] Dibrell's men received the same privilege when they were paroled on May 11, 1865.

The parolees of Dibrell's Tennessee brigade proceeded to ride in military order to their homes beyond the mountains in Tennessee. They marched unmolested until they were encamped on the banks of the Connesauga River in Polk County, Tennessee, an area of fiercely divided loyalties and a hotbed of anti–Confederate feeling. Here they were taken into custody by a squad of Union soldiers and a belligerent provost marshal.

Taken into Cleveland in adjacent Bradley County, each soldier was searched for pistols, cartridges, belts, buckles and anything that might bear the "U.S." imprint on it. Citizens appeared and made claims against the soldiers for horses, cattle, and other property. Simeon E. Browder appeared and threatened suit for camping on his property the night before.

According to Dibrell, the paroled prisoners of war felt that they had fallen into a den of thieves until they were saved by Colonel Alfred T. Smith, commanding the 156th Illinois Infantry Regiment, who instructed the provost guard and citizens about the terms of the soldiers' paroles and sent the ex-Confederates on their way.

Leaving Cleveland late in the afternoon, Dibrell and his men marched through rain and mud and arrived the next day in Chattanooga, where they reported to the provost marshal, who said he had instructions to dismount all the private soldiers, contrary to the prevailing military convention.

Seeking a reversal of the marshal's instructions, Dibrell went to see Brigadier General Henry Moses Judah, whom he found engaged in a game of whist with Judge Richard Hilaire Rousseau of Louisville, Kentucky, a brother and prewar law partner of Major General Lovell H. Rousseau. Judah appeared to Dibrell to be too engrossed in his game to care about the injustice about to be committed. He declined to interfere with the provost marshal despite having the terms of the soldiers' paroles explained to him by Dibrell. So their horses, their own private property, were taken from the men, and the provost marshal stood with a guard on the bridge out of Chattanooga across the Tennessee River to delay and to inspect, one by one, the parole of each soldier as he passed on his way home.

Dibrell reported that application was made to Major General George H. Thomas in Nashville for the return of the horses. According to Dibrell, Thomas ordered their return, and a party was sent to Chattanooga for them. But Dibrell wrote that, except for the best of the horses, which were seen in possession of officers who had them branded "U.S." and would not release them, most had been placed by the quartermaster in dry lots without food or water, several had died, while many were so starved that they could scarcely walk. Few were recovered.[128]

Similarly, George B. Guild reported that the horses of the men of Baxter Smith's/Paul Anderson's Fourth Tennessee Cavalry were confiscated on the way home from North Carolina at Sweetwater, Tennessee, by order of Major General George Stoneman, who was headquartered in Knoxville and had spent time in a Confederate prison in 1864.

Indeed, Stoneman received instructions from George H. Thomas on May 13, 1865, that Colonel James T. Wheeler's Sixth Tennessee Cavalry Regiment, paroled May 3 at Charlotte, North Carolina, and on its way home, would not be permitted "to go in a body into Middle Tennessee." Thomas stated that it was "not understood here that any such agreement was entered into between generals Johnston and Sherman which was ratified." Further since "the horses upon which the soldiers are mounted are supposed to have

The five Fisher brothers after the war: Clockwise from top left: John Franklin, Elisha Monroe, James Wesley, Thomas Burr, and William Stratton.

belonged to the Confederate government," they now belong to the United States, or so Thomas believed.

Stoneman was further instructed to insure that the paroles of all the soldiers were in order. He was also to "compel them [members of Wheeler's regiment] to disband before coming further into this state."

Guild wrote that, in order to partially rectify the injustice done to the dismounted soldiers, the Federal government forty years later recompensed the surviving soldiers who were dismounted counter to the prevailing convention and thus deprived of their property. They were paid $125 for each horse and $10 for saddles and bridles.[129]

Although there are no muster rolls of Company D of the Fourth Tennessee Cavalry for the closing months of the war, Federal reports provide fragments of service records of three men of the company who deserted in 1865. John W. Nelson deserted on January 28 and took the oath of allegiance on February 28. William J. McAdams deserted on February 7 and took the oath on March 24. George W. Goodwin of Giles County, Tennessee, deserted on April 24 and took the oath on May 2. Although there is no indication in the records as to where each soldier deserted or surrendered, each took the oath in the Headquarters of the Provost Marshal General, Department of the Cumberland, in Nashville.[130]

An analysis and comparison of total recorded casualties suffered by Company D of the Fourth and Company C of the Eleventh are found in Chapter 11.

A final word is due about Joseph Wheeler following his capture on May 9, 1865, near Atlanta and his subsequent imprisonment at Ft. Delaware. With the war over, Wheeler married in 1866 and went into the hardware and carriage business in New Orleans in the late 1860s. He removed to Alabama in 1870, became a lawyer, and was first elected to the United States Congress in a contested election in 1880. Thereafter he was reelected term after term until after the war with Spain. In 1898, at the age of 61, he was commissioned a major general of volunteers and served in Cuba. In 1899, he served in the Philippines. In his final years, he was a popular national hero and was much sought after as a public speaker. He died on January 25, 1906, in Brooklyn, New York, while visiting in the home of his sister. His funeral was held in St. Thomas Episcopal Church on Fifth Avenue in New York. As a symbol of national reunification, he was buried with honors in Arlington National Cemetery, Arlington, Virginia.[131]

Yet the story of the last months of the war as experienced by the Fisher brothers and their comrades of the Eleventh Tennessee Cavalry in the remaining portion of the Western cavalry has yet to be told. In November 1864, after being members of the command of Major General Joseph Wheeler for a year, they, along with what remained of their battle-tested regiment, left Georgia to facilitate the Army of Tennessee's march back to Tennessee under their celebrated cavalry leader, Nathan Bedford Forrest, whom they rejoined at last.

Chapter 7

Hood's Tennessee Campaign: Debacle at Spring Hill, November 16–29, 1864

Forrest once again reported for duty with the Army of Tennessee on November 16, 1864, after a year of brilliant fighting which included the Battle of Brice's Crossroads in Mississippi, a textbook performance adding luster to his already formidable military reputation. He had created a new command which had wreaked havoc on opposing Union forces sometimes several times its size and put out of action nearly three times its own number.[1]

In an address to his troops on January 23, 1865, Forrest commended members of his command who served with him during 1864 and listed their accomplishments. He said that they had fought 50 battles, killed and captured 16,000 enemy soldiers, as well as taken 67 field pieces, 10,000 stands of small arms, 2,000 horses and mules, 300 wagons, and 50 ambulances; and they had destroyed 40 blockhouses, 36 railroad bridges, 200 miles of track, 6 locomotives and 100 railroad cars. Altogether, they had destroyed $15 million worth of property.[2]

On the Tennessee River, Forrest's troops had taken or destroyed four gunboats and fourteen transports. Both Grant and Sherman were astonished that Forrest could successfully take on heavily armed gunboats with cavalry. Grant termed this "a very remarkable feat . . . the accomplishment of which is very hard to account for."[3] His command had never exceeded 5,000 troops, 2,000 of whom were killed or wounded and 200 captured.[4] Given the size of his force, his victories could hardly have been more complete or more devastating to the enemy.

But Forrest's attack on April 12, 1864, against a garrison of 557 officers and men, a force made up of West Tennessee Unionists, both black and white, defending Fort Pillow on the banks of the Mississippi, led to a congressional inquiry which, critics said, produced a well-circulated report that was important to the war party in the North in the elections of 1864. The report and its attendant use made Forrest's attack on Fort Pillow *the* atrocity of a war which was replete with charges of atrocities by both sides.[5] Over a

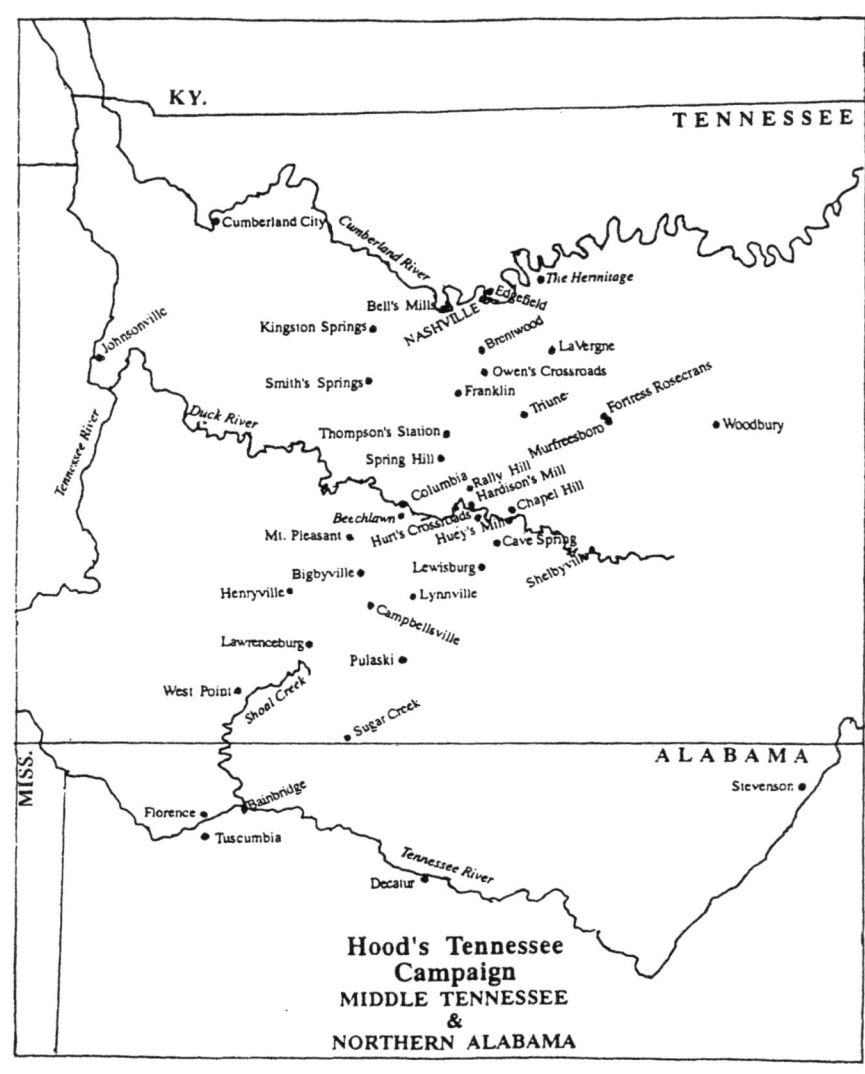

Hood's Tennessee Campaign
MIDDLE TENNESSEE
&
NORTHERN ALABAMA

hundred years later, the report of the Fort Pillow Massacre continues to sully Forrest's name.

Immediately after the attack on Fort Pillow, there were reports of killings of black troops and their white officers after they had surrendered. Major General W.T. Sherman noted the stories when, writing from Nashville on April 15, he expressed exasperation that there had been a garrison at Fort Pillow at all, a position not worth defending in his estimation. Sherman was angry at Major General Stephen A. Hurlbut for the latter's timidity in sequestering himself in Memphis while Forrest seemed to have free rein wherever he struck in West Tennessee and Western Kentucky.

Grant received Sherman's communication at 2:30 P.M. on April 15. At 8 P.M. Grant replied, from Culpeper, Virginia, directing Sherman, commanding the Military Division of the Mississippi at Nashville, to relieve Hurlbut of his command of the XVI Corps.[6]

The garrison at Fort Pillow numbered 557, of whom 253 were blacks. Forrest reported that he captured 164 Federals and 75 black troops and about 40 black women and children. Estimates of Union casualties in the battle are 50 to 60 percent of the defenders, a high rate but not unusually high for America's Civil War. For example, at Gettysburg on July 2, 1863, the First Minnesota Infantry had casualties of 82 percent, as did the First Texas at Antietam in a few hours of combat. During the war, no less than 63 Federal and 52 Confederate regiments had casualties of over 50 percent in a single engagement.[7]

At Fort Pillow and in other Civil War engagements, black soldiers, who were treated as fugitive slaves by the Confederate government, may have been killed in disproportionate numbers because of their understandable reluctance to be captured. While the suggestion smacks of blaming the victims, the high casualty rate at Fort Pillow may have been the result of a failure of command within the fort rather than the result of undisciplined, frenzied troops on a mindless, vicious rampage. Outnumbered by close to three to one and facing a master of military tactics, Fort Pillow's commander, Major Lionel F. Booth, and his second, Major W.F. Bradford, were mere martial amateurs and no match for Forrest.

Forrest struck the exterior fortifications at dawn, and by 9:00 A.M. Booth had been killed by a Confederate sharpshooter.[8] Forrest came upon the field at about 10 A.M. By eleven, Forrest's troops approached and took possession of rifle pits abandoned earlier in the day by the fort's defenders. The firing died down early in the afternoon while Forrest awaited the arrival of his ordnance wagons. When the latter arrived, Forrest sent in a demand for surrender at 3:30 P.M. with a promise to treat the troops as prisoners of war but with a typically intimidating ascription: "Should my demand be refused, I cannot be responsible for the fate of your command."

The surrender option was refused by Major Bradford. Within minutes after Forrest received the refusal to surrender, the charge was sounded and Forrest's troops attacked, scaled, and entered the fort and proceeded to overwhelm its defenders.

When further resistance became useless, the defenders failed to surrender, according to Confederate participants. Many fled to the river where they were caught on three sides by deadly fire from their attackers who were in the fort above the defenders and under the river bluff both above and below the fort. Having no other exit, and with the fort's flag still flying, many plunged into the river. Forrest, upon entering the fort, ordered the fort's flag to be lowered and firing to cease, only twenty minutes after the final assault began.⁹

As for what happened within the fort and under the river bluff, the Report of the Joint Select Committee on the Conduct of the War described a scene of absolute horror, involving indiscriminate slaughter with Forrest reportedly taking part by ordering his soldiers to shoot defenseless victims.¹⁰

Eyewitness accounts which related the most inhumane atrocities must be weighed against Forrest's strongly-worded refutations of the same as well as accounts of Confederate soldiers who participated in the assault. The congressional committee's report is inconsistent with Forrest's accustomed conduct in combat as well as that of his troops, always well disciplined while under his command, and with Forrest's efforts the day after the battle to parole the badly wounded Federals at Fort Pillow and have them placed aboard the U.S. Steamer *Silver Cloud*, a vessel which had stood off the bank and shelled Forrest's troops on the morning of the battle. Evacuation of the wounded to the steamer was accomplished by Charles W. Anderson, Forrest's aide-de-Camp, in cooperation with Acting Master W. Ferguson of the *Silver Cloud*. Three officers, 43 white privates and 14 blacks were received by Ferguson.

The compilation of statements of witnesses is also inconsistent with Forrest's reputation for dealing with black soldiers in the field as well as dealing with his own slaves. With respect to the latter, Forrest took 45 slaves with him into the war as teamsters, promising them that if the South won and they had served faithfully, he would set them free. Forrest related that a year and a half before the war ended, he correctly surmised that the South would lose and, fearing that he might be killed, gave all but one their free papers.

Forrest's testimony was corroborated by the youthful George W. Cable, the future Louisiana novelist and neo-abolitionist, who prepared some of Forrest's manumission papers while serving as a clerk in Forrest's headquarters. Cable, however, corrected Forrest's account, saying that Forrest's teamsters were freed shortly before the end of the war rather than a year and a half earlier.

The prevalent Northern view of Forrest both during and after the war is reflected in Grant's criticism of Forrest's conduct at Fort Pillow. Grant wrote in his memoir: "I will leave Forrest in his dispatches to tell what he did with them [the Ft. Pillow garrison]: 'The river was dyed,' he said, 'with the blood of the slaughtered for two hundred yards. The approximate loss was upward of five hundred killed, but few of the officers escaping. My loss was about twenty killed. It is hoped that these facts will demonstrate to the Northern people that negro soldiers cannot cope with Southerners.' Subsequently Forrest made a report in which he left out the part which shocks humanity to read."

Grant refers here to two reports from Forrest to his superior officer, Leonidas Polk: (1) a hasty, exuberant report dated April 15, 1864, dashed off three days after the attack on Fort Pillow, describing the success of Forrest's recent operations in West Tennessee, and (2) a well-defined, detailed, and comprehensive report of the action at Fort Pillow *only* dated April 26.[11]

Despite Forrest's manifestly prejudiced stereotyping of the fighting abilities of blacks in his report of April 15, a flawed stereotype he shared with large numbers of whites both north and south, Grant's imputations of misconduct drawn from Forrest's reports by no means would be shared by observers who had not formed a prejudgment of Forrest's guilt.

Nevertheless, the reported enmity between Unionists and Confederates in West Tennessee complicates resolution of the issue and impels one to the view that circumstances existed on the battlefield at Fort Pillow which might indeed have led to the illegal killing of enemy soldiers. As in the instance of the killing of captured black troops and their white officers at Saltville, Virginia, in October 1864, in which Forrest's command played no part, the possibility of excessive bloodshed at Fort Pillow remains.

Of course, the blot on Forrest's name and conduct remains and no doubt does so partially because of Forrest's connection with the Ku Klux Klan in the late 1860s. Without condoning the purposes or results of the Klan's activities in the 1860s, one may acknowledge that, from the point of view of most white Southerners of the time, the original 1860s Klan represented a resistance movement against Federal military occupation of the late secessionist states, the political empowerment of local Unionists, white and black, as well as northern Radical Republicans, and the disfranchisement and political neutering of ex–Confederates.

Fed by passionate hatred, the conduct of many Klansmen, however, became so outrageous, murderous, and ungovernable as to prompt Forrest to order the dissolution of the Klan. It is likely that Forrest, believed to be the order's commander, concluded that the Klan's depredations harmed prospects for the South's economic recovery. In his testimony in 1871 before the Joint Select Committee of Congress to Inquire into the Condition of Affairs in the Late Insurrectionary States, Forrest stated at one point that he "suppressed" the Klan in 1869. Otherwise he appeared to obfuscate the issue of his Klan connection to avoid facing federal criminal charges.

The twentieth-century Ku Klux Klan, inspired by prejudice and misinformation, American racism, nativism, and Thomas Dixon's novel, *The Clansman*, published in 1905 and made into the motion picture *The Birth of a Nation* in 1915, has no lineal succession from the Klan of the 1860s.[12]

Baffled by Forrest's military genius and his uncanny ability to win in battle against daunting odds, Forrest's wartime adversaries may have concluded that Forrest won *not* because he was a superior military leader but because he did not adhere to fair or "civilized" rules of warfare.

By 1864, so closely was Forrest's name linked with fear and cunning that, on Monday, November 7, 1864, the day before the national election, fantastic stories were reported from Danville, Springfield, and Chicago in Illinois, and from Cincinnati in Ohio about Forrest being in disguise in Canada, Michigan City, and Chicago with 14,000 men under his command who would, at Forrest's direction, spring into action, take over the city of Chicago, mobilize Southern sympathizers, and subject the city to a thorough sacking, looting and killing at will.

Adding to the appearance of a grave conspiracy, a number of Southern sympathizers, rebel officers, and escaped prisoners of war reportedly were arrested on Sunday night, the sixth, in Chicago. They were alleged to be in possession of caches of arms with which they planned to force the release of prisoners of war at Camp Douglas in Chicago.[13]

But on Forrest's last military strike before rejoining Hood's Army of Tennessee, the devastating amphibious strike on November 4, 1864, against Johnsonville, Tennessee, the railhead on the Tennessee River at the western terminus of the Nashville & Northwestern Railroad, which had been a vital link in Sherman's line of communications with the North, Forrest commanded only 3,000 men. These he took with him in November to Florence, Alabama, where he joined them with the 2,000 cavalry which Hood brought out of Georgia for his thrust northward into Middle Tennessee.

Hood had decided in early October to return to Tennessee. But he lost several weeks' valuable time. His army needed shoes and clothing which he hoped to get via rail at Tuscumbia. But upon his arrival there, he found rail service still disrupted and continuing delays in repairing the road despite his request weeks before for repairs to be made. Then he was dogged by rains which made the Tennessee River rise and crossings quite perilous. And Hood could not move until Forrest had reported for duty. But Forrest was still in West Tennessee when Hood would have liked to commence.

From November 17 to 21, Forrest's cavalry bivouacked at Shoal Creek, east of Florence, Alabama, on the north side of the Tennessee River. During this time, his troops had several sharp skirmishes with Union cavalry which altogether numbered 4,300 troops in four brigades under Brigadier General Edward Hatch. In one encounter, one of Forrest's wagon trains was taken, then recaptured in the next engagement.

When Hood was finally able to begin his offensive on November 21, Forrest led his cavalry out ahead of the infantry toward Nashville. He led the remnants of three divisions under the commands of Abraham Buford, James R. Chalmers, and William H. Jackson. Characteristically, Forrest wasted no time in pressing northward beyond the line of the Tennessee River in Alabama, an area occupied by Federal troops, both infantry and cavalry, in substantial numbers. The boldness and celerity of Forrest's initial attacks, despite being hampered by abysmal weather, tended to carry the day against enemy troops, most of whom had seen recent action with Sherman in Georgia and against Forrest in his raid of North Alabama and Middle Tennessee in September and October last.

As Hood's army started north, the weather turned worse, with freezing rains, sleet, and snow which, with alternating thaws and freezes, turned the roads into quagmires and impeded movement. These happenings gave Major General George H. Thomas in Nashville more leeway in preparing his defense and time in assembling an unbeatable military force.[14]

The 32,000-man Army of Tennessee was opposed by a force aggregating 71,000 under the command of Thomas, headquartered in Nashville. The force figures are the maximums for the respective armies that faced each other in the campaign. Thus the numerical strength of the Confederate force is reckoned as of the time it started north from Florence, Alabama, on November 21, before spectacular casualties at Franklin reduced its number substantially. The strength of the Union force is reckoned as of the time it moved out of its fortifications in Nashville on December 15 to attack Hood's army. Thus while Thomas's strength increased during the campaign, Hood's diminished.

Thomas drew the strength of his army from various quarters. First, there were about 10,000 troops more or less permanently under arms holding Nashville against any threats that might be brought against the citadel which had been in Union hands since February 1862.

Thomas also had at his command a number of garrisons within 200 miles of his headquarters, including 5,000 men at Chattanooga under Major General James B. Steedman, another 5,000 at Murfreesboro, Tennessee, under Major General Lovell H. Rousseau, and 4,000 at Decatur, Alabama, under Major General Gordon Granger.

Two divisions totalling 14,000, under Major General A.J. Smith, were ordered to return from Missouri where they had been sent from Georgia to oppose Major General Sterling Price's incursion in the state in September and October 1864. And Sherman had detached two corps under his command in Georgia to return to Tennessee just prior to his cutting loose for Savannah and the sea. They were the IV Corps, under Major General David S. Stanley, numbering 12,000, already at Pulaski, Tennessee, seventy-five miles south of Nashville and close to the path Hood would take north; and the XXIII Corps, under Major General John M. Schofield, another 10,000 troops, also at Pulaski.[15]

In addition, Thomas had cavalry under Brigadier General James H. Wilson aggregating 10,000. Wilson had been sent west from the Army of the Potomac by Grant to take command of Sherman's cavalry, which had hitherto proved itself much inferior to Wheeler's cavalry. But when Sherman started for the sea, he took with him only 4,500 horse soldiers, whom he placed under the command of Major General Judson Kilpatrick. He sent Wilson back to Nashville with the remainder of his cavalry to aid Thomas in defense of Middle Tennessee.[16]

Wilson, barely twenty-seven years old, was quite successful in upgrading the Federal cavalry, which gave a good accounting of itself at the

Battle of Nashville as well as later in the war in the West, when its superiority over a diminished and crumbling enemy became manifestly overwhelming. Wilson proved to be one of the better Union cavalry officers in the war.

The Army of Tennessee left Florence, on the north bank of the Tennessee River, on the morning of November 21, marching in three columns behind Forrest's three cavalry divisions and headed for Columbia, Tennessee, seventy-five miles northeast of Florence.

Forrest's left column of cavalry under Chalmers marched via West Point, Kelly's Forge, Henryville, and Mt. Pleasant to Columbia. On their way, Chalmers' men made contact near Henryville in Lawrence County, Tennessee, with Colonel Horace Capron's brigade of Hatch's command in the first major fighting of the campaign.

With a frontal demonstration and attacks on both flanks and the rear of the enemy at Fouche Springs, and with Forrest present and in the lead, the Confederates routed Capron's brigade and took 45 prisoners. In the evening, Colonel Edmund W. Rucker further pressed a frontal assault and drove Capron's force back upon an ambuscade in its rear which consisted of Forrest and his escort. Fifty prisoners were taken, and the enemy continued to fall back.[17]

Also on the twenty-third, the troops of the Eleventh Tennessee Cavalry, in Bell's brigade of Jackson's division, having reached Lawrenceburg, turned east to approach Pulaski, sixteen miles away, only to find that the IV and XXIII corps under Schofield had abandoned their advanced position and were hurrying north to Columbia. Jackson's and Buford's divisions together turned north on obscure secondary roads paralleling the Pulaski-Columbia turnpike. From noon to night of the next day, they had several sharp encounters with units of Hatch's cavalry covering the withdrawal of the infantry to Columbia. One of the encounters was at the village of Campbellsville, where the Confederates took 100 prisoners.[18]

Meanwhile, Chalmers' left wing had driven the Union cavalry opposing them through and out of Mt. Pleasant, where they seized a substantial cache of small-arms ammunition, 35,000 rounds. Then they began a push at two in the morning of November 24 to seize the crossings of Duck River to the north at Columbia and squeeze Schofield's withdrawing forces between the river and the advancing Army of Tennessee.[19]

Chalmers' rapid advance was checked only by the timely diversion by Brigadier General Jacob D. Cox of his infantry division, which had encamped eight miles south of Columbia on the road to Pulaski on the night of the twenty-third. The following morning Cox took a connecting road three miles south of Columbia to the Mt. Pleasant highway to face and halt Chalmers. Cox's efforts made it possible for Schofield's corps to march into Columbia on the twenty-fourth before Hood's cavalry arrived and to remain there for three days until Hood's infantry came up via Mt. Pleasant.

Dug in for three days in Columbia, Schofield's army skirmished with

Forrest's ubiquitous sharpshooters. Men of Chalmers' division took a valuable flour mill less than three miles from town and kept it operating.

Schofield evacuated Columbia by night on the twenty-seventh after Hood's infantry arrived from the south that morning. His withdrawal was completed by 5 A.M. on November 28. He then set fire to Columbia's bridges, but stayed no more than a mile and a half from the north bank of the river, not withdrawing further to the north for the time being.[20]

Advanced units of the Eleventh Tennessee Cavalry were reported across on the north side of the Duck River on the twenty-sixth. In a report from Hardison's Mill in eastern Maury County, Colonel Horace Capron stated that T.C.H. Miller, the Fisher brothers' company commander, with a regiment [sic] of cavalry, was seen at eight in the evening of November 26 going north six miles from Chapel Hill in the direction of the Nashville & Chattanooga Railroad.

And from Kingston Springs on the twenty-ninth, there was a Union report of a skirmish with the Eleventh Tennessee Cavalry at Smith's Springs in Williamson County on the South Harpeth River.[21]

Hood used several companies of the Eleventh for a variety of details in his Tennessee campaign. The troops were all from the Middle Tennessee counties of Coffee, Davidson, Giles, Marshall, Rutherford, Warren, and Williamson, and their knowledge of the country and acquaintance with the people was believed to be of value to the army.

But desertion was a problem with the officers and men so close to their homes. Lieutenant William W. Braden, 30, a prewar resident of Marshall County, deserted on November 27. Braden, said to have a family, likely went home and hid out until he surrendered and took the oath of allegiance in Nashville on March 8, 1865.[22]

On the evening of November 27, Hood held a meeting with Forrest and his infantry division commanders at Beechlawn, the home of Mrs. Cornelia Francis Warfield, three miles south of Columbia on the Pulaski Pike, and reportedly laid out a sound and feasible plan for the entrapment of Schofield's two corps.

The historian Thomas Lawrence Connelly cast doubt on just what Hood's plan was. If it were to head off Schofield at Spring Hill, as commonly believed, it was poorly planned. Hood's advance units reached Spring Hill with little ammunition or artillery, most of the latter being held south of the Duck River around Columbia with two divisions of Stephen Lee's corps. Nevertheless, pursuant to a plan, whatever it was, Forrest's cavalry, in a flanking movement, was to force its way across the Duck River by nightfall on the twenty-eighth.[23]

Forrest's divisions proceeded as follows: Chalmers on the left forded at Carr's Mill, Jackson crossed at Holland's Ford, while Forrest with Biffle's regiment crossed at Owen's Ford, all points seven miles and more above

Columbia to the east. Buford's division, crossing still further upstream near the Lewisburg-Franklin turnpike, was delayed in getting across the river until daybreak on the twenty-ninth owing to stiffer than anticipated resistance from the Union cavalry under its youthful new commander, James H. Wilson.[24]

Before he crossed the river, Forrest sent his escort east to Shelbyville to scout and destroy the railroad spur there.[25] Once across the river, Chalmers' division struck at the enemy at Hurt's Crossroads, home of John Fisher's late wife, Sarah Hurt, on the morning of the twenty-ninth. Jackson's division had already begun to pressure Wilson's cavalry up the Franklin-Lewisburg pike in a northeasterly direction away from Schofield's two corps.[26]

From Hurt's Crossroads, at one in the morning of November 29, Wilson sent a message to Schofield advising him to get back to Franklin with all due haste since Hood's army would soon be crossing the river on pontoons that were even now being laid down for the purpose.[27]

Schofield received Wilson's urgent message at 7:30 A.M. on the twenty-ninth. Thereupon he directed two divisions of infantry, his supply trains, and most of his artillery to depart for Franklin, going through the village of Spring Hill, twelve miles north of Columbia.[28]

Meanwhile, before dawn, Hood began crossing Duck River on pontoons at Davis's Ford, five miles above Columbia. Here both Stewart's and Cheatham's corps, as well as Edward Johnson's division from Lee's corps, crossed near where Forrest had crossed the day before. But Hood left two divisions from Stephen Lee's corps as well as nearly all of his artillery and ammunition wagons in Columbia to demonstrate across the river from Schofield to convince the latter that the bulk of Hood's army was still in Columbia rather than attempting a flanking movement on Schofield's left.[29]

Also left behind upstream in Marshall County only a few miles from Cave Spring was a contingent of Company C of the Eleventh Tennessee Cavalry, which included Thomas Fisher, with orders to guard Huey's Mill on the Duck River to insure that the mill continued to grind out flour for the use of Hood's army as it advanced northward toward Franklin and Nashville.[30]

It is likely that local indigenous personnel operated the mill the troops guarded and that the men of the Eleventh were posted as guards to be alert to any attempt by the enemy to close down the mill's operations and to insure that the supply of grain coming into the mill was not interrupted. The troops would also have guarded commissary wagons going to the front and assisted in the army's efforts to scout and forage in the Duck River valley.

Forrest's cavalry continued to press Wilson's cavalry five miles north of Hurt's Cross Roads on the Franklin-Lewisburg Pike to Mount Carmel Church. Wilson noted that at that point the rebel cavalry ceased its pursuit and broke off. But Wilson was convinced that Forrest was headed for Nashville, and he notified Thomas in Nashville of his surmise and promised to arrive to help defend the capital against Forrest. He continued north to Franklin and beyond after Forrest had broken off.[31]

Forrest left Ross's 600-man Texas brigade of Jackson's division to follow Wilson as the latter continued to retire to Franklin to the north. Forrest, with the remainder of his command, returned down the Franklin-Lewisburg Pike to Rally Hill, then turned west toward Spring Hill, arriving just after noon of the twenty-ninth on the perimeter of a hastily drawn-up Union semicircular defensive line to the east of the village and about two miles from its center.

The line was manned by Wagner's division of Stanley's IV Corps supported by artillery. Near a tollgate on the Rally Hill road more than a mile and a half from Spring Hill, Forrest opened the action by ordering Frank Armstrong's brigade of Jackson's division, a portion of his Kentucky brigade, and the Fourteenth Tennessee Cavalry Regiment, both of Buford's division, to form in line of battle and charge what was thought to be cavalry concealed among some trees.

But the enemy was not moved. Brisk and rapid bursts of fire surprisingly revealed that there was a strong concentration of infantry in the woods, not cavalry.

At this point, Forrest dismounted his whole command and moved against the enemy. Going to a high hill to reconnoiter, Forrest could see the Federals moving up the Franklin Pike.

In order to get to the pike, he ordered a mounted attack by Colonel Andrew L. Wilson's Twenty-First Tennessee Cavalry Regiment, of Buford's division, against the enemy's right flank. Forrest reported that Wilson was wounded three times in the charge through an open field but refused to leave his command.

Next Forrest sent Tyree Bell's brigade, of which the Eleventh Tennessee was now a part, to attack dismounted on the left in order to get as close as possible to the turnpike. Bell's attack began to make headway.[32]

Just past the middle of the afternoon, Hood's infantry, virtually without artillery support, approached the village up the Rally Hill Pike from the southeast with Cheatham's corps in the lead, followed by Stewart's corps and Edward Johnson's division of Lee's corps closing the rear. They faced only Wagner's division but most of Schofield's artillery at Spring Hill along with Schofield's train of 800 wagons.

Lee's other two divisions were still in Columbia, along with most of the Confederate artillery, demonstrating and causing Schofield to keep a substantial number of his infantry before Columbia. Hood's plan for entrapping Schofield's army neared the logical point of execution of the final phase. But Schofield's success in getting infantry units to Spring Hill rapidly, so that the road north was kept open to his corps, effectively blocked whatever plans Hood may have had for entrapment of his enemy.

Hood ordered Pat Cleburne's infantry division into the fight on the left of Bell's brigade. Cleburne and Forrest personally led their troops into battle. Bell's brigade was almost out of ammunition but pressed its attack with promptness, energy, and skill.

When Cleburne's troops attacked the Union defenders on their right flank, the latter gave way on the run until eight Federal field pieces unloaded shrapnel on their attackers. The pursuit was halted, and a shorter Union line was formed at about four thirty in the afternoon.[33]

At this point, execution of the Confederate strategy began to unravel rapidly and puzzlingly amidst orders that were not relayed properly or which were contradictory, as well as misunderstandings between senior staff. And in retrospect, recollections of some participants were irreconcilable.

Cleburne, first of the infantry commanders to see action, re-formed his troops to renew his attack and seize the vital turnpike he faced. But he soon received an order from Cheatham to delay his attack until he had received further orders, orders which never came. Soon after sundown, he went into bivouac for the night, holding his line of battle.[34]

Hood ordered the division of a civilian general, William B. Bate, Governor of Tennessee after the war (1883-1887), the second of Cheatham's divisions to come up, to press forward to the vital artery to the west, get on it and face southward to block the withdrawal of elements of Schofield's army still on the road from the vicinity of Columbia. Bate was also ordered by Hood to keep in touch with Cleburne's left.

But about the time Bate's division advanced to within a hundred yards of the pike at the Nat Cheairs home, a bit over a mile south of Spring Hill, he received an order from Cheatham to halt and to form his line at Cleburne's left. Bate was hesitant to obey the order until it was repeated. But he could clearly see Schofield's troops passing north on the pike unimpeded and saw the advantage of immediately advancing to the road in line of battle. Nevertheless, he fell back as ordered and went into bivouac after 9 P.M.

John C. Brown, another civilian general (Governor of Tennessee 1871-1875), commanded the third and last of Cheatham's divisions which came upon the scene. He was ordered to fall in on Cleburne's right and to attack when the order was given. But upon inspecting the situation confronting him when he arrived at about 5 P.M., he stopped short, noting that the Federal line facing him extended menacingly to his right and that elements of Forrest's cavalry, which he had been assured would cover his right, either had been withdrawn to another part of the field to rest and feed their horses or were north of Spring Hill with William H. Jackson's division.

Brown reported his misgivings to Cheatham who, with Hood, approved Brown's decision to hold back from the battle line until Stewart's corps should arrive to his right, at which time he would advance, at a moment's notice, to attack the enemy directly in front of him. Brown was to open the attack and Cleburne and Bate would immediately follow suit on their fronts to Brown's left.

But the order for Brown to advance never came. Nor did Stewart's corps come to the front on Brown's right. Hood previously had ordered it to stay two miles distant down the Rally Hill Pike until well after dark, then ordered it forward but with no order to attack.[35] Later Cheatham and Stewart were called to Hood's headquarters where Hood announced that he had changed his mind. The attack would come in the morning at daylight.

Stewart, when he finally was ordered up after dark, was sent not to the right of Cheatham's corps as expected, but to advance around the Union perimeter to the north of Spring Hill to block Schofield's withdrawal to Franklin. As it turned out, his troops, once put in place in total darkness, did not face the turnpike to intercept Schofield's withdrawing army as they should have, but faced away from it.[36]

Stewart came across Forrest in the darkness of the night and learned something of the tactical situation as it had progressed from the general officer who had been on the scene at Spring Hill that day longer than any other. Not being content with the way matters were progressing, Stewart and Forrest went together to Hood's headquarters at the Absalom Thompson house, about three miles southeast of Spring Hill, to try to make sense out of what was transpiring.

Stewart explained to Hood that he had put his men into bivouac owing to inexplicable changes in orders he had received. Hood was content to let Stewart's men rest but wanted to know if Forrest's cavalry might undertake the assignment of blocking Schofield's withdrawal.

Forrest reported to Hood an acute shortage of ammunition within his command. Buford's and Chalmers' divisions were without a cartridge. The army's ammunition wagons were still back in Columbia, and Cheatham's and Stewart's infantry corps were so short that they could not spare ammunition for the cavalry, as Hood suggested they might.

William H. Jackson's cavalry had captured some ammunition during the day. With the captured ammunition, and Jackson's division, Forrest promised Hood that he would do his best to prevent Schofield's escape.[37]

Jackson received orders from Forrest about ten at night to march four miles north of Spring Hill to staunch the flow of Schofield's army through Spring Hill to Franklin to the north. He took with him Brigadier General Lawrence S. Ross's Texas brigade of only 686 men and Frank Armstrong's somewhat larger brigade of about 1,000, a weak force indeed to accomplish its assigned task.[38]

By ten at night, the last of Schofield's 22,000-man army, infantry guarding a train of 800 wagons, began leaving Spring Hill on its twelve-mile march north to Franklin. The last wagon left Spring Hill almost six hours later with Wagner's infantry covering the rear of Schofield's train.[39]

Jackson's pitifully small cavalry division moved north, somewhat more than the stipulated four miles, and made an attack on the train at 11 P.M., just north of Thompson's Station at the Fitzgerald farm.

Brigadier Ross made the only report of the engagement by a Confederate officer. He reported attacking and destroying or capturing thirty-nine wagons, stampeding teamsters and guards, and blockading the pike for thirty minutes. Then, to avoid being overwhelmed in an infantry pincer trap which he saw forming and in which he would be greatly outnumbered, Ross stated that he withdrew his men to hills overlooking the pike and watched the procession of wagons and infantry recommence up the pike toward Franklin.[40]

Although Jackson made no report of the engagement, Forrest reported that Jackson's command fought from 11 P.M. until near daylight. But receiving no support, Jackson retired after inflicting damage to the wagon train.[41] Forrest's intelligence was quite at variance with Ross's report.

All through the morning of the thirtieth, the hindermost parts of Schofield's army marched into Franklin, virtually untouched by Hood's army. There they strengthened the strong Union position behind formidable defensive emplacements in anticipation of possible frontal assaults in force.

Hood's plan (if indeed it was his plan to entrap Schofield's army, laid out to his senior staff at his headquarters at Beechlawn, three miles south of Columbia on the evening of Tuesday, November 27) had failed in its accomplishment because of the speed of Schofield's withdrawal up the pike to and past Spring Hill, Hood's failure to prepare his army properly for battle, and his uncharacteristic decision to avoid battle in the dark of the night of November 29 at Spring Hill.[42]

Even if it were not his plan, Hood nevertheless had a golden opportunity to entrap Schofield's army at Spring Hill but failed. For the only time in his Nashville campaign, his army had outnumbered the Union army which faced him on the field. There is every reason to believe that, despite the obstacles, he might have defeated, captured, or at the very least, destroyed the effectiveness of the forces facing him had he boldly opted for a night fight on the twenty-ninth. By attacking and winning, he would have substantially weakened the Nashville position of Thomas, commanding the Army of the Cumberland, and might have created consternation, perhaps panic, among people in the Midwestern states who would have felt threatened by a victorious Confederate army on the loose in Tennessee headed north.

Hood's failure meant that the following day, he and his army, frustrated, chagrined, and angry, and without the support of their artillery, still far down the road toward Columbia, would face, across a two-mile long, naked, gently undulating plain, their escaped quarry, reinforced and fighting behind a well-fortified position, with excellent artillery support, high morale, and a growing confidence of their ability to win in battle.

The officers and men of the Army of Tennessee, on the other hand, had a commander whose leadership they had distrusted from the beginning of his command before Atlanta five months earlier on July 17. Hood, minus a leg and with a disabled arm, was an ambitious, impetuous soldier whose mental state was quite likely worn to a frazzle by his physical disabilities as well as his limitations in military command. And now Hood commanded an army whose numbers had steadily dwindled from death, wounds, disease, capture, and desertions and whose members had unremittingly and increasingly suffered discouragement from losses in battles and losses of homeland to a relentless invader.

Then there was the soldiers' anger at not being paid, not getting leave to go home, poor food, clothing, and equipment, as well as substandard medical and spiritual care, insufficient ammunition, and suspect leadership. It was an army in the final throes of defeat but still capable of giving a punishing account of itself in battle. Against prohibitively superior forces, it demonstrated the most reckless abandon and aggressive fighting behavior in the slaughter pen at Franklin on the last day of November 1864.

Chapter 8

Hood's Tennessee Campaign: Disasters at Franklin and Nashville, November 30–December 16, 1864

Hood's beleaguered army followed Schofield's army north from Spring Hill to Franklin on the morning of Wednesday, November 30. After the cavalry, Stewart's corps led, followed closely by Cheatham's corps. Stephen Lee's corps, with all but two batteries of Hood's artillery, marched all the way from Columbia considerably to the rear of the others.

The Confederate cavalry, in the lead, marched at daybreak with borrowed ammunition from Walthall's infantry division supplying Buford's and Chalmers' divisions. Forrest led his cavalry up the main turnpike accompanied by Jackson's and Buford's divisions. Chalmers' cavalry was on the west advancing on Franklin up the Carter's Creek Pike.

Forrest caught up with Schofield's rear guard just north of Thompson's Station and pressed them on to Winstead's Hill two miles south of Franklin. The Federals made a stand at the hill until about two in the afternoon when advanced elements of Stewart's infantry came up. The defending forces then withdrew two miles across the open plain to their entrenchments just south of the town.[1]

Schofield was not convinced that Hood would frontally attack his fortifications at Franklin. He believed his main threat came from Forrest flanking his position, crossing the Harpeth River, and attacking his rear. Accordingly, he moved his 800-wagon train through Franklin, across the planked-over railroad bridge over the Harpeth, and on to Nashville as speedily as possible. He planned to withdraw his infantry across the bridge after sundown if Hood did not attack.[2]

Hood arrived at Winstead's Hill just ahead of Stewart's corps and met with Forrest who pointed out to Hood the strength of the Federal position at Franklin and advised a flanking movement. Forrest proposed leading his cavalry, augmented by a division of infantry, to the east of the town. He promised that in two hours, he would flank Schofield's army out of Franklin. But Hood did not want to let Schofield's army withdraw to Nashville where, as

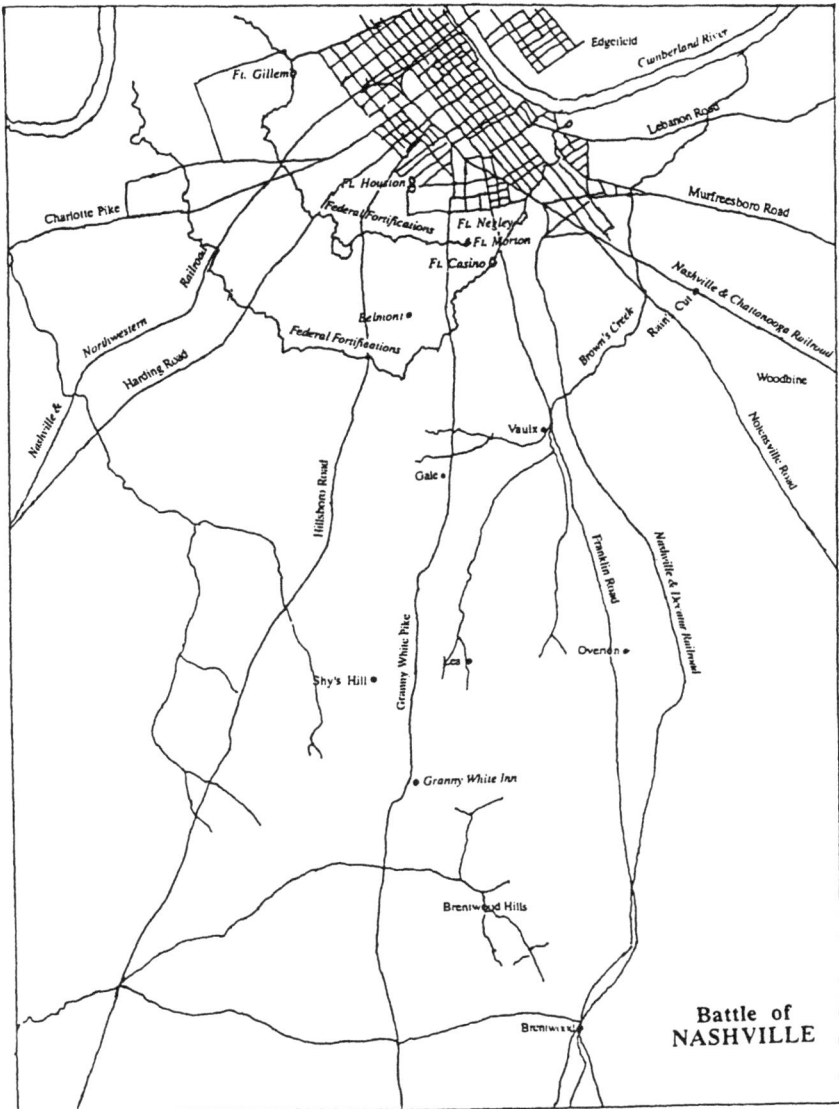

Battle of NASHVILLE

a part of Thomas's much larger Army of the Cumberland, they would be able to fight him with greater advantage.[3]

There was some logic in Hood's reasoning. But there would have been more logic in Hood attacking Schofield the previous night at Spring Hill where he had more leverage than he had now in front of Franklin. Considering Schofield's protected defensive position and Hood's exposed attacking position at Franklin, Hood had little reason to believe that he would be successful in a frontal assault at Franklin. He had lost his tactical advantage twelve miles back down the road.

Notwithstanding the appearance of the situation, the attack was ordered to be made at about four in the afternoon, mainly by Stewart's and Cheatham's corps.

Forrest's cavalry was divided.[4] Chalmers' division, now joined by Biffle's brigade, advanced dismounted on the left flank of Cheatham's corps below the town. There they became engaged with a Federal infantry force which fought from behind the protection of a stone wall strengthened by breastworks of earth. Unable to dislodge the infantry, Chalmers ordered his men to continue their firing for as long as their ammunition held out and thus hold down the infantry and prevent them from retreating to the main Union line in front of the Carter house to reinforce the enemy there.[5]

Buford's division, also dismounted, moved forward on the right flank of Stewart's corps above the town where they engaged both infantry and cavalry posted well out on the Union left and drove them back.

Forrest led a flanking movement on the Confederate right with which he would like to have gained the Nashville turnpike, now strongly protected by cavalry under Wilson which outnumbered his force by at least two to one. He sent Jackson's division, which remained mounted, across the river at Hughes' Ford, three miles above Franklin, to take a hill from which artillery was assaulting Hood's advancing troops on the south side of the Harpeth.

Jackson's troops exhausted their ammunition in trying to take the Union battery. By nightfall, Jackson had failed in his objective and had sustained heavy losses which were especially severe in Armstrong's brigade.

Opposed by Edward Hatch's Fifth Division and Brigadier General Richard W. Johnson's Sixth Division on Schofield's left and with limited ammunition, Forrest and Jackson were joined on the north side of the Harpeth River by Buford's troops who had driven back Federal infantry and cavalry on Schofield's left across the Harpeth River and followed across.

Initially opposed by Brigadier General John Croxton's brigade, which he drove back, Forrest made scant headway when Johnson sent in Colonel Thomas J. Harrison's First Brigade of the Sixth Division alongside Horace Capron's brigade. Forrest managed to hold on north and east of the Harpeth for over two hours until darkness closed in. His cavalry was strongly opposed by Wilson's cavalry which had been heavily concentrated on the Union army's left flank north and east of the Harpeth River to oppose Forrest's expected flanking movement.[6]

His three divisions at Franklin were spared the heavy loss of life sustained by Hood's two infantry corps, which advanced in the center of the battle line up to and over the heavily armed and well-manned center of the Federal fortifications.

The Battle of Franklin represented the most desperate and deadliest five hours' fighting of the war. Advancing two miles over an exposed plain, with no artillery support, Stewart's and Cheatham's corps were pounded mercilessly by a massive barrage of Federal artillery from which there was no shelter. Up closer to the Federal breastworks where the attacking troops were funneled and concentrated, the rifle fire was murderous. At the center of the Federal fortifications, the attackers climbed over the parapets and into the trenches where hand to hand combat took a devastating toll of soldiers on both sides.

Fewer than 16,000 soldiers carried the main burden of the attack against 22,000 defenders lodged behind breastworks. The attackers suffered about 6,500 casualties in killed and wounded, including many of their division, brigade, and regimental commanders. The defenders suffered about 2,300 casualties. And all this within five hours' time and within a few hundred yards of the Carter house at the center of the Union line.

The attackers lost 1,750 killed and about 4,750 wounded. In casualties from all causes, the Army of Tennessee lost two major generals (division commanders), ten brigadiers, and fifty-four regimental commanders.[7] The loss of Patrick Cleburne, perhaps the most effective division commander in the army, was a crippling blow to the Confederate cause. Cleburne was irreplaceable.

Toward midnight of the thirtieth Schofield undertook another night march, this time eighteen miles north to Nashville, leaving his dead and wounded on the bloody battlefield to the battered Confederates.[8]

Thus Hood accomplished with frightfully heavy losses what Forrest had promised him early in the afternoon he could do quickly and with little expense by a flanking action. Hood had virtually destroyed his army.

Forrest's cavalry, on the perimeters of the fighting, sustained some heavy losses but had escaped the worst of the carnage. While the survivors from Stewart's and Cheatham's corps attended to their wounded and buried their dead on December 1, the cavalry was up at daybreak and headed for Nashville. Buford's and Jackson's divisions, with Forrest in command, crossed the Harpeth River east of Franklin and took the Wilson Pike northward to Brentwood, twelve miles south of Nashville, where they expected to converge with Chalmers' division marching up the Hillsboro Pike to the west and hoped there to interfere with the Union withdrawal.

Schofield's army, however, had stolen the march on the Confederates to such an extent that by noon, it was marching into the protective perimeter of fortifications erected south of Nashville. Thus it was not to be interfered with at Brentwood or anywhere else in its withdrawal.

Wilson's cavalry protected the passage of the infantry back to Nashville and engaged in sharp skirmishing with Forrest's cavalry on the Wilson Pike at Owen's Crossroads. But the withdrawal of the Union infantry from Franklin was accomplished almost without incident.[9]

After covering the army's withdrawal into Nashville's defenses, Wilson's cavalry was posted on the Nolensville Road at Thompson's Chapel. On

December 2 it withdrew through Nashville and crossed the Cumberland River on the railroad bridge, going into Edgefield. Here it spent the next ten days preparing for its role in Thomas's attack on Hood's army.[10]

As planned, Chalmers' division met Forrest at Brentwood, although Schofield's corps had already passed north of that point. Then Forrest's combined command, including Buford's, Chalmers' and Jackson's divisions, moved up the main Franklin Road north of Brentwood and encamped four miles south of Nashville in the area of Brown's Creek on the night of December 1. Here Forrest learned that Schofield's corps had already reached the protection of Nashville's outer defensive perimeter. A few miles south, Lee's corps, which hardly had been engaged at Franklin, had come on early with Hood's artillery and was now in bivouac.

On December 2 Forrest ordered Chalmers to go west to picket the Hillsboro and Harding roads while he, with Buford's and Jackson's divisions, advanced north to the suburbs another mile, where he was within sight of the state capitol perched high atop Cedar Knob within the city.[11]

By December 1 Thomas had at Nashville an army of 60,000, which would grow to 71,000 by the fifteenth. Hood brought up a force of 25,000 to besiege the Tennessee citadel, then detached Bate's infantry division and Forrest's cavalry, except for Chalmers' division, to demonstrate against a reinforced Federal garrison of 8,000 at Murfreesboro under Major General Lovell H. Rousseau, thus further weakening his command.[12]

On the morning of the second, Chalmers' division, about 1,500 strong, began to patrol the Hillsboro, Harding, and Charlotte pikes on the left flank of the army in a no-man's land between the Cumberland River below Nashville four miles south to where, by now, Hood's infantry had begun to establish a line anchored on the Hillsboro Pike, a line which ran east across the southern approaches to the city.

On December 2 Colonel David C. Kelley, of Chalmers' division, commanding 300 men of the Third (Forrest's old) Tennessee Cavalry Regiment, not to be confused with Forrest's Old Brigade (now split between Georgia and Tennessee), took four field pieces and set up a blockade of the Cumberland River across from Bell's Mills twelve miles below the city.[13] Despite some lively opposition, Kelley was able to maintain his blockade until the day the Battle of Nashville began.

Thus for two weeks, Kelley cut off Nashville's primary avenue of supplies, which came from the north by way of the river. The Federals' flow of rail traffic via the Nashville & Northwestern Railroad west to the Johnsonville wharves on the Tennessee River was yet unrestored after Forrest's bold destruction of the wharves on November 4, 1864.

Of course, the rail line north from Nashville to Louisville and Cincinnati remained open. Two attempts to dislodge Kelley by Federal gunboat attacks failed. But Thomas was at no great pains to dislodge the pesky Kelley as long as the rail line north to Louisville was kept open and operating.

Upon reaching Nashville's southern suburbs, Forrest began to patrol the roads leading south from the city with Buford's and Jackson's divisions as far east as the State Hospital on the Murfreesboro Road. Upon being relieved by the infantry during the next forty-eight hours, however, Forrest was ordered to Murfreesboro on December 4. But he was ordered by Hood to leave 250 men to picket between the Murfreesboro Road and the Cumberland River above Nashville. Colonel George H. Nixon of Bell's brigade was left to command the pickets.[14]

Forrest started for Murfreesboro on the fifth, proceeding down the Nashville & Chattanooga Railroad, destroying stockades, blockhouses, and bridges, capturing a train and taking prisoners as he went. Forrest was to meet Major General William B. Bate's infantry division, which had previously been sent by Hood from Franklin to destroy the railroad between Nashville and Murfreesboro.

The latter town for a long time had been considered by Federal authorities as a strategically vital point of their defensive position in Middle Tennessee. The Federal strong point had been heavily fortified with a defensive position known as Fortress Rosecrans which sat athwart both Stones River and the Nashville Turnpike one to two miles northwest of Murfreesboro.[15]

Forrest's cavalry and Bate's infantry met on December 5 about four miles southeast of LaVerge. Together, under Forrest's command, they proceeded to Murfreesboro via the main road while one of Jackson's brigades moved down the Wilkinson Pike.

Meanwhile two members of Company C of the Eleventh Tennessee Cavalry, Andrew Jackson Cole and John A. Morris, were captured at Shelbyville, Tennessee, on December 5. Cole and Morris likely were a part of the contingent of Company C which guarded the Duck River mills and sought to maintain the flow of grain thereto. Cole, an original enlistee in his company and a prewar resident of Marshall County, was transferred after a month to Louisville by his captors on his way to Camp Chase where he arrived on January 14, 1865. He languished there until well after the end of hostilities. He took the oath of allegiance at Camp Chase on June 12, 1865, and was released. Morris, on the other hand, reportedly escaped from his guards while enroute from Nashville to Louisville. There are no military service records to show what happened to him subseqently.[16]

In the morning on December 6, Forrest's command reached Fortress Rosecrans, which enclosed about 200 acres on the approach from Nashville just outside Murfreesboro. Forrest ordered Bates' brigade in line of battle to advance on the enemy's works. When the enemy showed no interest in fighting, Forrest made a detailed reconnaissance of the enemy fortifications, a reconnaissance which convinced him that, outnumbered as he was, it would be folly for him to try to attack the Union garrison heavily protected within its fortress and armed with 57 big guns.

With the arrival on the evening of the sixth of two infantry brigades under brigadier generals Claudius W. Sears and Joseph B. Palmer totaling 1,600 men, Forrest had a force of about 6,500 while Rousseau had some 8,000.

On the morning of December 7, Forrest was confronted by a Federal sortie consisting of two brigades totaling 3,325 soldiers. The Union force, with six guns, was under the command of Major General R.H. Milroy. From Fortress Rosecrans, Milroy's troops moved out Salem Pike intent upon giving battle to the Confederates. Forrest moved his troops out to the Wilkinson Pike to form a line at a position more favorable than the one he held earlier in the morning.

The battle was joined on the same grounds where the much larger Battle of Murfreesboro or Stones River had been fought just after Christmas in 1862, but with the differences that the armies each faced in a direction exactly the opposite of the direction each faced in the earlier battle, and the number of troops involved now numbered less than 8,500 vis-à-vis about 85,000 in the earlier battle.

Forrest chose a defensive position so as to have his infantry receive the attack of Milroy's infantry, and he planned to have his cavalry in reserve to attack Milroy's flanks and hinder his return to the fortress. He wanted Buford to protect his left flank. Instead Buford, along with Morton's artillery, had gone around Murfreesboro independently and entered the town from the east by way of the road to Woodbury and delivered a surprise attack within the heart of the town.

On the field near the banks of Stones River, the Federal infantry joined battle and drove in the left flank of Bate's infantry with such force as to produce a precipitous retreat or rout, which both Bate and Forrest personally tried in vain to stem, Forrest with threats, imprecations, and bludgeonings of terrified soldiers within his range which expressed his fierce anger at their manifest panic. Only Brigadier General Thomas Benton Smith's brigade had stood firm.

Acting through his adjutant, Major J.P. Strange, Forrest sent orders to Jackson's two cavalry brigades under Armstrong and Ross to charge the enemy promptly to check his advance. This being done, Milroy's force gave up its pursuit of Bate's infantry and withdrew to Fortress Rosecrans.

Meanwhile, Buford had indeed entered Murfreesboro from the east to the very center of the town. He trained and fired Morton's guns on Federal troops in the Rutherford County courthouse and public square. Making a speedy recovery following their initial surprise, however, the defenders managed to kill the mule teams pulling the guns but were unable to capture the guns and caissons, which the Confederates brought away by hand.[17]

Forrest's command, with some changes in units, continued to operate quite superfluously around and about Murfreesboro right up to the outbreak of the Battle of Nashville on December 15 while Rousseau holed up in his fortress. On the ninth, Bate's division went back to Cheatham's corps on the line of siege just south of Nashville and was replaced in Forrest's command by James A. Smith's infantry brigade commanded by Colonel Charles H. Olmsted.

Meanwhile, Forrest, using Smith's infantry, destroyed what remained of the railroad north out of Murfreesboro as far as LaVergne. South of Murfreesboro, Jackson's division intercepted and burned a train of 17 cars carrying 60,000 rations, bound for Murfreesboro from Stevenson, Alabama, capturing the rations and 200 guards of the Sixty-First Illinois Regiment of Infantry, commanded by Lieutenant Colonel Daniel Grass.[18]

On December 11 Forrest sent Buford's division north to the Cumberland River near the Hermitage, the late President Andrew Jackson's home, to picket the area and prevent a flanking movement from that quarter which might threaten Forrest's command. The river was patrolled in the area by a fleet of a dozen heavily-armed Union gunboats operating upstream from Nashville, a fleet posted to prevent Hood, or more likely Forrest, from crossing the river and flanking the Union position in Nashville.[19]

While the Confederate Army of Tennessee, uneasily camped just three miles south of Nashville and, operating ineffectually around Murfreesboro, was in the most desperate straits possible, Union commanders in the North, beginning with President Lincoln and Secretary of War Edwin M. Stanton, were apprehensive in the extreme because of their perception of Hood's threat to Nashville, Kentucky, and the Middle West.

Grant, deep in Virginia, was insistent that Thomas attack Hood before Hood received reinforcements that might make him unbeatable. Wilson, commanding Thomas's cavalry, later suggested that Grant's fears were fed by Thomas's weakness, relative to Grant's and Sherman's, two generals who had largely stripped Thomas of much of his army's strength so that it might be used in the East in Virginia, Georgia, and the Carolinas.

Grant wired Thomas of his fear that Forrest would move down the Cumberland, cross the river, and flank Thomas out of Nashville. He then ordered Thomas to attack immediately. Thomas was in his headquarters in a Nashville hotel named for the Parisian suburban town, St. Cloud. At four in the afternoon of December 6, he promised Grant he would attack the next day, *if ready!* But, of course, he was not. He told Grant that he wanted to have 6,000 to 8,000 mounted cavalry to cover his flanks when he attacked Hood, because, he explained, Forrest had 12,000 horsemen.[20]

Forrest, in fact, had fewer than 5,000, most of whom were unavailable to Hood by Hood's own design since he had detailed them to demonstrate against the Federal garrison at Murfreesboro and keep it from being used at Nashville against Hood's main army.

About 1,500 of Forrest's command, under Chalmers, were covering Hood's left flank. On the twelfth, Chalmers would be left with only about 900, Rucker's brigade, when Hood ordered Biffle's cavalry brigade to take a position on the Confederate right in support of Buford, who was patrolling the river in the vicinity of the Hermitage.

When Chalmers complained to Hood of his weakness in numbers and the four-mile front he had to defend, Hood on the fourteenth sent him Brigadier General Matthew D. Ector's brigade of infantry, 700 strong, under the command of Colonel David Coleman of the Thirty-Ninth North Carolina Infantry Regiment.[21] Ector had lost a leg at Atlanta, and his brigade had been hit hard at Franklin. Their small numbers would prove to be of no use whatever to Chalmers when he was attacked by Wilson's 12,500 cavalry corps the following day.

At six-thirty in the evening of December 6, 1864, when Thomas received orders from Grant to attack, Thomas's cavalry was still in Edgefield making preparations. Horses were seized and brought to Edgefield from over a wide area while arms, clothing, and equipment were issued to Thomas's dismounted cavalry now organized into brigades.[22]

Secretary Stanton urged Grant not to permit Thomas to wait for Wilson to strengthen his cavalry before attacking, saying that the time required might be interminable. Stanton wired his message at ten twenty on the morning of December 7, the day Thomas had promised to attack.

But Thomas's attack did not come that day. He still was not ready. He was risking his command and his career by waiting. He might attack, he said, by the ninth or tenth. But he did not.

At one thirty in the afternoon of the eighth, Grant, having heard nothing of Thomas's promised attack, wired the Army Chief of Staff, General Henry W. Halleck, to the effect that if Thomas had not yet attacked, he should be relieved and his command given to Schofield.

After conferring at headquarters, Halleck replied to Grant that if he wanted Thomas removed, he (Grant) would have to give the order and assume the responsibility therefor as no one in headquarters wanted Thomas replaced. Although Grant still wanted Thomas removed, he was unwilling to assume responsibility for the action at that time.[23]

On December 8, Thomas set daylight of the tenth as the time for his attack. But on the morning of the ninth, an ice storm hit Nashville and lasted for four days, during which time it became very treacherous indeed to conduct large-scale military movements. Freezing rain brought a heavy coat of ice that covered everything. The attack date was postponed to await the cessation of the icing conditions.

Grant still grew impatient. An order was drawn up in the War Department on the ninth, though not delivered, to put Schofield in command of Thomas's army. Major General John A. Logan, a civilian general, started for Nashville on the thirteenth pursuant to orders to relieve Thomas of command. Then Grant himself started for Nashville from City Point, Virginia, on the fifteenth.[24]

Thomas, "Rock of Chickamauga," was not given the credit he had earned and deserved by his betters at the top. Grant's continuing alarm had been fed perhaps by a telegram sent from Nashville to Washington at eight in the evening of December 8 which mentioned the activity of Brigadier General Hylan B. Lyon, a Kentuckian, reputedly of imperfect manners, who broke away from Chalmers' cavalry division with two field pieces and a hundred and fifty men and was reported to be seventy miles downstream of Nashville about Cumberland City.

This isolated and not-very-threatening sally by Lyon was interpreted by skittish Union generals hundreds of miles away as a portent of a massive Confederate movement into Kentucky, flanking Nashville and threatening the growing Federal force waiting there to move methodically and destructively against Hood's battered barefoot army.[25]

It was later reported that Schofield authored one or more telegrams to Grant commenting critically on Thomas's reluctance to attack. Three days before the battle, Thomas became aware of Schofield's efforts to have him relieved and Schofield put in command. Major General James B. Steedman was the source of the latter information several years later.[26]

With the ice storm still upon them, Wilson's cavalry, having confiscated as many mounts as they were able, left Edgefield and crossed the Cumberland River using both the railroad and pontoon bridges. They marched west of Nashville and massed between the Harding and Charlotte pikes in anticipation of the command to attack.[27]

When the storm broke, the weather warmed, and rain began to fall on the fourteenth, Thomas sent a telegram to General Halleck in Washington, informing him of the change in weather and saying that the army would attack the enemy the next morning.[28]

As promised this time, Thomas sent his magnificently prepared army out to attack Hood's ill-equipped, outmanned, extremely vulnerable, and largely barefoot military force on the morning of December 15 in a dense fog which delayed the army's movement but which lifted by noon.

The main attack went against the Confederate left, primarily against Stewart's infantry corps, which was pushed back a mile or more from the Hillsboro Pike on the left, east to the Granny White Pike on the first day by an attack by infantry strongly supported by artillery under major generals Thomas J. Wood, who had the largest corps, 14,171 troops, headquartered at the Belmont estate, and Andrew Jackson Smith, with 10,461 men. Brigadier General James H. Wilson, with 9,000 mounted and 3,500 dismounted cavalry, operated farther out on the Federal right.[29]

Major General James B. Steedman's division, 7,541 strong, consisting of predominantly black Tennessee troops supported by U.S. regular army troops, demonstrated against Cheatham's corps on the Confederate right at Rain's Cut in Woodbine on the Nashville & Chattanooga Railroad. Cheatham's and Lee's corps, the latter in the center at the Franklin Pike, were largely unmoved at the end of the first day of fighting. Indeed Lee's corps had hardly been engaged. But Cheatham's corps was kept busy most of the day. Late in the afternoon, Hood ordered reinforcements of Cheatham's officers and men to be sent to relieve the hard-hit Stewart on the Confederate left.[30]

But on the night of the fifteenth, after a day of fighting, Hood had to shorten and pull back his lines. He also rearranged his corps, switching Cheatham from right to left along the Granny White Pike, the new left, placing Stewart in the center, and leaving Lee at the Franklin Pike, which became the new right. Instead of the line facing the enemy around Brown's Creek as on the opening of the first day, the line was pulled back two miles to just north of the "knobs," the Brentwood Hills around the Overton and Lea properties. John Overton's home served as Hood's headquarters when he came up to besiege Nashville.[31]

Chalmer's cavalry division of about 900, the only Confederate cavalry operating on the field on the first day, was guarding the Harding and Charlotte pikes, far to the north and west of the Confederate infantry lines, up in the four-mile gap between Cumberland River and the main infantry forces south of Nashville. It was hit by Wilson's cavalry, numbering 9,000 mounted rifles plus 3,500 on foot, the latter awaiting mounts, yet still participating in the push. Wilson advanced on a wide swinging arc against the Confederate left.

Chalmers' men stood and fought until Chalmers found that he had been flanked and was isolated from his own command with the enemy two miles in his rear, out on the Harding Road to the west. He thereupon broke off contact with the enemy and withdrew out the Harding Road to a road that crossed east to the Hillsboro Road. Thus he regained contact with his own army, bringing out Colonel Kelley and his 300 river blockaders across from Bells' Mills. This he accomplished before daylight of the sixteenth, joining the left flank of Hood's army northwest of the Brentwood Hills and pathetically extending Hood's flank west perhaps the better part of a mile to the Hillsboro Pike.[32]

Ector's infantry force of 700, which had been sent to reinforce Chalmers on the day before the battle began, fired a few volleys against Wilson's attack, but quickly retired without capture when faced with a sea of advancing bluecoats. Chalmers complained that Ector's brigade, under Colonel David Coleman, withdrew without notifying him. Chalmers said that, owing to Coleman's failure to communicate, Wilson's cavalry was two miles out the Harding Road in his rear before he learned of its presence.[33]

Ector's brigade made its way in good order across the Harding Road south and east, whence they had come so recently, to the left flank of the main Confederate infantry lines on the Hillsboro Pike, lines which were bent farther toward the south and east by the great wheel of the Federal right as it turned during the first day's fighting.[34]

At the end of the first day, Thomas thought the battle was ended and sent orders to Schofield simply to press the retreating enemy the next day. But Schofield knew Hood from their West Point days and rode into Nashville to tell Thomas that he believed Hood would be ready to fight in the morning.

Thomas decided to play it safe and renew his attack on the morning of the sixteenth.[35] His opponent, Hood, however, was apprehensive about the outcome of renewing the fight. Early in the morning of the sixteenth, he ordered his wagons south to the Harpeth River at Franklin and instructed Lee that his corps should assure a safe withdrawal by way of the Franklin Pike in the event the infantry could not hold its line, orders which were not calculated to inspire confidence in his battered troops.[36] Still the officers and men of the Army of Tennessee, shivering, wet, freezing, and ill-clothed, held their ground and awaited the expected assault from overwhelmingly superior forces.

Thomas attacked both right and left flanks of Hood's army as he had done the previous day. But the first assault by Steedman's troops, beginning at about nine in the morning against Hood's right, was more than the demonstration delivered the day before on this flank. It involved a heavy assault for the purpose of wresting the Franklin Pike from the enemy by regular army infantry as well as troops of the Twelfth and Thirteenth U.S. Colored Infantry regiments, both organized in Nashville in 1863.

The attack produced heavy casualties on both sides, but it failed. Lee's corps clung to its positions until the late afternoon when the Confederate left was routed and many of the defenders streamed through Lee's troops on their way south via the Franklin Pike.[37]

On their left flank, the Confederates had a strong point on a hill just west of Granny White Pike which the Federals bombarded furiously and lethally beginning in the morning, a bombardment which both Union and Confederate observers praised as a model of intensity, accuracy, and effectiveness. The Federal infantry outflanked the Confederate position, then assaulted the hill after four in the afternoon and took it from its defenders, an infantry brigade led by twenty-six-year-old Brigadier General Thomas Benton Smith of Bate's division.[38]

After the battle, Smith suffered brain damage from blows to his head, which cut through to expose brain tissue, from his own sword, reportedly wielded repeatedly by a victorious officer, Colonel William Linn McMillen of the Ninety-Fifth Ohio Volunteer Infantry.[39] McMillen had experienced a checkered career during the war. He had been accused of cowardice and unsoldier-like conduct against the enemy at Richmond, Kentucky, on August 30, 1862, for which he had been court-martialed, tried, and acquitted. Action in this instance involved Union infantry which panicked, resulting in the capture of half the Union force by Colonel John S. Scott's Confederate cavalry brigade, of which Starnes' Fourth Tennessee Regiment was a part. McMillen was captured and reportedly wounded in the action.

In a less sanguinary mode, on June 18, 1864, in Memphis, McMillen was ordered to report himself under arrest and to relinquish his sword by order of Major General C.C. Washburn as a result of an occurrence the previous evening when McMillen refused, upon request, to produce an admission ticket while viewing a performance in a Memphis theatre. McMillen insisted that his word was sufficient to establish that he had a ticket.

But on May 26, 1865, McMillen was appointed by brevet a brigadier general in the Volunteer Force of the U.S. Army, the appointment to date from December 16, 1864, "for gallant and distinguished services" in the Battle of Nashville. Two years later, July 16, 1867, McMillen was appointed a brevet major general, to date from March 13, 1865, for "gallant and meritorious services."

One of McMillen's accusers in his 1862 court-martial, Lieutenant Colonel James B. Armstrong, his second in command in his regiment, noted that McMillen had a passing good social position in Ohio which served him well.[40]

While McMillen was recovering from ignominious accusations and realizing increasingly higher career success, Thomas Benton Smith spent virtually the remainder of his life, 1876 to 1923 when he died, in a state hospital for the insane near Nashville. Thomas Fisher served as chaplain at the state hospital in 1904–1908 and became well acquainted with Smith.[41]

Smith's obituary writer in the *Confederate Veteran* recorded that all did not go well with McMillen henceforth. He wrote that when McMillen's causative role in Smith's injuries became known, the Grand Army of the Republic post in New Orleans, where McMillen was living, relieved McMillen of his official position in the post and required him to surrender his membership.[42]

One of the fatalities of the fight on the hill was Colonel William Shy, one of Smith's regimental commanders, whose name was given to the hill, now and ever since the battle known as Shy's Hill.[43]

The whole Confederate resistance began to crumble as soldiers of Cheatham's and Stewart's corps sought the most expeditious routes south of their positions in the direction of Brentwood. Lee's corps, as planned, fell back in an orderly manner down the Franklin Pike toward Brentwood, protecting the army's exposed rear. But Hood stated that, when he observed the collapse of his left wing, he beheld "for the first and only time a Confederate army abandon the field in confusion."[44]

Chalmers' cavalry, now consisting only of his escort and Rucker's brigade, had spent most of the day of the sixteenth, twelve miles out from Nashville on the Hillsboro Road where the road from Brentwood intersects, guarding against the contingency of a Federal flanking movement that might threaten capture of all of Hood's infantry.

Late in the afternoon, Chalmers with his escort and Forrest's "Old Regiment" under Colonel Kelley, moved east toward Brentwood to the Granny White Pike. They were later joined by the bulk of Rucker's brigade, minus the Seventh Tennessee Cavalry Regiment, which had been ordered south to

Franklin via the Hillsboro Road after the latter had skirmished on the road with troops of Brigadier General Richard W. Johnson's Sixth Division, U.S.A.

Chalmers had been ordered to move east on the road to Brentwood and to form a rear guard on the Granny White Pike, where early in the evening his troops formed a barricade astride the road just north of where the road to Brentwood intersects and saw their first significant action of the day.

In the gathering darkness, Federal cavalry under brigadier generals Edward Hatch and John Croxton and Colonel John H. Hammond came south down Granny White Pike in such force that, upon seeing the barricade and receiving warning shots, they decided directly to form in line and charge the Confederate defensive position.

Rucker being temporarily away, his undersized brigade was led by Colonel David C. Kelley, the physician-divine-artillerist-staff officer who would play a brief but important role in Thomas Fisher's professional life after the war. Although hopelessly outnumbered, Kelley and his men put up a furious struggle in hand-to-hand combat in the dark. When Rucker came upon the scene, he received a gunshot wound in his sword arm just after engaging in a fierce saber fight, resulting in his capture and the subsequent loss of his arm in a Nashville hospital.

In the end, the Confederate defenders were driven from the scene well into the night. They had suffered heavy losses, but they retired in order a mile east to Brentwood where they remained until the last of Hood's train, infantry, and artillery had passed in retreat. Then they camped on the Franklin Pike with Lee's rear guard for the remainder of the night, undisturbed by Wilson's cavalry, now in bivouac.[45]

But Hood's army was quite generally shattered and disorganized as it swept south in the drenching rain, snow, and sleet. Efforts to get it to regroup or to form a line of battle were unavailing. Not until they were south of Brentwood, nine miles south of their line on the first day of battle, did they bivouac, and fragments of commands were reunited. By then pursuit by the Union cavalry had been called off for the day because of darkness, inclement weather, weariness, and the stout defense of the soldiers of Chalmers' and Lee's commands.[46] It would be renewed the next day.

Thomas reported that he captured 4,462 Confederate soldiers in the two-day fight, and he gave his own losses as 387 killed, 2,562 wounded, and 112 missing. Hood reported that his losses in killed and wounded were small, but he gave no numbers.[47]

Since Hood's troops were fighting defensively from behind breastworks on both days of the battle and usually were giving way to superior numbers and firepower rather than fighting to the death, it is not unlikely that Hood's losses, except for captures, were less than those of Thomas. But Hood left fifty-four artillery pieces behind, testimony to a lack of attention to military detail egregiously aggravated by the muddy and frozen condition of the terrain and the virtual impassability of roads.[48]

Hood had ill-advisedly divided his cavalry so that it was unable to support his army in performing the intelligence gathering, destruction of enemy supplies, and fighting dismounted as infantry duties that Forrest's cavalry performed so splendidly. And the dispatch of Forrest with the bulk of his cavalry, along with a brigade of infantry, a total of about 6,500 troops, to demonstrate before Fortress Rosecrans at Murfreesboro and damage the Nashville & Chattanooga Railroad was a gratuitous weakening of his forces before Nashville which also deprived Hood of the skill and advice of probably the most capable military tactician produced in the war, Forrest.

It may be acknowledged, however, that, even with the strongest force that he was capable of assembling before Nashville, Hood faced a virtually impossible task in winning the fight, owing to the relative strength of his and Thomas's armies. His only hope lay in getting reinforcements in sufficient numbers and with sufficient firepower to be able to challenge Thomas's burgeoning war machine. But reinforcements, of course, did not arrive.

Hood now faced the prospect of his whole army being captured or destroyed.

Chapter 9

Hood's Tennessee Campaign: Retreat, December 16–27, 1864

From the field on December 17, Schofield advised Thomas that citizens were reporting that Forrest had been killed at Murfreesboro. And another report alleged that Rousseau "reports Forrest killed and fifteen hundred of his men captured at Murfreesborough."[1]

Hood informed Forrest in the evening of the fifteenth that the battle at Nashville had commenced and that he should hold himself in readiness to move at any moment. Sensing the tide of battle, Forrest, on the morning of the sixteenth, moved his entire command operating in the vicinity of Murfreesboro to Wilkinson's Crossroads at the terminus of the Wilkinson Pike six miles west of Murfreesboro preparatory to moving south.[2]

Except for the 250 pickets under Colonel George Nixon left by Forrest east of Nashville on December 5, reinforced by Jacob Biffle's brigade on December 10 and by Buford's division on the eleventh, which were still patrolling about the Cumberland River near the Hermitage, Forrest had his troops assembled and ready to march with their prisoners and livestock on the sixteenth. Rousseau kept to his fortress and made no attempt to interfere with Forrest's departure.

On the night of the sixteenth, one of Hood's staff officers arrived with news of the disaster at Nashville and orders for Forrest to retreat south from Murfreesboro by way of Shelbyville and Pulaski, orders which would have removed Forrest from contact with Hood's main forces until they were virtually out of Tennessee and into Alabama, if they were fortunate enough to get that far.

Forrest sent word to Abraham Buford on the Cumberland to march south to La Vergne in order to protect Forrest's rear until he could move his artillery and wagon train. Then Buford was to make his way with all despatch cross country via secondary roads to join the rear guard of Hood's retreating army along the road south from Nashville to Franklin.

Since Forrest's sick, wounded, and wagon train were west of Murfreesboro at Triune, Forrest ignored Hood's orders to retreat south and moved instead to Triune. From the latter point, he ordered Frank Armstrong's brigade out of Jackson's division to proceed to join the rear guard of Hood's army as quickly as possible just as he previously had ordered Buford. Next he sent the remainder of Jackson's division to follow Armstrong.[3]

With his remaining straitened forces, including Brigadier General James A. Smith's infantry brigade, mostly barefooted, and Lawrence S. Ross's brigade of Texas horsemen, Forrest set out with prisoners and several hundred head of livestock, hogs and cattle, which, combined with virtually impassable roads, made his progress unavoidably slow. Forrest proceeded with the firm intention of intercepting Hood's army at Columbia where the Duck River, flowing toward the west, intersected the terrain and where Hood would briefly entertain the idea of halting his retreat and setting up winter headquarters.[4]

Biffle's brigade rejoined Chalmers at Brentwood on the night of the sixteenth. At daylight on December 17, Wilson's cavalry resumed its vigorous pursuit of the Confederate rear guard three miles south of Brentwood at Hollow Tree Gap in the most determined and threatening manner. Chalmers, whom Hood had placed in charge of the cavalry on the seventeenth, made a courageous stand, with his greatly outnumbered command, which held off Wilson's pursuit and gained time for the rear guard infantry to escape across the Harpeth River at Franklin. Here Buford's cavalry arrived from the Hermitage pursuant to Forrest's orders to reinforce the rear guard.[5]

Another stand was made two miles below Franklin near the crossing of the West Harpeth with the Columbia Pike. After bitter hand-to-hand fighting, the Confederate cavalry was outflanked and retreated five miles to a defensive position south of Thompson's Station and north of Spring Hill, where it went into bivouac for the night.

Lieutenant General Stephen D. Lee, commanding the rear guard, suffered a gunshot wound in the early afternoon of the seventeenth in a sharp encounter with Wilson's cavalry about four miles north of Spring Hill. The seriousness of his wound prompted him that evening to turn over his command to his second, Major General Carter L. Stevenson.[6]

On the eighteenth, Stevenson's men retreated south across Rutherford Creek, south of Spring Hill, on a bridge which they then destroyed. The creek was flooded and seemed to be unfordable.

There was little fighting that day, as Wilson had outrun his army's rations. Wilson's deficiency of rations provided the Confederates a propitious opportunity to change their rear guard. Lee's corps was replaced by Cheatham's. Brigadier Frank Armstrong's cavalry brigade and the remainder of Jackson's division, sent posthaste by Forrest from Triune, arrived and joined Chalmers' cavalry.[7]

Grant, stopping on the evening of the fifteenth in Washington on his way to take charge of Thomas's army in Nashville, wired Thomas that he would go no further and informed him that Union armies operating in front of Richmond had fired 200 guns in honor of his victory at Nashville. Major General

George Meade, before Petersburg, Virginia, ordered the firing of a 100-gun salute. And Major General Philip Sheridan from his headquarters in the Shenandoah Valley sent Thomas a congratulatory telegram informing the victorious general that his army had given him a 200-gun salute accompanied by unrestrained cheering.[8]

But Grant was still concerned about the threat of Forrest. He urged Thomas to take precautions that Forrest did not cross the Cumberland or Tennessee rivers on his way to inflicting further depredations against the Union war effort.[9]

The war, however, was at such a stage of Federal dominance that Forrest would never again be the threat to the tranquility of Union generals that he had been up to the end of 1864. Far from striking boldly and destructively at Federal armies or supply lines, on December 18, 1864, Forrest arrived in the evening on the north bank of the Duck River at Columbia, Tennessee, forty miles south of Nashville, at the head of Smith's infantry brigade, his own mounted staff, Ross's cavalry brigade, and his wagons, prisoners, and livestock. He would soon be reunited with his three cavalry divisions under Chalmers, Buford, and Jackson.

The next day, the nineteenth, Hood ordered Forrest to withdraw to Columbia, south of the river. Hood gave Forrest command of the rear guard on the twentieth. On the previous day, the last Confederate soldiers crossed to the south side of the Duck River at Columbia.[10]

At Columbia on December 19, 1864, the Fisher brothers of the Eleventh and other members of their detail, the remnant of Company C at Huey's Duck River mill in Marshall County, were reunited with the officers and men of the Eleventh Tennessee Cavalry after an interval of three painful weeks. After leaving the mill, they destroyed bridges over the swollen Duck River, forcing Wilson's attacking forces to wait for the arrival of pontoons to cross.

Yet Company C of the Eleventh lost another soldier to desertion on the seventeenth. He was Henry T. Drake, 35, who surrendered to Federal troops, then took the oath of allegiance on January 10, 1865, in Nashville. What happened to Drake thereafter is unknown. There is no subsequent military service record for Drake.

Hood had earlier decided to turn and make a stand at the river in Columbia. But then he observed the condition of his army, largely without shoes, stockings, overcoats, jackets, hats, and blankets, as well as tents and oilcloths. The inclement weather took its toll in shivering, fever, colds, and exhaustion in what was becoming a particularly bleak winter. So Hood gave up his hope for a stand at Columbia and pressed on to the wider safety of the Tennessee River in Alabama. He and the main body of his troops left Columbia for the south on the morning of December 20. He was going by way of Pulaski to Florence.[11]

When Forrest was given command of the rear guard, he told Hood that he would need some infantry to make the rear guard effective. He suggested that Major General Edward C. Walthall, a thirty-three-year-old Mississippian, be put in command of eight picked brigades to assist in holding off Wilson's hard-charging cavalry and infantry as they bore down on the rear guard of Hood's beleaguered army.

Hood agreed, and Walthall, under Forrest's command, on December 20 consolidated and reorganized his undermanned brigades, reducing their number from eight to four. They were commanded by brigadier generals Winfield S. Featherston, Daniel H. Reynolds, and Joseph B. Palmer, and Colonel Hume R. Feild. Personnel in the brigades were principally from Georgia, Mississippi, Tennessee, Texas, and Virginia. Although they came from over thirty regiments, altogether they numbered only 1,920 effective fighters, of whom 400 were without shoes.[12]

To keep his infantry in fighting trim and readiness, Forrest arranged for those without shoes to be transported in wagons until they were needed to fight. Upon command, they alighted and maneuvered appropriately to oppose the enemy. Again, upon command, when they were no longer needed to be in position on the field, they mounted wagons to be taken to the next point of action and, finally, to be taken to the pontoon bridge which took them to safety across the Tennessee River.[13]

Upon assuming command of the rear guard, Forrest was allowed some time to organize his command as a result of the inclemency of the weather. Heavy rains had so swollen the Duck River that Thomas's pursuing army was unable to cross the stream upon first approaching its banks. Not until December 22 were the Federals able to cross, using pontoons belatedly brought from Nashville to help fabricate a floating bridge. The bridge was built by infantry under Colonel Abel D. Streight.[14]

When the first Federal units under Edward Hatch reached the north bank of the Duck River, opposite Columbia, they commenced shelling the town on the afternoon of December 20. Under a flag of truce, Forrest parleyed with Hatch across the turgid, roaring waters of the river, requesting that the shelling cease, explaining that there were no Confederate soldiers in the town, only several hundred wounded soldiers of both sides and permanent residents. By agreement, the shelling stopped.[15]

Forrest had already sent Walthall's infantry down the road to Pulaski, while his reunited cavalry, reduced from 5,000 to about 3,000 men by the attrition of the Nashville campaign, covered the rear. He set up his headquarters and a picket line at Beechlawn, the Warfield home, three miles south of Columbia. The line engaged the attention, shot and shell of Federal artillery when the cutting edge of Thomas's infantry approached.[16]

Forrest sent Chalmers' division down the road to Bigbyville and Campbellsville, just west of the main road to Pulaski while Buford and Jackson covered the infantry's rear down the main road. Forrest fell back two miles to a gap in the hills through which the main road ran, giving him a natural defensive barrier where he checked the Union advance. Later in the day, he fell back another ten miles all the while keeping his wagons and livestock from being captured. He camped at Lynnville the night of the twenty-third.

On the morning of December 24, Forrest called for Walthall's infantry to return thirteen miles north to the village of Lynnville and rejoin him. At this point Chalmers' division also rejoined him. Together, infantry and cavalry marched three miles north, where they met the enemy and held him in check for two hours in a severe engagement. Then Forrest withdrew two miles and took position at Richland Creek where Hood's rear guard engaged in another heavy fight.[17]

On the twenty-fourth, William Stratton Fisher of Company C of the Eleventh Tennessee Cavalry rejoined his company and regiment in Bell's brigade of Jackson's division after being absent at home at Cave Spring and in transit. Will had gone home on November 28, in the evening of which Forrest's cavalry had crossed the Duck River headed north toward Spring Hill.

But Will and a contingent of the Eleventh had crossed the Duck River at Leatherwood Creek, upstream from Columbia, on November 24. They had camped at Hurt's Crossroads until the evening of the next day. Then they moved out toward Salem in Rutherford County and cut the telegraph wires and damaged the tracks of the Nashville & Chattanooga Railroad on November 26 before moving down to Chapel Hill to camp on the twenty-seventh.

Owing to his capture and ill health, Will had had two previous prolonged absences from duty, once in 1863, January 15 to June 29, when he contracted measles in prison, and again for forty days in the spring of 1864, with a respiratory problem. In Hood's Tennessee campaign, he had been in the vanguard of Forrest's cavalry north of the Duck River, cutting rail and telegraph lines when he became ill and left his command for home. On December 17, he reported back for duty to his company commander, Captain T.C.H. Miller, near the home of a Company C comrade, H.G. McCord of Chapel Hill. But two days later, he returned home for a day. Then, stopping in the homes of friends and acquaintances along the way, he began making his way back to Hood's army, retreating toward Pulaski.

On December 20, he stayed at the Crutchlaws'. The next day, he had lunch—he called it dinner—at the Hendersons' and stayed at the widow Abernathy's home. On the twenty-second, still proceeding in the direction of Pulaski, he stopped by the Parsons'. The next day found him in Pulaski while his regiment was just north at the village of Lynnville. On the twenty-fourth, he rejoined his regiment and stayed with it until the surrender in May 1865.[18]

In the engagement at Richland Creek on Christmas Eve, General Abraham Buford was wounded and relinquished his command to Chalmers, who now commanded both his own and Buford's division. Forrest's rear guard continued to fall back, this time to Pulaski, the last town of significance in Tennessee before the army retreated into Alabama. The improved macadamized turnpike ended at Pulaski. The dirt road from Pulaski to Bainbridge on the Tennessee River, now mostly a ribbon of deep mud ruts and hoof prints, was almost impassable.

At Pulaski on Christmas morning, Forrest destroyed all ammunition which Hood's infantry had been unable to take south, and he burned two railroad trains to prevent their being retaken, trains which had been captured at Spring Hill four weeks previously.[19]

The Nashville & Decatur Railroad ran from Nashville to Pulaski, but it had been so badly damaged by both armies that it was unusable on Hood's retreat from Tennessee. The line continued south of Pulaski to Decatur, Alabama. Thomas had sent a force under Steedman by rail from Murfreesboro to Decatur to block any attempt by Hood to cross the river there, so Hood, with his broken army, wisely chose not to provoke a fight in that direction. From Pulaski, Hood left the railroad and marched southwest, arriving on the banks of the Tennessee on December 25.

The next morning, the lead units of the infantry of the Army of Tennessee began crossing the Tennessee River across from the town of Bainbridge, east of Tuscumbia. A bridge was constructed from pontoons which had been transported all the way to Nashville and back, augmented by some pontoons captured earlier by Roddey's cavalry at Decatur and floated down the river to Bainbridge. Hood's army began to cross the river on the morning of the twenty-sixth.[20]

Jackson's division fought a brisk action at Pulaski on Christmas Day, after which Forrest took a position seven miles south at King's Hill where, in a heavy engagement, Forrest's soldiers killed and wounded 150 of the enemy and captured a large number of men as well as one field piece. Forrest had maneuvered his pursuers into an ambuscade in a V-shaped ravine where infantry, cavalry, and artillery poured in a withering frontal and enfilading fire prior to charging.[21]

The next day the rear guard had one last sharp confrontation with the pursuing army at Sugar Creek, where Hood's army ordnance wagon train had been stopped while its mules had been used to help haul the pontoons to the river. The rear guard infantry, Reynold's and Feild's brigades, and two mounted regiments of Ross's brigade, turned and faced their pursuers in a dense fog which concealed the Confederate line, while Forrest placed a few decoys out in front to draw in the attackers. When the attack came, the defenders, reacting savagely in adversity, sent a firestorm across the line, driving the attackers into the creek and taking prisoners and horses.

The action resulted in the rapid withdrawal of the Union column, whereupon the pursuers were pursued for two miles. Forrest cut off his pursuit when Union troops under Hatch showed no disposition to recommence the fight. Forrest reported that Union losses were 150 killed and wounded, many prisoners and horses captured, and 400 horses killed.[22]

Hood's ordnance wagons got away safely, and Forrest fell back in the fog and camped that night sixteen miles from the Bainbridge ferry. The next day, the twenty-seventh, he delivered what remained of his rear guard, unmolested during the last twenty-four hours, organizationally intact, and reportedly in surprisingly high spirits, to the pontoon bridge at the Tennessee River and crossed over in the evening.[23]

In summing up the role of his command in Hood's Tennessee campaign, Forrest reported his cavalry was engaged every day with the enemy from November 21 to December 27. His casualties were heavy. He managed to bring out three more artillery pieces than the number with which he came in. His command destroyed 16 blockhouses and stockades, 20 bridges, 4 locomotives, 100 cars and 10 miles of rails, and captured several hundred horses and mules, 20 yoke of oxen and 1,600 prisoners.

Forrest lost from his cavalry command 39 killed and 366 wounded, a total of 405 casualties. The hardest hit of Forrest's brigades was Frank Armstrong's, which suffered 20 killed and 127 wounded. Biffle's brigade of Chalmers' division had the lightest losses, with one killed and 17 wounded. Chalmers' division had the lightest losses of the three divisions: seven killed and 84 wounded. Jackson's division suffered most heavily: 21 killed and 158 wounded. But neither the Eleventh Tennessee nor the fragment of the Fourth with Hood were mentioned as sustaining any killed or wounded in the Return of Casualties for November/December 1864 compiled by the acting medical director of Forrest's corps, J.B. Cowan.[24]

While Forrest did not mention desertions in his report, Chalmers reported a heavy rate of desertion, but no numbers, in his division, beginning on December 16 when the army began its flight south from Nashville.[25]

Thus ended the last, pathetic, albeit courageous and spirited, flicker of John B. Hood's belated grand scheme to establish the Army of Tennessee on the banks of the Ohio, to end the war by threatening invasion of the Middle West or, turning east, by crossing the mountains and threatening the Army of the Potomac in front of Petersburg and Richmond so that it necessarily would be withdrawn and used to defend Washington from capture. In pursuit of his ambitious design, Hood had marched his army almost five hundred miles within six weeks and fought two major battles in which his army was badly mauled and quite nearly destroyed.

On December 29, 1864, George H. Thomas issued an order stating that the pursuit had come to a close ending a campaign which he described with apparent hyperbole as "brilliant in its achievements and unsurpassed in its results by any other of this war."[26]

The end of the campaign indeed seemed to sound the death knell of the Southern Confederacy. And the pursuit of the Army of Tennessee after the Battle of Nashville was like no other in the war in terms of its length of time (eleven days) and distance (125 miles).[27]

Despite Thomas's predictably decisive victory at Nashville, his pursuit of Hood had failed to prevent the escape of Hood's army, or what remained of it. Thomas's assessment of the results claimed that "with the exception of his rearguard, [Hood's] army had become a disheartened and disorganized rabble of half-armed and barefooted men...." To Forrest's rearguard, however, Thomas paid a gallant tribute. He wrote that it "was undaunted and firm, and did its work bravely to the last."[28]

Chapter 10

Redeployment and Wilson's Alabama Campaign, December 28, 1864–April 12, 1865

After crossing the Tennessee River on the evening of December 27, Forrest's cavalry rode through Tuscumbia and camped successively at Barton's Station, Alabama, and Iuka and Burnsville, Mississippi, on its way west to the environs of Corinth, where it took up duty picketing and foraging the country thereabouts as well as guarding the remnants of the infantry of the Army of Tennessee at Tupelo, fifty miles south.[1]

Roddey's brigade patrolled the south side of the Tennessee River from Decatur, Alabama, downstream to just across the river from the town of Waterloo at the Mississippi border,[2] where a major concentration of Wilson's cavalry would take place in March just prior to an unprecedentedly large cavalry operation against Confederate forces in Alabama.

On December 30, a Federal cavalry force of less than 600 men, under the command of Colonel William J. Palmer of the Fifteenth Pennsylvania Cavalry Regiment, slipped out of Decatur, Alabama, and went on a 265-mile raid south of the Tennessee River in northern Alabama. On the thirty-first, Palmer's cavalrymen drove off a small guard force of Roddey's cavalry from a wagon train after passing beyond Russellville. They captured and destroyed a train of Hood's pontoons which included 82 boats, 150 wagons, and 400 mules. The next day, after proceeding southwest through Nauvoo, Palmer overtook and destroyed another train consisting of 110 wagons and over 500 mules. Palmer reported he took 150 prisoners and destroyed from 750 to 1,000 stands of arms. Palmer thought it was odd that Forrest was easily within a day's march of him but did not pursue.[3]

On January 1, 1865, Forrest directed Chalmers to take Holman's Eleventh, Biffle's Nineteenth, and Wheeler's Sixth Tennessee cavalry regiments, Gantt's Ninth Tennessee Battalion (part of Gantt's Ninth was with Joseph Wheeler in South Carolina), the First Confederate, and that part of the Seventh Alabama Regiment that was mounted and consolidate them into four regiments to compose a brigade. Chalmers was to furlough for twenty

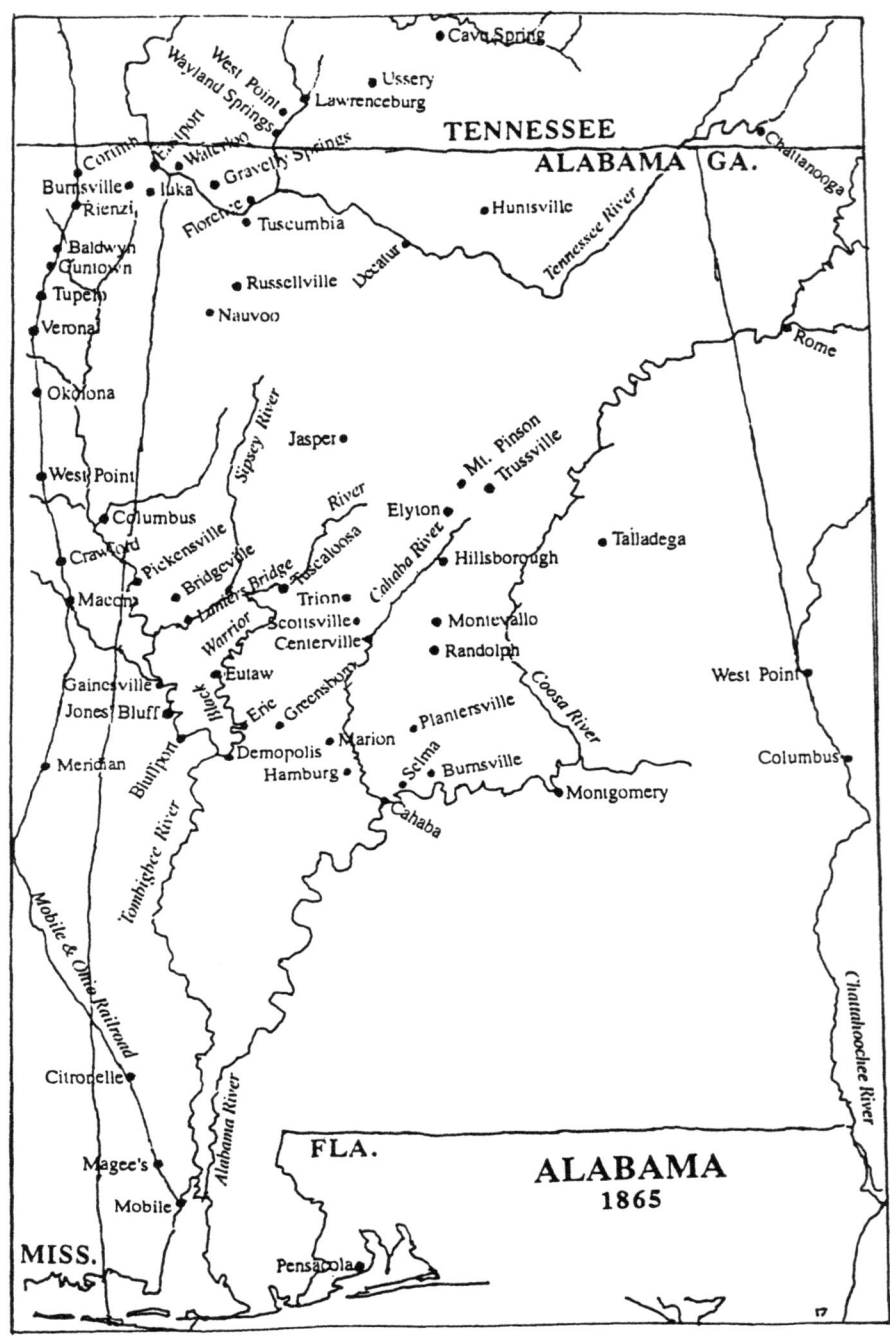

days the unmounted men of the Seventh Alabama so that they might return to their homes to get mounts, collect absentees, and find clothing for those left behind, after which they were to report back to Chalmers.

Chalmers was also directed to furlough for fifteen days the Fifth Mississippi Regiment. And he was ordered to furlough until the twentieth instant the newly consolidated Tennessee brigade with the promise that those who returned with a well-mounted recruit or deserter would get an additional twenty-day furlough later in the year.

Some of the brigade's troops joined the deserters and simply did not return to the army. Three soldiers from Company C of the Eleventh Tennessee Cavalry deserted during the period in January when the Tennessee brigade was furloughed. On January 5, J.W. Stilwell deserted, surrendered, then took the oath of allegiance at Columbia, Tennessee, on January 25. Theodore Riggs Adams, 22, an original enlistee of the company, deserted on January 11 but did not take the oath in Nashville until April 5, 1865. He was thereupon ordered to report monthly to the Provost Marshal General at Shelbyville beginning May 1, 1865. And Samuel Warner, a prewar resident of Marshall County, Tennessee, deserted on January 18. He took the oath, signing with his mark, on February 7 in Nashville. Warner had been captured at Morganton, Tennessee, on November 2, 1863, and had been imprisoned in Camp Chase and Ft. Delaware before being exchanged as recently as October 30, 1864.[4]

Fresh from disasters at Franklin and Nashville, the officers and men of the Army of Tennessee who did not desert showed surprising resilience. Within a few weeks of their arrival in Tupelo, they had rehabilitated themselves sufficiently to begin going off to fight other battles, although there was manifest reluctance among some to undertake arduous duties which they regarded as futile and unavailing in a cause already lost.

Still Forrest's cavalry aroused apprehension in the enemy. On January 2, 1865, George H. Thomas in Nashville was apprised by Rear Admiral Samuel P. Lee, the latter aboard his flag ship *Fairy* on the Tennessee River at Eastport, Mississippi, of his desire "that Forrest and his gang be entirely cleaned out of Western Kentucky and Tennessee." And Major General William T. Sherman, away in Savannah, Georgia, wrote on January 21 that he "would like to have Forrest hunted down and killed." But he doubted that this could be done at the time.[5]

Forrest's depleted cavalry was in need of everything a fighting force needs save military skills. Even its vaunted esprit de corps was sagging. On January 2, 1865, Forrest wrote dispiritedly from Corinth, Mississippi, to Richard Taylor, his departmental commander, regarding the poor state of his cavalry command, greatly reduced in strength and with insufficient numbers of serviceable animals. Forrest explained that in successfully covering Hood's retreat from Tennessee, it had become necessary for him to sacrifice his command. His losses in killed, wounded, and captured were large, and many of the soldiers he commanded had wandered off or gone home on their way out, often on the pretext that their mounts were lame.

Forrest stated that he needed help in procuring forage for his horses in northeastern Mississippi. The latter were subsisting on corn rations of only one third of their needs. He said that he might have to abandon his advanced position at Corinth and go south to Tupelo for forage for the animals. Otherwise the horses soon would become broken down. He was also short of horses to pull his artillery, of which he had only four batteries of four guns each. Explaining that he had never been to the capitol at Richmond, Forrest plaintively requested permission to go to Richmond to meet with leaders in the War Department there to explain the needs of the western army. Besides, he wrote, the visit would be recreation for him who had had no time off in over a year.[6]

When Forrest granted twenty days' leave to troops under Chalmers in the new Tennessee brigade, many reportedly were grateful to get time off to go home, although not a few did not thereafter return to the army. Most had had no furlough in over a year. Instead of returning to their homes, some preferred to travel to the few fashionable resorts that remained within Confederate lines such as Montgomery, Alabama, and the fleshpots thereof, or to visit displaced friends who had secure dwellings free of Yankee intruders.

Armed and alert to the likelihood of having to fight for their lives, some members of the Tennessee brigade, despite heavy concentrations of Federal troops between Corinth and their homes in Tennessee, managed to get home using stealth and inquiring of trusted informants along the way how to proceed without encountering Union soldiers in such numbers that they would risk capture or death. Doubtless some were able to get a new mount at home, badly needed because of the rigors of the Nashville campaign which either broke down or killed many horses. But there is no evidence that any were able to recruit well-mounted prospective soldiers to return to camp with them. Nor is it likely that many did.

There also is no evidence that the Fisher brothers returned to their home in January 1865 despite Forrest's order to furlough Chalmers' new brigade. William Stratton Fisher's diary indicates that he remained on duty in Mississippi with his command during the time others were furloughed. He does not mention where his brothers were or what they might have been doing until the twentieth of January when soldiers were to have returned to their commands.

In his memoirs, Thomas Fisher makes no mention of what he might have been doing during the period of the furlough. He states that his father, John Fisher, and the latter's son-in-law, Robert M. Haggard, planted all the corn they could get in the spring of 1865 because they believed that John's five sons would be home later in the year to cultivate and harvest it. They put in their largest planting ever, he wrote.[7]

One might believe that the decision to put in their largest corn crop was not one made solely by John Fisher and Robert Haggard without consulting with one or more of the five brothers who were expected to cultivate and harvest the crop. Such consultation might have taken place in January if the brothers had been at home on furlough at that time.

On the other hand, the consultation might have taken place late in 1864 when the brothers were on duty at the Duck River mill, only a few miles from their home in Marshall County. It is likely that the brothers, Monroe, Frank, and Tom, visited their home in the period November 29 to December 19, when Company C was detailed to guard the mill. On the latter date, the company left for Columbia to rejoin Forrest's rear guard. Will wrote that he was at home November 28 to December 20. He rejoined Forrest's rear guard at Lynnville on December 24, 1864.[8]

November–December 1864 probably was the first time since their enlistment almost two and a half years before that all four Fisher brothers from the Eleventh Tennessee Cavalry, Frank, Monroe, Tom, and Will, had been at home at the same time. Their visits had become very infrequent indeed since the summer of 1863 when the Army of Tennessee had retreated out of Middle Tennessee in the direction of Chattanooga. Thereafter their command had seen service primarily in East Tennessee and Georgia, retreating with Joe Johnston from Chattanooga to Atlanta just prior to their return to Middle Tennessee.

They may have just missed seeing their brother, Jim, with the Fourth Tennessee Cavalry, who, as previously noted, had leave to recruit enlistees and return stragglers found behind Federal lines in Middle Tennessee some time during the last half of 1864.

Jim might have been called upon, in concert with comrades-in-arms covertly operating nearby to play the partisan in military actions which might be destructive and disruptive to the occupying army. But by late 1864, partisan and guerrilla activity in Middle Tennessee had been curtailed by Federal authorities who moved against Confederate sympathizers, jailed or banished them, destroyed their property, or made them pay restitution for depredations against army personnel and local white Unionists. The Federals armed local Unionists to combat guerrillas and organized ex-slaves into Tennessee infantry regiments to guard railroads and waterways against attack, steps which strongly contributed to the success of their war effort.

George B. Guild, of Baxter Smith's Fourth Tennessee Cavalry, visited his home near Gallatin, well behind Federal lines, while on Wheeler's Middle Tennessee raid in August 1864. Guild believed there was extreme danger from armed Unionists, bushwhackers, and Federal soldiers as well as from ordinary-appearing citizens whom one could not trust when they were met on the road. As often as not, the latter might be informants or agents for the Federals.[9]

Thus the work that Jim Fisher had been sent to do was very difficult indeed in 1864 in Tennessee, a state almost entirely under military occupation.

And his work could be done with only meager success even by individuals with courage and conviction who were sufficiently alert to escape capture and sufficiently persuasive to occasionally break down the resistance of prospective recruits and delinquent soldiers to the idea of risking their lives in the service of a cause which had poor prospects of succeeding at this stage of the conflict.

There is no documentary evidence of when or where or even if Jim Fisher made contact with Forrest's cavalry when it returned to Tennessee in November 1864. If contact was made, he might have been told to fall in, to find and rejoin the fragment of his old regiment, the Fourth, that every possible effective soldier was needed in the army's advance. On the other hand, Jim might well have been thought valuable as a scout under the circumstances, garnering intelligence behind enemy lines and reporting back as directed. Many of his comrades who came into Middle Tennessee with Forrest who had good knowledge of the country and its people had been assigned to do exactly that.[10]

Then on January 20, 1865, Forrest ordered all fragmentary units in his army which were separated from any other fragment in the Carolinas to report there and consolidate their units.[11] Six companies of the Fourth, including Jim Fisher's own Company D, were then in South Carolina in Joe Wheeler's command. Whether Jim rode east to rejoin his company comrades is not known with certainty. But given the absence of evidence to the contrary, it is reasonable to believe that he did.

Jim's duty in Middle Tennessee was pursuant to a policy of the War Department in Richmond which was belatedly protested on March 18, 1865, by Forrest, with Richard Taylor's endorsement, in a communication to the department which pointed out that poor returns made the effort virtually useless. Further, the natural offspring of recruiting parties was, according to Forrest, "roving bands of guerrillas, jayhawkers and plunderers." Forrest believed that orders to send out recruiting parties represented "an exemption from duty for the war, a license to plunder, and a nest-egg of desertion." He stated that most men recruited behind enemy lines refused to come south to fight as members of the army where they were needed. Instead, they subsisted on plunder.

But in this matter Wheeler was in disagreement with Forrest. In his last report of the war, Wheeler, in summing up the condition of his command, stated his belief that "by discipline and by using every opportunity to recruit my ranks behind the enemy's lines in Kentucky and Tennessee, my rank and file was not only kept full, but gradually increased."[12] Wheeler, the West Point professional, normally reflected the views of headquarters more readily than did Forrest.

John Allan Wyeth, Forrest biographer and Civil War veteran, in writing of Forrest's furloughed soldiers going into occupied territory in January 1865, reported that some reverted to their partisan ranger character, a characteristic many of them never lost during the war; that they recklessly attacked isolated military blockhouses at bridges and waylaid small groups of Federal troops when the latter might be found to be vulnerable to surprise attacks. Some of these men reportedly captured supplies and horses and fired on Federal vessels operating on the Cumberland, Tennessee, and Mississippi rivers in the vicinity of their homes.[13]

But desertions from the Army of Tennessee became epidemic as an aftermath of the crushing defeats suffered at Franklin and Nashville. Some troops manifested a loss of confidence in their leaders. And the army's deplorable state of combat readiness was evidenced in wintertime shortages of shoes, clothing, field shelter, supplies, equipment, rifles, ammunition, and ordnance.

On January 14, Hood directed Forrest to be on the alert with picked bodies of cavalry to intercept deserters from the army. Hood hoped to make examples of some of the bolters in order to discourage others from taking the same course of action.

And on the same day, Hood, in a circular from headquarters of the Army of Tennessee, addressed a related problem, that of depredations by undisciplined armed soldiers in the vicinity of the army. Hood decreed that henceforth arms would be stacked and company rolls called frequently during the day to ascertain who might be absent from camp.[14]

The previous day, January 13, 1865, Hood, disabled in body and broken in spirit, requested of James A. Seddon, Secretary of War, to be relieved of command of his army. Ten days later, with Hood desiring to leave for Richmond, Lieutenant General Richard Taylor assumed command, by order of General G.T. Beauregard, Commander of the Military Division of the West, without waiting longer for a response from the War Department to Hood's request.[15] Taylor, chief of the Military Department of Alabama, Mississippi, and East Louisiana, commanded the army but a short time prior to its leaving, without most of the cavalry, for its final military duty in North Carolina.

Also on the thirteenth, Beauregard wrote from Meridian, Mississippi, to President Jefferson Davis that, judging from Richard Taylor's report of the disorganization and demoralization of the Army of Tennessee, plus the poor condition of roads and railroads east to Augusta, Georgia, in his considered judgment, it was unlikely that reinforcements could be sent in time to help General Hardee in South Carolina.[16]

But such help as was available would be provided for the last gasp of the Southern Confederacy as Sherman's juggernaut roared into North Carolina. Between January 20 and the end of the month, while 4,000 infantry were sent to Mobile, Alabama, to aid in its defense, what remained of the army, perhaps 15,000 infantry, was sent to North Carolina.

Lee's corps was the first to be sent east, alternately by rail, riverboat, and marching to Augusta, thence through upland South Carolina to its destination, the coastal plain of North Carolina. Cheatham's corps followed on the twenty-fifth, and Stewart's departed on the thirtieth.[17]

Pierre G.T. Beauregard, on January 22, recommended to General Samuel Cooper, Adjutant and Inspector General, C.S.A., in Richmond that Forrest be placed in charge of all cavalry in the Department of Alabama, Mississippi, and East Louisiana. Beauregard's recommendation was acceptable in Richmond as well as to Richard Taylor, the departmental commander. But Taylor went a step further. He not only made Forrest chief of all cavalry within his department, but gave Forrest command of all troops in the District of Mississippi and East Louisiana.[18]

Forrest assumed his new command on the twenty-fourth in Verona, a few miles south of Tupelo, and, on his own authority, added West Tennessee, site of his peacetime domicile and many of his successful wartime exploits, to the District of Mississippi and East Louisiana.[19]

Forrest, setting up his headquarters south of Corinth in West Point, Mississippi, sought to reorganize his new cavalry command on February 13, 1865, since depletions of manpower had reduced the old organizational designations to absurdly small units which could not operate effectively without a wholesale merging of units.

Tennessee troops, including those of the Eleventh Tennessee Cavalry, who, in Hood's Tennessee campaign, had been in either Bell's or Rucker's brigades, were aligned with Ross's brigade of Texans and the consolidated Eleventh and Seventeenth Arkansas regiments plus John W. Morton's battery, Leonidas Willis's battalion of Texans, and Joseph T. Cobb's company of Texas scouts to form a division commanded by Brigadier General William H. ("Red") Jackson.[20]

After the war, Jackson would enjoy international renown as successor to his father-in-law, William Giles Harding, in the operation of Belle Meade, near Nashville, the American turf's first and, in the 1870's and 1880's, most celebrated thoroughbred nursery. The influence of Belle Meade's stallions, Bonnie Scotland, Enquirer, Iroquois, John Morgan, Luke Blackburn, and Priam as well as the mares Ailene, Alaska, Tallulah, and Wanda, is still strongly felt through their progeny in America's thoroughbred racing industry.[21]

But Jackson's future was anything but promising at the reorganization of Forrest's command on February 13 when the Tenth and Eleventh Tennessee cavalry regiments were merged. The result was wholesale desertions, one officer and 21 men from Company C of the Eleventh alone, a high proportion of the already greatly diminished strength of the company. The deserters doubtless anticipated that consolidation of regiments presaged their participation in fresh combat with the enemy on new and unknown battlefields in a cause already lost.

On February 14 and 15, while in camps near Verona, Mississippi, the following Company C soldiers deserted:

2nd Lt. E.G. Hamilton	John L. Dillard
John Bailey	J.M. Dowdey
Robert Bailey, 25	J.P. Epperson
John Bomar, 32	James E. Farver
J.B. Bradley, 17	T.R. King
J.W. Bruce	G.W. Laughton
P.B. Call	Daniel Revis, 21
Joseph P. Cromer	James M. Smotherman
Francis M. Dillard	A.R. Snell
Isaac V. Dillard, 18	Robert Tanner
J.J. Dillard	John Trice

Thirteen of the deserters surrendered to the enemy and took the oath of allegiance at Nashville in either February or March 1865, according to their service records. Regarding the other nine, there are no records to indicate any subsequent service-related activity.[22]

Three brigades of Mississippi troops commanded by brigadier generals Frank C. Armstrong, Wirt Adams, and Peter B. Starke, as well as the Second Missouri Cavalry Regiment under the command of Colonel Robert McCulloch, were assigned by Forrest on February 6, 1865, to a new division commanded by James R. Chalmers.

Abraham Buford, wounded on his way out of Tennessee, was assigned on February 18 to command all the Alabama cavalry in the Department of Alabama, Mississippi, and East Louisiana. Buford consolidated the brigades of brigadier generals James H. Clanton and Phillip D. Roddey and Colonel Charles G. Armistead, plus other small unattached Alabama units into two brigades.

Forrest's promotion to the rank of lieutenant general was confirmed on March 2, 1865, and post-dated to February 28, 1865, by the Confederate Congress.[23] There was irony in the tardiness of the congress's approval of Forrest's final promotion until the last few fleeting days of the war after the South's defenses had eroded beyond restoration. And this for the one leader whose leadership placed him apart and marked him as perhaps least blameworthy for the South's crumbling military fortunes.

Brigadier General Daniel W. Adams was assigned by Taylor, his departmental commander, to command all troops in the District of Alabama on March 11. Meanwhile, on the same day, four more soldiers of Company C of the Eleventh Tennessee Cavalry deserted while in transit from Verona to West Point, Mississippi. The soldiers were J.M. Ramsey, 27; Thomas J. Snell, 18; J.A. Taylor; and Joseph K. Crosser. Ramsey, Snell, and Taylor, all prewar residents of Marshall County, surrendered to Federal authorities and took the oath of allegiance in Nashville on April 6. Crosser, of Bedford County, took the oath on March 24, 1865.

A week later the name of J.M. Bickman, a Company C straggler, appeared on a list of "prisoners of war, citizens, refugees, and Federal prisoners received at Eastport, Mississippi." The list was dated Headquarters, Fifth Division, Cavalry Corps, Military Division of the Mississippi [U.S.A.], Eastport, March 18, 1865.

Two days later, George W. Joice of Company C was captured near Fayetteville, Tennessee. How he happened to be there is unknown. A notation on his record stated: "Violating oath, captured." Joice had deserted in June 1863 and perhaps had taken the oath of allegiance and been released. His record was cleared, however, and he was permitted to take the oath of allegiance at Camp Chase in May 1865.[24] Forrest's District of Northern Mississippi and West Tennessee reportedly was in a deplorable state of lawlessness bordering on anarchy when Forrest took command. There were roving organizations of cavalry illegally assaulting the lives, rights, and property of citizens. Some were, according to Forrest, no more than "bands of deserters, absentees, stragglers, horse-thieves, and robbers."[25]

Forrest pledged himself and his command to arrest and exterminate the pillagers. On March 13, he sent his younger brother, Colonel Jesse Forrest, to sweep through more than a dozen counties in Northern Mississippi, to arrest and send deserters who ravaged the country to Brigadier General Marcus Joseph Wright at Grenada, commander of the District of Northern Mississippi and West Tennessee.[26]

Fatigue duty and boredom were commonplace in everyday life among Forrest's troops encamped in Mississippi for the better part of January, February, and March, 1865. Foraging, picketing, scouting, and resting in camp were the most common activities of the soldiers. The men of the Eleventh were in camp near Buena Vista for three days, January 24-26, in camp near Verona for thirty-eight days, January 28-March 6, and again in camp near West Point for two weeks, March 12-26.[27]

Life in camp was occasionally punctuated by activities which were out of the ordinary such as those involving Colonel David C. Kelley, second in command in Forrest's original battalion and regimental commands. Kelley was a Methodist clergyman who had served as a medical missionary in China prior to the war. He was to have a career after the war in Nashville and Middle Tennessee as an avant-garde gadfly with progressive views on race relations, higher education, liberal thought, and industrial democracy. He became a leader in a number of areas of developing social importance. Ironically, his career and that of Thomas Fisher clashed briefly in 1890 in a matter of canonical procedure when Kelley temporarily left his clerical appointment and made an unsuccessful race for governor of the state.[28]

Kelley preached to the troops at Verona on Sunday, February 12, accompanied by William H. Johnson, another Tennessee Methodist cleric, who also preached on Sundays, March 5 and 19. Johnson had served as a Confederate army chaplain and, prior to the war, had undertaken a ministry to slaves during 1846-1852. The venerable Bishop Robert Paine, in his sixty-sixth year, also preached to the troops on March 19 at West Point.

On February 16, the division was reviewed by its commander, William H. Jackson. This was followed four days later by a general review by the district commander, Nathan Bedford Forrest. On February 24, a very rainy day among many wet days, the four Fisher brothers and their comrades of the Eleventh underwent a general inspection.²⁹

On the twenty-eighth, there was a mass meeting at which Forrest's troops were urged to keep the faith and remain true to their cause by a number of speakers, principally Kelley and W.C. Whitthorne. The latter was a prominent state legislator from Maury County who had read law with the late President James K. Polk in Columbia, and had gone off to Virginia in July 1861 as Assistant Adjutant General to Brigadier General Samuel R. Anderson of Tennessee. Following the war, Whitthorne served in both the United States House and Senate. He had a reputation as an effective orator.³⁰

The troops heard more sermons in camp in Verona on March 1 and 5. And they were reviewed by their departmental commander, Richard Taylor, at West Point on March 24. Three days later, they were up and out of camp, on their way east to block an enemy incursion in Alabama.³¹

Within his district, Forrest commanded close to 10,000 troops of all kinds, infantry, artillery, and cavalry. But the territory encompassed within his district became of less importance militarily when both Richard Taylor and Forrest rightly divined that the likeliest target of a Federal strike would be Selma, Alabama.

At Selma were located ironworking plants, shops, arsenals, and navy yards, all of which were in the service of the Confederate government. Railroads and the Alabama River gave Selma's industry connections with other vital points of supply, including Alabama's coal and iron fields. Taylor's departmental headquarters were at Selma. Taylor had to be on the alert for possible attacks on Selma from the north by means of Wilson's cavalry, from the south from Union troops in the vicinity of Mobile or Pensacola, and from the west from troops as far away as Vicksburg on the Mississippi. Before the end of February 1865, he began to move his forces in the direction of Selma in a preemptive defensive move.³²

Owing to torrential rains, there was massive flooding in the Tennessee Valley in northern Alabama and Mississippi in late February and early March, which postponed and otherwise changed arrangements for an exchange of prisoners negotiated by Forrest and Colonel John G. Parkhurst, General Thomas's provost marshal general, February 23–28 at Rienzi, Mississippi.³³

The floods also delayed an unprecedentedly large expedition by Wilson's cavalry deep into the heart of Alabama in the direction of Selma. And still the rains came, covering much of the Gulf coastal plain in the central South. But before March 18, the Tennessee River had reached its crest just below Muscle Shoals. Between the eleventh and twenty-second, Wilson put across from Waterloo to the south side of the river 12,500 mounted men armed with Spencer repeating carbines and accompanied by three batteries of artillery, a train of 30 canvas boats, and 250 supply wagons. Wilson also placed 1,500 equally well-armed dismounted soldiers to guard the wagon trains. It was Wilson's plan that they would become mounted as soon as horses for them were impressed or captured.

Wilson's force was comprised of the First, Second, and Third Cavalry divisions of the Military Division of the Mississippi under brigadier generals Eli Long, E.M. McCook, and Emory Upton, respectively. It was the largest, best equipped, best manned, and best-led cavalry force ever assembled and organized in the United States. Wilson expected to be out on an expedition of sixty days' duration.[34]

Their Confederate adversaries had never come up against a force with as much firepower and staying power as this one. Wilson's Gargantuan force introduced an entirely new element in the fighting of the war. It had been assembled in response to the resourcefulness of Nathan Bedford Forrest, who would, or so George Thomas believed, be able to quickly dispose of any Union cavalry force short of one that was totally and crushingly overwhelming. U.S. Grant in Virginia had advised Thomas to send a force of 5,000 cavalry to demonstrate against Tuscaloosa and Selma. But in the face of Thomas's and Wilson's strenuous objections, Grant demurred and consented, and the larger force took the field to march to Selma.[35]

Assembled near Gravelly Springs, Chickasaw, and Waterloo, Alabama, and personally led by Wilson, the cavalry started south from the Tennessee River unmolested on three roads, coming together at Jasper, seat of Walker County. At Jasper on March 27, 1865, Wilson learned that Forrest was sending Jackson's division east on the right flank of Wilson's planned route of advance. Wilson thereupon ordered his command to leave their wagon train behind and move with the greatest speed in the direction of their target, Selma. Everything they carried for the use of each soldier would be either on their persons or on pack mules.[36]

They then marched to the town of Elyton, seat of Jefferson County and future site of the iron and steel center of Birmingham, arriving there on March 29–30. Here Wilson detached from McCook's Second Division, Brigadier General John T. Croxton's brigade of 1,800 to march southwest to Tuscaloosa to destroy government stores and supplies, as well as public buildings, including the buildings of the University of Alabama, where student cadets were trained. Croxton was expected to rejoin the main force at Selma by way of Centerville once his tasks were accomplished in Tuscaloosa.[37]

Emory Upton's Third Division, in the lead, proceeded south and reached Montevallo on the evening of March 30, where it proceeded to destroy four iron furnaces and other militarily useful property. Eli Long's First Division, along with La Grange's brigade out of the Second Division, crossed the Cahaba River at Hillsborough on the railroad bridge and followed Upton to Montevallo, arriving on March 31.[38]

Here Wilson learned that there was a Confederate force just below the town, a force which Wilson believed to be Forrest, who, Wilson assumed, would be intent as always upon striking the first blow. But Wilson determined that he himself would strike first and thus gain the initial advantage Forrest usually claimed.

The Confederate force Wilson encountered, however, was not Forrest, but consisted of a part of Abraham Buford's Alabama cavalry, without Buford, P.D. Roddey's brigade, and a fragment of Lyon's brigade of Kentuckians led by Colonel Ed Crossland, plus a few hundred infantry under Brigadier General Daniel W. Adams, Alabama district commander, up from Selma, a force of about 1,500.[39]

Forrest still was miles to the west, although advancing rapidly with his 75-man escort and a picked company of 200 of Frank Armstrong's brigade in the direction of the projected route of Wilson's advance. And Forrest had ordered his division commanders, Chalmers, en route to Selma from Mississippi with two brigades, and Jackson, at Tuscaloosa, to proceed with all speed so that they might either intercept or follow in the wake of Wilson's column so that the latter might be hit front, rear, and flank.

Wilson struck first, on March 31, 1865, at Six Mile Creek below Montevallo, and began what would turn out to be the beginning of the last battle of the war for those members of Forrest's command who were able to get to the scene of the action, a running battle which lasted forty-eight hours and ended with the capture and destruction of Selma.[40]

Forrest's battle plan was revealed to Wilson by the capture of one of Forrest's couriers on April 1. With the information he gained, Wilson took counter action which resulted in Jackson's never arriving at Wilson's rear, as Forrest had planned, and taking no part in the two-day action.[41]

On March 23, Forrest had ordered two components of Chalmers' division to Selma, Frank Armstrong's brigade and Captain Alfred B. Hudson's Mississippi battery, the latter originally known as the Pettus Flying Artillery until Hudson was killed at Shiloh in April 1862. Hudson's battery was now commanded by Lieutenant Edwin S. Walton.

Two days later, Forrest ordered Brigadier General Peter B. Starke's brigade, also of Chalmers' division, to Selma. Starke and his brigade, however, never arrived.

Chalmers' Third Brigade under Wirt Adams was left behind in Mississippi to guard the north-south railroad that ran virtually the entire length of the state south from the Tennessee border, through Corinth, Tupelo, Meridian, and into Alabama to Mobile near the Gulf of Mexico.

Jackson's division of Tennesseans, Texans, and Arkansans had been ordered by Forrest to go from their Mississippi headquarters to Selma via Tuscaloosa to get closer to Wilson's approaching army.[42]

Taylor, upon learning of the Union advance south of the Tennessee, wrote to Forrest on March 26 that he looked to Jackson's division, now at

Tuscaloosa, in concert with Hylan B. Lyon's small command, to "meet, whip, and get rid of that column of the enemy as soon as possible."

As late as March 28, Taylor still had no idea what sort of behemoth force he faced to the north. He expressed a hope that he could turn back Wilson's raiders in three or four days. Then he would be free, he anticipated, to turn his forces to aid in the defense of Mobile at the south from attack from Union forces at Pensacola.[43] But such a scenario was not to be.

Forrest advanced from his headquarters at West Point, Mississippi, into Alabama, with a well-conceived but ill-starred strategy for dealing with Wilson's invading force. He had crossed the bridge over the Cahaba River at Centerville when he soon heard the sound of fighting near Six Mile Creek on the afternoon of March 31, 1865.

He hurried forward in the company of a force of 275 and struck Wilson's troops just north of the fighting, stampeded and fought through a portion of the column, then turned and struck the most advanced troops to the south, took prisoners, talked to the wounded to gather information, swung off to the east again, made a circuit of Wilson's most advanced forces, and in the evening came into the Confederate camp below Randolph, sixteen miles south of Montevallo, to which the pitifully small resistance had been pushed by Wilson's troops in less than half a day's fighting. He was but a short distance from where Emory Upton's division camped that night fourteen miles below Montevallo.[44]

In the evening, Forrest wrote a message to Jackson, describing the movement of the enemy and urging him to proceed in such a manner as to be able to participate in attacks on Wilson's force. But he told Jackson not to bring on a general engagement alone since he believed Wilson's force was too large for him to take on. Jackson was to avoid engaging unless he found the balance of Confederate forces within supporting distance.[45]

But the next morning, April 1, all three Union divisions met Forrest's force of less than 1,500, pushed them back, and captured Forrest's courier.[46]

Thus Wilson firmly seized control of events and assured his victory against an enemy which never could bring to bear against him the full but inconsiderable weight of its depleted forces. In order to assure that Jackson's division did not interfere with his progress toward Selma, Wilson sent McCook, with Colonel Oscar H. La Grange's brigade replacing Croxton's, to cross the Cahaba River at Centerville, join with Croxton's brigade advancing on Tuscaloosa, attack and break up Jackson's force, then rejoin Wilson's main force via Centerville.[47]

And Chalmers, commanding Forrest's other division, already greatly depleted in strength, was at Marion on April 1, having made slow progress eastward against the ravages of the high water which delayed his crossing flooded swamps and streams with no bridges.[48]

Wilson had an advantage in terms of the flooding owing to his coming from the north in his invasion. Once past the mighty Tennessee, which he crossed March 11–22, 1865, unopposed except by the swirling, turgid waters near their crest, his path southward to Selma, took the high ground and went with the flow of the streams except for his having to cross the upper reaches of the Cahaba in Jefferson County where the comparatively slim volume of the headwaters was no great obstacle.

When Forrest established his first defensive position near Randolph on April 1 to oppose Wilson's advance, he had fewer than 2,000 men to oppose 9,000, the latter equipped with repeating rifles, which gave them many times the firepower of their enemy. Wilson's force consisted of Emory Upton's Third Division numbering 3,900 and Eli Long's First Division of 5,127.[49]

At Bogler's Creek on the first, Forrest received his fourth wound of the war pursuant to a saber charge upon his headquarters by four companies of the Seventeenth Regiment of Indiana Cavalry, a charge which was met defiantly by Forrest and his escort using their revolvers two to a man as they mixed with the charging Indianans in lethal hand-to-hand conflict. Forrest's wound was inflicted on his arm by saber hacks from the hand of Indiana Captain J.D. Taylor, whom Forrest killed with his pistol, not without a considerable loss of the general's blood.[50]

Forrest's meager force was pushed back twenty-four miles on the first day Forrest was personally in command and stopped at Plantersville in the evening, only nineteen miles north of Selma, after taking severe assaults at Bogler's Creek or Ebenezer Church, only five miles from Plantersville.[51]

The next day, April 2, Forrest arrived in Selma and prepared as best he could a nondescript force of 3,000 regulars, militia, old men, and boys to defend Selma's entrenchments against Wilson's army, in the flush of victory, after he saw Richard Taylor, departmental commander, escape by train to Demopolis from his headquarters in Selma.[52]

Wilson's advanced skirmishers began to appear before the town by two in the afternoon. A bit after 5 P.M., Wilson's force began its full 9,000-man attack against Selma's defenders.[53]

The night before, Wilson had found at Plantersville an English civil engineer named Millington who said that he had planned and constructed the defenses of Selma. Wilson said that Millington was quite willing to reconstruct for him on paper the detailed plan of the defenses. Selma was fortified with a single line of entrenchments surrounding the town in horseshoe shape and terminating above and below the town at the Alabama River.[54]

Armed with the plans of Selma's defense and commanding a cavalry force of overwhelming size, Wilson had every reason for confidence in attacking Selma just before dark on April 2. Forrest had a vastly inferior force with which to engage him. Jackson's and most of Chalmers' divisions were still west of the Cahaba River, and Buford's division was split with Roddey's and a part of Lyon's brigade at Selma. But the remainder of Buford's division was with Buford south of the Alabama River scouting for the reported approach of a Federal force from Pensacola.

With the state militia manning the center of the Confederate defenses, it did not take long for Wilson's attacking force to cave in the center, taking 2,700 prisoners and 26 field guns, according to Wilson, and pushing back the troops on the flanks.[55]

A fierce assault was made by Brigadier General Eli Long on Frank Armstrong's brigade of 1,432 men on the Confederate left, resulting in over three hundred casualties among Long's men. Long, together with three of his brigade commanders and four colonels, was among the wounded.[56]

Forrest, with his escort, together with Armstrong and Roddey and fragments of their brigades, cut their way out of Selma and out the Burnsville road to the east. On his way out of Selma, Forrest slew an unknown Federal soldier who assailed him, the thirtieth and last such slaying by Forrest in hand-to-hand combat since his first engagement at Sacramento, Kentucky, on December 28, 1861, when Forrest personally brought down three of the enemy.[57]

Still within sight of the flames rising above Selma, Forrest's escort captured a vidette of the Fourth United States Regular Cavalry who informed his captors that there were soldiers of his unit on the nearby property of one M. Godwin. Lieutenant George Cowan, head of Forrest's escort, wanted to surround and capture the troops. But the escort refused to mount the attack if Forrest led them. They insisted, probably because of Forrest's most recent battle wound, that he stay a quarter of a mile back with the horse-holders. The general agreed.

Forrest's troops stealthily approached the house, but their discovery led to a bloody exchange of shots resulting in the killing or capturing of virtually the entire contingent of soldiers lodged in the house. A Federal account of the action refers to it as an unprovoked attack upon sleeping men whose cries for surrender went unheeded. The day after the attack, the Godwin house reportedly was burned to the ground by angry Federal soldiers.[58]

The Fourth United States Regular Cavalry had previously engaged with Forrest's "Old Brigade" on April 10, 1863, on the Lewisburg Pike south of Franklin, Tennessee, when Captain Samuel L. Freeman, in charge of Forrest's artillery battery, was captured, then shot and killed when his captor, anxious to disengage, could not carry him away as his prisoner. This incident created among Forrest's soldiers a deal of ill feeling against the Fourth U.S. Cavalry which, it is said, was not forgotten.

The report of Wilson's Medical Director, Surgeon Francis Salter, U.S.A., alleged that there was an element of wanton brutality in the attack at the Godwin house. But the testimony of Confederate soldiers present was that there was nothing improper in the conduct of members of the attacking party, who made prisoners of Union soldiers who surrendered.

Wilson, the Federal commander, wrote that the attacking party killed "the last one" of the contingent of the Fourth U.S. in the Godwin house and, echoing the conventional Unionist view of Forrest's alleged brutality at Fort

Pillow, was critical of Forrest for permitting such atrocities. Otherwise, Wilson seemed in his writings to be quite in awe, indeed fond, of Forrest.[59]

On the morning of April 3, Forrest and his fellow survivors reached Plantersville to the north of Selma, where they turned west in the direction of Marion. A mile out of Plantersville, they met advanced elements of McCook's Second Division, which Wilson had sent to join Croxton two days earlier beyond the Cahaba River at Centerville, where they were to attack and deflect Jackson's division. McCook's force was now returning, escorting a wagon train, to rejoin Wilson's main force.

Forrest ordered a charge, actually a feint, which took McCook by surprise. But Forrest did not press his attack with his outnumbered force. His main goal was to join forces with his two lost divisions commanded by Jackson and Chalmers on the west side of the Cahaba.

Forrest withdrew his attacking force before McCook had opportunity to throw his men into line of battle. Then he drew off into woods to the left and continued his march toward Marion that day and night, reaching his destination on the morning of April 4, after three consecutive all-night rides and day fights for him and his command.

At Marion, Forrest found both Jackson and Chalmers with Starke's brigade, and his wagon train and artillery, the latter fresh from Mississippi. Jackson's command, unable to cross the Cahaba at Centerville, had come on south on the west side of the river and met Chalmers.[60]

Except for a portion of Buford's division, Forrest now had back what was left of his main cavalry force in the waning days of the war. But his troops would see no more fighting.

On April 5, Taylor, Confederate departmental commander, still looking to the future, wrote to Forrest: "It is useless to fight the enemy until we are strong enough to whip him. Hang on his flanks and rear, cut off small parties, and delay his movements till you can get your whole force in hand."[61] This was sound advice which Forrest would instinctively pursue.

Wilson, who was waiting at Selma for Croxton to rejoin him, proposed a meeting with Forrest under a flag of truce to discuss arrangements for an exchange of prisoners held by both armies. At noon on Saturday, April 8, in the town of Cahaba on the Alabama River below Selma, the meeting was held. It was the day before the surrender of Lee's army at Appomattox.

Cahaba, onetime Alabama state capital and the site of a wartime military prison in a converted cotton warehouse, was chosen for the meeting because it was easily accessible by both generals. Forrest rode down a spur rail line from Marion directly to Cahaba. Wilson took a captured river steamer from Selma a few miles down the Alabama River to the town.

Wilson was anxious for news of Croxton, whom he had sent off to take Tuscaloosa over a week earlier. He reported that Forrest appeared with his arm in a sling, depressed about the course of the war. But Wilson was reassured in his conversations with Forrest that Croxton was not among the dead, wounded, or captured, as he and Forrest, retiring to the parlor of the home of a local Unionist, Joel E. Matthews, a 56-year-old well-to-do land and slave holder, "treated each other like old acquaintances, if not old friends," according to Wilson, who came to know Forrest better after the war when both were engaged in the building of railroad systems.[62]

Following his meeting with Forrest, which failed to effect a prisoner exchange, Wilson completed destruction of the militarily useful works at Selma, and finished the mounting of his unmounted men who numbered fifteen hundred when he began his thrust toward Selma on March 18.[63]

He ordered that 25 horses be relinquished to Confederate surgeons on April 8, explaining that "General Forrest allowed our surgeons to retain their horses, and this is a reciprocal act of courtesy."[64] Then he had some 500 surplus horses destroyed to prevent their falling into the hands of the Confederates. The carcasses of many stayed as carrion to feed the scavengers of Selma. Others were disposed of in the Alabama River where they raised a stench for miles downstream.[65]

On April 10, the day after Lee's surrender in Virginia, Wilson and his unprecedentedly large cavalry force headed east toward Montgomery, the state capital and first capital of the Confederacy, crossing the swollen Alabama River on pontoons. Montgomery's defenders left the city without a fight. The city fell to Wilson on the fourth anniversary of the firing on Fort Sumter, Wednesday, April 12. Continuing eastward, Wilson advanced against scant opposition in a campaign of destruction to Columbus, Georgia, then to West Point and Macon, where on May 20, he was finally joined by Croxton's 1,800-man brigade which had been dispatched to destroy Tuscaloosa by Wilson from Elyton on the thirtieth of March.[66]

Meanwhile, as noted earlier, it was Wilson's cavalry, continuing eastward and flooding central Georgia, which, on May 10, 1865, effected the capture of the fugitive president of the Southern Confederacy, Jefferson Davis, as the latter fled south following the last meeting with his cabinet in Washington, Georgia, six days earlier.

On his way from Elyton to Tuscaloosa, Croxton had engaged Jackson's division near Trion on the morning of April 1. Jackson's troops, including the Eleventh Tennessee Cavalry, had left camp near West Point, Mississippi, on March 27. The next day, Samuel A. Smith of Company C of the Eleventh deserted, headed north, surrendered, then took the oath of allegiance in Nashville on April 15.

The balance of Jackson's troops proceeded on their way via Columbus, Mississippi, where they camped on the first night out. They crossed the state line and camped near Pickensville, Alabama, on the twenty-eighth. Proceeding via Bridgeville, they crossed Laniers Bridge over the Sipsey River where a drumhead court had sentenced two men to be shot for desertion on March 29, and the bodies of the deserters or victims had been placed on display by the sides of the road for all the troops to see.[67]

Jackson's division reached Tuscaloosa on March 30 and camped for the night. Forrest had written to Richard Taylor on January 2 of the need for draft animals to pull his artillery. Apparently the need persisted, and Jackson accordingly impressed horses belonging to the battery of the Corps of Cadets of the University of Alabama while encamped in the vicinity.

Colonel Landon Cabell Garland, superintendent and university president, a Virginian who in 1875 would become the first chancellor of Vanderbilt University in Nashville, lost no time in protesting to Jackson the impressment in the strongest possible terms. Also taken were two horses belonging to the mess hall which Garland said he sorely needed to keep the cadets fed. Jackson replied to Garland the next day, the thirty-first, disclaiming responsibility because, he said, he was acting on Forrest's orders. But he added that the impressment was as clear a case of military necessity as he had ever seen. The horses were needed to move Forrest's artillery in the present emergency of rushing to stop Wilson's raid. But Jackson graciously offered to return the two mess hall horses if Garland would send over someone to point them out.[68]

The next day, Jackson left Tuscaloosa on his way to Plantersville and camped that night nine miles northwest of Centerville. That day, March 31, Croxton's force intervened by chance between Jackson's fast-charging cavalry and his artillery and wagon train. The latter was struggling to keep up with the cavalry but was some four miles to the rear.

Croxton decided to follow the rebel cavalry and did so until it camped for the night. The morning of April 1, Jackson's scouts discovered the presence of Croxton's cavalry in camp at Scottsville. Jackson ordered a charge. His troops engaged the enemy heatedly, took prisoners, and pursued them for several miles in the direction of Trion.[69]

The next day, April 2, Jackson, still intent upon crossing the Cahaba River in accordance with Forrest's plan for hitting Wilson's main force, reversed his direction after chasing Croxton and found another enemy force, this time McCook's Second Division augmented by LaGrange's Second Brigade of the First Division, in the direction of Centerville.

Once again Jackson's men fell upon the enemy in camp in the morning, engaged them warmly, and drove them fifteen miles in a running skirmish into Centerville where they retreated across the Cahaba River and burned the bridge.[70]

McCook's force rode east to Randolph, near which they came across a Union wagon train going south. They fell in and escorted the train the rest of the way to Selma.[71]

Unable to cross the flooded river plain now that the bridge was burned, Jackson turned south, full of frustration, still on the west bank of the river, and camped that night eight miles south of Centerville on the road to Marion.[72]

Thus the capture of Forrest's courier the previous day, which led Wilson to send McCook to engage Jackson's division, played a decisive role in ensuring the success of Wilson's lightning thrust at Selma. Jackson was unable to join Forrest at Plantersville or to deter Wilson's main force in any way.

The four Fisher brothers of Company C of the Eleventh saw their last fighting of the war on April 1 and 2, the latter date the day Selma was taken. They were in action against elements of McCook's division in which they drove two forces of the enemy from the field, the first to Trion on the first, the second in the opposite direction to Centerville on the second.

Perhaps they took with them a sense of satisfaction that they ended their fighting on a winning note against a crack cavalry outfit which was not easily beaten. Will Fisher recorded in his diary that they (the men of Jackson's division) "routed the Yankees" (Croxton's cavalry) in the direction of Trion on April 1. Then they "routed the enemy" (McCook's cavalry) in the direction of Centerville on April 2.[73]

Jackson's division continued on south via Marion to Hamburg where the soldiers of Company C of the Eleventh Tennessee Cavalry picketed on April 3 and 4 while the rest of their regiment camped a mile away. Jackson's command proceeded to Marion Station on April 5, when Forrest and the remnant of his command which had fought at Selma returned. The same day, the men of Company C went to picket Johnson's Ferry on the Cahaba, where they remained through the tenth.[74]

Meanwhile, Croxton, after narrowly escaping from his confrontation with Jackson's division, came into and destroyed Tuscaloosa on April 3 and 4 with scant opposition from the home guards there. He had been ordered to come on south to Selma after destroying Tuscaloosa. But he dared not go through Centerville, the shortest way, because of the presence of Jackson's division in that direction. So he decided to try a roundabout route to the southwest of Tuscaloosa.

On April 6, after venturing all the way to Bridgeville, Croxton turned back and was engaged just after crossing the Sipsey River by troops under Brigadier General Wirt Adams about thirty miles southwest of Tuscaloosa. He escaped with the loss of two officers, 32 men, and two ambulances.[75]

Next Croxton decided that a more northerly route might harbor fewer obstacles. So he proceeded north of Tuscaloosa in the direction of Jasper, which he bypassed. On April 19, he was informed that Wilson had taken Montgomery and was headed east. He decided that it would be the better part of valor to push east across North Alabama and into Georgia and there rejoin Wilson's command. This he did via Mt. Pinson, Trussville, and Talladega in Alabama and Carrollton, Newnan, Zebulon, and Forsyth in Georgia, completing his odyssey in Macon on May 20.[76]

James Harrison Wilson (1837-1925), leader of the Federal thrust to Selma and a descendant of the Harrisons of Virginia, was born in Shawneetown, Illinois, attended McKendree College a year, then entered the United States Military Academy, graduating in 1860. After the war he engaged in building railroad systems in the 1870s. Back in the service, he went to Cuba in 1898 and to China during the Boxer Rebellion. He turned to writing and wrote his autobiography and a biography of Grant.

Wilson had been placed in charge of the cavalry of the Military Division of the Mississippi by U.S. Grant, who told Sherman, commanding officer of the division, whose cavalry heretofore had performed poorly, that Wilson would increase the efficiency of his cavalry by 50 percent. Subsequently Wilson congratulated himself that his campaign "from the Tennessee River through Selma, Montgomery, and Columbus may be fairly claimed as the most rapid, far-reaching, and successful cavalry campaign of modern times." And Richard Taylor, commanding Confederate forces in Alabama, wrote that "of all the Federal expeditions of which I have knowledge, his [Wilson's Alabama campaign] was the best conducted."[77]

The campaign introduced a new element in warfare, that of conducting "a great campaign with an army of mounted men." At its end, Wilson had almost 17,000 infantry and cavalry, including 3,600 colored infantry. Every cavalryman was mounted, and there were 8,000 horses and mules for its teams and for later distribution as needed. Wilson's command consisted of three divisions and six brigades with from three to five regiments to a brigade and a battery of horse artillery for each division. Wilson claimed it could march at an average speed of 35 miles per day.

His cavalry and its campaign, Wilson believed, had destroyed the means whereby the South might carry on its struggle to throw off the Northern invader. Wilson observed that, following his campaign, most of the combatants in the Confederate army were either prisoners of war or had deserted. The South's industry and transportation were in ruins. There was no possible way for the South to continue the conflict.

Revealing a degree of class consciousness, Wilson concluded that "'The rich man's war and the poor man's fight' had been fought to a finish. It was ended for good and all." Wilson's consciousness of class was similar to Sherman's who, in his march to the sea, enjoined his troops to discriminate "between the rich who are usually hostile, and the poor or industrious, usually neutral or friendly." The property of the rich, who instigated the war, was subject to confiscation and destruction.[78]

Indeed, the end of the war seemed almost in sight. But Forrest's command still had to maintain itself as a force in being, always watchful and on the alert for incursions by other Yankee army elements into the ever-smaller portion of Alabama that it occupied.

Chapter 11

An Army in Bivouac; Surrender and Home, April 12–May 25, 1865

Following his meeting with Wilson at Cahaba at noon on April 8, Forrest returned to Marion Junction. Two days later he decided to establish his headquarters at Gainesville, Alabama, on the Tombigbee River near the Mississippi border at the terminus of a rail spur of the Mobile & Ohio Railroad.[1]

Forrest wrote to Brigadier General William H. Jackson on the tenth directing him to assume command of all his (Forrest's) forces and to move them to the vicinity of Gainesville via Greensboro. Forrest had set out by rail, via Demopolis and Meridian, for Gainesville.[2] But on April 12, Taylor wrote to Forrest and directed him to prepare to intercept a Federal cavalry force which reportedly was advancing north from the vicinity of Mobile up the west bank of the Alabama River.[3]

Accordingly, Forrest, also on the twelfth, directed Jackson to halt his command near Greensboro and forage, but to send his wagons to Gainesville to pick up 100 rounds of ammunition per man and 400 rounds of shot and shell for each field piece.

The next day, Forrest's order of the twelfth was amended to say that, instead of Jackson sending wagons to Gainesville to pick up ammunition, Forrest would have the ammunition shipped by boat, the steamer *Lilly*, to Finch's Ferry or Demopolis. The amendment was occasioned by continued flooding, which made it difficult or impossible to get wagons to and from Greensboro and Gainesville.

Forrest also directed Jackson to send a scout to Montevallo and to keep open communications east to Talladega. This mission was expanded the next day when Jackson was directed to establish a telegraph line from Talladega to a safe point on the Georgia Railroad north of Montgomery so as to restore communications with the east.[4]

During this period, members of the Confederate Congress from adjoining and western states, displaced in Richmond, came into the remaining

Confederate lines in Alabama as refugees from Northern troops. They had left Richmond hurriedly in early April and were hard pressed to escape capture on the way to Alabama. They were reported much jaded with fatigue and anxiety and were eager to receive news of the latest developments.[5]

Forrest directed Jackson to send Captain Addison Harvey's scouts after Wilson and have them report on the latter's activities. And Jackson was ordered to impress much-needed able and fit horses for the command by exchanges of animals with locals. Exchanges were to be accomplished in all cases under the supervision of a trustworthy officer.

Addison Harvey and his scouts pursued Wilson to Montgomery, coming into town on the fourteenth as Wilson was leaving and skirmishing with the latter's rear guard. At Columbus, Georgia, on April 19, while aiding the local commandant in restoring order following Wilson's departure for West Point and Macon, Harvey was killed by a citizen of Columbus.[6]

Forrest wrote to Brigadier General Peter B. Starke on the twelfth, directing him to send a scout to Tuscaloosa to look for Croxton. If he found Croxton, Starke was to move his brigade up to drive him away.[7]

On April 15, Taylor acknowledged his desertion problem by issuing a general order which alerted all officers to be vigilant and attentive to the needs of their men in order to prevent "the worst of military crimes — desertion." The same day, Taylor wrote to Forrest to direct him to have Jackson move Forrest's command to Gainesville instead of facing south to oppose the Union cavalry reportedly coming from Mobile, a Union column which did not materialize.[8]

On Sunday, April 16, Colonel Kelley held services near Greensboro for such of the troops as desired to attend.[9] The date was the last Easter that Forrest's cavalry would be in the service of the Southern Confederacy. One might believe that the terminal stages of the war served to create a need among the troops for spiritual succor and that Kelley's services were well attended.

The same day, Forrest ordered the steamer *Marengo* to transport Jackson's division across the Tombigbee River at or near Finch's Ferry. But on Tuesday the eighteenth, Jackson reported that high water had delayed his crossing. On April 23, Brigadier General Tyree H. Bell's brigade crossed the river via the *Marengo*. And Forrest's Assistant Adjutant General, Major J.P. Strange, reported that there were other boats at Bragg's Bluff which would complete the crossing of Forrest's command.[10]

Thus from the fifteenth to the twenty-fourth, Forrest concentrated his troops in camps in the vicinity of his headquarters. Pursuant thereto, members of Company C of the Eleventh Regiment of Tennessee cavalry discontinued their picketing of Johnson's Ferry on the Cahaba and rejoined their command at Marion preparatory to moving west on April 11. Until the seventeenth, Forrest's troops had camped in several locations in the vicinity of Greensboro, about twenty miles west of Marion.

On Monday the seventeenth, Jackson's division moved further west and camped near Erie on the east bank of the Black Warrior River. Beginning on April 19, units of the division began crossing by boat to the west bank of the still swollen stream.

The Eleventh Tennessee became waterborne on the twenty-second, going upstream almost nine miles before landing. The next day, troops of the regiment marched still further up the river and camped near Eutaw.

On April 25, the regiment proceeded west in the direction of the Tombigbee River and camped some six miles from Bragg's Bluff. The next day, officers and men of the Eleventh moved with their mounts down to the river and boarded *The Reindeer*, which took them fifteen miles downstream to Bluffport, on the west side of the river. There they moved out two miles on the road to Livingston and camped. The next day, Thursday, April 27, they marched up the river to camp near Jones Bluff. This camp site would be their last prior to the surrender, the receipt of their paroles, and their departure for home.[11]

Rumors about what lay ahead were rife among the troops, as was the news that both Lee and Johnston had surrendered. There was a rumor on April 27 that not only had President Lincoln been assassinated, but also Secretary of State William H. Seward and his son. Later the troops learned that Seward had been wounded by an assailant.[12]

The Confederate central government was still operating, although no longer in Richmond. The president, cabinet members, and other key officials had gone first to Danville, Virginia, then to Greensboro, North Carolina, via the Richmond & Danville Railroad. On April 25 Forrest had felt constrained to address his troops and urge them to stand fast and do their duty regardless of what rumors might influence them to believe or want to do. Forrest expressed doubt that Lee had surrendered.[13] On April 30, William H. Jackson, the Eleventh's division commander, addressed his troops encamped on the banks of the Tombigbee to urge them to put no stock in unfounded rumors.[14]

Taylor wrote to Forrest on April 30 that an armistice existed while he met with Major General E.R.S. Canby, the Union commander in Alabama and Mississippi, at Magee's farm, twelve miles north of Mobile, a city which had been in Union hands since April 12, when Major General Dabney H. Maury's Confederate contingent of 5,000 evacuated the city.

Taylor and one officer, Colonel William Levy, later a member of the U.S. Congress from Louisiana, attended the meeting with Canby wearing well-worn, "rusty suits of Confederate gray" after riding a handcar, powered by two black servants, on the Mobile & Ohio Railroad from Meridian, Mississippi, south to the Magee farm.

Taylor noted that the meeting graphically demonstrated the differences in fortunes of the two causes of the attendees. Canby was escorted by a brigade with a military band and a celebratory retinue of officers in dress uniforms. A bountiful luncheon was served and consumed amidst joyous poppings of corks from champagne, provided by the victors, of course.

When the band played "Hail, Columbia," Canby graciously had it change its tune to "Dixie." Not to be outdone in civility and camaraderie, Taylor insisted that the band return to the tune of "Hail, Columbia," and expressed the hope that Columbia would again become a happy land, a sentiment which was enthusiastically approved with libations.[15]

The agreement and terms entered into by Canby and Taylor on April 29 were similar to the broad and liberal compact for surrender of the Army of Tennessee made by generals Sherman and Johnston in their first convention signed on April 18 near Durham Station, North Carolina.

In writing to Forrest, Taylor said that hostilities had ceased subject to renewal on forty-eight hours' notice only if the agreement were disavowed by either government. Taylor directed Forrest that no troop movements were to be made, scouting outside his lines would cease, and an officer under a flag of truce would be sent to notify Croxton of the truce.

But the government in Washington predictably disapproved of the agreement and terms as it had the first terms agreed to by Sherman and Johnston. Canby so informed Taylor. Their truce would terminate within 48 hours. Taylor then informed Canby that he wished to negotiate a surrender of his forces.[16]

Isham G. Harris, Tennessee's Confederate wartime governor in exile, addressed Forrest's troops on May 2, confirming reports of the surrenders of Lee and Johnston, and strongly recommending that officers and men stand fast and not give way to panic, stampede, or wild rumor.

Within days and with a price on his head, Harris would head for Mexico, thence to England. By 1868, however, he had returned to his legal practice in Memphis, only to receive appointment to the United States Senate in 1878, where he served until his death in 1897 in his seventy-ninth year.[17]

On May 4, Taylor again journeyed down the railroad, this time to Citronelle, forty miles north of Mobile where, in meeting again with Canby, he agreed to terms approved by the government in Washington for Lee's and Johnston's troops.

Thus Taylor surrendered the last Confederate forces in an operational mode east of the Mississippi. They consisted of the remainder of Forrest's cavalry at Gainesville and Maury's former Mobile garrison, fewer than 10,000 officers and men.

On May 4, Brigadier General Tyree H. Bell announced to troops of his brigade, of which the Eleventh was a part, that final terms of surrender had been agreed upon. Taylor promulgated the surrender instrument from his headquarters on Saturday, May 6, and commended its terms to the troops under his command.[18]

William T. Sherman was sure that men with temperaments such as Forrest's would not accept surrender and the life of a peaceful civilian. He had written to U. S. Grant from Raleigh on April 25 suggesting that Forrest, John Mosby, Red Jackson, and others, after the war had ended, would likely lead guerrillas, bands of desperadoes who care nothing about death or danger and its consequences, and there would be no peace.[19] But the man Forrest revealed in his address to his troops at war's end was a citizen totally amenable to reason and the facts.

In Forrest's camp in and about Gainesville, when the surrender order was received on May 5, there was more desperate talk about striking out for Texas or Mexico. And there was talk of carrying on the fight in small guerrilla bands, living dangerously, striking suddenly and disappearing quickly, but being a constant menace to Federal forces.

Forrest himself was uncertain at first where his duty was, to those who had stood loyally with him and wanted to carry on the fight, or to those who now wished to abandon a hopeless and beaten cause and who needed to be led into the ways of peace. He counselled about the matter with his assistant adjutant and inspector general, Major Charles W. Anderson, who, in their talks, came down on the side of peace.[20]

The momentum of the sentiment which favored peace continued to increase among the troops as they remained in their camps from April 27 to May 7. Then on the eighth of May, they were marshaled for the last time and relinquished possession of their arms at the brigade ordnance train.[21] There was no turning back now for most of Forrest's men.

Talk among his troops of further resistance was allayed by Forrest's farewell address on May 9. Surveying the hopelessness of further resistance, Forrest marshaled a strong argument for peace: "That we are beaten is a self-evident fact.... Reason dictates and humanity demands that no more blood be shed.... It is your duty and mine to lay down our arms, submit to 'the powers that be,' and to aid in restoring peace and establishing law and order throughout the land. The terms upon which you [were] surrendered are favorable to all...."

Forrest further warned: "Those who neglect the terms and refuse to be paroled may assuredly expect when arrested to be sent North and imprisoned." Soldiers who had experienced imprisonment during the war would almost surely be swayed by Forrest's warning.

The following day, May 10, 1865, Forrest's steadfast remnant of a once unbeatable force of mounted soldiers, most of whom had been prevented from participating in their leader's last losing battle of the war because they could not get across the flooded Cahaba River to Wilson's line of march, received their paroles pursuant to Forrest's concluding argument for peace. He said: "I have never on the field of battle sent you where I was unwilling to go myself, nor would I now advise you to a course which I felt myself unwilling to pursue. You have been good soldiers, you can be good citizens."[22]

The four Fisher brothers of the Eleventh were among the parolees on the tenth. As previously indicated, the fifth Fisher brother, James Wesley, is believed to have been making his way home from Georgia, having been dispersed by order of President Jefferson Davis on May 4. Without clear evidence to the contrary, it is presumed that Jim was with one of the last remnants of Forrest's Old Brigade under Brigadier General George G. Dibrell, which rode south from North Carolina as escort to Jefferson Davis and his cabinet as far as the site of the Confederate government's last meeting place in Washington, Georgia.

Thomas Fisher was still youthful at 21, but he must have deeply regretted the failure of the cause to which he had given his life for almost three years. Doubtless he and his brothers accepted the inevitable as stoically as they could. But committed soldiers who had stayed and fought to the bitter end, who had invested so much of themselves in the cause and fight, suffered a crushing and devastating depression which moved many of them to tears at the surrender which capped their failure to oust and dispatch an intrusive invader from their homeland and, as they believed, to achieve the goal of freedom from unjust coercion which they so earnestly sought.

The surrender terms were similar to those by which the Army of Tennessee was surrendered, one of which provided that transportation and subsistence were to be furnished at public cost for officers and men. Accordingly, each prisoner of war was provided ten days' rations to see him home. Enlisted men kept their horses but not their rifles.[23]

Thomas Fisher recalled that "tears were shed when we were marshaled for the last time and laid down our arms." The men waited impatiently in camp to receive their paroles. In defeat, the men of Company C must have given the appearance of crestfallen, depressed, malnourished, sickly-appearing soldiers dressed in tattered, soiled butternut. Once they had been awesome and splendid, with a hundred finely mounted soldiers.

The service records of the officers and men of Company C of the Eleventh comprise a total of 149 soldiers who served in the company at one time or another during the war. Appendix B provides the name of each soldier. Strangely, *not one* was recorded as having been killed in action. Only two were wounded in action against the enemy. Forty-four were captured. Four were reported missing. Forty-eight deserted, 30 in 1865 alone. Of those captured, 37 were incarcerated in military prisons, and seven of them died therein. Twenty of the captured soldiers were exchanged.

A comparison of casualties suffered by Company D of the Fourth Tennessee Cavalry Regiment (see Appendix A for names of company personnel) reveals both similarities and a few minor contrasts with those of Company C of the Eleventh. By coincidence, the number of service records of officers and men who served in each of the companies at one time or another is the same, 149. But Company D suffered two soldiers killed or mortally wounded in action (both in 1863), six wounded in action (all also in 1863), 19 captured, 25 missing (of whom one was wounded and presumed dead), 28 deserted, and seven dead of unreported causes. Of those captured, 12 were incarcerated in military prisons, where only one died (of variola). Six of the captured soldiers were exchanged. One company member was executed by firing squad for desertion and resisting arrest in a gunfight in which he mortally wounded an arresting soldier.

Seven soldiers of Company C of the Eleventh died during the war, *all* in Federal prisons. The company's death rate in prison was 18.9 percent, compared with an overall death rate of 12.1 percent of Confederate prisoners in Northern prisons and 15.5 percent of U.S. soldiers in Southern prisons.

Eleven soldiers of Company D of the Fourth died, two as a result of enemy action, seven from unrevealed causes, one of disease in a Federal prison (a prison death rate of only 8.3 percent), and one who was court-martialed and executed.

Company C of the Eleventh suffered total casualties (killed, wounded, captured, missing, deserted, died from unknown causes) of 98, a casualty rate of 65.8 percent. Desertions, 48, and captures, 44, accounted for all but six of the casualties.

Company D of the Fourth had total casualties of 87, a rate of 58.4 percent, the leading sources of which were desertions, 28, missing, 25, and captures, 19. It is believed that Company D's figures, particularly for desertions and total casualties, are understated, owing to there being no surviving muster rolls for the company in 1865 when desertion rates in the Confederate army were highest.

The desertion rate for Confederate armies during the war was approximately 14 percent, well below the rates for these two cavalry companies. Company C of the Eleventh had a desertion rate of 32.2 percent. Company D of the Fourth had a rate of 18.8 percent, a rate which, as indicated above, may be considerably understated.

Civil War infantrymen frequently complained of the relatively safe life of the cavalry and of the latter's perceived reluctance to fight. The figures for the two companies above tend to confirm the justice of the infantry's complaint.

Following Hood's Tennessee campaign, Forrest reported that his cavalry had been engaged every day with the enemy from November 21 to December 27, 1864, and that his losses were heavy. He had lost 39 killed and 366 wounded, a total of 405. Compared with the losses of Hood's infantry during the same campaign, however, Forrest's cavalry losses appear to be almost minuscule. Consider that Hood lost 6,500 killed and wounded out of an engaged force of less than 16,000, virtually all infantry, in the Battle of Franklin alone.

Including only soldiers actually engaged, a soldier's chances of being killed in action in the Federal army in the Civil War have been estimated at one in 42.7 (2.3 percent); of being captured, one in 10.2 (9.8 percent); of being wounded, one in 6.7 (14.9 percent). There are less reliable figures for Confederate soldiers for these classifications of casualties.

In Company C of the Eleventh, the chances respectively worked out to be one in 149 (0.0 percent) of being killed, one in 3.4 (29.4 percent) of being captured, and one in 74.5 (1.3 percent) of being wounded. In Company D of the Fourth, the chances worked out to be one in 74.5 (1.3 percent of being killed; one in 7.8 (12.8 percent) of being captured; and one in 24.8 (4.0 percent) of being wounded.

Only in being captured did members of the two companies exceed the overall chances estimated for Federal soldiers. Otherwise in terms of being killed or wounded, members who served in the two companies were much less likely to be harmed than were Federal army participants in the war. Nevertheless attrition from total casualties ran high. Both Company D of the Fourth and Company C of the Eleventh rapidly diminished in size as the war wore on.

Owing to their depleted rolls, the Tenth and Eleventh Tennessee cavalry regiments were consolidated on February 13, 1865. The consolidated regiment reported only 312 officers and men present for duty at its surrender on May 4, 1865, only 207 of whom were effectives,[24] a sharp drop indeed from the year 1862 when their combined number had been close to 2,000.

The last word on Company D of the Fourth is unavailable now owing to there being no extant muster roll after December 31, 1864, and no records of paroles of the company's complement at its surrender. The company was in the Tennessee brigade of Brigadier General George G. Dibrell in Georgia and the Carolinas. But the Compiled Military Service Records in the National Archives contain no records of paroles for *any* of the officers and men of Company D of the Fourth who served in the company to the end. Accordingly, there is no way to know with certainty which officers and men were serving in the company at its final surrender on May 5, 1865.

In summarizing the casualty rates for the two companies, the low rates of death or wounding in action against the enemy, coupled with the high rates of desertion and capture lead one to believe that the soldiers of the two companies might have tended to be rather more careful of their personal safety than one would expect of intrepid Confederate cavalrymen, especially those who served under Forrest and Wheeler.

One might argue that some of the duty they drew did not expose them to the degree of risk to life and limb as other kinds of duty would have. A case in point might be the assignment of the Eleventh to Johnston's, then Hood's, headquarters where they operated a good part of the time behind the battle lines in the summer of 1864 at Atlanta. Or again in Hood's Tennessee campaign, Company C of the Eleventh, or a contingent thereof, was assigned the duty of guarding the Duck River mill while the remainder of the cavalry went north to Nashville and Murfreesboro where portions of it actually engaged the enemy.

Of course, the high rates of capture, particularly in Company C of the Eleventh, would seem to indicate that the soldiers of the two companies got a fair share of exposure to the enemy. In 1863, Company C had a total of 24 men captured in three encounters with the enemy, at Middleton in February (14), at Morganton in November (6), and at Jacksboro in December (4). But in none of the encounters did the company lose a soldier to enemy fire.

Surprisingly, in the Battle of Chickamauga, where both the Fourth and the Eleventh were reportedly in the thick of the fight on the right flank, neither company D of the Fourth nor Company C of the Eleventh reported any casualties in action against the enemy.

The Fourth Tennessee Cavalry Regiment went in December 1862 with Forrest into West Tennessee, where it engaged with the enemy. Both Company D of the Fourth and Company C of the Eleventh were with Forrest in 1863 in several severe fights in Middle Tennessee, then in protecting Bragg's army retreating to Chattanooga. Both companies were in the siege of Knoxville and reported no casualties. They were in a number of running skirmishes in upper East Tennessee in the winter of 1863-1864. And they were with Wheeler in May and June of 1864, falling back before Sherman from Dalton to Atlanta. Their engagement in these actions with no recorded casualties causes one to question the accuracy of the service records. On the other hand, perhaps it was the inherent nature of cavalry duty combined with elements of skill and blind luck that enabled the two companies to suffer such light casualties in action against the enemy.

The brothers Fisher and other soldiers from Middle Tennessee took up a line of march homeward in military order until they crossed the Tennessee River.[25] From their camp on the Tombigbee River south of Gainesville, they rode through the latter town across the state line into Mississippi via an unimproved road and camped the first night, May 12, ten miles south of Macon. The second day, now following the Mobile & Ohio Railroad, they made about 24 miles and camped near the town of Crawford. Thirty miles more on the fourteenth and they camped seven miles north of West Point. Passing through Okolona, they traveled about twenty-eight miles on their fourth day out and camped seven miles south of Verona. May 16 found them proceeding through Verona and camping two miles south of Guntown, a march of thirty miles.[26]

At Guntown, a road led off to the west to Brice's Crossroads where a conspicuously brilliant victory had been won by Forrest's cavalry on June 10, 1864, almost a year earlier. The noted nineteenth-century British soldier and military commentator, Field Marshal Viscount Wolseley, quite characteristically understated his estimate of Forrest's victory here as "a most remarkable achievement, well worth attention by the military student."[27]

On May 17, the brothers and their comrades proceeded via Baldwyn, then left the rail line and started cross country on their way to Iuka. The next day, they passed through Iuka and the Federal garrison of mounted troops camped by the road. The passage through Iuka proceeded without incident. Fourteen more miles brought them to Eastport where they crossed the Tennessee River by ferry and camped in Alabama.[28]

Once across the river, they little by little broke up into squads composed of those who lived in the vicinity of appropriate intersecting roads that took them home.

On May 19, the members of Company C who had stayed together, traveling in the direction of Lawrenceburg, Tennessee, and doubtless wishing to avoid any more Union troops, traversed a few miles of Alabama soil on their way into Wayne County, Tennessee, where they spent the night in camp on the banks of Butler's Creek. The next day, they rode via Wayland Springs, West Point, and Lawrenceburg, and camped two miles from Williams' Mills in the direction of Campbellsville in Giles County.

The next morning, Sunday, May 21, after proceeding only a mile, Will Fisher decided that his pain was so severe and his strength so limited that he could no longer hold himself steadily on his horse. He wrote that he was very sick.[29] His complaint suggests that he may have suffered from an ailment which could have been tuberculosis of the bowels or genitourinary tract.

Frank Fisher, Will's oldest half-brother, said he would stay with Will. The two of them stopped at the home of William Usry (or Ussery) on Big Creek a few miles west of Campbellsville.[30] They were within twenty-five miles of Cave Spring and home.

Usry's son, E.R., 31, had been paroled in April at Greensboro, North Carolina, as a member of Company D, the Third Tennessee Volunteer Infantry Regiment, C.S.A. He had been a property owner prior to the war while still living with his parents.[31] Will wrote that he was "very kindly treated" by the Usry family.[32]

In accordance with the code of etiquette of that time and place and the commonality of their wartime experiences, Frank and Will indeed would have been graciously received by members of the Usry family who would try to make their guests feel as easy as possible. William Usry probably assured them that they should stay as long as it was necessary to get Will back on his feet and fit to travel. And one might believe that the Usrys were an attractive family in the eyes of Frank and even Will, as sick as he was. The head of the household, William, a farmer of modest means, was 68. His wife, Rebecca, was 63. They had three daughters, Frances, 21, Sarah, 19, and Eliza, 17.[33]

Frank and Will stayed with the Usrys until Thursday, May 25. During their hiatus, it is not unlikely that Frank, when not attending to Will's needs and in accordance with his own code of etiquette, might have aided his hosts as recompense for their kindness by performing some long-neglected chores about the farm.

On the twenty-fifth, Will, feeling well enough to get home, mounted up. With many and profuse thanks, he and Frank left their Usry benefactors and took up a twenty-four mile ride home, finally rejoining their family at Cave Spring in the evening.[34]

Victorious Northern armies were honored in Washington in a Grand Review on May 23-24. On the twenty-sixth, the Confederate Army of the Transmississippi Department, under General Edmund Kirby Smith, received terms of surrender in New Orleans from Major General E.R.S. Canby, who was in charge of both the Army and the Division of West Mississippi, U.S.A. Many of the Southern troops in the Transmississippi reportedly anticipated the surrender and disbanded prematurely without waiting to receive paroles.

And eight days later, on Friday, June 2, 1865, in Galveston, Texas, Smith agreed to the capitulation of the last army and territorial fragment of the Southern Confederacy. Included was the Confederate District of Texas, New Mexico, and Arizona under the command of Major General John Bankhead Magruder who, fearing the worst of Yankee reprisals, fled to Mexico.

Also included in the surrendered territory was the District of the Indian Territory, in present-day Oklahoma, with armed Cherokees, Choctaws, Arapahos, and Sioux under the command of Brigadier General Douglas Hancock Cooper, who after the war won legal actions against the Federal government claiming wartime losses for the Indians.[35]

And the virtually expired hopes of the nation yet flickered in the Confederate cruiser, C.S.S. *Shenandoah*, still sinking United States shipping until June 28 in the Arctic Ocean. The ship did not lower its ensign until November 6, 1865, in Liverpool, England, after a 17,000 mile cruise around Cape Horn from the North Pacific to the North Atlantic via the South Pacific and the South Atlantic.

The cruise to the ship's home port began on August 2 after the vessel, then in the Pacific Ocean, overtook the H.M.S. *Barracouta*, a British bark fourteen days out of San Francisco. The *Shenandoah*'s captain, Lieutenant James I. Waddell, learned of the collapse of his government from San Francisco newspapers aboard the bark. After deliberate and painful weighing of alternative courses of action urged upon him by his officers and men, Waddell decided to disarm his ship and to stow his armament, so as not to be taken and treated as a pirate vessel and crew. Still flying his Confederate flag, Waddell headed for the ship's home port as a fugitive, all the while successfully avoiding a meeting on the high seas with United States Navy cruisers. The ship, which had earlier reached the Pacific Ocean via the Atlantic and Indian oceans, circumnavigated the globe on this, her maiden voyage.[36]

Ever since early April when they had encamped about Marion, Alabama, and then moved toward Gainesville, Forrest's soldiers, more certainly than before, came to realize that their fighting days were over. Officers and men were assailed with gloom and an uncertainty about what lay ahead. Even the excited talk about carrying on the fight as desperadoes, or west of the Mississippi in Texas, or going to Mexico, could not dispel their preponderant anxiety.

Further, their enforced retirement from fighting combined with their isolation from the rest of the world, gave them time to entertain rumors as well as to ruminate over their experiences in the army. Many of them had been troubled by the recent case of the execution of two presumed deserters at Lanier's Bridge over the Sipsey River in Alabama on March 29, 1865.

The army obviously faced a serious problem with desertions, as indicated by the records of officers and men of the two companies closely followed in the present narrative. The problem was exacerbated when the troops in Richard Taylor's department who were bivouacked along the Mobile & Ohio Railroad, just inside Mississippi near the Alabama line, began to be ordered in late February to move east to Selma. Many soldiers thought the order meant that they were to follow their comrades in the Army of Tennessee who had been sent to North Carolina in January to oppose Sherman's march north from Savannah.

The order to consolidate the Tenth and Eleventh Tennessee cavalry regiments on February 13, 1865, seemed to many of the troops to presage a dangerous and unacceptable move. Hence the sudden desertion of 22 members of Company C of the Eleventh on February 14–15, 1865.

Orders were issued to guards at bridges to arrest any soldier moving unattached through the country without proper written authority. This meant that any white male of military age who might be found in transit was precariously in the position of being stopped, questioned, accused, tried, and shot if he could not give an accounting of his status that established that he was not a deserter. But if he looked as though he might be a soldier and he did not bear on his person written authority for detached duty, the presumption was that he was indeed a deserter.

At Lanier's Bridge over the Sipsey River between Carter's and Colter's ferries, two men were arrested as deserters. They acknowledged previous army service and asserted that they were on their way home to Kentucky. A drumhead court-martial, i.e., a summary court-martial held in the field to try offenses committed during military operations, was convened to try the men. They had no papers on them to establish the truth of their assertions relative to their leaving the army. With nothing to support their word, the two were found guilty and promptly shot. Their bodies were laid one on either side of the road under a tree and a placard nailed to the tree which said: Shot for Desertion.

The soldiers of Jackson's division saw the cruel spectacle as they passed, crossing the river on the twenty-ninth and thirtieth of March. Many were deeply angered by the killings. The two soldiers were buried on the morning of March 31 after having been in death a largely useless and ineffectual object lesson for two days to all soldiers of an already defeated army who rode by and saw their bodies.

The anger and revulsion felt by hardened soldiers at the scene of the executions was exacerbated when, according to Forrest's biographer, John A. Wyeth, word circulated among the troops that the men had been shot unjustly, that every particular of what they told the court-martial had been true. It was said they had been members of Tyree Bell's brigade, of which the brothers Fisher had been a part since February, and had been granted leave to return to their homes. Either they thoughtlessly left in haste without securing written authority or their papers were lost. Members of the court, acting in haste, did not take time to check out the stories of the accused. Instead they cleared their docket with alacrity.[37]

Veterans of the Western cavalry could bring up from memory some of the times when they, their comrades, and their horses, had been hungry. They were more often hungry than not all through the war. When Wheeler's cavalry had been stationed at Covington, Georgia, forty miles east of Atlanta in July and August of 1864, there had been no dry grain for their horses, creatures which could not long subsist on green vegetation. And the men, as usual, were in straits relative to their own diets.[38]

But they were not to be totally denied, owing to their resourcefulness and, in the case of the men of the Eleventh, the help of their forage master, John Jordan of Murfreesboro. The men more or less successfully foraged for food for man and beast and did not stand on formalities relative to where the food came from or from whom it was taken. They were hungry for meat for themselves and dry corn for the horses. Sometimes they settled for chickens and eggs for the men. And they were detested by their civilian compatriots for whom they fought but from whom they stole both food and fence rails.

Through the years thereafter, Thomas Fisher did not forget the cooking practices of troops in the field in wartime. Some of the soldiers who volunteered for cooking duties were really quite good at making the most out of scarcity. Members of each company usually messed together and shared the chores, cooking, the drawing of water and rations, the wood for the fire, and seeing that their mounts were combed, watered and fed, all incident to chowing down.

Tom related how one day a soldier had brought in some red pepper to season the food for the company mess. Everyone looked forward to the addition of the pepper to spice the taste of the soup they would eat. Their food, in addition to being predictably scarce, was generally quite bland in taste. But no chef could please all his soldier clients at any given time. There were always those who would have used either more or less pepper.

On this particular day, Frank Fisher offered suggestions to the cook about how he might better prepare the soup then being heated in an ample baling vessel over a roaring open fire.

After feeling thoroughly abused by what seemed to him to be a lengthy succession of unjustified criticisms, the cook advanced toward Frank and, with his large stirring spoon upraised for emphasis, he snarled, "Now if you think you can do it better than I can, then by God, just take hold and do it yourself!"

A few minutes later, when each soldier had tasted his tin cupful of soup, Frank remained, as before, the critic. "Why did you put so much pepper in it?" he asked.

Calmly, the cook, obviously enjoying his creation, disdainfully said to Frank: "If you don't like it, you needn't to eat it."

Frank slowly thought of the question and his answer before giving his measured response: "I *have* to eat it to get my share," he said with emphasis.[39]

And so he did.

The Confederate army's policy which seemed to encourage the stealing of horses by cavalrymen was troubling. The policy was that horse soldiers provided their own mounts. On the other hand, the Federal army furnished mounts for their soldiers. But some Confederate cavalrymen, when their horses were wounded, broken down, worn-out, or killed, might seek out privately-owned horses in pastures or towns in the vicinity and take them without recompense to their owners.

Despite problems deriving from private ownership of horses by Confederate cavalrymen, George Guild, Adjutant of Baxter Smith's/Paul Anderson's Fourth Tennessee Cavalry, asserted his belief that ownership of their own horses caused Confederate horsemen to give better care to their mounts than Federal horsemen gave to theirs. Further, the Southern horseman gave more care to his *selection* of a mount, insisting generally on "the best blood and make-up that could be found." According to Guild, Federal horses were "pretty much of the rough order, large, inactive, and easily broken down and worn out." To Guild, these factors plus the Southerners being "born, as the saying is, upon horseback," explained his assessment that "the Confederate cavalryman did more effective and better service than the Federal cavalryman."[40]

But horse-thievery was only one despised consequence of living off the land which was a part of the everyday life of the Western cavalry. The cavalry under Wheeler was conspicuous in continued and grave complaints lodged by citizens against them for their depredations against the property of civilians. The complaints were of such gravity that Wheeler felt constrained to issue a General Order, Number 7, while his cavalry corps was headquartered in Beaufort District, South Carolina, on December 29, 1864, eight days after Sherman had completed his march to the sea and occupied the city of Savannah, during which march Wheeler's cavalry was about all the opposition that Sherman's army met.

Wheeler emphasized to his troops that all general orders from army or corps headquarters relative to discipline and depredating upon the property of civilians would be rigidly enforced. Officers and soldiers were forbidden to enter any dwellings under any pretext whatever, unless invited by the occupants. Further, care would be taken to insure that no fence rails were burned for fuel. Troops and mounts would eat subsistence and forage issued by commissaries and quartermasters except in instances where a command might be without wagons. In the latter instance, forage and rations would be procured and legal vouchers given the owners or sellers.

Each division commander was ordered to select an exemplary regiment commanded by a strict officer to act as division provost guard and protect every house along the division's line of march and within the division's camp sites. At each level, commanders were to be held strictly accountable for the conduct of their commands.[41]

Another troubling Confederate army policy was one which provided that when a soldier found himself dismounted, he was entitled to a thirty-day furlough to go home to secure another horse. A common complaint arose that cavalrymen might sell their horses so that they could go home for thirty days.[42]

Most men who served in the cavalry had been forced to remount more than once during the war, even those who loved their horses, took great care in their treatment, and tried to avoid, despite the urgency of their missions, riding their horses to death as soldiers sometimes did. Horse lovers were genuinely pained to witness the suffering of cavalry mounts in combat, animals which were larger targets than their riders and more often victims of gunshot and shrapnel wounds amidst cavalry operations.

Perhaps the most excruciating physical pain many veterans of the Fourth and Eleventh felt and remembered from their war experiences was the numbing, blistering cold of the winter of 1863–1864 in upper East Tennessee. Some of their comrades reportedly froze to death, a fate to which others believed they had come perilously close.

But quite unforgettable was duty as a vidette in sub-zero temperatures with inadequate protection from the cold and wind, icicles hanging from one's nose and whiskers, the wheezing and shortness of breath that one experienced at the slightest exertion in the extreme cold, and having a comrade pump one's arms and legs to restore circulation and feeling.

Many soldiers came very close to death, in these circumstances, as did their horses. Will Fisher became so ill with a respiratory problem that he went home on a forty-day furlough in March 1864. The circumstances seemed to precipitate a spate of desertions from the army.[43]

Many veterans remembered most poignantly the violent deaths of comrades in sanguinary battles or minor skirmishes, the anguish and the heartache of loss and separation, the revulsion at the disfigurement caused by gunshot, shell, or shrapnel, the repellent sight and odor of open abdominal, head, and leg wounds, and death, the heavy physical exertions of digging shallow graves in the unyielding, irresilient earth with inadequate tools, covering the bodies with dirt, sand, and rock until they finally disappeared from view.

Only slightly less tragic were the disabilities inflicted on soldiers who were maimed for the rest of their lives, some physically, others mentally. Of the latter, Thomas Fisher remembered Brigadier General Thomas Benton Smith of William B. Bates' division during Hood's Tennessee Campaign in November–December 1864.

After surrendering at Shy's Hill on the second day of the Battle of

Nashville, Smith was repeatedly struck on the head with his own sword, reportedly wielded by Colonel William Linn McMillen, commander of the Ninety-Fifth Ohio Volunteer Infantry Regiment.[44] The assault resulted in brain trauma when the blows cut through to expose brain tissue. Smith was not expected to live. But he recovered sufficiently to spend most of the remainder of his life in a state hospital for the insane near Nashville where he died in 1923.

Thomas Fisher served as chaplain at the hospital in 1904–1908 and became well acquainted with Smith. Fisher reported that the general began a correspondence with him, writing him a letter almost every week during his chaplaincy. Fisher recalled that the first few lines of Smith's missives would always appear to be those common to any personal letter between friends. But before the end, the tone usually would reflect that of a general military order concluding with some such ascription as: "By order of General T.B. Smith, Commander, Theodore Roosevelt, Adjutant." Smith's adjutant would change from time to time. But always it would be the name of a person of prominence.

Fisher recalled that Smith was a fine looking man with a military air and bearing. He was well-bred, and there was never anything coarse or vulgar in what he said or wrote. This was quite unlike the discourse of some other inmates in the hospital with whom Fisher became acquainted.

On a visit to the hospital in 1921, Fisher saw Smith for the last time. Smith did not know Fisher when the latter first spoke to him, after an absence of twelve years. But when Fisher told him his name, the general seemed to recall him quite fully. Later during his visit, Fisher was called by Smith to come over to where he was seated. Fisher took a seat on the general's left, and the two chatted amiably.

Directly, Smith asked Fisher: "Didn't I give your baby boy [Howard] a silver dollar as a birthday present when you were here?"

"You certainly did," Fisher replied.

"Well, tell me about him," he said.

At some length, Fisher related how, after his mother's death, Howard went to Oklahoma to live with his aunt, Lillian Boone Fentress, his half-sister, Mary, and his uncle, Howard H. Boone, who was Mary's husband. The three adults, with Howard, combined their households in 1916 in Clinton before moving to Oklahoma City two years later. By 1920, Howard had returned to Tennessee as a student at Sawney Webb's distinguished Webb School in Bell Buckle.

When Fisher had done giving as many details about Howard as he could, Smith said, "Well, give Howard my love!"

Fisher assured him he would.[45]

Within two years, both Fisher and Smith were dead, the latter, unhappily, after 47 years in an institution owing to his war-related injuries. Smith died on May 21, 1923, and as Tennessee's last surviving Civil War general, received official honors and a lying-in-state in the Capitol prior to burial in Confederate Circle in Mt. Olivet Cemetery in Nashville.[46]

After the surrender, when Confederate veterans encountered Union troops on their way home, as the men of the Eleventh did at Iuka, Mississippi, they were never more aware of the differences in operational readiness and appearance of Union and Confederate soldiers.

It seems that the former were resplendent in well-fitted, unsoiled, and impressive uniforms made of durable, well-cut and well-stitched cloth appropriate to the season of the year, carrying modern weapons of the latest design and maximum accuracy and repeating fire power, mounted on well-groomed horses with expensive burnished saddles and bridles to match, and accoutrements of virgin-wool blankets and effective foul-weather gear which were the envy of their adversaries whose factionalized states-rights governments, with their dearth of manufactures, embargoed imports, and regional agricultural economy could never afford.

Passing through the U.S. garrison at Iuka on their way home, the brothers Fisher and their comrades had not been paid for over a year, were in tatters and had been so for virtually the entire length of their enlistments. Yet their fighting elan, skill, courage, intrepidity, and ingenuity are yet praised over a hundred years after they laid down their arms.

But the most obvious contrasts in appearance of Federal versus slave-state soldiers seemed to confirm the conclusions of the renegade North Carolina editor and author, Hinton Rowan Helper, who warned Southern slave holders in 1857 in his book, *The Impending Crisis of the South*, and declared his belief that slavery produces poverty and free labor wealth.

Confederate soldiers who might have read Helper's book before the war doubtless had done so more often than not with chagrin and half-suppressed anger, not ready to concede anything of the author's argument. But after over three and a half years of fighting in the most sanguinary war America ever fought, those with a bent toward candor may have been ready to concede some of Helper's conclusions.[47]

One of the crippling maladies noted by observers of the war was the petty infighting that went on among the top commanders of the Army of Tennessee. While the war was yet in progress, some of the differences between Bragg, Polk, and Hardee were known, as well as something of the role that Jefferson Davis played in the army politics that served to weaken the execution of the army's military plans.

But it was not until after the war with the publication of often self-serving memoirs and apologiae by some of the principals that the extent of the organizational infighting and cliquishness became evident. Then it became clear that the army's leadership, men like Beauregard, Joe Johnston, whom his troops trusted and loved, Longstreet, Polk, Kirby Smith, Cheatham, Breckinridge, and the gallant Cleburne, Wheeler, McCown, and others had competed with and against each other for personal preferment or out of personal preferences and prejudices, or were professionally inept or had character defects which did not serve the army or the nation well.[48]

On balance, the evidence overwhelmingly indicates that the leadership of the Army of Tennessee was poor and ineffective and that Confederate authorities in Richmond consistently shortchanged those who fought outside the Washington-Richmond theatre. The armies in the West consistently operated on short food rations, shoes and clothing, guns and ammunition, horses and mules, while the Army of Virginia had first call on everything usable even within the geographical areas the Army of Tennessee was defending.

Commissary depots, first in Nashville, then in Atlanta, were required by the government to supply the army in Virginia while western armies had to live off the country. The priorities of Confederate officials in Richmond were questionable and, in the end, contributed substantially to the collapse of the struggle for Southern independence.

One might question whether the Southern Confederacy would have had a better chance of succeeding if the capital of the Confederacy had remained in Montgomery or moved to another interior point, but not to Richmond. Then the defense of Richmond, located so perilously close to the Potomac River and the Chesapeake Bay, both held by Union forces throughout the conflict, would not have been of such transcendent importance to top officials at the seat of government. There could have been more balance in defensive priorities which conceivably might have resulted in all the Confederate states being more effectively defended.

The remote strategic location of the capital in Montgomery or another interior location would have rendered the defense of the capital less costly to the Confederates and its capture by Union forces a more expensive and tenuous operational and logistical undertaking.

In Virginia, the war was fought essentially between the two cities of Washington and Richmond, only a hundred miles apart, plus rather narrowly contiguous counties within eighty miles of each city. On the other hand, there were vastly too few arms, troops, and support resources to defend hundreds of miles of strategic territory in the West, natural and commercial resources across the Confederacy's primary breadbasket, ordnance, livestock, and transportation citadels in the central South, and the strategic Mississippi River, all of which successively and predictably fell into the hands of Federal armies and gunboats.

On balance, it appears reasonable to conclude that the war was essentially won by the North and lost by the South in the areas defended by the Army of Tennessee. And the victory of the North in the crucial central South, utilizing troops which became stronger as the war wore on, stronger in numbers, equipment, training, leadership, and firepower, even as the South became progressively weaker, made the eventual collapse of the Confederacy a predictable conclusion.

The struggle in Virginia, played on a smaller stage with a larger cast and finally brought to an end by a progressively weakened resistance and by U. S. Grant, appears to have been largely a costly holding operation and an extravagantly sanguinary diversion to the strategically decisive losing struggles of the Confederate Army of Tennessee and the winning struggles of the Federal Army of the Cumberland, Army of the Tennessee, Army of the Ohio, and Army of the Mississippi, the results of whose battles, as the war wore on, increasingly tended to be overwhelmingly decisive.

Indeed the war seems to have been essentially ended with the decisive Confederate defeat at Nashville, coupled with the Army of Tennessee's inability to mount effective opposition to Sherman's military juggernaut as it progressed from Atlanta to the sea and from Savannah to North Carolina.

Ralph Henry Gabriel placed the assured demise of Confederate arms as indicated in early November 1863, over a year before Hood's disaster at Nashville and Sherman's successful march to the sea, when Grant decisively defeated Bragg in the Battle of Chattanooga. After this disaster, he wrote, the South's chances of victory were "almost hopeless."[49]

Nevertheless, the results of military operations after December 1864, from the Federal siege of Richmond and Petersburg to Wilson's lightning dash to Selma and beyond, seem now to have been wholly predictable. After December, the Confederate government in Richmond was isolated and fatally untenable, with virtually all the national resources which enabled it to function now firmly in the hands of the enemy.

But Confederate authorities in Richmond did not see the war being fought according to the western view. They consistently gave priority in men, animals, forage, materiel, and strategic importance to the Army of Northern Virginia and thus forced enormous losses upon the South which could not be sustained, losses of manpower in Virginia and losses of land, industry, natural resources, armies, materiel, and reserve manpower throughout the balance of the Confederate states.[50]

Thus it was likely a costly and fatal day for supporters of Southern independence when the Provisional Congress, meeting in Montgomery on Monday, May 20, 1861, approved moving the capital to Richmond.

The third Sunday in May 1865, the twenty-first, Monroe and Thomas Fisher arrived home. They approached by way of the old Rock Creek camp ground, about a mile from their home, just as the congregants were coming out of the shelter under which their service had been held. It was the annual May meeting at which hundreds of people gathered every year.

Monroe and Tom knew a fair number of the people there. As they dismounted and received the greetings of well-wishers, they were quite embarrassed by their appearance. They would have preferred to have reached home and changed into more presentable clothing before greeting neighbors and friends, some of whom they had not seen in three years.

Of course, they wore no medals for gallantry by which victorious nations bestow their appreciation and admiration on those who defend home, hearth, and heartland. Their government conferred no such awards.

But those who greeted them let it be known almost immediately that they cared not about the returning soldiers' appearance. They were genuinely interested in the two men as products of the neighborhood, as friends and loved ones, and as returning war heroes who had gone away selflessly to defend the lives and property of neighbors and countrymen.

The warmth of their welcome soon managed to elicit smiles from Monroe and Tom and the acknowledgment that they were glad to be home among friends and neighbors. The boys almost forgot the thinness of and the holes, rips, and rents in their trousers and jackets which exposed their bare, soiled, and suntanned flesh to the eyes of others.[51]

Thomas was greeted in the crowd of people at Rock Creek camp ground by a young woman who had been a special friend before the war. And after the assembled friends expressed a desire to accompany the two veterans the balance of the way to their home, Thomas and the young woman fell in with each other and rode together.

Monroe and Tom were met at the fence gate by their parents, John and Mildred, and their thirteen-year-old brother, Bascom. After embraces were warmly exchanged and Mildred's apprehensions about the absences of Frank and Will were addressed, family members and friends came into the house for more camaraderie and talk.

Outside, Tom and his friend sat and talked together at one end of the front veranda and spoke of a romantic promise they had once made to wait for each other. Did she remember the promise? Thomas ventured. "Just as well as if it had been made only yesterday," she replied.

Tom wrote that he "was almost sorry she remembered so distinctly."[52] He was not ready to renew his commitment to her. In the months that followed, references were made to their relationship. But he proposed no plans.[53] They each may have wondered uncertainly of what their relationship was to be now that Tom was home from the war and unencumbered by responsibilities which might interfere with the culmination of a warm romance and ultimately for them, marriage.

At home after two and a half and more years of learning and practicing the military arts, and presumably becoming skilled and resourceful horse soldiers, the five Fisher brothers left behind them the skills they had learned so well and fitfully attempted to cope with life in peaceful pursuits in a wrecked economy of scarcity.

And, although penniless, with nothing to show for their military service except defeat and memories, no unemployment compensation provided by a grateful nation to tide them over from service separation to permanent employment, no pensions for the disabled or elderly, widows or orphans, no medical care for the sick and disabled was in the offing, and without job prospects for the future other than what they or their families might provide from their accumulated scarcity, they were, in a way, indeed quite fortunate.

They returned home as paroled prisoners of war. But, more than that, they were survivors.

Of five brothers, who, between them, might have been responsible for the deaths or wounding of scores of the enemy, all returned without loss of life or limb. Their survival, of course, may not appear unusual given the number of deaths from all causes of the two companies in which the brothers served, seven in one and eleven in the other. But it appears quite unusual in the great war that was most costly to Americans in casualties, a veritable bloodbath of epic proportions not likely to be repeated save by a future nuclear holocaust.

One is reminded that more Americans died in the Civil War (618,000) than in all other American wars combined, beginning with the French and Indian wars in the 1750s through the Korean conflict in the 1950s (total: 606,000). The war produced over a million total casualties when the population of the United States was only 31.4 million (1860 census).[54]

To realize the enormity of casualties if today the United States should engage in a war and sustain casualties proportionate to those of the Civil War, American dead would amount to 4,895,000 out of a population of 248.7 million (1990 census). Total killed and wounded would be close to eight million.

The capacity of Americans to continue the killing and maiming in the 1860s evinced a strength of purpose, a hardness of heart, a desperation of spirit, or a lack of knowledge of what was transpiring that is difficult to understand in retrospect. Preservation of our federal Union became the lofty rhetorical purpose for which the war was waged in the North. One cannot lose sight of individuals, however, virtually all in the North, who made a great deal of money from government contracts, federal debentures issued to finance the war, and the rising prices of manufactured goods.

Their government failed to fight wartime profits with drastic imposts and, shortly after the end of the war, abolished a moderate tax on incomes and shifted the burden of paying increased government obligations to excise taxes paid by consumers. Further indications of the heightened national influence of prewar Whigs turned Republicans, an influence induced by their new and enhanced fortunes and material contributions to the war effort were (1) the increase of the tariff to an all-time high to protect domestic manufacturers and (2) the payment of federal subsidies to facilitate the growth of transportation and commerce, subsidies which became lavish in the immediate postwar period.[55]

The unprecedented growth of industry and banking in support of the war effort began the accrual of substantial personal fortunes while the fighting raged and thus promoted for many in the new capitalist/industrialist class a vested interest in the continuation of the war.

On the other hand, there were, to be sure, individuals who refused to become directly involved in the war, as well as peace parties on both sides made up of people who, in the name of humanity, would have staunched the unprecedentedly massive effusion of blood in the fighting had they had the political power to do so. But they were outnumbered, outspent, and out-leveraged.

Among the war's survivors, the five Fisher brothers began their lives again with virtually nothing save the scant material support lent by their parents' 275-acre farm. They had little education, few marketable skills, and virtually no cash, property, or investments.

They faced a future, not of promise and hope, but full of foreboding in the financially ruined South of a federal Union industrially revolutionized by the war in the Northeast, held together by a vast and growing rail system, and otherwise much changed by the war, socially, economically, and occupationally.

Epilogue

The violence and rigors of the war did not break the hold of John Fisher and his family on the land which gave them sustenance and an incorruptible degree of independence in the rural society of which they were a part. The end of the war simply brought a continuation of the economic hard times which had been accentuated by the privations, political disorganization, and economic isolation of secession and the hostilities of 1861–1865. Again the rural South was populated by survivors, economic survivors now, whose crops, livestock, and services were depressed in price and demand for well over a generation to come.

Family members who survived the war were typical of thousands from small slaveholding families who had gone off to defend home and hearth and the Southern Confederacy. Coming home, they lived in a genteel poverty that they shared with most property holders, artisans, mechanics, tradesmen, and professionals who lived in areas of moderate-sized farms and general agriculture in the South and indeed through much of rural America.

Later their progeny would leave their inexpensively capitalized family farms. Most moved to towns and cities and went to work for others. But most, including those with an entrepreneurial bent, endured a prolonged period when moneylending was normally monopolistic, privileged, and usurious, a condition which made scarce investment capital the scarcer.[1]

After the war, New South advocates favored industrial development as *the* cure for the South's old problem of poverty. But industrial development in the South was small-scale, depending largely upon scarce local capital and locating in small towns and crossroads. Southern cities continued to be small by comparison with those in the North, as did the banks, businesses, personal fortunes, and wages. Even in the North, where improvements in production technology, productive capacity, and productivity were apparent over time, the economy was marked by recurrent financial panics and recessions or depressions in every decade prior to World War II. But the South's relative poverty, no longer reinforced by discriminatory rail freight rates after 1945, continued well past the war years of 1939–1945.[2]

Public policy initiatives, beginning in the fourth decade of the twentieth century, however, began to expand and democratize the nation's economy, then virtually paralyzed by the collapse of laissez faire capitalism. The initiatives created progressive economic forces and conditions, e.g., a stable yet competitive money-lending sector, long-term amortized mortgages which, together with the government's investment in mortgage insurance, encouraged and made possible popular home ownership; the extension of electricity and telephones to rural America, and mass collegiate education and vocational training gave impetus to the emerging middle class. The initiatives encouraged unprecedented competition and extended to Americans economic opportunities, options, and freedoms in the post–Depression period hitherto unknown and unavailable to most people.

Economic freedom was expanded with the passage of the Social Security Act, which provided for the first time a means by which most Americans might retire with earned benefits paid pursuant to law without groveling or prostituting oneself. In addition to providing income for the elderly, widows, orphans, and, later by amendment, the disabled, the act gave impetus to the establishment of large supplementary pension funds, both public and private. These funds, together with Social Security trust funds, made available unprecedentedly large sources of capital for lending to business and government, the investment of which in turn greatly expanded economic opportunities for Americans.[3]

Concurrently, substantial and continuing public investment in broadly-based initiatives and programs which produce economic growth, e.g., investment in transportation, housing, water resources, power production, medicine and health care, as well as investment in wars and in preparation therefor made customarily severe and recurrent financial downturns appear to be a thing of the past during much of the last half of the twentieth century.[4]

Such investments, coupled with progressive fiscal and tax policies, recognition and protection of rights of wage earners, and legal reforms in investment and banking practices, provided the impetus and opportunity for substantial numbers of descendants of Civil War veterans, among others, to begin to share more equitably in the nation's wealth and income and to accumulate capital in significant amounts in the period following the Great Depression, a period which became the golden age of the American economy.

But the changes came too late to help the returning Civil War veterans. America's relatively open and prosperous post–World War II economy was far from the postwar economy of the rural South to which the Fisher brothers returned in 1865.

The paternal grandfather of the fighting Fisher brothers, Jacob Fisher, born March 31, 1784, in Mecklenburg County, North Carolina, died while the war yet raged, on April 7, 1863. His widow, John Fisher's stepmother, Nancy Helm Fisher, born July 8, 1802, lived until July 29, 1873. Nancy and Jacob had continued to live on their farm in the Grantsburg Township, Johnson County, Illinois, to which they had moved from Tennessee in 1854.[5]

John and Mildred Stratton Fisher continued to live on their farm on the

Verona-Farmington road in Marshall County, Tennessee, to which their five sons returned following the war. In 1870, John reported sharp declines in the value of his farm, farm implements, and livestock.

The cash value of his farm was reduced from $5,500 in 1860 to $2,300 in 1870. The value of his farm implements dropped from $90 to $40. And the value of all his livestock declined from $1,795 to $1,420. The acreage of his farm was 265 in 1870, down from 275 in 1860. But he had 120 acres in cultivation in 1870 as opposed to only 80 in 1860.

He produced 500 bushels of Indian corn in 1870, 320 bushels of oats, and 191 of winter wheat. In 1860 he had produced 750 bushels of corn and 200 of wheat. He had produced no oats in 1860. Now he attempted to compensate for declining prices by producing oats but less corn.[6]

As John and Mildred's sons married following the war, they each moved away from the family farm and settled elsewhere. But none went far from the family homestead.

Jim was the first to go, in early 1866, but he went no farther than a farm near Farmington, three to four miles away. Monroe initially went a few miles west to Berlin, still in Marshall County, when he married in 1869. The next year he was in Farmington where he was in charge of the academy. By 1880 he was living on the farm of his wife's parents in adjoining Maury County. He made a fourth move, this time to Longview, Texas, in the 1890s.[7]

Will moved away to the north to a farm near Franklin in adjoining Williamson County. Thomas left for good in 1869 when he graduated from Union University and began itinerating among communities none of which was more than seventy-five miles from home until he undertook a brief Oklahoma sojourn in 1909–1911.

Frank stayed on the family farm longer than the other veterans of the war. He stayed until 1879, when he moved three miles away to Farmington following the death of his brother, Jim.[8]

The family patriarch and matriarch, John and Mildred, grew old on their farm finally accompanied only by their youngest son, Bascom Hurt, born October 25, 1852, too late to be a soldier in the war. His parents both died in 1882, John of uremia, Mildred of unknown causes. The same year, Bascom's cousin, Bettie Haggard, who was caring for his parents, died. Bascom's wife, Sally Hill, also died in 1882, an extraordinarily grievous year for Bascom, who was left alone with three children. He was helped in this crisis by Melinda, 47, still living in the household, who became "black mammy," a surrogate mother, to his children.

Bascom became head of the household and continued to live on the family farm until 1898 when he moved to a home near Lewisburg, seat of Marshall County. He combined farming and teaching careers.

Bascom was married in 1876 to Sally Hill and had three children, Fay, Jose Burr, and Kate. After Sally's death in 1882, Bascom married Addie Ewing in 1886. Addie died in 1889 without issue. Bascom married Mollie Craig in 1890 and had four children, Lewis Craig, Commodore Bascom, Mattie Mildred, and Margaret Fisher. Bascom succumbed February 28, 1917, to tuberculosis of the lungs and was survived for thirty years by his widow, Mollie.[9]

The Fisher brothers' only surviving sister, Mary Charlotte Fisher Haggard (1833–1896), was married to Robert M. Haggard (1820–1902), a widower with six children, all minors. Robert became a member of the Tennessee Conference of the Methodist Episcopal Church, South, in 1854. Mary itinerated with her husband among a number of localities in Middle Tennessee, but never lived far from home.

She had a daughter, Bettie, and four sons, Barry Stevens, William Thomas, Frank M., and Elisha Bascom Haggard, who lived to adulthood. She also reared the four youngest children, Mary, Martha, George, and Robert P., born to Robert M. Haggard and his first wife, Barbara.[10]

Although most Southern whites were anything but prosperous after the war, the freedmen and women were even more in extremis economically owing to their treatment as serfs and peasants expected to perform the most arduous labor with no future, labor which others wished to avoid and which was unrelieved by technological improvement. They were denied capital and were at the mercy of crop failures, extortionate storekeepers, low prices for their labor and production, and unsympathetic, often brutal employers, or employers who loved but patronized them.[11]

Their prospects of making a living with dignity and accumulating savings and property were the least promising of all Americans. For lack of opportunity, the vast majority barely subsisted in grinding and unending poverty. They were denied economic and political rights as well as educational opportunities commensurate with need or with that made available to whites. They were further hurt by the absence of medical care, by hookworm and other contagious, disabling, and debilitating diseases.[12]

When the war ended and the slaves were free, two, or possibly all three, of the adult black women still lived on the Fisher farm. The eldest of the original three women, name unknown, who had been married to a venerable slave of Jonathan Thomas, probably died in the 1860s, following the death of her husband.

One of the younger black women went with her two children to live with her husband, who continued to live on the land of his former owner, Elihu Hunter, with whom Tom and Monroe lived in 1866 while attending Captain James J. Finney's classical school only a few miles north of the Fisher farm.

Melinda, with her three children, continued to live in the Fishers' home after the war. But her husband was not enumerated with her in postwar decennial censuses. One might guess that either he died a soldier's death in the war or died of other causes, or the couple separated by mutual consent, or he found no employment on the property of his former owner and may have had to leave the community in search of work. In the latter case, he likely became a sharecropper or moved away to a town or city. If so, his temporary separation from his family seems to have become permanent. Melinda raised their daughter, Louisa, and their two sons, Robert and Dudley. She continued to live at the Fishers' after both John and Mildred Fisher died in 1882. She worked in the employ of Bascom Hurt Fisher, new head of household, until she moved to Nashville to live with her son, Robert. She died tragically in 1893 in a fire in Robert's home.

When Melinda died, Robert sought Thomas Fisher, who lived at 211 Meridian Street in East Nashville, to conduct his mother's funeral. Unable to find Fisher, he located William Thomas Haggard, a cleric and son of Fisher's sister, Mary Charlotte. Haggard conducted Melinda's funeral.[13]

The five Fisher brothers who served in the Western cavalry came home in 1865 well enough to make a fresh, albeit unpromising, start. Little is known now of their personalities, skills, interests, and motivations. Most of what is known of them now is found in Thomas Fisher's memoirs, in legal records, and in a scant oral tradition inherited by their progeny.

Only one of John Fisher's sons who had served in the Western cavalry, James Wesley, had been seriously wounded, and he was the first to die, though not before he had married, started a family, and made a modest living working a forty-acre farm near Farmington, only a few miles from where he had been born and reared.

His brother, Thomas, wrote that Jim was bugler of Starnes' Fourth Tennessee Cavalry and always rode at the front armed with rifle and pistols. Returning home from the war, Jim was sought after as a suitor by two local women, according to Thomas's narrative. But by December 1865, Jim's irrevocable marital decision was made, and he and Mollie Dryden plighted their troth. Thomas described a joyous "infare" or wedding reception for the couple which was unspoiled even by a dangerously destructive ice storm which damaged trees and plants in the area of Cave Spring.

Born February 1, 1838, to Sarah Hurt, who died giving him birth, Jim succumbed October 13, 1878, at the age of forty, from the effects of the gunshot wound in his right thigh, received when Nathan Bedford Forrest's Old Brigade was ambushed by the Fourth U.S. Cavalry at Douglas Church on the Lewisburg Pike near Franklin, Tennessee, on April 10, 1863. He suffered recurring pain from the minié ball lodged in his leg over a period of years. But Thomas recorded that he derived strength and consolation from his abiding faith in a merciful God who he believed would make all things right.

Jim lived in a period over fifty years before the development of antibiotics, and his wound reportedly continued to drain. The infection sapped his strength and eventually overcame his body's defenses. He was survived by his widow, Mollie Dryden of Farmington, two sons, Robert Lee and John Franklin, and three daughters, Ella, May, and Sally, the last named daughter having been born only three weeks before Jim's death.[14]

William Stratton, born December 7, 1842, only fourteen months older than Thomas, was the next brother to die. He married and pursued a career as a farmer in adjoining Williamson County near Franklin. Will was forty-one when he succumbed on May 17, 1884, from his wartime experiences. He was imprisoned early in 1863 at Ft. McHenry, Maryland. Shortly after his release, he was hospitalized with measles at Ringgold, Georgia. His health was undermined by exposure, medical neglect, and poor diet that accompanied his military duty.

He had taken leave and came home once in 1863 to convalesce from an attack of measles, a major cause of death in the army. Then he took leave twice in 1864 because he was not well. But each time, he returned to the army. He had been ill on the way home after receiving his parole as a prisoner of war at Gainesville, Alabama, on May 10, 1865. He kept a valuable wartime diary during 1864-1865.[15]

After the war, Will and his young family lived on a farm east of Franklin on the road to Murfreesboro with his wife Margaret's parents, William A. and Eliza Marshall. His health remained delicate until his death, perhaps from tuberculosis, at which time he left his widow, Margaret Marshall of Williamson County, and two daughters, Fannie Ellen and Margaret Ophelia.

William and Thomas, with only fourteen months separating their births, had been inseparable as boys on the farm. They had compatible personalities and a close affinity. As a child, William was unusually shy, a personality characteristic which Thomas believed led to his being a sometime school truant.

During the years 1890-1893, Thomas took Fannie Ellen (Nellie) Fisher, one of Will's daughters, into his home in Franklin and gave her two years in the Tennessee Female College in Franklin where she received her diploma. Thomas is credited with introducing Nellie to her future husband, William Henry Lovell.[16] In 1895 Thomas memorialized his brother by naming his fourth son for Will ten years after the latter's death.

In the 1890s, two more of the Fisher brothers died. The first was Elisha Monroe. Born on July 29, 1836, he grew up on his father's farm, taught school at Cave Spring, then served in the war. Monroe was elected a lieutenant in the Eighth Tennessee Cavalry Battalion in November 1861. But his illness from measles caused him to resign his commission and return home to recover after his battalion was moved to Chattanooga in February 1862. He took up arms again in September 1862 when he joined T.C.H. Miller's company of partisan rangers along with his brothers John Franklin, William Stratton, and Thomas Burr. He remained in the army until surrendered and paroled in May 1865.

Following the war, Monroe returned to school, then was a teacher and schoolmaster for thirty years. He married Olivia Williamson on July 29, 1869. He and Olivia lived first at Berlin, then at Farmington, where he conducted the local academy. After a few years, they moved to the home of Olivia's parents, J.J. and C.B. Williamson, on a farm in Maury County, adjacent to Marshall County, prior to their removal to Texas in 1894.

Monroe succumbed on June 18, 1896, in Longview, Texas, where he had gone to teach only two years earlier. He had followed one of his daughters, who went to Longview to teach and had married there. At his death, he was within thirty-five days of his sixtieth birthday and left his widow, Olivia Williamson, and two daughters, Minnie and Susie, who both taught school in Longview.

Thomas described his brother Monroe as having a "highly nervous" temperament, which revealed itself in degrees of manic-depressive behavior, "capable of highest ecstasy and deepest despair." Concurrently, Thomas observed, Monroe was "a dear good brother with lots of influence." By his own example, Monroe had influenced Tom to return to school after the war. As a country schoolmaster, he had the power to "inspire his students with enthusiasm for study." As a churchman and devotee of revivalistic religion, Monroe would assume the role of an exhorter and effectively move his students to expressive manifestations of their frontier religion.

During his final illness, he arranged to have his remains returned from Texas for burial in the family cemetery at Cave Spring, an indication, Thomas believed, of his brother's "ardent temperament and family affection."[17] Since teachers barely subsisted on marginal wages in that place and time, the fulfillment of Monroe's last wish was a luxury that his survivors, who continued to live in Texas, likely could ill afford.

John Franklin, the first child (born August 19, 1831) of John Fisher and his first wife, Sarah Hurt, died on June 23, 1898, less than two months short of his sixty-seventh birthday. Following the war, Frank had come home to live and work on his father's farm. But following the death of his brother, Jim, in 1878, Frank went to manage the farm of Jim's widow, Mollie Dryden. He stayed and soon married his sister-in-law, Mollie, and became stepfather to her children by his brother, Jim. Frank and Mollie lived on her farm near Farmington in Marshall County and became parents of two children, Emma Elizabeth and Thomas Monroe.

According to Tom, Frank's personality was reticent and reserved, and "he lacked the qualities of leadership. . . ." But he was a good man and a worthy churchman, who, remembering how communicants in his youth had to *merit* receiving the Sacrament of Holy Communion, never felt that he was good enough. Thus he never received the sacrament even after standards were relaxed and casual churchmen were doing so regularly.

One might question whether Frank's taciturn temperament was a perverse reaction to pressures to succeed and to be an exemplar for the younger children sometimes felt by a family's eldest sibling. On the other hand, there is no evidence as to what expectations or behavioral requirements Frank's parents may or may *not* have placed upon their first son.

Apparently Frank maintained a continuing interest in the Southern Confederacy and the soldiers thereof. In April 1896, the *Confederate Veteran* reported that J.F. Fisher of Farmington, Tennessee, had contributed $1.00 to the Sam Davis Memorial Fund, strongly supported by the magazine, which

Thomas Burr Fisher, October 1920.

eventuated in the erection of an heroic statue of Davis on the grounds of the state capitol funded, according to the sponsors, by contributions from people of every state in the American Union. The Davis monument was unveiled in Nashville on April 29, 1909, long after Frank's death.[18]

Thomas managed to outlive all his siblings, including his two older half-sisters, Mary Charlotte Fisher Haggard (1833-1898) and Frances Elizabeth Fisher Hunter (1835-1855), as well as his younger brother, Bascom Hurt (1852-1917), his junior by eight years.[19] He was the only one of John Fisher's veteran sons who lived into the twentieth century and who, in his final illness, received what would have been considered modern medical care in a large city hospital, or for whom an official death certificate was issued, both of which were results of Thomas's relative longevity. But beyond that, he appears to have developed intellectually and socially into a significantly modern product of the early twentieth century.

He may have been the first member of his family to learn to speak and write standard English, an elitist fulfillment at the time. He wrote that his brother, Monroe, although a schoolmaster and, he believed, a competent scholar, did not achieve mastery of "elegant grammatical English" owing to "disadvantages which prevented his attainment of a polished education."

Coming home from the war from which losers normally emerged with no material resources at all, Tom and Monroe were enabled to enroll in a classical school operated by a war veteran, Captain James J. Finney, only five miles north of their home. Thomas did not reveal how the means were found which permitted him and Monroe to attend Finney's school. He simply wrote that "arrangements were somehow made and we started."

Then Finney encouraged Thomas, a good student, to seek the advantages of a college education and made arrangements for him to enroll in Finney's alma mater, Union University in Murfreesboro, Tennessee, a town in the patrician heartland of Middle Tennessee. Fisher wrote that Finney traveled to Murfreesboro and arranged with Union's faculty to extend him credit. Thomas would attend school and pay later. Thomas then dealt with the matter of room and board while he would attend Union. Contacting his wartime regimental forage master, John Jordan, the only man he said he knew in Murfreesboro, Fisher laid before Jordan his plans and his problem.

Jordan, a 36-year-old retail grocer and merchant of modest means, lived with his wife, Fanny, 24, and their two children, ages one and five, and others, including a black domestic, Lucy Miller, 27; a black plasterer, John Ready, 27; and three other minor whites, Robert Jordan, 16; W.B. Boone, 15; and C.F. Tate, 16.

Fisher refused Jordan's offer to board him, thus acknowledging Jordan's limited resources in meeting the current demands on him from his extended family. Jordan then agreed to find affordable lodgings for Fisher in the town and subsequently reported that William A. Ransom would provide room and board for $21.00 per month, *payment to be made at Fisher's convenience.*

Ransom, 46, was a well-capitalized retail grocer and lumber dealer, who lived in Murfreesboro's Third Ward with his wife, Sarah, 37, six children ranging in age from two to 13, a white domestic, Sylvia Burt, 37; a black porter, Henry Brown, 27; and Knox Ridley, 16, white, who worked as a clerk in Ransom's grocery. This was the Ransom household in which Thomas Fisher lived while attending Union University.

Thus, through the kindness of strangers, Fisher attended college. While a student at Union, Fisher accepted a loan of $100 from the Ministerial Educational Aid Society of the Tennessee Conference of the Methodist Episcopal Church, South, the only source of money made available to him during his school days mentioned by Fisher in his memoirs. He graduated from Union in 1869.[20]

Union University dated from September 1845, when it began classes under the auspices of Tennessee Baptists. In 1850 it had occupied a new college hall designed and built by Adolphus Heiman (1809–1862), a Nashville architect originally from Potsdam, Brandenburg, Prussia, who sided with the South and died in uniform during the war.

The school closed in the fall of 1861 owing to the pressures of war. Its work was revived after the war with a faculty of three, Duncan H. Selph, president and professor of moral philosophy and theology; Thomas Treadwell Eaton, professor of mathematics and natural science; and George W. Jarman, professor of ancient languages. Thomas paid tribute to his professors at Union as being men of character and ability. A victim of hard times, Union University in Murfreesboro closed its doors permanently in 1873.[21]

Upon graduating from Union, Thomas was admitted on trial to the Tennessee Conference of the Methodist Episcopal Church, South, in 1869, and, pursuant to the appointive system of the church, served pastorates and district superintendencies during 49 years in a number of communities in Middle Tennessee, including two rural circuits in Bedford and Giles counties early in his career, then in Nashville, Fayetteville, Chapel Hill, Lebanon, Franklin, Springfield, Gallatin, Spring Hill, Erin, and Hendersonville. He served an additional year in Piedmont, Oklahoma, in 1910–1911.[22]

Tom did not marry the young woman who had waited for him through the war years. Instead, his deferment of marriage while he attended school resulted in the object of his first romantic attachment terminating their relationship.[23]

On September 22, 1872, Tom married Sallie Roberts of Chapel Hill, with whom he had four children, Wilson Phillips, Fannie, John Roberts, and Mary. After Sallie died of cancer on May 20, 1889, he married Mollie Eastham of Nashville on December 2, 1890, and had two sons, Thomas Waterston and Will Stratton. Mollie died of cancer on April 17, 1903.

Fisher's first wife, Sallie, died at home in Chapel Hill. She had been under the care of Duncan Eve, a surgeon from Nashville whose father, Paul Eve, had a remarkable career as medical educator/military surgeon in both

Europe and America, and as president of the American Medical Association (1857–1858). Duncan's brother, Paul Eve, Jr., was likewise a surgeon.

Duncan Eve rode 40 miles out from Nashville to the Fishers' Chapel Hill home. He brought with him a retinue of assistants and performed exploratory surgery ostensibly to relieve fluid forming in the abdominal cavity. What he found was possibly a malignant ovarian tumor which was observed to be beyond effective treatment by surgery.

Fisher's second wife, Mollie, was diagnosed with cancer of the breast and in March 1903 underwent a mastectomy performed by Richard Douglas, a specialist in gynecology and abdominal surgery who operated an infirmary in Nashville and was on the faculty of the Vanderbilt Medical Department. Following the surgery, it was found that the malignancy had spread to the liver. Death came within a few weeks.[24]

Thomas married Letitia (Lula) Boone of Gallatin on December 22, 1904, and with her had a son, Howard Boone.

During 1909–1911, Fisher lived among several of Lula's siblings in Clinton and Piedmont, Oklahoma, in an unsuccessful attempt to find a congenial climate for his wife, whose health was failing. He returned to Tennessee in 1911 to his parish ministry and was superannuated in November 1920 at the age of seventy-six. Lula had preceded him in her death from tuberculosis on December 10, 1913.[25]

Because of the two memoirs he wrote, there is more information available about Thomas Burr Fisher than about all his siblings combined. Further, he left either outlines or extensive notes of about 200 sermons that he delivered during his ministry, and there are letters and newspaper accounts which shed light on his work and persona, and books from his personal library remain.

There is no evidence in Thomas's writings of any deep or abiding animosity toward Yankees growing out of the South's defeat in the Civil War such as has colored the Southern white ethos since the war. Although he wrote that he never agreed with the manner in which slavery was abolished, there is no evidence that he retained any bitterness relative to abolitionism or emancipation.[26]

As a soldier in the war, he likely developed the mutual respect that seemed to characterize soldiers on both sides of the conflict. His attitude was conspicuously at variance with some of the verbal abuse hurled by both sides in postwar confrontations of detestation and abhorrence that sometimes characterized sectional relations after 1865.

As a cleric of a sectionally divided church in which slavery had been a major social issue beginning with the church's organization in 1784, Thomas surely was aware of the ill feeling that was sometimes manifested between members of the Methodist Episcopal Church, North, and the Church, South, beginning in 1844 when the sectional split took place. During the war, representatives of the northern church, mistakenly believing a Northern victory would destroy the raison d'etre of the church's disunion, came south and, with the aid of the U.S. War Department, laid claim to properties of the southern church.[27] Those who did so were premature. The sectional split in Episcopal Methodism was not healed until 1939.

But Fisher's memoirs and sermons are silent on a number of issues of importance during the early years of his life. He did not address the class consciousness in the antebellum South or in the Confederate army which was revealed in responses to the Tennessee Civil War Veterans Questionnaire, reportedly the only effort by a state of the American Union to preserve the memories of its Civil War generation.

According to Fred Arthur Bailey's analysis of responses to the questionnaire, choice of service in the war, either infantry, cavalry, or artillery, was a function of class distinctions. While most Confederate soldiers from each social level, whether (using Bailey's classifications) elite, slaveholding yeomen, non-slaveholding yeomen, or poor, were in the infantry, the cavalry attracted a disproportionate share of wealthy Confederates.

Responses also indicated that, of Tennessee Confederate soldiers captured and released before the end of the war, those from the most affluent class were far more likely to return to active duty than were those of poorer classes who had less to gain and perhaps more to lose by returning. Allied to this perception is the suggestion of cumulative responses that each Southern setback in the war reduced the resolve of the soldiers to persist in the fight. "Long before the actual end of the war, thousands of Tennesseans, especially the poor and the yeomen, had given up the cause."[28]

Although Fisher did not address class-consciousness in the antebellum South or in the Confederate army, he reflected a consciousness of class in twentieth century society in a number of his sermons.

Prior to the war, a patrician and nationally influential society had developed over a period of eighty years in the heartland of Middle Tennessee. During the war, the heartland endured the worst of social, economic, and physical destruction at the hands of the Union army, the desertion of slaves from their masters, internecine warfare between Union and Confederate families, and outbreaks of banditry, jayhawking, and bushwhacking practiced by men within their communities who did not hesitate to use violence. Only parts of occupied and fought-over Virginia suffered as much destruction and social disorganization during the period.

Commerce all but ceased to exist. Hunger became endemic. The livestock, grain, silage, and produce of farmers was stolen. Fences and farm buildings were destroyed. Townspeople were unemployed since the means of commerce were no longer at hand. The poor suffered most pitiably. The rich were inconvenienced and sometimes jailed for their southern sentiments. They lost investments in Confederate debentures and bore the expense of rebuilding farms and businesses which were damaged or destroyed during the war. Most, however, managed to retain their privileged positions at the top of the social and economic pyramid. There were few people with sufficient influence to displace them.

Of course, Fisher was in the army while most of the domestic destruction occurred. Apparently the disorganization of life in occupied wartime Middle Tennessee was not burned into his consciousness sufficiently to cause him to comment upon it when he wrote his memoirs late in his life.

During the war, race relations changed dramatically. Beginning in 1862, slaves in Middle Tennessee, both men and women, emboldened by the presence of occupying troops, walked away from their masters. Under the wartime Unionist government in Nashville, enforcement of the state's slave code was dismantled in a series of judicial rulings. Thereafter, slaves might sue their masters, open schools, work for wages, and join the army.

Following the war, race relations deteriorated. The hostility of poor whites against blacks increased when the latter received schooling and the vote and began to get the jobs, working for lower wages, of some poor whites. Most whites of all classes expected freedmen and women to be submissive servants without rights. Despite new laws to protect blacks, the latter could not expect to be dealt with justly in courts of law or in the workplace, where fraud became commonplace against blacks who worked under contract or for crop shares. White employers used their leverage to see that blacks voted the right way. When they did not, they might expect to be fired or evicted. Black tradesmen commonly were boycotted. And, of course, violence was used against blacks to keep them submissive.[29]

Fisher was in school during most of the immediate postwar racial turmoil. And while he wrote little about the details of what had transpired then in race relations, he reflected in his memoirs a consciousness of what had gone on when he wrote empathetically of the black servants who had worked for him and his family.

Thomas Fisher was stationed in Gallatin, Tennessee, in October 1904 and was host to Bishop Earl Cranston (1840–1932) of Athens, Ohio, a prelate of the northern church and a proponent of church reunification. Cranston was in town to preside over the Tennessee Annual Conference of the Colored Methodist Episcopal Church. Thomas invited the bishop to speak on a Sunday evening at his church, the leading Methodist church in Gallatin.

Thomas wrote that Cranston was "a lovable man" and that he delivered "a great sermon . . . one we all enjoyed." Since the appearance of a bishop in a local pulpit was a treat widely appreciated in towns big and small, Cranston spoke "to a crowded congregation of delighted hearers," according to Fisher.[30]

With his invitation, Thomas may have advanced the cause of mutual understanding and forbearance and perhaps played a role in binding up the wounds of sectional antipathy which were still quite open in 1904.

Despite what Thomas might have done to heal sectional strife, he once made reference to "the period of the *miserable* Carpet Bag Rule of the South" (italics added) when he related an instance of actual racial equity on the occasion of his accepting an invitation to dine with one of his father's former slaves.

When he wrote the passage about Reconstruction in 1920, he likely was under the influence of Columbia University's Professor William A. Dunning, whose revisionist school ably stated the conservative Southern white view of Reconstruction which for many years dominated opinion of the period both in the North and South.[31]

While Thomas did *not* express belief in white supremacy, there is no evidence that he took to the streets to oppose it when it was quite openly and unapologetically the modus vivendi in America.

He described himself in 1921 as a "chastened optimist," one who had endured much of sadness as well as material deprivation but who "believed that the world is growing better" and more rapidly so. He wrote that he believed there was "more good than bad, more health than sickness, more joy than sorrow, more love than hate, more life than death." Here he was reflecting the optimism of contemporary progressive religionists who, around the turn of the twentieth century, saw the new century as the beginning of a new and promising epoch.[32]

In the spirit of the times, an ecumenical periodical was named *The Christian Century* in 1900, its current name, in anticipation of a hundred years of human progress. The optimism of its editors and readers was severely tested by two world wars in the first half of the new century.

Thomas was strongly solicitous of the welfare of his family. He wrote that he felt the need for a mother for his motherless children after the deaths by cancer of both Sallie Roberts in 1889 and Mollie Eastham in 1903. This felt need caused him to remarry twice. Following the death of Lula Boone in 1913, he arranged, at age 69, in a wrenching decision, to have his son, Howard, eight, live with relatives in Oklahoma. But he made sure that close family ties remained in spite of spatial distance.[33]

In homiletics, he was a scriptural and humanistic preacher who lived long enough to come under the influence of late nineteenth- and early twentieth-century theological authors such as Henry Drummond, Harry Emerson Fosdick, Shailer Mathews, Theodore T. Munger, Walter Rauschenbusch, and Josiah Strong, all of whom may be counted as theologically and socially progressive. Their written works were in his library.

Fisher's library also contained a copy of Volume IV of *The Fundamentals: A Testimony to the Truth*, one of a series of 12 volumes, paperbound, published by the Testimony Publishing Company in Chicago, 1910–1912. The publisher's notice stated that the series of books was being sent to every pastor, evangelist, missionary, theological and college professor, theological student, Y.M.C.A. and Y.W.C.A. secretary, and editor of a religious paper in the English-speaking world whose addresses could be obtained. The effort was sustained with the material support of two unnamed laymen.

This series of volumes gave its name to fundamentalism, the post–World War I theological and religious reaction which has shown remarkable endurance. The insistence of fundamentalists on establishing their own rigid and unquestioned doctrinal standards, however, was out of harmony with Methodist history, tradition, and interest and not in keeping with the liberal or liberal evangelical theology that early in the twentieth century became, and largely remains, the most influential theological standard among the American church's clergy and laity. Accordingly, fundamentalism never found fertile ground in Methodism.[34]

Nor did fundamentalism seem to inspire Thomas Fisher in his writings or homilies. In an untitled sermon delivered on Sunday, December 10, 1916, in Trinity Church, Nashville, Fisher said of the Christian religion, "[It is] not a book religion, but a life religion. It centers in a person.... The Bible is its servant, not its source. In a *primary* sense, Christ gives us the Bible. No Christ, no Bible. [But the] converse [is] not true."

Hardly using the words of one who believed in the inerrancy of the scriptures in every detail, Fisher spoke of biblical criticism and said, "[It] aims to eliminate everything imperfect or untrue, and leave only that which cannot successfully be assailed." He finished his sermon by commending to his listeners the work of the British and American Bible Societies.[35]

Fisher grew out of a rural-based, mid-nineteenth-century religious culture which favored revivalism as its principal modus operandi. Although he alluded to his father's religious proclivities only in a general way, Fisher made it clear that his mother was an ardent churchwoman who shared in the uninhibitedly joyous religious expressions of the revivalism of the frontier.[36]

It seems clear, however, from a reading of his sermons and notes, that Fisher moved beyond his bucolic roots to a view of religion marked by a common sense approach to belief systems enlightened by modern critical scholarship and, for him, a preoccupation with an inclusive humane, urbane, and ethically mature theistic understanding of the message of Jesus.

There is circumstantial evidence that Fisher may have been influenced by Horace Bushnell's view of "Christian nurture" to abandon sole reliance upon revivals and their insistence upon a specific emotional experience of conversion. Bushnell (1802–1876), a Congregationalist graduate of Yale College and Divinity School, author, theologian, and pastor of North Church in Hartford, believed that a child might grow up in a Christian environment in such a way that the child might never require a conversion to turn him or her away from the path of sin and death.

Fisher was in possession of Theodore Munger's biography of Bushnell, published in 1900.[37] His surviving homilies reflect that he used a Christian nurture approach to building the faith of his hearers rather than an attempt to convict his hearers of their unforgiven sins, a conviction which might concern them sufficiently to cause them to turn to God and experience a wrenching conversion experience.

Fisher seems to have been implicitly a theist and a believer in the divinity of Christ without feeling the need to argue either point. But he betrayed no normative interest in theological terms, opinions, or creeds and no interest at all in such contemporary theological interests as millennialism, holiness, or anti–Darwinism.

In a period when temperance, as the country's most widely debated social reform, often stood at center stage in America's consciousness, Fisher left no notes of sermons dealing exclusively with the issue. He mentioned temperance and sobriety briefly in a few sermons which dealt principally with broader social and economic issues pursuant to scriptural insights.

During the last three or four years of his active ministry, some of his sermons indicate that he supported: (1) President Wilson's decision to seek U.S. involvement in World War I; (2) a postwar international progression toward representative government and world federation; (3) resolutions by church bodies calling the attention of the world's political leaders to the burden of maintaining armies and navies "and the crime of killing men *even in war*" (italics added); (4) improvements at home in terms of social justice, including closer relations between capitalists and laboring people, who he observed had begun to talk together of living wages, profit sharing, worker pensions, and the desirability of a more equitable distribution of the fruits of one's labor, e.g., he preferred to "make 20,000 men [employees] prosperous and contented instead of a few multimillionaires."

In a sermon on "Labor Conflicts of 1919," he referred to strikes of steel workers, coal miners, railroad employees, and longshoremen which resulted in egregiously heavy losses of wages and corporate profits. He believed that the church should stand for the workers' right to organize for collective bargaining within ethical constraints and due regard for the public interest. The church should take this position because (1) it is right and prudent, and (2) the manhood and freedom of the workers are at stake.

Relations between employers and workers, he believed, should cease to be adversarial. We need, he said, to move to a new economic code which substitutes the Golden Rule for destructive competition. The new code should be "recognized and applied to stockholders, directors, presidents and workers of all classes." It would involve the creation of more democratically organized workplaces, a living wage, and improved, closer human relations between employers and workers wherein "employers visit the homes of workers in time of sickness or death and sit side by side with workers and their families in church."[38]

He expressed no regret for his participation in the War between the States and wrote of his and his brothers' participation in the war in a matter-of-fact way with neither rancorous self-pity nor jingoistic pride. But a reading of his memoirs reveals that he had some of the genteel white Southerner's defensiveness about slavery, i.e., he wanted to make it clear that his father's slaves had been well-treated, that he was kindly disposed toward, and had cordial relations with, blacks, and that he was aware of the injustices visited upon blacks every day.[39]

In an undated sermon dealing generically with the Kingdom of Heaven, Fisher enumerated "some visible effects of Christianity on human society." He credited Christianity with "(a) the development of a sense of human brotherhood, (b) belief in the sacredness of human rights, (c) the destruction of slavery . . . [and] (i) . . . transforming the hostility of races into brotherly love."

And in another sermon which purported to answer the question, "What Is True Christian Fellowship?" Fisher closed with these words: "The one blood of the race is the natural basis for [our] unity. The fellowship of believers would efface every line of division between nations, churches, [and] individuals, and make the world one united glorious brotherhood."

Time and again in his sermons, he returned to the theme of the brotherhood of mankind. In one such sermon, the internal evidence of which indicates that it was delivered just after the end of World War I, he emphasized mankind's common interests, obligations, and interdependence "so that no one can say to his fellows: 'I need nothing from you. I owe nothing to you.'"

In an undated sermon on "Doing the Greatest Good," Fisher made clear his belief in the Christian religion's strong identification with the poor. He based this conviction upon his reading of the exemplary model of Jesus's life and teachings as well as the examples of the mendicant friars, followers of St. Francis of Assisi, the early English Methodists, and the Salvation Army. And he added: "Part of the church's work [is] to remove grinding poverty and preventable diseases."[40]

Fisher opposed vigilantism and lynch lawlessness in an undated homily titled, "Law and Order," the body of which seems to describe both violent strikebreaking in the North and the lynching of blacks in the South. Of course, the ultimate injustice to blacks and whites alike is the wanton taking of their lives by lynching, rioting, or other mob violence, a problem of substantial dimensions during the period 1865–1940 in America.

Fisher lived during the abuse and killing of blacks by the Ku Klux Klan in the 1860s, race riots in 1866 between black troops and city police in Memphis which cost 46 black lives and the destruction of black-owned property, and a disturbance in New Orleans in July 1866 in which 200 blacks and a dozen policemen were killed.

Other race riots which resulted in lynchings, together with public apathy among Northern whites toward the enforcement of civil rights in the South, assured that violence against blacks decade after decade would be a frequently recurring problem during Fisher's adult life first in the South and then, as black seeking work moved into northern cities, in the North.

Fisher seems to have been aware of the unemployment, economic helplessness, and homelessness of white workers in economically depressed cities of America. Such conditions culminated in the Thompkins Square police charge on unemployed people seeking relief in New York City on January 13, 1874. Later the same year, there were outbreaks of violence in the anthracite coal fields of eastern Pennsylvania which resulted in the suppression, jailing, and execution of strike leaders.

In the railroad strikes of 1877, Federal troops were called out to intervene and suppress labor discontent. And on May 3, 1886, a clash between strikers and strikebreakers at the McCormack Harvester plant in Chicago resulted in the deaths of four people. The next day, a peaceful protest of working men in Haymarket Square was in the process of breaking up when a bomb exploded amidst a detachment of 200 policemen. Police shots fired into the workers were answered, and both sides sustained casualties. Anarchists were blamed for the bombing. The police rounded up eight self-confessed anarchists, and the eight were tried and convicted despite there being no evidence to connect any of the eight with the bombing.

Six years later, when Governor John Peter Altgeld of Illinois pardoned the convicted felons on the basis that they had not received a fair trial, Altgeld's act of simple justice was attacked across the country because of widespread fear and hatred of anarchists.[41]

In dealing homiletically with such incidents of extralegal violence, Fisher described the American government as better than those of antiquity but subject to improvement in the way it deals with such violence. Fisher said our government "can be made far better than it is if every good citizen will rise up and say: 'The law shall be obeyed and enforced.'"

He acknowledged that "the period through which we are passing is, to say the least, one of evolution. To many peoples, it is one of revolution. The old order is passing and a new order is being introduced." Forces are conspiring to throw off "restraints ... [and] appropriate everything in sight, disregarding the rights and interests of others. Even human life is nothing ... to many [people] if it stands in the way of their selfish greed."

In retaliation, "we rise up and in our righteous wrath ... wreak vengeance on the offender by hanging, shooting, and burning," Fisher said. "Thus we are destroying the very shelter to which we must look for protection in the evil day."

Noting that many people blame "hoodlums" and "riffraff" for inciting and leading "the mobs in their savage work while the good citizens are at home and know nothing of the cruelty and murder until it is done," Fisher argued that officers of the law working with law-abiding citizens need to organize for the prevention of mob violence and to insist upon timely legal justice for the criminals responsible for "these dark and bloody incidents."[42]

Fisher stated that he was always opposed to slavery, but he did not make clear his view of a racially egalitarian society. Nevertheless he recorded that one of the women who was his father's slave invited him and Monroe to share a meal with her in her new home after emancipation. She had gone to live with her husband and children on the property of her husband's former owner. He wrote that he accepted her invitation and enjoyed her hospitality. "I went and have always been glad of it."

The racial etiquette of the time, during Reconstruction when there was talk of establishing racial equality, *but seldom by Southern whites*, would have precluded both the invitation and the acceptance thereof since both rested upon an assumption of social equality of the two parties.[43] Tom and his hostess apparently were amenable to a different sanction.

Thomas felt a particular debt to a black domestic servant, Bitha Holt of Nashville, whom he engaged shortly after Sallie Roberts was taken by death in 1889. He wrote that "Aunt Bitha" became "black mammy," a surrogate mother, to his children, Wilson, John, and Mary. "She was always there, kind and patient and trustworthy."

In 1896, he engaged a black woman, Josie Holman of Lebanon, who had been recommended to his wife, Mollie Eastham, by Susan Tarver, wife of Benjamin Tarver, a lawyer and former judge of the chancery court of Tennessee. Of "Aunt Josie" he wrote: "She was old enough to have been a slave, was never married, yet she adopted and reared more than one of her own race. One of those whom she reared was at that time a professor in the Meharry Medical School in South Nashville. . . . He visited her twice while she was with us, and I greatly enjoyed talking with him, finding him easy master of faultless English, and familiar with all that was taught in his department."

Josie Holman was given charge of both the laundry and the culinary arts in the home and was entrusted with the milking and feeding of the family's cow. Thomas noted that she was especially fond of their youngest son, Will, who was hardly a year old when Josie came. She would have Will eat with her at the kitchen table where she patiently and lovingly saw that he was fully satisfied at mealtimes.

Tom recorded that Josie went with him and his family when they moved to Springfield in 1898. She stayed as long as she was able to work, then returned to Lebanon to spend her last days. Tom's wife, Mollie, visited her in Lebanon and found Josie confined to her bed but glad to receive her. Tom wrote that "soon after she went to her reward, which I doubt not will be more glorious than that of many of us who had better advantages."[44]

Thomas was a strong believer in education. All but one of his offspring were college-trained. Two, Wilson and John, became pedagogues by profession. Wilson was teacher of Greek and Latin and a high school principal in the Nashville public school system. John was professor of modern languages at Randolph-Macon College in Ashland and department head at the College of William and Mary in Williamsburg, Virginia. Students of Wilson and John remember each of them with affection and gratitude.[45]

Tom regretted that during his years in the Confederate army, he lost the opportunity to form classes with other soldiers under the tutelage of college graduates. During World War I, he urged the young men he knew who were going off to war to take college courses in their training camps. He was delighted to learn that the United States Army in 1917–1918 provided for such courses. The army, he said with apparent hyperbole, was "the greatest literary school in the land."[46]

As to his approach to the ministerial profession, he commented about his ministry in Springfield, Tennessee, 1898–1902: "I tried to lead . . . by example," he said, "and in my pulpit ministrations, to a deeper and more thorough consecration of life, and time, and possessions to God, and to the interests of humanity." He sought to bring the churches of the community together, to eliminate denominational competition and to foster cooperation instead. For his trouble, he wrote that he and his family became recipients of various acts of Christian charity.[47]

In 1890, Thomas Fisher's career was severely tested when it clashed with that of an old comrade-in-arms, David C. Kelley, "the petted idol of the fashionable Methodists at Nashville." In 1890 Kelley made a run for governor of Tennessee and temporarily left his clerical appointment to do so. Fisher showed something of his commitment to his calling in the incident and in subsequent repercussions thereto.

When Kelley ran for governor, his character was challenged by a colleague, George W. Winn, Nashville city missionary, who alleged, at the Tennessee Annual Conference in Pulaski in October 1890, that Kelley had left his appointment, a pastorate in Gallatin. Bishop Robert K. Hargrove, presiding, appointed Fisher to chair a committee to investigate the charge.

Fisher wrote that friends urged him to refuse to serve on the committee, owing to Kelley's popularity. If the committee found against Kelley, Fisher's future in the conference might be dimmed. Fisher preferred *not* to serve but, once appointed, felt it his duty to do so.

Frustrated by Kelley in their efforts to obtain information needed to resolve the dispute, Fisher and his committee members returned a finding that they deemed a trial of the charge necessary.

Fisher became a pariah to Kelley partisans when the Tennessee Conference temporarily suspended Kelley after finding him guilty as charged of leaving his station. Kelley appealed the verdict to the General Conference of 1894, a body which reversed the action of the Tennessee Conference. Fisher, of course, did not serve on the conference committee which found Kelley guilty. But he chaired the committee which recommended that the charge against Kelley go to trial, as in a grand jury indictment.

In 1894, when Fisher was appointed to Elm Street Church in Nashville, a station that Kelley had just vacated, parochial Kelley partisans tried to have Fisher's appointment rescinded. When the appointing bishop, William Wallace Duncan, refused their request, disaffected members cut Fisher's salary to $1,200 for the year. They also cut their financial contributions and their involvement in the work of the parish for the balance of the year. In 1895, Fisher was relieved when appointed by Bishop Alpheus Waters Wilson to the Lebanon District as presiding elder.

Fisher wrote in 1921 that Kelley, who died in 1909, was cool to him after Kelley's trial in 1890 until some years later when the two had occasion to work together. The occasion may have been when Kelley officiated and Fisher assisted at the funeral of Edward H. East (1830-1904), member of the Nashville bar, member of the state legislature both before and after the war, Tennessee Unionist in 1861-1865 who served as Tennessee's wartime Secretary of State, judge of the Davidson County Chancery Court in 1869-1872, and first president of the Vanderbilt University Board of Trust, beginning in 1872.

Fisher had been East's pastor in 1870-1873 at Trinity Church, then a mission, and, as an unmarried cleric, had boarded in the East family home on the Dickerson road four miles north of Nashville in 1870. Fisher's ties with East and his personable and enthusiastic wife, Tennessee, remained intact for over thirty years. Their divergent political views during the 1861-1865 war were no impediment to their friendship.[48]

Fisher was a clergyman of a church which did not ordain women. Indeed women only gained equal rights with men to vote and hold *lay* offices in the church in 1918, just two years prior to the ratification of the woman's suffrage amendment of the United States Constitution. In 1939 the Methodist Episcopal Church, South, at last sanctioned the exercise of sacerdotal duties by women when it merged with the Methodist Episcopal Church and the Methodist Protestant Church, both of which had previously approved the ordination of women.[49]

The ordination of women was a theme that Fisher did not directly address in his writings or sermons. Nevertheless, he may have inadvertently struck a small blow in behalf of women's clerical rights in an undated sermon in which he dealt with the universality of Jesus. "The humanity of Jesus," he said, "[is] elemental, [and] transcends all surface distinctions of country or rank, temperament or sex. *A woman might have done anything He did* [italics added]. Among his friends [were] as many women as men." Here Fisher seems to have struck upon an adequate summation of a brief for women's ecclesiastical rights.[50]

Within Fisher's communion during his adulthood were leaders with advanced theological, social, and cultural views who labored hard to liberate their people. Such leaders were found at all levels, national, regional, and local. Their reputations made it possible for Fisher and other like-minded clergy to be less uncomfortable espousing advanced views on theology, race, education, missions, government, or labor-management relations.

Fisher's intellectual liberality grew naturally out of his manifest love of learning, his reliance upon empirical reason or common sense, his enthusiasm for knowledge and objectivity, and his commonsense rejection of prejudice, propaganda, misinformation, stereotypes, ideological dogma, egocentrism and ethnocentrism, authoritarian pontifications, and other defective habits of mind which serve as poor substitutes for knowledge and inductive reasoning. Surely Fisher sometimes fell short of perfection in his habits of intellect. But his resources of mind and heart seem to have caused him to deal respectfully and honestly with people without being manipulative.

Although the forces of darkness, division, and disaffection are always persistent, enlightened clergy and lay people in the Methodist Episcopal Church, South, were by no means alone during Fisher's professional years. In the capital of Tennessee alone, Fisher could find strength in the company of such contemporaries as Chancellor James Hampton Kirkland of Vanderbilt University, who, as a Methodist in the 1890s, believed in a "broad" or "liberal" religious identity for the university and had a personal openness to the historical method and the higher criticism as well as a Christian accommodation to Darwinian evolution.[51]

Kirkland fought the good fight of reasoned enlightenment through his 44 years as chancellor, beginning with his election in 1893. His admiring biographer, Edwin Mims, wrote of him that "by reason of his organization of the Southern Association of Colleges and Schools (1895) and of the Southern University Conference (1935), by his participation in the work of the Conference for Education in the South and the Southern Education Board, he was generally referred to as the 'Chancellor of Southern Education,' 'the greatest educational statesman the South has ever produced.'"

At Vanderbilt's semicentennial celebration in 1925, James R. Angell, President of Yale University, hailed Kirkland for having encouraged at Vanderbilt complete freedom of instruction and investigation and for having steadily pushed forward intellectual and academic standards.

In an address on the same occasion in 1925 before a convocation which included many of the leading figures in American academia, Kirkland spoke of "Vanderbilt University: Retrospect and Prospect." In his words, Kirkland drew a sharp distinction between stiflingly narrow religious dogma and the open intellectual atmosphere on the Vanderbilt campus to which he contributed so much.

He said: "The answer to the episode at Dayton [the unsuccessful legal challenge to the antievolution law heard earlier the same year] is the building of new laboratories on the Vanderbilt campus for the teaching of science. The remedy for a narrow sectarianism and a belligerent fundamentalism is the establishment on this campus of a School of Religion, illustrating in its methods and in its organization the strength of a common faith and the glory of a universal worship."[52]

Two of Fisher's sons, Wilson and John, were Vanderbilt students and graduates at the turn of the century while Kirkland was chancellor. Their majors were both in languages, Kirkland's specialized field, more broadly, philology or linguistics, and they each taught languages.

Dean Wilbur Fisk Tillett of the School of Religion, an acquaintance and correspondent of Fisher in the Tennessee Conference, and Professor Edwin Mims, chair of the English department, Kirkland's biographer, represented the best in free inquiry and thought unfettered by prejudgments and ideology. And bishops Eugene R. Hendrix and Edwin Mouzon, university trustees, were supportive of the forces of freedom in the church-university struggle of 1901–1914. Hendrix also was a founder and the first president of the ecumenical Federal Council of the Churches of Christ in America in 1906,[53] an unusual achievement and distinction, one would believe, for a Southern churchman. All of these men had reputations for the highest character and intelligence in the community and had been drawn to Nashville in part by their joint labors in behalf of a free and enlightened Vanderbilt University.

The church-university struggle of 1901–1914, or "Vanderbilt Crisis," a regrettable aberration in the record of the church's polity, pitted one group of churchmen against another. On the one hand were those who wanted Vanderbilt to be not unlike a denominational college, such as most American churches have established and supported, whose staff and curriculum affirm the doctrines and discipline of the church and whose graduates would be committed to the interests of the church and its religious views. These Methodists largely represented conservative social and religious views.

On the other hand were those who had a vision of Vanderbilt as a free and unfettered university community whose first allegiance would be to free research and the discovery of truth. While they would not desire a libertine or a person of dubious character on the university's teaching staff, they would not insist on an ideological test for professors. These Methodists largely represented liberal social and religious views.

In 1914, Bishop Elijah Embree Hoss, 1849–1919, who had wished to rein in the liberal leaders of the university, led a cadre of conservative churchmen to walk away from Vanderbilt after losing a suit against the university trustees in which the general conference of the church, through its bishops, both inspired by Hoss, sought to establish two contentions: (1) that the conference had the right to elect the trustees, and (2) that the bishops had the right of visitation, which amounted to having a veto over the actions of the board, which would include, of course, faculty appointments. Such rights, according to Edwin Mims, would have been unprecedented. They had neither been exercised nor claimed during Vanderbilt's forty-year history, nor had they been asserted over any other organization related to the church.

Vanderbilt's church affiliation could have been resumed on its previous basis, i.e., pursuant to the school's charter, following the decision of the State Supreme Court of Tennessee. But when the petitioners lost their court case, they proceeded to sever connections with Vanderbilt and to set out to support the establishment of two new universities in Vanderbilt's place.

It is ironical that within ten years, provision had been made for not two but three new church-affiliated universities. In 1915, Emory College, founded in 1836 in Oxford, Georgia, was elevated to university status with a new campus in an Atlanta suburb. The same year, a new institution of higher learning, Southern Methodist University, opened its doors to students in Highland Park, a suburb of Dallas, Texas. And in 1924, James Buchanan Duke announced that he would provide funds to build upon Trinity College, founded in 1838, a university with a new campus in a western suburb of Durham, North Carolina. Trinity College became Duke University.[54]

Had the church's leaders learned from the Vanderbilt unpleasantness? The administration of none of the new universities was hobbled by an attack upon its freedom such as Vanderbilt had so recently survived.[55]

While Fisher left no writing in which he directly addressed the Vanderbilt issue in the church, he left several sermons wherein he supported the raising of money for the church's schools. Given his personal alignment with progressive Christianity, he discussed education and schools and stated a case for education with a scripturally-based moral and ethical cast by which graduates might develop an abiding consciousness of God in their lives.

In one such homily, Fisher referred approvingly to the example of his nephew, Commodore Bascom Fisher, a recent graduate of Maryville College, a Presbyterian school in Maryville, Tennessee, who was influenced by family, his college environment, and the Student Volunteer Movement for Foreign Missions to seek a vocation in missions, a desirable form of service for committed Christians in America early in the twentieth century. He and his wife, Franke, a classmate, had gone out to Persia (Iran) in 1920 as educational missionaries in the service of the Presbyterian Church in the U.S.A.

Fisher's sermon appears to have been delivered in support of a denominational campaign launched by approval of the General Conference of 1918, the "Christian Education Movement," which aimed at raising $13 million for the schools and colleges of the Methodist Episcopal Church, South.[56] In his sermon, Fisher supported the liberal arts college in the service of the church vis-à-vis secular schools.

In yet another sermon delivered during World War I, Fisher discussed the balanced development of human capabilities present in all men and women and alluded to the role of higher education therein. He reviewed statistics from the annual report for 1910 of the United States Commissioner of Education on contributions to American higher education made by (1) state schools, (2) non-sectarian private schools, and (3) denominational schools.

From the statistics, Fisher fashioned an argument that denominational schools were doing heroic work, producing more graduates, and doing so with deficient endowments, smaller annual budgets, and often inferior equipment and facilities. But he insisted that, on balance, their work was "broad and thorough" and included the teaching of the belief "that the sacrificial life is more noble than the selfish [life]." Fisher's treatment of his subject makes it appear that the latter sermon, as with the previous one, was delivered with a view to encouraging parishioners to increase their financial support for denominational schools and colleges.

In yet another sermon delivered during World War I which dealt with individuals as citizens of the state, Fisher expressed his belief that for a government to have legitimacy, it must be supported by a citizenry that has "intelligence, morality, [and] patriotism." He noted that the American "government [was] under heavy strain now, [with] so many aliens, and the war." And he believed that, since the schools mould the citizen, "[the] highest aim of eduation should be to develop character." And the best standard for developing character was the Bible. "The Bible ought to have the highest place in our schools," he said.

"[One] cannot understand and appreciate English literature without knowledge [of the Bible]," he said, noting that in Shakespeare's works, there were 700 biblical allusions. Tennyson's poetry contained 500, he said. "All great orators and writers get inspiration and imagery from it. Philosophy and religion rest on it. The Bible has made us what we are as a nation." The burden of Fisher's argument was that the Bible should be in schools for use as an inspirational and edifying literary and cultural resource but not as a tool to indoctrinate students or as an object of bibliolatry.

Fisher finished his sermon by summarizing "the results of right education" as (1) fruitful sons, (2) cultured womanhood, (3) a prosperous nation with (4) an open and safe transportation system, and (5) a free, happy, contented, non-rebellious citizenry which knows no class distinctions and therefore no reason to complain of such or to take up arms to achieve. In other words, "[the] Kingdom of God on earth."[57]

Other intellectual and spiritual leaders of the Methodist Episcopal Church, South, increasingly had undertaken to show a sense of responsibility for improving the lot and lives of blacks for several decades during Fisher's professional life. The first to gain a national reputation for his work in the field was Atticus Greene Haygood of Georgia. Haygood became a leading proponent of black education through his platform appearances in both the North and South as well as through his books, some of which received critical acclaim and gained national repute. Haygood's *Our Brother in Black*, published in 1881, was a seminal assessment of the current and future condition of blacks in the South.

In 1882, Haygood became the first agent of the John F. Slater Fund, the first foundation established to aid black education exclusively. Haygood was elected bishop twice, in 1882, when he declined the office, and again in 1890. His work in behalf of blacks and his reputation therefor seem to have played an affirming role in the enthusiastic elections he received to the office.[58]

Two of Haygood's books were in Thomas Fisher's personal library. One might surmise that Fisher was influenced by Haygood in terms of the latter's race relations work.

But there were other leaders in the church in addition to Haygood who well might have influenced him, including Bishop Charles B. Galloway, who was both a Slater and a Vanderbilt trustee, and Will W. Alexander, a colleague of Fisher in the Tennessee Conference and head of the Commission on Interracial Cooperation, organized in Atlanta in 1919. The commission became a major force for better race relations in the South.

David C. Kelley, also of the Tennessee Conference, was a vocal force within the denomination in urging upon whites reasoned and informed views of blacks and relations between the races.[59]

In 1883, Fisher had a brief sojourn in the company of Bishop Holland Nimmons McTyeire while Fisher was presiding elder of the Gallatin District. McTyeire was father and architect of Vanderbilt University, shaping the university before its birth as a central university for the Methodist Episcopal Church, South. In its formative years, McTyeire continued to shape Vanderbilt in such a way that it might become a liberal seat of learning and a university of the first rank.

McTyeire obtained the financial backing of Cornelius Vanderbilt, the New York transportation tycoon, perhaps the richest man in America at the time, whose second wife, Frank Crawford, was a cousin and devoted friend of McTyeire's wife. The university opened its doors to students in 1875. Its initial financial resources (two gifts from "The Commodore" of $500,000 each and two more gifts of $100,000 each from the founder's son, William H. Vanderbilt) greatly exceeded those of any other institution of higher learning in the former Confederate states and placed Vanderbilt in a privileged and elite class of American universities together with a few of the oldest private colleges in the Northeast plus two latecomers, Cornell University (1865) in Ithaca, New York, and Johns Hopkins University (1876) in Baltimore.

As president of the board of trustees, McTyeire lived on the university campus in Nashville and closely attended to the affairs of the fledgling school until his death in 1889. At the same time, he did not neglect his episcopal duties. In the 23 years from his consecration in 1866 to the year prior to his death, McTyeire conducted 125 annual conferences for the church.[60]

In 1883, Fisher and McTyeire came together in Burkesville, Kentucky, located on the Cumberland River in Cumberland County, where the bishop had gone to conduct a district conference. Fisher had engaged McTyeire to preside at the Gallatin District Conference at Livingston in Overton County, Tennessee. There being no rail connections in the vicinity of this rugged and primitive section of the Cumberland Plateau, Fisher arduously conveyed McTyeire in his horse-drawn buggy across more than thirty miles of uncomfortable terrain from Burkesville to their destination.

Fisher admitted to being in awe of his influential and accomplished guest who had a reputation for austerity. He had previously seen McTyeire conduct two Tennessee Annual Conferences, first in 1873, when McTyeire had appointed him to the church in Fayetteville, then in 1881, when Fisher received appointment to Brentwood and Johnson Chapel. In 1885, McTyeire would conduct the Tennessee Conference for the last time.

Fisher wrote that McTyeire did not live up to his reputation for austerity when he was with him. Fisher was profuse in his praise of the good bishop, noting his warmly human qualities. As the two journeyed together, McTyeire revealed himself to be "open and confiding, appreciative and sympathetic." Fisher had daytime and evening appointments along the way. But McTyeire seemed to be glad to indulge Fisher by accompanying him on his rounds.

The two talked. Fisher revealed that he had been separated from his wife and children for several months and did not expect to see them again for an extended period, altogether a year. Owing to problems inherent in presiding over the Gallatin District, Fisher had returned his family to the Chapel Hill home of his wife's uncle, Ewing Wilson, when he received his Gallatin appointment in October 1882. The problems inhered in the great size of the district, the difficulty of travel owing to poor roads throughout much of the district, and the absence of a parsonage.

McTyeire was sympathetic when Fisher expressed a desire for an appointment near Chapel Hill at the next annual conference so he could attend to his wife's property interests in Ewing Wilson's estate. Wilson died in 1883 and left the bulk of his estate to Sallie Roberts Fisher. McTyeire promised to write Sallie a consoling letter upon his return to Nashville, and did so, according to Fisher.

After McTyeire conducted the Gallatin District Conference in Livingston, Fisher and the bishop made their way westward a distance of well over fifty miles to New Middleton in Smith County where McTyeire preached and he and Fisher parted.

In their brief time together, McTyeire seemed to take a fancy to Fisher's horse, John. Thereafter when they met, the bishop would inquire after Fisher's family and then would ask about John, the horse.[61]

As an inveterate horseman, Thomas had a favorite horse, Pat (not John), a gift to him from his wife's uncle, Ewing Wilson. When Thomas and Sallie Roberts went to live with Wilson in 1877, Wilson had perhaps twenty horses, mules, and colts running on his pastures. Among them Tom noticed a horse, three years old, about the color of a grey fox, small and well-built, and showing saddle qualities in all his movements. Further, the horse had common sense to a remarkable degree, never fretted, was never startled, never lost direction or refused to pull, would hold a buggy on a grade, work to anything, and carry anything on his back.

Thomas told Wilson that he wished to buy the horse. Instead, Wilson *gave* him the horse, Pat, and told Thomas to use the money he *would* have paid Wilson to buy himself books that would be professionally useful to him.

Thomas wrote that Wilson's gift meant much to him in more ways than one. In addition to having the faithful service of the horse, Tom learned something about Wilson for which he was always grateful. Wilson never counted Fisher his debtor because of his gift. Quite the contrary, he seemed to value Fisher's friendship and always wished him well. Second, Wilson showed his estimate of books and their value to a cleric. Third, Wilson showed his desire to see Fisher succeed in his chosen vocation.

Pat gave his owner 23 years of more than satisfactory service and, according to Tom, was the ideal horse for family and ministerial use. He met engines in narrow lanes when most horses would have been very frightened. Pat would pass them without concern. He never hestitated when being led or driven onto a ferry.

One day Pat was subjected to a severe test when one predictable move might have resulted in agonizing injury or death. He was grazing in the yard with several adults about him when Tom's son, Wilson, three years old, ran up and threw his arms around his hind legs and held Pat as tightly as he could.

Pat did not move.

The grey horse was the subject of an amusing and instructive story which Thomas related to more than one audience. It seems that Pat, after being hitched to the family's empty barouche one Sunday evening and awaiting the family members' boarding, calmly made his way alone to church when the family delayed too long over their evening meal. Noting Pat's absence, Thomas rapidly strode to the church and found Pat and the empty barouche standing at Pat's accustomed hitching post. The incident served to remind family members to eschew dawdling.

The horse proved so good for him and his family that Thomas quite early determined to keep him for as long as he lived and, at the end, to give him a decent burial. Pat had become a beloved family pet. After 23 years, Pat could no longer ingest enough food to keep him strong enough to work. Tom bought another horse. But he kept Pat and gave him all the ground feed and hay and grass that he could eat.

In 1904, the family was at Arlington Church six miles out of Nashville on the Murfreesboro road. Tom had come home after filling his appointment and was at table when his son, John, told him that Pat had come up to the barn and entered his stall. He lay down and rolled, he said, showing that he was suffering. John observed that Pat then went out, again returned and lay down, for the last time. "I expect Pat is dead by now," John said. They went out together and indeed found Pat dead. Pat was 30. Tom said there were tears of sorrow shed by every member of the family.

Pat had only recently been shod, and John suggested that they remove his shoes so they might be used again. But Will, only nine years old, with tears welling up in his eyes, insisted that they not disturb Pat and that he be buried with his shoes on.

To Will's entreaty they acceded. The next day, Monday, they solemnly buried Pat in the pound of the Arlington parsonage with grateful thanks for his life and the qualities of deportment that he exemplified for the edification of all who knew him. Patience, gentleness, and steadfastness suited him and us, Tom said.[62]

Late in his life, Fisher relinquished his habitual reliance upon the horse for transportation. In 1921 he purchased the first and only automobile he ever owned. He purchased a Ford, a black four-door T-Model soft-top touring car, and enjoyed the enhanced comfort, convenience, and freedom that the car provided. The lives of his son, Will, and daughter-in-law, Estelle, who shared his home in Nashville at 918 North Fifth Street, were enhanced substantially by the purchase. The family had entered the age of the automobile.[63]

Toward the end of his second year at Alex Erwin Church in Nashville in 1920, Fisher, in his seventy-seventh year, began to doubt his ability to work full-time for another year. He complained of what he believed to be rheumatism, which made standing and walking painful. He decided to seek the status of a superannuate at the Tennessee Annual Conference to be held in Shelbyville, October 6–9, 1920. With Bishop James Atkins (1850–1923) presiding, Fisher was one of 25 clerics who sought retirement at the conference.

The church offered little in retirement income. A resolution was offered on the fourth day of the conference by James H. Parkes, a Nashville printing executive and partner in the Foster & Parkes Company, which noted the "shameful inadequacy" of conference retirement funds and recommended the collection of a onetime offering early in the conference year to benefit "worn-out preachers . . . and widows of deceased preachers." The resolution was adopted and the budget item for conference claimants for 1920–1921 became $18,000, up from $11,693 in 1919–1920, still quite inadequate.

Fisher's first payment as a superannuate was the sum of $100 in 1920. He was one of 78 conference claimants who received benefits totalling anywhere from $25 to $250 each during the year 1919–1920. Eight widows of deceased clergy were paid an average sum of $338 each as a one-time death payment.[64]

Undoubtedly Fisher was more fortunate than most of his contemporaries and colleagues in a time when there was no social security, virtually no pension funds, public or private, and no health insurance. When he retired, he purchased a "quiet home" at 918 North Fifth Street in Nashville which he shared with his youngest adult son, Will, and Will's beautiful bride, Estelle. Will was a salesman with the Davie Printing Company and a future executive vice president of Ambrose Printing Company.[65]

In retirement, Fisher began writing his second memoir, undertook temporary ministerial duties when asked which included the performance of numerous marriages and funerals (for which he received honoraria, except for funerals, which were gladly received by a penurious superannuate), became involved in an industrial ministry for the first time, and found that his rheumatism abated.

For several months in 1921, he filled the pulpits of Brentwood and

Johnson Chapel for W.H. Baird, pastor, who underwent prostate surgery which resulted in an extended convalescence, then retirement.

His industrial ministry was sponsored by the Young Men's Christian Association. He began to go once a week, sometimes twice, at noontime to shops and factories in Nashville to speak to and counsel members of the workforce. Fisher wrote that, at the time, there were fifteen such places of business where he had freedom to go. He mentioned only two in his writings, the L. & N. Railroad shops and "the casket company."

He had misgivings initially about the industrial ministry. But as he participated, he gained confidence and came to enjoy his visits, getting acquainted with the workers and finding that they listened and spoke with him with genuine interest and pleasure.[66]

Although Fisher had served pastorates during five decades where he had affluent and influential community leaders and members of their families as congregants, it was fitting at the end of his professional life that he found he had not lost the common touch that he so valued. By serving an industrial ministry of workers from varying trades and with different degrees of skills, he gave renewed emphasis to some of the social and religious concerns that he expressed to audiences through the years.

Thomas Fisher died of acute prostatitis with cystitis following influenza, according to his physician, Stanley R. Teachout, in St. Thomas Hospital in Nashville, March 2, 1922, in his seventy-ninth year. Obsequies were held in McKendree Church, Nashville, the city's oldest church, with the Methodist ministers of the city serving as pallbearers. Interment was in the Boone family lot in the public cemetery in Gallatin, Tennessee. At his death, an obituary writer in the *Nashville Banner* credited him with being "universally loved and respected throughout Middle Tennessee."[67]

Fisher was survived by six children, Wilson, John, Mary, Thomas, Will, and Howard, in whose memories, without exception, their father remained a pleasant, gentle, and beloved source of strength, love, and rectitude.

Of Thomas's seven children, Howard Boone Fisher was the last surviving. He died on April 18, 1991, in Dallas, Texas.[68]

Howard was the last surviving child of John Fisher's five sons, an American Civil War generation, who, as they perceived it, served their country in the Western cavalry.

Appendix A

Soldiers Who Served in Company D, Fourth Tennessee Cavalry Regiment, from November 1861 to May 1865

Adams, Samuel J.
Allen, Thomas J.
Anderson, Francis M.
Anderson, James
Anderson, John
Armstrong, Samuel
Baldin, William
Barnes, John
Bartlett, Andrew J.
Bartlett, James M.
Beck, Calvin B.
Bills, Gashan A.
Bills, John A.
Blakemore, J.M.
Blanton, W.H.
Brotherton, George
Brown, Samuel C.
Bryant, R.H.
Bryant, Thomas J.
Bugg, John E.
Burrow, Hiram W.
Call, Henry C.
Carpenter, John
Coffee, A.N.
Coffee, Thomas W.
Collins, William H.
Collins, Willis M.
Cook, James F.
Cook, Thomas
Cowper, J.T.
Crabtree, William
Cunningham, W.M.
Darnell, Allen
Davidson, Elijah A.

Davidson, H.B.
Davis, N.C.
Doyle, Eli J.
Duling, John A.
Dwiggins, H.C.
Dysart, Alfred A.
Dysart, George D.
Dysart, James M.
Dysart, John H.
Dysart, Robert A.
Dysart, Thomas J.
Dysart, William A.
Endsley, Alexander M.
Fisher, Elisha M.
Fisher, Jacob C.
Fisher, James W.
Fonville, Josh
Foster, Simm
Freeman, James H.
Gates, Woodson C.
Gentry, William C.
Gibbs, R.T.
Glasscock, Henry H.
Glasscock, Nathan
Goodwin, George W.
Graves, James K. Polk
Harrison, Elisha P.
Harrison, Richard A.
Harrison, William
Hobbs, R.C.
Hopper, Newton
Hopper, Thomas
Horton, John N.
Houston, John L.

Hunter, George W.
Hunter, Thomas N.
Hunter, W.A.
Hunter, W.L.
Jones, David
Kerr, Marshall V.
Killough, James M.
Lawwell, Ethan
Lawwell, Henry
Layne, Jesse R.
Ledford, W. Pinckney
Lentz, Benjamin F.
Long, Benton W.
Long, Richard T.
Loving, William R.
McAdams, John J.
McAdams, William J.
McCullough, Allen P.
McCullough, Delliston S.
McCullough, William W.
McCurdy, William A.
McLane, G.A.
Meadows, William M.
Moffatt, Jonathan
Monnigan, Daniel
Muse, Melchizedec B.
Neill, John T.
Nelson, John W.
Nowlin, James O.
Patton, Elisha A.
Pendergrass, Jasper
Peyton, John W.
Powell, James M.
Price, Reuben S.

Puckett, John W.
Pyland, J.H.
Pyland, William N.
Rambo, William C.
Rankin, R.S.
Redman, J.H.
Reeder, William H.
Reese, Robert
Reynolds, Ezekiel E.
Robinson, William M.
Russell, Thomas E.
Rutledge, James
Sawyer, W.P.
Stegall, Douglas M.
Stegall, Milton C.

Slucer, John
Smith, Benjamin A.
Smith, George
Smith, Gustavus J.
Smith, J.G.
Smith, William R.
Speruce, J. Jackson
Sumey, A. Franklin
Sutt, J.W.
Sutton, Samuel J.
Sweeney, Adolphus N.
Sweeney, Littlebury J.
Sweeney, Warren L.D.
Sweeney, William D.
Tennison, Hiram

Tennison, J.F.
Thomas, Christopher C.
Thomas, George C.
Thomas, Isaac A.
Tinsley, H.B.
Walker, George W.
Walker, William W.
Webb, Francis M.
White, John H.
Wiggs, William W.
Willis, Joseph G.
Yopp, Jeremiah
Young, G.C.
Yunt, Thaddeus

Appendix B

Soldiers Who Served in Company C, Eleventh Tennessee Cavalry Regiment, from September 1862 to May 1865

Adams, Theodore Riggs
Aldridge, J.M.
Alford, J.H.
Allen, J.G.
Ashworth, T.J.
Bailey, John
Bailey, Robert
Bickman, J.M.
Billington, Joseph A.
Bomar, John
Boyce, William M.
Boyd, Thomas A.
Braden, William W.
Bradley, J.B.
Brittain, J.F.
Bruce, John H.
Bruce, J.W.
Bryan, Jesse N.
Bugg, Joseph
Call, P.B.
Carter, John
Cartwright, A.W.
Cathey, T.J.
Chapman, T.M.
Chrisman, W.D.
Cole, Andrew Jackson
Corlett, David R.
Crafton, G.H.
Crockett, J.E.
Cromer, Joseph P.
Crosser, Joseph K.
Crutcher, T.R.
Davis, J.B.
Davis, J.T.

Davis, W.G.
Davis, W.H.
Devan, D.W.
Dillard, Isaac V.
Dillard, John L.
Dillard, Francis M.
Dillard, J.J.
Dowdey, J.M.
Drake, Henry T.
Drumwright, James T.
Epperson, J.P.
Epperson, James T.
Epperson, Thomas J.
Ezell, G.W.
Ezell, Hugh Frank
Ezell, J.B.
Farver, James E.
Fisher, E.M.
Fisher, J.F.
Fisher, T.B.
Fisher, W.S.
Gates, L.C.
Giles, Thomas P.
Goodrich, J.T.
Hamilton, Edward G.
Hardison, J.J.
Harper, W.C.
Hay, John H.
Hazelwood, W.R.
Henderson, W.N.
Higginbottom, R.M.
Hill, James
Holland, R.T.
Holt, J.H.

Hunter, J.Z.B.
Hunter, T.H.M.
Johnson, J.M.
Joyce, George W.
Jones, J.B.
Jones, Redding
Jordan, J.W.
King, B.W.
King, Elias
King, T.R.
King, W.T.C.
Lamb, J.M.
Laughton, G.W.
Laws, G.C.
Leonard, L.J.
Little, J.W.
Loftin, J.H.C.
Loftin, T.B.
McConnell, Peter M.W.
McCord, H.G.
McCullough, C.R.
McCullough, D.S.
McFadden, W.H.
Miller, T.C.H.
Morris, John A.
Nancy, James
Neely, J.I.
O'Neal, H.M.
Owen, J.G.
Owen, W.J.
Pate, William J.
Patterson, S.H.
Poindexter, J.W.
Primrose, Benjamin C.

Putman, D.V.
Rainey, N.E. Frank
Rambo, M.V.
Ramsey, J.L.
Ramsey, J.M.
Ramsey, T.J.
Ransom, Whitman
Reese, William B.
Reid, L.W.
Revis, Daniel
Reynolds, W.G.
Rickman, W.C.
Robinson, Aaron B.
Rone, W.N.
Royster, Edward D.
Royster, J.W.

Sheffield, E.V.
Sheffield, E.W.
Shelton, W.D.
Shepherd, R.L.
Smith, J.C.
Smith, Samuel A.
Smotherman, James M.
Smotherman, R.N.
Snell, A.R.
Snell, James T.
Snell, Thomas J.
Stegall, P.M.
Stilwell, J.W.
Tanner, Robert
Taylor, J.A.
Taylor, N.R.

Taylor, W.C.
Taylor, W.R.
Trice, John
Turner, J.C.
Warner, Samuel
Wilhoit, J.B.
Williams, James Chesley
Williamson, F.M.
Williamson, W.H.
Wilson, John H.
Wilson, Joseph
Wood, D.T.
Woodall, W.P.
Wynn, Joseph B.
Wynn, W.S.

Notes

Introduction

[1] "Compiled Service Records of Union and Confederate Soldiers," National Archives & Records Administration, Washington, D.C. Hereinafter cited as "Service Records."
[2] *Ibid.*; *Tennesseans in the Civil War*, part 1; *Military Histories* (Nashville: Civil War Centennial Commission, 1964), p. 62.
[3] "Service Records"; *Tennesseans in the Civil War*, part 1, p. 78.
[4] *United States Census of Population:* Eighth, 1860 (Schedule 4). Hereinafter cited as *U.S. Census.*
[5] Lyman Draper, *Kings Mountain and Its Heroes* (Baltimore: Genealogical Publishing Company, 1971), p. 304; "Revolutionary War Pension Records," National Archives and Records Administration, Washington, D.C.
[6] Thomas Jefferson, *Notes on Virginia* (1781–1782) in Andrew A. Lipscomb (ed.), *The Writings of Thomas Jefferson* (Washington, D.C.: The Thomas Jefferson Memorial Association, 1905), vol. 2, p. 229.
[7] *U.S. Census:* Eighth, 1860 (Schedule 4); Blanche Henry Clark, *The Tennessee Yeomen, 1840–1860* (Nashville: Vanderbilt University Press, 1942), p. 60.
[8] Commodore Bascom Fisher manuscript, undated, quoted in William L. Jones (comp.), *The Fisher Scrap Book, 1730–1972* (Milan, Tenn.: Privately printed, n.d.), p. 42. Hereinafter cited as Jones, *Fisher Scrap Book.* C.B. Fisher (1894–1987), son of Bascom Hurt Fisher, was a Presbyterian educational missionary in Iran and professor at Maryville College, Maryville, Tennessee.
[9] Thomas Burr Fisher, untitled memoir (unpublished, 1915), p. 1. Page citations refer to typescript transcribed and edited by Estelle Carr Fisher in 1966. Hereinafter cited as Fisher, "1915 Memoir." Thomas Burr Fisher, "Life on the Common Level" (unpublished, 1921), p. 3. Page citations refer to the typescript transcribed and edited by Estelle Carr Fisher in 1966–1967, hereinafter cited as Fisher, "Life on the Common Level"; Matthew Simpson (ed.), *Cyclopedia of Methodism* (Philadelphia: Everts & Stewart, 1878), p. 92; Donald G. Mathews, *Slavery and Methodism: A Chapter in American Morality, 1780–1845* (Princeton, N.J.: Princeton University Press, 1965), pp. 95, 105, 266 ff.
[10] See *To Give the Key of Knowledge: United Methodists and Education, 1784–1976* (Nashville: The National Commission on United Methodist Higher Education, 1976), pp. 14–15, 18–19, 46, 47–48, 87, 91.
[11] See Frederick C. Gill, *The Romantic Movement and Methodism* (London: The Epworth Press, 1937), pp. 13–38; Henry Sloane Coffin, "Religion in the Last Hundred Years," in *A Century of Social Thought* (Durham: Duke University Press, 1938), pp. 61–62, 64–65.
[12] See Harold H. Titus, *Living Issues in Philosophy* (New York: American Book Company, 1946), pp. 243–44, 274; Warren E. Steinkraus (ed.), *Representative Essays of Borden Parker Bowne* (Utica, N.Y.: Meridian Publishing Company, 1980), pp. iii–ix; Vergilius Ferm (ed.), *An Encyclopedia of Religion* (New York: Philosophical Library, 1945). p. 576.

[13] Herbert Welch (comp.), *Selections from the Writings of the Rev. John Wesley, M.A.* (Nashville: Abingdon-Cokesbury, 1942), p. 9.

[14] Lea & Febiger, a medical publisher established in Philadelphia in 1785, was the oldest American book publisher prior to its discontinuance in 1993. The name is now one of three imprints of Williams & Wilkins, book publishers of Baltimore. See *Literary Market Place: LMP, 1995, The Directory of the American Book Publishing Industry with Industry Yellow Pages* (New Providence, N.J.: R. R. Bowker, 1994), pp. 249-250.

[15] On Mott, see Williston Walker, *A History of the Christian Church* (New York: Charles Scribner's Sons, 1959), pp. 538-540.

[16] For sources of the history, doctrine, and polity of American Methodism and its British antecedents, see Kenneth E. Rowe (comp. & ed.), *United Methodist Studies: Basic Bibliographies* (Nashville: Abingdon Press, 1987), pp. 22-73. For official Methodist views of doctrine, see *The Book of Discipline of the United Methodist Church, 1972* (Nashville: United Methodist Publishing House, 1973), pp. 39-52, 68-82.

[17] See William Jones, "Land Grant in Fisher Family for 186 Years," in *The Lewisburg Marshall Gazette*, November 18, 1969, p. 7.

[18] Fisher, "Life on the Common Level," p. 14.

[19] See Jones, *Fisher Scrap Book*, pp. 35-36, 165.

[20] *Report of the Adjutant General of the State of Illinois, Containing Reports for the Years 1861-1866*, vol. VIII (Springfield: Journal Company, 1901), pp. 626, 644, 646, 662-63, 664-65; *Annual Report of the Adjutant General of the State of Illinois* (Springfield: Baker & Phillips, 1863), pp. 57, 76, 378.

1. The Beginning, Secession through 1862

[1] "Service Records"; E.B. Long, *The Civil War Day by Day: An Almanac, 1861-1865* (Garden City, N.Y.: Doubleday & Co., 1971), p. 83. Hereinafter cited as Long, *Civil War*.

[2] *History of Tennessee* (Nashville: Goodspeed Publishing Company, 1887), pp. 532-34. Hereinafter cited as Goodspeed, *History of Tennessee*.

[3] Stanley J. Folmsbee, Robert E. Corlew, and Enoch L. Mitchell, *Tennessee: A Short History* (Knoxville: University of Tennessee Press, 1969), p. 316; Goodspeed, *History of Tennessee*, pp. 358-59.

[4] Folmsbee, Corlew, and Mitchell, *Tennessee: A Short History*, p. 317.

[5] Goodspeed, *History of Tennessee*, p. 517.

[6] *Ibid.*

[7] *Ibid.*, pp. 517-32.

[8] Joseph Howard Parks, *John Bell of Tennessee* (Baton Rouge: Louisiana State University Press, 1950), pp. 397-402.

[9] Goodspeed, *History of Tennessee*, p. 535.

[10] *Ibid.*, pp. 536-41.

[11] Thomas Lawrence Connelly, *Civil War Tennessee* (Knoxville: University of Tennessee Press, 1979), p. 16. Hereinafter cited as Connelly, *Civil War Tennessee*.

[12] *War of the Rebellion: A Compilation of the Official Records of the Union and Confederate Armies* (Washington, D.C.: Government Printing Office, 1894-1927), Serial No. 3, pp. 272-73, 304; Serial No. 4, pp. 196-97. Hereinafter cited as *O.R.*

[13] Thomas Lawrence Connelly, *Army of the Heartland: The Army of Tennessee, 1861-1862* (Baton Rouge: Louisiana State University Press, 1967), p. 40. Hereinafter cited as Connelly, *Army of the Heartland*.

[14] Stephen V. Ash, *Middle Tennessee Society Transformed, 1860-1870: War and Peace in the Upper South* (Baton Rouge: Louisiana State University Press, 1988), pp. 73-75, 77; "Service Records."

[15] "Service Records"; Fisher, "Life on the Common Level," pp. 34-35, 56; Robert M. McBride and Dan M. Robison, *Biographical Directory of the Tennessee General Assembly*

(Nashville: Tennessee State Library and Archives and the Tennessee Historical Commission, 1975), vol. I, pp. 806-7.

[16] See *Tennesseans in the Civil War*, part 1, pp. 55-64.

[17] *Ibid.*, p. 62; "Service Records." For a review of the opposition of Unionists in East Tennessee to the Southern Confederacy, see Goodspeed, *History of Tennessee*, pp. 477-512.

[18] "Service Records"; *U.S. Census*, Ninth (1860); Jones, *Fisher Scrap Book*, p. 34.

[19] H.H. Cunningham, *Doctors in Gray: The Confederate Medical Service* (Baton Rouge: Louisiana State University Press, 1957), pp. 163-65.

[20] *O.R.*, Serial No. 22, pp. 883-84, 938-39.

[21] *Ibid.*, p. 933; Connelly, *Army of the Heartland*, p. 216.

[22] Connelly, *Army of the Heartland*, pp. 243, 251-52, 256, 258.

[23] Robert Selph Henry, *The Story of the Confederacy* (Garden City, N.Y.: Garden City Publishing Company, 1931), p. 199. Hereinafter cited as Henry, *Story of the Confederacy*.

[24] "Service Records." Soldiers of the Fourth and Eleventh Tennessee Cavalry regiments whose ranks or rates are not stated herein were rated privates. Others are designated by rank or rate.

[25] *O.R.*, Serial No. 29, pp. 6-7.

[26] John Allan Wyeth, *Life of General Nathan Bedford Forrest* (New York: Harper, 1899), pp. 117, 125-44. Hereinafter cited as Wyeth, *Life of Forrest*.

[27] "Service Records."

[28] *Ibid.*; *U.S. Census*, Ninth (1860).

[29] *O.R.*, Serial No. 23, pp. 876-77.

[30] *Ibid.*, Serial No. 127, pp. 1095-97.

[31] Connelly, *Army of the Heartland*, pp. 11-12.

[32] *Ibid.*, pp. 97-99.

[33] *Ibid.*, pp. 20-21.

[34] Albert Dilahunty, "Shiloh" (Washington, D.C.: National Park Service, 1955), pp. 19-20.

[35] Long, *Civil War*, pp. 195-96, 198.

[36] *Ibid.*, pp. 202-3.

[37] *Ibid.*, p. 256.

[38] See Fisher, "Life on the Common Level," pp. 8, 14.

[39] Quoted in William Graham Sumner, *Folkways: A Study of the Sociological Importance of Usages, Manners, Customs, Mores, and Morals* (New York: Mentor Books/The New American Library, n.d.), pp. 243-44.

[40] "Service Records"; *Tennesseans in the Civil War*, Part 1, pp. 78-79.

[41] Fisher, "Life on the Common Level," p. 3; *Journal* of the 109th Session of the Tennessee Annual Conference of the Methodist Episcopal Church, South (1922), p. 24. Hereinafter cited as Tennessee Conference *Journal*.

[42] "Service Records."

[43] Robert Selph Henry, *"First with the Most" Forrest* (Indianapolis: Bobbs-Merrill, 1944), pp. 106-8. Hereinafter cited as Henry, *Forrest*.

[44] See Glenn Tucker, "Forrest — Untutored Genius of the War," *Civil War Times* (June 1964), pp. 7-8, 35-36; Robert Selph Henry (ed.), *As They Saw Forrest: Some Recollections and Comments of Contemporaries* (Jackson, Tenn.: McCowat-Mercer Press, 1956), pp. 17-53; Wyeth, *Life of Forrest*, pp. 633-53.

[45] Wyeth, *Life of Forrest*, pp. 264-71.

[46] William Shakespeare, *King Henry V*, Act III, Scene 1, Lines 3-9.

[47] Horn, *Army of Tennessee*, pp. 196-98.

[48] John P. Dyer, *From Shiloh to San Juan: The Life of "Fightin' Joe" Wheeler* (Baton Rouge: Louisiana State University Press, 1961), p. 64. Hereinafter cited as Dyer, *Life of Wheeler*.

[49] *Ibid.*, pp. 65-68.

[50] *O.R.*, Serial No. 29, pp. 958-60; Dyer, *Life of Wheeler*, pp. 68-69.

[51] Connelly, *Autumn of Glory*, pp. 63-65.

[52] Stanley F. Horn, *The Army of Tennessee: A Military History* (Indianapolis: Bobbs-Merrill Company, 1941), pp. 209-10. Hereinafter cited as Horn, *Army of Tennessee*.

2. The Year 1863 through Streight's Raid, January 3-May 3, 1863

[1] *O.R.*., Serial No. 29, pp. 959-60.
[2] *Ibid.*, p. 961.
[3] *Ibid.*; Dyer, *Life of Wheeler*, pp. 73-78; Wyeth, *Life of Forrest*, pp. 145-53.
[4] "Service Records"; *O.R.*, Serial No. 24, p. 26.
[5] *Tennesseans in the Civil War*, part 1, pp. 321, 324.
[6] *O.R.*, Serial No. 23, pp. 557, 566-67; Ezra J. Warner, *Generals in Blue: Lives of the Union Commanders* (Baton Rouge: Louisiana State University Press, 1964), p. 116. Hereinafter cited as Warner, *Generals in Blue*.
[7] *O.R.*, Serial No. 24, pp. 24-26; "Service Records"; Fisher, "Life on the Common Level," p. 8; Jones, *Fisher Scrap Book*, p. 186.
[8] *Tennesseans in the Civil War*, part 1, pp. 78-79; T.C.H. Miller's Company Report, Atlanta, June 30, 1864, in "Service Records"; Daniel Wilson Holman, "Eleventh Tennessee Cavalry," in John Berrien Lindsley (ed.), *The Military Annals of Tennessee* (Nashville: J.M. Lindsley & Company, 1886), p. 690. Hereinafter cited as Lindsley, *Military Annals of Tennessee*; Henry, *Forrest*, pp. 104, 127.
[9] Henry, *Forrest*, p. 127.
[10] *Ibid.*
[11] *Ibid.*; *Tennesseans in the Civil War*; part 1, p. 40.
[12] Thomas Lawrence Connelly, *Autumn of Glory: The Army of Tennessee, 1862-1865* (Baton Rouge: Louisiana State University Press, 1971), pp. 81-85, 87-91. Hereinafter cited as Connelly, *Autumn of Glory*.
[13] *O.R.*, Serial No. 34, pp. 116-18, 120-21.
[14] Fisher, "1915 Memoir," p. 4; *U.S. Census*, Ninth (1860); "Service Records."
[15] *O.R.*, Serial No. 34, pp. 187-89.
[16] Fisher, "Life on the Common Level," p. 5; Newton Cannon, *Reminiscences* (Jackson, Tenn.: McCowat-Mercer Press, 1963), p. 26; Henry, *Forrest*, pp. 136-37.
[17] "Service Records"; Fisher, "Life on the Common Level," p. 5.
[18] *O.R.*, Serial No. 34, pp. 239-40.
[19] Fisher, "1915 Memoir," p. 5; Wyeth, Life of Forrest, pp. 185-89; *O.R.*, Serial No. 34, p. 285.
[20] *O.R.*, Serial No. 34, pp. 286-87; Wyeth, *Life of Forrest*, pp. 187, 189.
[21] *O.R.*, Serial No. 34, p. 287; Henry, *Forrest*, pp. 142, 144.
[22] Wyeth, *Life of Forrest*, pp. 190-91.
[23] *Ibid.*
[24] *Ibid.*, p. 191.
[25] Henry, *Forrest*, p. 145.
[26] *Ibid.*
[27] Wyeth, *Life of Forrest*, pp. 193-94.
[28] Henry, *Forrest*, pp. 146-47.
[29] Wyeth, *Life of Forrest*, p. 198; Fisher, "1915 Memoir," p. 4; "Service Records."
[30] Wyeth, *Life of Forrest*, p. 200.
[31] *Ibid.*, p. 201.
[32] *Ibid.*
[33] *O.R.*, Serial No. 34, p. 289.
[34] *Ibid.*, p. 290.
[35] Henry, *Forrest*, p. 149.
[36] Wyeth, *Life of Forrest*, pp. 206-7.
[37] *Ibid.*, p. 207.

³⁸ *Ibid.*, pp. 208-12.
³⁹ *O.R.*, Serial No. 34, p. 291.
⁴⁰ Henry, *Forrest*, pp. 153-55.
⁴¹ *Ibid.*, p. 155.
⁴² Wyeth, *Life of Forrest*, pp. 215-17.
⁴³ *O.R.*, Serial No. 34, p. 292.
⁴⁴ Henry, *Forrest*, pp. 156-57.
⁴⁵ *Ibid.*, pp. 157-58.
⁴⁶ *O.R.*, Serial No. 34, p. 294. Cooper was the highest-ranking general in the army and intended by Jefferson Davis to be "the Chief of Staff of the whole army." Davis was progressive in perceiving the need for a modern army command system. But he erred in choosing Cooper as the army's chief of staff. Cooper reportedly was not up to the task. See Steven E. Woodworth, *Jefferson Davis and His Generals: The Failure of Confederate Command in the West* (Lawrence: University Press of Kansas, 1990), p. 23. Hereinafter cited as Woodworth, *Jefferson Davis and His Generals*.
⁴⁷ *O.R.*, Serial No. 118, pp. 844-45.
⁴⁸ *Ibid.*, Serial No. 34, pp. 285, 293.
⁴⁹ *Ibid.*, p. 293.
⁵⁰ Fisher, "Life on the Common Level," pp. 5, 8; Fisher, "1915 Memoir," p. 4; "Service Records."

3. Through the Chickamauga Holocaust, May 4-October 29, 1863

¹ Fisher, "1915 Memoir," p. 4; Cunningham, *Doctors in Gray*, pp. 200-1.
² "Service Records."
³ Fisher, "1915 Memoir," p. 4; Cunningham, *Doctors in Gray*, p. 186.
⁴ Robert G. Hartje, *Van Dorn: The Life and Times of a Confederate General* (Nashville: Vanderbilt University Press, 1967), pp. 309-19.
⁵ *U.S. Census*, Ninth (1860), and Tenth (1870); Hartje, *Van Dorn*, p. 320.
⁶ Henry, *Forrest*, p. 167.
⁷ *U.S. Census*, Ninth (1860); "Service Records."
⁸ "Service Records."
⁹ G.G. Dibrell, "Eighth Tennessee Cavalry," and Daniel Wilson Holman, "Eleventh Tennessee Cavalry," in Lindsley, *Military Annals of Tennessee*, pp. 657, 692.
¹⁰ "Service Records."
¹¹ Lindsley, *Military Annals of Tennessee*, pp. 657, 692.
¹² Fisher, "1915 Memoir," pp. 4-5.
¹³ *Tennesseans in the Civil War*, part 1, p. 78; "Service Records"; *History of Tennessee with an Historical and Biographical Sketch of Maury, Williamson, Rutherford, Wilson, Bedford & Marshall Counties* (Nashville: Goodspeed Publishing Company, 1887), pp. 996-97, hereinafter cited as Goodspeed, *Tennessee with Sketch[es] of Counties*.
¹⁴ Lindsley, *Military Annals of Tennessee*, pp. 657-58; "Service Records."
¹⁵ Woodworth, *Jefferson Davis and His Generals*, pp. 230-33; Henry, *Forrest*, p. 117; Connelly, *Autumn of Glory*, pp. 169, 185.
¹⁶ "Chickamauga and Chattanooga Battlefields" (Washington, D.C. National Park Service, 1956), p. 24.
¹⁷ "Service Records."
¹⁸ Henry, *Forrest*, p. 183.
¹⁹ *O.R.*, Serial No. 51, p. 20; Lindsley, *Military Annals of Tennessee*, p. 693.
²⁰ *O.R.*, Serial No. 51, pp. 528-29.
²¹ *Ibid.*, p. 524; Henry, *Forrest*, pp. 183-84.
²² *O.R.*, Serial No. 51, p. 524; Henry, *Forrest*, p. 184.
²³ *O.R.*, Serial No. 51, p. 14; Henry, *Forrest*, pp. 184-85.

[24] O.R., Serial No. 51, pp. 20, 525.
[25] Lindsley, *Military Annals of Tennessee*, p. 693.
[26] Wyeth, *Life of Forrest*, pp. 251-52.
[27] O.R., Serial No. 51, p. 289.
[28] *Ibid.*, p. 145.
[29] *Ibid.*, p. 525.
[30] Lindsley, *Military Annals of Tennessee*, p. 694.
[31] *Ibid.*
[32] *Ibid.*, p. 660.
[33] Woodworth, *Jefferson Davis and His Generals*, p. 237; Henry, *Forrest*, p. 193; Wyeth, *Life of Forrest*, p. 267; Lindsley, *Military Annals of Tennessee*, p. 660.
[34] Lindsley, *Military Annals of Tennessee*, p. 695.
[35] *Ibid.*
[36] Wyeth, *Life of Forrest*, p. 264.
[37] *Ibid.*, p. 255.
[38] O.R., Serial No. 51, p. 20.
[39] Fisher, "1915 Memoir," p. 5; "Service Records."
[40] Dyer, *Life of Wheeler*, pp. 97-98; Henry, *Forrest*, pp. 196-97.
[41] O.R., Serial No. 51, pp. 722-25.
[42] *Ibid.*, p. 723.
[43] Bob Womack, *Call Forth the Mighty Men* (Bessemer, Ala.: Colonial Press, 1986), pp. 298-99. Hereinafter cited as Womack, *Call Forth the Mighty Men*.
[44] O.R., Serial No. 51, pp. 723-24.
[45] Womack, *Call Forth the Mighty Men*, pp. 300-1; George B. Guild, *A Brief Narrative of the Fourth Tennessee Cavalry Regiment* (Nashville: privately printed, 1913), pp. 42-43. Hereinafter cited as Guild, *Fourth Tennessee Cavalry*. Guild wrote of Baxter Smith's/Paul Anderson's regiment, not Starnes'/McLemore's Fourth.
[46] O.R., Serial No. 51, p. 673.
[47] Guild, *Fourth Tennessee Cavalry*, p. 43.
[48] Dyer, *Life of Wheeler*, p. 106; "Service Records."
[49] Henry, *Forrest*, pp. 198, 200-1.
[50] O.R., Serial No. 55, pp. 662-63.
[51] Wyeth, *Life of Forrest*, pp. 265-66.
[52] *Ibid.*, pp. 267-68; O.R., Serial No. 56, pp. 603-4.
[53] Wyeth, *Life of Forrest*, p. 271.

4. Chattanooga, Knoxville, and into the Atlanta Campaign, October 30, 1863–July 22, 1864

[1] Long, *Civil War*, pp. 436-38; Woodworth, *Jefferson Davis and His Generals*, pp. 248-55.
[2] Horn, *Army of Tennessee*, pp. 284-85, 294-95; Woodworth, *Jefferson Davis and His Generals*, pp. 238-39, 248.
[3] O.R., Serial No. 56, pp. 890-92.
[4] *Ibid.*, Serial No. 55, p. 662.
[5] *Ibid.*
[6] *Ibid.*, p. 631.
[7] *Ibid.*, Serial No. 56, pp. 807, 891; Guild, *Fourth Tennessee Cavalry*, pp. 49-50, 54, 59-60; Lindsley, *Military Annals of Tennessee*, pp. 696-99.
[8] Lindsley, *Military Annals of Tennessee*, pp. 695-96; "Service Records." The United States Department of Veterans Affairs furnished data relative to Finn's Point National Cemetery.

[9] Dyer, *Life of Wheeler*, p. 113; O.R., Serial No. 54, p. 540, and Serial No. 56, pp. 687, 688.
[10] *Ibid.*, Serial No. 54, pp. 540-41.
[11] *Ibid.*, pp. 541-42.
[12] Fisher, "1915 Memoir," p. 5; O.R., Serial No. 56, p. 704; Dyer, *Life of Wheeler*, p. 114.
[13] Fisher, "1915 Memoir," p. 5; O.R., Serial No. 54, p. 542.
[14] O.R., Serial No. 54, p. 542.
[15] Lindsley, *Military Annals of Tennessee*, p. 697.
[16] *Ibid.*
[17] "Service Records."
[18] What is now the University of Tennessee was, in the Civil War period, East Tennessee University, the classes of which were suspended early in the war during a session begun September 12, 1861. Classes were not resumed until 1866. Locus of the school was College Hill, occupied by Union troops during Longstreet's siege. Fort Sanders was three quarters of a mile northwest of College Hill. Wounded Confederate soldiers from the Battle of Fishing Creek, Kentucky, were cared for in school facilities in January 1862. Burnside later used school buildings as a hospital. After the war, the school collected $18,500 from the Federal Government for wartime property damages. Its faculty had divided loyalties during the war. See James Riley Montgomery, Stanley J. Folmsbee, and Lee Seifert Greene, *To Foster Knowledge: A History of the University of Tennessee, 1794-1970* (Knoxville: University of Tennessee Press, 1984), pp. 65-72.
[19] O.R., Serial No. 54, pp. 277-78, 352-53; Lindsley, *Military Annals of Tennessee*, p. 663.
[20] O.R., Serial No. 54, pp. 461, 462.
[21] Lindsley, *Military Annals of Tennessee*, pp. 663-64, 697-98.
[22] "Service Records."
[23] Lindsley, *Military Annals of Tennessee*, pp. 664, 698.
[24] O.R., Serial No. 54, p. 462; Henry, *Story of the Confederacy*, p. 325.
[25] Dyer, *Life of Wheeler*, pp. 115-16.
[26] O.R., Serial No. 56, pp. 807, 891.
[27] Lindsley, *Military Annals of Tennessee*, p. 698.
[28] "Service Records."
[29] Lindsley, *Military Annals of Tennessee*, p. 664; O.R., Serial No. 58, pp. 508-9, 598, 605; Dyer, *Life of Wheeler*, p. 119.
[30] "Service Records."
[31] Lindsley, *Military Annals of Tennessee*, pp. 664-66, 699-700; O.R., Serial No. 57, p. 410.
[32] O.R., Serial No. 57, p. 632; Serial No. 58, pp. 634, 681-82.
[33] *Ibid.*, Serial No. 34, p. 295; Wyeth, *Life of Forrest*, pp. 279-88.
[34] O.R., Serial No. 54, pp. 549-50.
[35] *Ibid.*, Serial No. 58, p. 803.
[36] Lindsley, *Military Annals of Tennessee*, pp. 664, 700-1.
[37] "Service Records."
[38] *Ibid.*; Goodspeed, *Tennessee with Sketch[es] of Counties*, p. 1147.
[39] "Service Records."
[40] "Service Records"; William Stratton Fisher, "Diary," in Jones, *Fisher Scrap Book*, pp. 81-95. Fisher kept his diary in the period April 19, 1864-May 25, 1865.
[41] Lindsley, *Military Annals of Tennessee*, p. 702.
[42] "Service Records."
[43] O.R., Serial No. 54, p. 871.
[44] Horn, *Army of Tennessee*, pp. 322-25.
[45] Dyer, *Life of Wheeler*, p. 124.
[46] William T. Sherman, *Memoirs of General William T. Sherman, By Himself* (New York: D. Appleton & Company, 1875), vol. 2, pp. 32-33. Hereinafter cited as Sherman, *Memoirs*; Dyer, *Life of Wheeler*, p. 125.

⁴⁷ Lindsley, *Military Annals of Tennessee*, p. 667.
⁴⁸ Horn, *Army of Tennessee*, p. 323.
⁴⁹ Dyer, *Life of Wheeler*, p. 125.
⁵⁰ *Ibid.*, p. 128.
⁵¹ *O.R.*, Serial No. 59, pp. 866-73; Serial No. 74, p. 646.
⁵² *Ibid.*, Serial No. 74, p. 666.
⁵³ *Ibid.*, p. 945.
⁵⁴ Dyer, *Life of Wheeler*, p. 129.
⁵⁵ Lindsley, *Military Annals of Tennessee*, p. 702.
⁵⁶ Dyer, *Life of Wheeler*, p. 128; "Service Records."
⁵⁷ Lindsley, *Military Annals of Tennessee*, pp. 702-3.
⁵⁸ *O.R.*, Serial No. 74, p. 946.
⁵⁹ *Ibid.*, p. 615.
⁶⁰ *Ibid.*, p. 946.
⁶¹ *Ibid.*, p. 616; Dyer, *Life of Wheeler*, p. 130; Gilbert E. Govan and James W. Livingood, *A Different Valor: The Story of General Joseph E. Johnston, C.S.A.* (Indianapolis: Bobbs-Merrill, 1956), pp. 276-77.
⁶² *O.R.*, Serial No. 74, p. 616.
⁶³ Dyer, *Life of Wheeler*, p. 130.
⁶⁴ *Ibid.*, pp. 130-31.
⁶⁵ *Ibid.*, p. 131.
⁶⁶ Lindsley, *Military Annals of Tennessee*, p. 703.
⁶⁷ *Ibid.*, p. 704; *O.R.*, Serial No. 74, pp. 616, 724-26.
⁶⁸ *O.R.*, Serial No. 74, pp. 724-26.
⁶⁹ *Ibid.*, p. 948.
⁷⁰ *Ibid.*, p. 949.
⁷¹ Horn, *Army of Tennessee*, p. 331.
⁷² Jones, *Fisher Scrap Book*, p. 82; Horn, *Army of Tennessee*, p. 331.
⁷³ Lindsley, *Military Annals of Tennessee*, p. 704.
⁷⁴ Jones, *Fisher Scrap Book*, p. 83; Cunningham, *Doctors in Gray*, pp. 184-217; John K. Stevens, "Hostages to Hunger: Nutritional Blindness in the Confederate Armies," *Tennessee Historical Quarterly* (Fall 1989), pp. 131-43.
⁷⁵ Cunningham, *Doctors in Gray*, p. 125; Jones, *Fisher Scrap Book*, p. 83.
⁷⁶ Horn, *Army of Tennessee*, p. 332; Womack, *Call Forth the Mighty Men*, pp. 379-80.
⁷⁷ Horn, *Army of Tennessee*, pp. 48-49; Woodworth, *Jefferson Davis and His Generals*, pp. 26-30, 238-43.
⁷⁸ Horn, *Army of Tennessee*, pp. 332-33.
⁷⁹ *O.R.*, Serial No. 73, pp. 820-23.
⁸⁰ "Service Records"; Jones, *Fisher Scrap Book*, p. 83.
⁸¹ Horn, *Army of Tennessee*, pp. 335-37.
⁸² Jones, *Fisher Scrap Book*, pp. 83-84.
⁸³ "Service Records."
⁸⁴ Horn, *Army of Tennessee*, pp. 338-39.
⁸⁵ "Service Records": *Confederate Veteran*, vol. XII, no. 3 (March 1904), p. 121.
⁸⁶ Horn, *Army of Tennessee*, pp. 339-40; Lindsley, *Military Annals of Tennessee*, p. 668.
⁸⁷ Jones, *Fisher Scrap Book*, p. 84; Walter T. Durham, *Nashville: The Occupied City* (Nashville: Tennessee Historical Society, 1985), pp. 27, 86, 250.
⁸⁸ Connelly, *Autumn of Glory*, pp. 416-21.
⁸⁹ Sam R. Watkins, *"Co. Aytch:" A Side Show of the Big Show* (Wilmington, N.C.: Broadfoot Publishing Co., 1987), pp. 131-35, 167-68.
⁹⁰ *Ibid.*, pp. 132-34. George Guild, Adjutant of Baxter Smith's/Paul Anderson's Fourth Tennessee Cavalry Regiment, expressed similar sentiments. See Guild, *Fourth Tennessee Cavalry*, pp. 58-59.

Notes (pages 84–99)   267

⁹¹ Connelly, *Civil War Tennessee*, p. 87.
⁹² Horn, *Army of Tennessee*, p. 345.
⁹³ *Ibid.*, p. 350.
⁹⁴ *O.R.*, Serial No. 74, p. 951.
⁹⁵ Dyer, *Life of Wheeler*, p. 137; Lindsley, *Military Annals of Tennessee*, pp. 668-69.
⁹⁶ Horn, *Army of Tennessee*, pp. 350-51.
⁹⁷ *Ibid.*, pp. 352-54.
⁹⁸ Dyer, *Life of Wheeler*, p. 138.
⁹⁹ Horn, *Army of Tennessee*, pp. 354-55.
¹⁰⁰ Dyer, Life of Wheeler, pp. 139-40.
¹⁰¹ *O.R.*, Serial No. 74, p. 953.
¹⁰² Horn, *Army of Tennessee*, pp. 358-59.
¹⁰³ *Ibid.*; Womack, *Call Forth the Mighty Men*, pp. 400-1; *Tennesseans in the Civil War*, part 1, pp. 219-20, and part 2, p. 98.

5. The Siege of Atlanta and Wheeler's Tennessee Raid, July 23–September 2, 1964

¹ Horn, *Army of Tennessee*, pp. 359-60.
² Jones, *Fisher Scrap Book*, p. 84.
³ Horn, *Army of Tennessee*, p. 360.
⁴ *Ibid.*, pp. 360-61.
⁵ *O.R.*, Serial No. 73, p. 915; Sherman, *Memoirs*, vol. 2, p. 87.
⁶ *O.R.*, Serial No. 73, pp. 761-62; Serial No. 72, p. 75.
⁷ Sherman, *Memoirs*, vol. 2, p. 88; *O.R.*, Serial No. 72, pp. 75-76.
⁸ Dyer, *Life of Wheeler*, p. 141; *O.R.*, Serial No. 73, p. 804.
⁹ *O.R.*, Serial No. 74, p. 953; Serial No. 73, p. 804.
¹⁰ *Ibid.*, Serial No. 73, pp. 914, 915.
¹¹ Dyer, *Life of Wheeler*, pp. 141-42.
¹² *O.R.*, Serial No. 73, p. 916.
¹³ Henry, *Story of the Confederacy*, pp. 426-27; Sherman, *Memoirs*, vol. 2, pp. 154-86.
¹⁴ *O.R.*, Serial No. 73, p. 914.
¹⁵ *Ibid.*, Serial No. 72, p. 114.
¹⁶ *Ibid.*, Serial No. 73, p. 925.
¹⁷ *Ibid.*, pp. 762-63.
¹⁸ *Ibid.*, Serial No. 74, pp. 953-55; Serial No. 76, p. 939.
¹⁹ *Ibid.*, Serial No. 73, pp. 763-64.
²⁰ *Ibid.*, Serial No. 74, pp. 955-57.
²¹ *Ibid.*, Serial No. 72, p. 77; Serial No. 74, pp. 956-57.
²² Sherman, *Memoirs*, vol. 2, pp. 96-97.
²³ Jones, *Fisher Scrap Book*, p. 86.
²⁴ Dyer, *Life of Wheeler*, p. 146; "Service Records."
²⁵ Dyer, *Life of Wheeler*, pp. 146-48.
²⁶ "Service Records."
²⁷ *O.R.*, Serial No. 74, p. 957; Dyer, *Life of Wheeler*, p. 148.
²⁸ Dyer, *Life of Wheeler*, pp. 148-49; Lindsley, *Military Annals of Tennessee*, p. 669.
²⁹ Dyer, *Life of Wheeler*, p. 149.
³⁰ *O.R.*, Serial No. 74, p. 958.
³¹ Lindsley, *Military Annals of Tennessee*, p. 669.
³² *O.R.*, Serial No. 74, p. 959.
³³ *Ibid.*
³⁴ *Ibid.*; Dyer, *Life of Wheeler*, p. 150.
³⁵ *O.R.*, Serial No. 73, p. 493; Serial No. 78, pp. 837, 874.

³⁶ *Ibid.*, Serial No. 73, p. 490.
³⁷ *Ibid.*
³⁸ Lindsley, *Military Annals of Tennessee*, pp. 670-71; *Tennesseans in the Civil War*, part 1, p. 400; "Service Records"; Guild, *Fourth Tennessee Cavalry*, p. 99.
³⁹ Dyer, *Life of Wheeler*, pp. 151-52.
⁴⁰ "Service Records"; *O.R.*, Serial No. 98, p. 1132; Serial No. 104, pp. 1124-26; Lindsley, *Military Annals of Tennessee*, pp. 669-70; Dyer, *Life of Wheeler*, pp. 151-52.
⁴¹ The account of Sam Davis's capture, trial, and execution is based upon *O.R.*, Serial No. 54, pp. 208-11; "Sam Davis," in John Trotwood Moore, *Ole Mistis and Other Songs and Stories from Tennessee* (Nashville: Cokesbury Press, 1925), pp. 231-38; and John Bakeless, *Spies of the Confederacy* (Philadelphia: J.B. Lippincott Company, 1970), pp. 217-42.
⁴² *O.R.*, Serial No. 74, pp. 957-61; Dyer, *Life of Wheeler*, p. 152.
⁴³ Dyer, *Life of Wheeler*, pp. 152-53.

6. The Fall of Atlanta, Sherman's March, and Surrender in the East, August 25, 1864-May 19, 1865

¹ Connelly, *Autumn of Glory*, p. 458.
² *Ibid.*, pp. 462-66; Horn, *Army of Tennessee*, pp. 364-65.
³ Horn, *Army of Tennessee*, pp. 365-66.
⁴ *O.R.*, Serial No. 73, p. 393.
⁵ Jones, *Fisher Scrap Book*, p. 87.
⁶ *O.R.*, Serial No. 74, p. 663.
⁷ Sherman, *Memoirs*, vol. 2, pp. 25-26, 109-10.
⁸ Horn, *Army of Tennessee*, p. 368.
⁹ Sherman, *Memoirs*, vol. 2, pp. 130-36.
¹⁰ Horn, *Army of Tennessee*, p. 368.
¹¹ *Ibid.*, p. 367.
¹² *O.R.*, Serial No. 74, pp. 683. Brigade strengths are estimates based upon manning charts of the Army of Tennessee in August and September 1864.
¹³ Sherman, *Memoirs*, vol. 2, pp. 111-12, 117-29; Horn, *Army of Tennessee*, pp. 369-70; Woodworth, *Jefferson Davis and His Generals*, p. 282.
¹⁴ Horn, *Army of Tennessee*, p. 370.
¹⁵ Sherman, *Memoirs*, vol. 2, pp. 137-40.
¹⁶ *O.R.*, Serial No. 77, p. 801; Jones, *Fisher Scrap Book*, p. 87; Connelly, *Autumn of Glory*, pp. 477-78.
¹⁷ Horn, *Army of Tennessee*, p. 372.
¹⁸ Sherman, *Memoirs*, vol. 2, p. 144.
¹⁹ Horn, *Army of Tennessee*, p. 375.
²⁰ Jones, *Fisher Scrap Book*, p. 87.
²¹ Horn, *Army of Tennessee*, p. 375.
²² Jones, *Fisher Scrap Book*, pp. 87-88; *Tennesseans in the Civil War*, part 2, p. 391; "Service Records." Also see Chapter 10, herein regarding other furloughed Company C troops in Chalmers' command who deserted in January 1865.
²³ Sherman, *Memoirs*, vol. 2, pp. 145, 152; Horn, *Army of Tennessee*, p. 377.
²⁴ Warner, *Generals in Gray*, p. 123.
²⁵ *O.R.*, Serial No. 78, pp. 849, 859.
²⁶ *Ibid.*, Serial No. 77, p. 562; "Service Records"; Guild, *Fourth Tennessee Cavalry*, p. 99.
²⁷ *O.R.*, Serial No. 77, pp. 554-57.
²⁸ Guild, *Fourth Tennessee Cavalry*, p. 100.
²⁹ *O.R.*, Serial No. 77, pp. 556-57.
³⁰ Lindsley, *Military Annals of Tennessee*, p. 671.

31 *O.R.*, Serial No. 77, pp. 554-55.
32 "Service Records."
33 *O.R.*, Serial No. 77, pp. 560-61, 567.
34 Thurman Sensing, *Champ Ferguson: Confederate Guerilla* (Nashville: Vanderbilt University Press, 1985), pp. 29-30, 40, 177, 208, 243. Hereinafter cited as Sensing, *Champ Ferguson*.
35 *U.S. Census*, Ninth (1860); Sensing, *Champ Ferguson*, pp. 36, 37.
36 *Tennesseans in the Civil War*, part 1, pp. 15-16.
37 *U.S. Census*, Ninth (1860); "Service Records."
38 *Tennesseans in the Civil War*, part 1, p. 42.
39 Sensing, *Champ Ferguson*, p. 180; Guild, *Fourth Tennessee Cavalry*, pp. 102-4.
40 Sensing, *Champ Ferguson*, pp. 188, 247, 251, 253; *Tennesseans in the Civil War*, part 1, pp. 401-2.
41 Sensing, *Champ Ferguson*, p. 254.
42 *O.R.*, Serial No. 78, pp. 837-38, 849, 861.
43 Dyer, *Life of Wheeler*, p. 157.
44 *Ibid.*
45 Lindsley, *Military Annals of Tennessee*, p. 705; *Tennesseans in the Civil War*, part 1, pp. 405-6.
46 *Tennesseans in the Civil War*, part 1, p. 406.
47 Connelly, *Autumn of Glory*, p. 480; Horn, *Army of Tennessee*, p. 379.
48 Dyer, *Life of Wheeler*, p. 158.
49 Sherman, *Memoirs*, vol. 2, p. 152.
50 *Ibid.*, pp. 162, 177-78; Henry, *Story of the Confederacy*, p. 424.
51 Dyer, *Life of Wheeler*, p. 159.
52 Henry, *Forrest*, p. 383.
53 Dyer, *Life of Wheeler*, pp. 162-63.
54 Sherman, *Memoirs*, vol. 2, pp. 174-76.
55 *O.R.*, Serial No. 79, p. 918.
56 Sherman, *Memoirs*, vol. 2, pp. 171-72; Dyer, *Life of Wheeler*, p. 162.
57 *O.R.*, Serial No. 92, pp. 406-7, 886.
58 Dyer, *Life of Wheeler*, p. 162.
59 *O.R.*, Serial No. 92, p. 407.
60 *Ibid.*, pp. 407-8; Lindsley, *Military Annals of Tennessee*, p. 672.
61 *O.R.*, Serial No. 92, pp. 408-9; Lindsley, *Military Annals of Tennessee*, pp. 672-73.
62 *O.R.*, Serial No. 92, p. 409; Sherman, *Memoirs*, vol. 2, p. 271; Lindsley, *Military Annals of Tennessee*, pp. 672-76.
63 *O.R.*, Serial No. 92, pp. 409-10.
64 *Ibid.*, p. 410.
65 Dyer, *Life of Wheeler*, pp. 165-69.
66 *O.R.*, Serial No. 92, pp. 410-11.
67 Lindsley, *Military Annals of Tennessee*, pp. 673-74.
68 *Ibid.*, p. 674.
69 *O.R.*, Serial No. 92, p. 411.
70 *Ibid.*, pp. 737-38; Sherman, *Memoirs*, vol. 2, pp. 195-99, 210, 216-17.
71 *O.R.*, Serial No. 92, pp. 771-74; Sherman, *Memoirs*, vol. 2, pp. 218-21, 230-40.
72 Sherman, *Memoirs*, vol. 2, pp. 206, 223-24.
73 *Ibid.*, pp. 219-20, 221, 232-37.
74 *Ibid.*, pp. 237-38.
75 *Ibid.*, pp. 238-40.
76 *Ibid.*, pp. 255, 256.
77 "Service Records"; Fisher, "Life on the Common Level," p. 21; James I. Robertson, Jr., *Soldiers Blue and Gray* (Columbia, S.C.: University of South Carolina Press, 1988), pp. 135-37.

[78] Lindsley, *Military Annals of Tennessee*, p. 674; Sherman, *Memoirs*, vol. 2, p. 272; Dyer, *Life of Wheeler*, pp. 170-71.
[79] Sherman, *Memoirs*, vol. 2, pp. 275-76.
[80] *Ibid.*, pp. 280, 286-87.
[81] *Ibid.*, p. 288.
[82] Dyer, *Life of Wheeler*, pp. 171-72; *O.R.*, Serial No. 98, pp. 43, 1058.
[83] *O.R.*, Serial No. 98, pp. 1018-20.
[84] Sherman, *Memoirs*, vol. 2, p. 291.
[85] *O.R.*, Serial No. 98, p. 3.
[86] Horn, *Army of Tennessee*, pp. 422-25.
[87] *O.R.*, Serial No. 94, p. 800; *Tennesseans in the Civil War*, part 1, p. 64.
[88] *Ibid.*, Serial No. 99, p. 994.
[89] Lindsley, *Military Annals of Tennessee*, p. 672.
[90] *Ibid.*, pp. 673-75.
[91] *Ibid.*, p. 675; Dyer, *Life of Wheeler*, p. 175; *O.R.*, Serial No. 98, p. 1130.
[92] Sherman, *Memoirs*, vol. 2, p. 294.
[93] *O.R.*, Serial No. 98, pp. 1126-27, 1130.
[94] *Ibid.*, pp. 1057, 1130-31.
[95] *Ibid.*, pp. 1131-32; Sherman, *Memoirs*, vol. 2, p. 305; Lindsley, *Military Annals of Tennessee*, p. 676.
[96] Horn, *Army of Tennessee*, pp. 425-26.
[97] Sherman, *Memoirs*, vol. 2, pp. 306-7; *O.R.*, Serial No. 98, p. 98.
[98] Sherman, *Memoirs*, vol. 2, pp. 324-31.
[99] *Ibid.*, pp. 333, 342-44.
[100] Lindsley, *Military Annals of Tennessee*, p. 676.
[101] Sherman, *Memoirs*, vol. 2, p. 344; John G. Barrett, *Sherman's March through the Carolinas* (Chapel Hill: University of North Carolina Press, 1956), p. 225.
[102] Lindsley, *Military Annals of Tennessee*, p. 676.
[103] *O.R.*, Serial No. 98, p. 1132; Barrett, *Sherman's March*, p. 258.
[104] Long, *Civil War*, p. 674.
[105] Sherman, *Memoirs*, vol. 2, pp. 347-50.
[106] *Ibid.*, pp. 352-54, 364-67.
[107] *Ibid.*, pp. 328-31, 356-57.
[108] *Ibid.*, p. 363.
[109] *Ibid.*, p. 370.
[110] Dyer, *Life of Wheeler*, p. 180.
[111] Lindsley, *Military Annals of Tennessee*, p. 676.
[112] *O.R.*, Serial No. 100, p. 841.
[113] *Ibid.*, pp. 841, 846.
[114] Dyer, *Life of Wheeler*, pp. 180-81.
[115] *Ibid.*
[116] Basil W. Duke, *Reminiscences of General Basil Duke, C.S.A.* (Garden City, N.Y.: Doubleday, Page & Co., 1911), pp. 380-85. Hereinafter cited as Duke, *Reminiscences*.
[117] Michael B. Ballard, *A Long Shadow: Jefferson Davis and the Final Days of the Confederacy* (Jackson: University Press of Mississippi, 1986), pp. 122-23. Hereinafter cited as Ballard, *A Long Shadow*.
[118] *Ibid.*, pp. 127-28.
[119] Lindsley, *Military Annals of Tennessee*, p. 677; Duke, *Reminiscences*, p. 389.
[120] Ballard, *A Long Shadow*, pp. 131-32.
[121] *Ibid.*, p. 130.
[122] *Ibid.*, p. 132.
[123] *Ibid.*, pp. 133-35; Lindsley, *Military Annals of Tennessee*, p. 677.
[124] *O.R.*, Serial No. 103, pp. 537-51; Serial No. 104, pp. 846, 857-58.
[125] *Ibid.*, Serial No. 103, pp. 539-41; Ballard, *A Long Shadow*, pp. 142, 152.

[126] Lindsley, *Military Annals of Tennessee*, p. 677; *O.R.*, Serial No. 103, p. 555.
[127] *O.R.*, Serial No. 103, pp. 685–87.
[128] Lindsley, *Military Annals of Tennessee*, pp. 677–78. Colonel Smith was identified in "Service Records," General Judah in Warner, *Generals in Blue*, pp. 255–56, and Judge Rousseau in *National Cyclopedia of American Biography*, vol. 12, p. 185.
[129] Guild, *Fourth Tennessee Cavalry*, pp. 151–52; *O.R.*, Serial No. 103, p. 754.
[130] "Service Records."
[131] Dyer, *Life of Wheeler*, pp. 192–259 passim.

7. Hood's Tennessee Campaign: Debacle at Spring Hill, November 16–29, 1864

[1] Henry, *Forrest*, p. 382.
[2] *O.R.*, Serial No. 93, p. 759.
[3] U. S. Grant, *Personal Memoirs* (New York: Charles L. Webster & Company, 1886), vol. 2, p. 347.
[4] *O.R.*, Serial No. 93, p. 759.
[5] Henry, *Forrest*, p. 248.
[6] *O.R.* Serial No. 59, pp. 366, 367.
[7] *Ibid.*, Serial No. 57, p. 616; Lonnie E. Maness, "The Fort Pillow Massacre: Fact or Fiction," *Tennessee Historical Quarterly* (Winter, 1986), pp. 308–10; James I. Robertson, "The Civil War" (Washington: U.S. Civil War Commission, 1963), p. 35.
[8] Henry, *Forrest*, pp. 250–51.
[9] *Ibid.*, pp. 251–56; *O.R.*, Serial No. 57, p. 596.
[10] Hondon B. Hargrave, *Black Union Soldiers in the Civil War* (Jefferson, N.C.: McFarland & Company, 1988), pp. 169–76. See statements and testimony relative to the treatment of Union prisoners captured at Ft. Pillow in *O.R.*, Serial No. 57, pp. 519–40, 556–72, 594–99.
[11] *O.R.*, Serial No. 57, pp. 598–99, 614–15; Henry, *Forrest*, pp. 14–15; Arlin Turner, *George W. Cable: A Biography* (Baton Rouge: Lousiana State University Press, 1966), p. 299; Brian Steel Wills, *A Battle from the Start: The Life of Nathan Bedford Forrest* (New York: HarperCollins, 1992), p. 316; Grant, *Personal Memoirs*, vol. 2, p. 138; *O.R.*, Serial No. 57, pp. 609–11, 613–17.
[12] See Henry, *Forrest*, pp. 442–51; Stanley F. Horn, *Invisible Empire: The Story of the Ku Klux Klan 1866–1871* (Boston: Houghton Mifflin Company, 1939), pp. 25–41, 312–25, 356–77; Raymond Allen Cook, *Fire from the Flint: The Amazing Careers of Thomas Dixon* (Winston-Salem, N.C.: John F. Blair, 1968), pp. 126–49, 163–83, 195–97. Jack Hurst, in his biography of Forrest, found evidence that following the war Forrest's racial views changed from mainstream white American prejudice *against* blacks to a genuinely progressive esteem *for* blacks which was far in advance of the views of most white Americans of the time. See Jack Hurst, *Nathan Bedford Forrest: A Biography* (New York: Alfred A. Knopf, 1993), pp. 366–67, 385–86.
[13] *O.R.*, Serial No. 79, pp. 694–97.
[14] Wyeth, *Life of Forrest*, pp. 534–35; Horn, *Army of Tennessee*, pp. 380–81; Henry, *Forrest*, pp. 382–84.
[15] *O.R.*, Serial No. 79, p. 576; Horn, *Battle of Nashville*, p. 1.
[16] Henry, *Forrest*, p. 387.
[17] Wyeth, *Life of Forrest*, pp. 535–37.
[18] Henry, *Forrest*, p. 386.
[19] Wyeth, *Life of Forrest*, p. 538.
[20] *O.R.*, Serial No. 93, pp. 144–47, 763; Wyeth, *Life of Forrest*, p. 538.
[21] *O.R.*, Serial No. 93, pp. 1097–98, 1109, 1161.

²² Lindsley, *Military Annals of Tennessee*, p. 706; "Service Records."
²³ Connelly, *Autumn of Glory*, p. 491.
²⁴ Henry, *Forrest*, p. 387.
²⁵ *O.R.*, Serial No. 93, p. 752.
²⁶ *Ibid.*, p. 763.
²⁷ *Ibid.*, p. 1143.
²⁸ *Ibid.*, pp. 113, 147–48, 341–42.
²⁹ Henry, *Forrest*, p. 388.
³⁰ Fisher, "1915 Memoir," p. 6.
³¹ *O.R.*, Serial No. 93, pp. 550, 558, 1145–46.
³² Henry, *Forrest*, p. 389; *O.R.*, Serial No. 93, pp. 113, 148, 753.
³³ Henry, *Forrest*, pp. 390–91.
³⁴ *Ibid.*, p. 391.
³⁵ *Ibid.*, pp. 391–92.
³⁶ *Ibid.*, pp. 392–93.
³⁷ *Ibid.*, p. 393.
³⁸ *O.R.*, Serial No. 93, p. 753.
³⁹ Henry, *Forrest*, p. 394.
⁴⁰ *O.R.*, Serial No. 93, p. 770.
⁴¹ *Ibid.*, p. 753.
⁴² Henry, *Forrest*, p. 392.

8. Hood's Tennessee Campaign: Disasters at Franklin and Nashville, November 30–December 16, 1864

¹ Henry, *Forrest*, pp. 396–97.
² *Ibid.*, p. 397.
³ Horn, *Army of Tennessee*, pp. 397–98.
⁴ *Ibid.*, pp. 398–99.
⁵ Wyeth, *Life of Forrest*, p. 545.
⁶ *Ibid.*, pp. 545–46.
⁷ Henry, *Forrest*, pp. 399–400.
⁸ Horn, *Army of Tennessee*, p. 404.
⁹ Henry, *Forrest*, p. 401.
¹⁰ *O.R.*, Serial No. 93, pp. 560–61; Stanley F. Horn, *The Decisive Battle of Nashville* (Baton Rouge: Louisiana State University Press, 1956), p. 47. Hereinafter cited as Horn, *Battle of Nashville*.
¹¹ Wyeth, *Life of Forrest*, p. 547.
¹² Henry, *Forrest*, p. 402.
¹³ Wyeth, *Life of Forrest*, pp. 547–48.
¹⁴ *O.R.*, Serial No. 93, pp. 754–55.
¹⁵ Henry, *Forrest*, p. 403.
¹⁶ Wyeth, *Life of Forrest*, p. 548; "Service Records."
¹⁷ *O.R.*, Serial No. 93, pp. 613, 617–19, 746–47, 755, 756.
¹⁸ *Ibid.*, p. 756; Horn, *Battle of Nashville*, p. 39.
¹⁹ *O.R.*, Serial No. 93, pp. 36, 756; Horn, *Battle of Nashville*, p. 39.
²⁰ Horn, *Army of Tennessee*, pp. 410–11; Henry, *Forrest*, pp. 406–7; Wyeth, *Life of Forrest*, p. 549.
²¹ *O.R.*, Serial No. 93, pp. 764–65; Horn, *Battle of Nashville*, p. 40.
²² *O.R.*, Serial No. 94, p. 70.
²³ *Ibid.*, pp. 84, 96, 97.
²⁴ *Ibid.*, pp. 114, 115, 171, 195.
²⁵ *Ibid.*, pp. 98, 99.

[26] Horn, *Battle of Nashville*, pp. 53-54.
[27] *Ibid.*, p. 58; Henry, *Story of the Confederacy*, p. 431.
[28] *O.R.*, Serial No. 94, p. 180.
[29] Horn, *Battle of Nashville*, pp. 1, 73-80.
[30] *Ibid.*, pp. 1, 74-77.
[31] Horn, *Army of Tennessee*, p. 415.
[32] *O.R.*, Serial No. 93, pp. 562-64, 765.
[33] *Ibid.*, p. 765.
[34] Horn, *Battle of Nashville*, p. 81.
[35] Horn, *Army of Tennessee*, pp. 414-15.
[36] *Ibid.*, p. 415.
[37] *Ibid.*, pp. 416-17; *Tennesseans in the Civil War*, part 1, pp. 397-98.
[38] Horn, *Battle of Nashville*, pp. 118-20.
[39] Warner, *Generals in Gray*, p. 284.
[40] "Service Records."
[41] Warner, *Generals in Gray*, p. 284; Fisher, "Life on the Common Level," p. 77.
[42] *Confederate Veteran*, (July 1923), p. 247.
[43] Henry, *Forrest*, p. 408.
[44] Quoted in Horn, *Battle of Nashville*, p. 129.
[45] *Ibid.*, pp. 150-52.
[46] Wyeth, *Life of Forrest*, pp. 556-59.
[47] *O.R.*, Serial No. 93, pp. 105, 655.
[48] Horn, *Army of Tennessee*, p. 418.

9. Hood's Tennessee Campaign: Retreat, December 16-27, 1864

[1] *O.R.*, Serial No. 94, pp. 233, 252.
[2] Henry, *Forrest*, p. 410.
[3] *O.R.*, Serial No. 93, p. 756; Wyeth, *Life of Forrest*, pp. 561-62.
[4] *O.R.*, Serial No. 93, pp. 655, 756; Horn, *Battle of Nashville*, pp. 160-61.
[5] Wyeth, *Life of Forrest*, pp. 562-63.
[6] Henry, *Forrest*, p. 411.
[7] Wyeth, *Life of Forrest*, p. 566; *O.R.*, Serial No. 93, pp. 566, 766.
[8] *O.R.*, Serial No. 94, pp. 195, 230, 248.
[9] *Ibid.*, p. 248.
[10] Horn, *Battle of Nashville*, p. 161.
[11] *Ibid.*; "Service Records."
[12] *O.R.*, Serial No. 93, pp. 724-30, 757.
[13] Horn, *Battle of Nashville*, p. 162.
[14] Henry, *Forrest*, p. 413.
[15] *Ibid.*
[16] Horn, *Battle of Nashville*, p. 162.
[17] *O.R.*, Serial No. 93, pp. 757-58; Horn, *Battle of Nashville*, pp. 162-63.
[18] Jones, *Fisher Scrap Book*, pp. 89-90; Fisher, "Life on the Common Level," p. 8; "Service Records."
[19] Henry, *Forrest*, p. 414.
[20] Horn, *Battle of Nashville*, p. 163.
[21] Wyeth, *Life of Forrest*, pp. 570-71.
[22] Henry, *Forrest*, p. 416; *O.R.*, Serial No. 93, p. 758.
[23] Henry, *Forrest*, p. 416.
[24] *O.R.*, Serial No. 93, pp. 760-62.
[25] *Ibid.*, p. 767.

²⁶ *Ibid.*, p. 50.
²⁷ Henry, *Forrest*, p. 416.
²⁸ *O.R.*, Serial No. 93, p. 42.

10. Redeployment and Wilson's Alabama Campaign, December 28, 1864–April 12, 1865

¹ *O.R.*, Serial No. 94, pp. 748, 756.
² Wyeth, *Life of Forrest*, p. 578.
³ *O.R.*, Serial No. 93, pp. 642–44.
⁴ *Ibid.*, Serial No. 94, pp. 751–52; "Service Records." Regarding other troops on furlough who deserted in January 1865, see two examples in Chapter 6.
⁵ Quoted in Wyeth, *Life of Forrest*, p. 579.
⁶ *O.R.*, Serial No. 94, pp. 756–57.
⁷ Jones, *Fisher Scrap Book*, pp. 90–91; Fisher, "Life on the Common Level," p. 11.
⁸ Fisher, "1915 Memoir," p. 6; Jones, *Fisher Scrap Book*, p. 89.
⁹ Stephen V. Ash, "Sharks in an Angry Sea: Civilian Resistance and Guerrilla Warfare in Occupied Middle Tennessee, 1862–1865," *Tennessee Historical Quarterly* (Fall 1986), pp. 227–29; Richard P. Gildrie, "Guerrilla Warfare in the Lower Cumberland River Valley," *Tennessee Historical Quarterly* (Fall 1990), pp. 169–70; Guild, *Fourth Tennessee Cavalry*, pp. 75–96.
¹⁰ Lindsley, *Military Annals of Tennessee*, pp. 706–7.
¹¹ *O.R.*, Serial No. 94, p. 800.
¹² *O.R.*, Serial No. 104, pp. 1124–26; Serial No. 98, p. 1132.
¹³ Wyeth, *Life of Forrest*, pp. 578–79.
¹⁴ *O.R.*, Serial No. 94, p. 783.
¹⁵ *Ibid.*, pp. 781, 805. Note that Beauregard sometimes dropped his first name, Pierre, in signing correspondence and orders.
¹⁶ *Ibid.*, p. 780.
¹⁷ Horn, *Army of Tennessee*, pp. 422–23.
¹⁸ *O.R.*, Serial No. 94, p. 804; Serial No. 103, p. 938.
¹⁹ Henry, *Forrest*, p. 420.
²⁰ *Ibid.*, p. 422.
²¹ Margaret Lindsley Warden, "Belle Meade's Glory Days," *Nashville Magazine* (November 1977), pp. 81–85.
²² "Service Records"; Jones, *Fisher Scrap Book*, p. 91.
²³ *O.R.*, Serial No. 103, pp. 962, 972, 992; "Service Records."
²⁴ *O.R.*, Serial No. 103, p. 1049; "Service Records"; Jones, *Fisher Scrap Book*, p. 92.
²⁵ *O.R.*, Serial No. 103, pp. 930–31.
²⁶ *Ibid.*, pp. 950, 1032, 1057–58.
²⁷ Jones, *Fisher Scrap Book*, pp. 91–93.
²⁸ See Kelley in Hunter Dickinson Farish, *The Circuit Rider Dismounts: A Social History of Southern Methodism, 1865–1900* (New York: DaCapo Press, 1969), pp. 97–98, 187, 199, 263, 270–71, 299–301, 320–21, 349–51. On social and economic reform, see Kelley in Paul E. Isaac, *Prohibition and Politics: Turbulent Decades in Tennessee, 1885–1920* (Knoxville: University of Tennessee Press, 1965), pp. 65–66.
²⁹ Jones, *Fisher Scrap Book*, pp. 91–92; *Journal of the Eighty-Fourth Session of the Tennessee Annual Conference of the Methodist Episcopal Church, South* (Shelbyville, Tennessee, October 20–25, 1897); Roy Hunter Short, *Chosen to Be Consecrated: The Bishops of The Methodist Church, 1784–1968* (Lake Junaluska, N.C.: Commission on Archives and History, 1976), p. 112.
³⁰ Jones, *Fisher Scrap Book*, pp. 91–92; Goodspeed, *Tennessee with Sketch[es] of Counties*, p. 962.

31 Jones, *Fisher Scrap Book*, p. 92.
32 Henry, *Forrest*, pp. 422, 425.
33 *Ibid.*, pp. 423-25.
34 Wyeth, *Life of Forrest*, p. 586; Henry, *Forrest*, p. 427.
35 Wyeth, *Life of Forrest*, p. 585.
36 *Ibid.*, p. 587.
37 Henry, *Forrest*, p. 429.
38 *O.R.*, Serial No. 103, pp. 383-84.
39 Henry, *Forrest*, pp. 429, 431.
40 *Ibid.*, pp. 429, 430.
41 *Ibid.*, p. 430.
42 *O.R.*, Serial No. 104, pp. 1146-47, 1155. Regarding Hudson's Mississippi Battery, see *Confederate Veteran* (May 1927), p. 187.
43 *O.R.*, Serial No. 104, p. 1160; Henry, *Forrest*, p. 428.
44 Henry, *Forrest*, pp. 428, 430; Wyeth, *Life of Forrest*, p. 593.
45 Wyeth, *Life of Forrest*, p. 594.
46 Henry, *Forrest*, p. 430.
47 Wyeth, *Life of Forrest*, pp. 593-96.
48 Henry, *Forrest*, p. 430.
49 Wyeth, *Life of Forrest*, p. 598.
50 *Ibid.*, pp. 599-602.
51 Henry, *Forrest*, pp. 430-31.
52 Wyeth, *Life of Forrest*, pp. 602-3; Richard Taylor, *Destruction and Reconstruction* (New York: Longmans Green, 1955), pp. 268-69.
53 Wyeth, *Life of Forrest*, pp. 603-4.
54 Wilson did not report Millington's first name. But it seems quite plausible that the English civil engineer was John Millington (1779-1868) who came to America in 1829, taught at the College of William and Mary beginning in 1837, and published *Elements of Civil Engineering* (Philadelphia, 1839), perhaps the first treatise on the subject published in America. He became professor of natural sciences at the University of Mississippi and Mississippi state geologist in 1848. He became professor of chemistry and toxicology at Memphis Medical College in 1853. He retired in 1859 and moved to La Grange, Tennessee, "La Belle Village," an idyllic residential community about 45 miles east of Memphis. Millington was pauperized by the Civil War. In his eighties, he may have found needed employment in his adopted South in designing and constructing fortifications, although none of the known sources of his life, all sketchy, mention such activity. After the war, he lived with a daughter in Richmond. He died July 10, 1868, and was buried in Bruton Parish churchyard in Williamsburg. *Dictionary of American Biography* (1961 ed.) vol. 6, p. 647.
55 Wyeth, *Life of Forrest*, pp. 587-88, 603-4; *O.R.*, Serial No. 103, pp. 359-61.
56 Wyeth, *Life of Forrest*, p. 604.
57 *Ibid.*, p. 605.
58 *Ibid.*, pp. 607-10.
59 *Ibid.*; *O.R.*, Serial No. 103, p. 406; James Harrison Wilson, *Under the Old Flag* (New York: D. Appleton and Company, 1912), vol. 2, p. 240. Hereinafter cited as Wilson, *Under the Old Flag*.
60 Henry, *Forrest*, p. 433.
61 *O.R.*, Serial No. 104, pp. 1206-7.
62 Henry, *Forrest*, pp. 433-34; *U.S. Census*, Ninth (1860); Wilson, *Under the Old Flag*, vol. 2, p. 241.
63 Henry, *Forrest*, p. 434.
64 *O.R.*, Serial No. 104, p. 272.
65 Henry, *Forrest*, pp. 434, 533.
66 *Ibid.*, pp. 434-35.

67 Jones, *Fisher Scrap Book*, p. 93; Wyeth, *Life of Forrest*, pp. 588-89.
68 *O.R.*, Serial No. 104, pp. 1177-78, 1182.
69 *Ibid.*, Serial No. 103, p. 420; Wyeth, *Life of Forrest*, pp. 590-91; Jones, *Fisher Scrap Book*, p. 93.
70 *O.R.*, Serial No. 103, pp. 416-17; Wyeth, *Life of Forrest*, pp. 591-92; Jones, *Fisher Scrap Book*, p. 93.
71 *O.R.*, Serial No. 103, p. 417.
72 Jones, *Fisher Scrap Book*, p. 93.
73 *Ibid.*
74 *Ibid.*
75 Wyeth, *Life of Forrest*, p. 592.
76 *O.R.*, Serial No. 103, pp. 368, 419-24.
77 Wilson, *Under the Old Flag*, vol. 2, p. 294; Taylor. *Destruction and Reconstruction*, p. 269.
78 Wilson, *Under the Old Flag*, vol. 2, pp. 295-96. See Lloyd Lewis, *Sherman: Fighting Prophet* (New York: Harcourt, Brace and Company, 1958), p. 444.

11. An Army in Bivouac; Surrender and Home, April 12-May 25, 1865

1 *O.R.*, Serial No. 104, p. 1224.
2 *Ibid.*, pp. 1224-25.
3 *Ibid.*, pp. 1227-28, 1234.
4 *Ibid.*, pp. 1229, 1235, 1236.
5 Taylor, *Destruction and Reconstruction*, p. 272.
6 *O.R.*, Serial No. 104, pp. 1229, 1245, 1271-72.
7 *Ibid.*, p. 1229.
8 *Ibid.*, pp. 1240, 1243.
9 Jones, *Fisher Scrap Book*, pp. 93.
10 *O.R.*, Serial No. 104, pp. 1248, 1251, 1261.
11 Jones, *Fisher Scrap Book*, pp. 93-94.
12 *Ibid.*, p. 94.
13 Wyeth, *Life of Forrest*, p. 611.
14 Jones, *Fisher Scrap Book*, p. 94.
15 *O.R.*, Serial No. 104, p. 1270; Taylor, *Destruction and Reconstruction*, pp. 274-75.
16 *O.R.*, Serial No. 104, p. 1270; Taylor, *Destruction and Reconstruction*, pp. 275-76.
17 Jones, *Fisher Scrap Book*, p. 94; Folmsbee, Corlew, and Mitchell, *Tennessee, A Short History*, pp. 354, 393.
18 Taylor, *Destruction and Reconstruction*, pp. 276-77; Jones, *Fisher Scrap Book*, p. 94; *O.R.*, Serial No. 104, pp. 1283-84.
19 Letter quoted in Henry, *Forrest*, p. 436.
20 *Ibid.*, p. 437.
21 Jones, *Fisher Scrap Book*, p. 95.
22 *O.R.*, Serial No. 104, pp. 1289-90.
23 See Sherman, *Memoirs*, vol. 2, pp. 356-57, 370; also Chap. 6 herein.
24 Fisher, "Life on the Common Level," p. 33; "Service Records"; *O.R.*, Serial No. 104, p. 1240; James M. McPherson, *Ordeal by Fire: The Civil War and Reconstruction* (New York: Alfred A. Knopf, 1982), pp. 451n, 468; *O.R.*, Serial No. 93, pp. 760-62; Frederick Phisterer, *Statistical Record of the Armies of the United States* (New York: Charles Scribner's Sons, 1883), pp. 71-72; James I. Robertson, Jr., *Soldiers Blue and Gray* (Columbia: University of South Carolina Press, 1988), pp. 20, 135.
25 Fisher, "1915 Memoir," p. 7.
26 Jones, *Fisher Scrap Book*, p. 95.

²⁷ Quoted in Henry, *As They Saw Forrest*, p. 46.
²⁸ Jones, *Fisher Scrap Book*, p. 95.
²⁹ *Ibid.*
³⁰ *Ibid.*
³¹ "Service Records"; *U.S. Census*, Ninth (1860).
³² Jones, *Fisher Scrap Book*, p. 95.
³³ *U.S. Census*, Ninth (1860).
³⁴ Jones, *Fisher Scrap Book*, p. 95.
³⁵ *O.R.*, Serial No. 102, pp. 600–3; Warner, *Generals in Gray*, p. 62.
³⁶ See James D. Horan (ed.), *C.S.S. Shenandoah: The Memoirs of Lieutenant Commanding James I. Waddell* (New York: Crown Publishers, 1960), pp. 175–82; *Official Records of the Union and Confederate Navies in the War of the Rebellion* (Washington: Government Printing Office, 1894–1927), series 1, vol. 3, pp. 791–836; *Civil War Chronology, 1861–1865* (Washington: U.S. Naval History Division, 1971), part 5, pp. 110–11, 122, 128.
³⁷ See Wyeth, *Life of Forrest*, pp. 588–89.
³⁸ Dyer, *Life of Wheeler*, p. 147.
³⁹ Fisher, "Life on the Common Level," p. 2.
⁴⁰ Dyer, *Life of Wheeler*, pp. 161–62; Guild, *Fourth Tennessee Cavalry*, pp. 168–69.
⁴¹ *O.R.*, Serial No. 92, pp. 1002–3.
⁴² See Dyer, *Life of Wheeler*, pp. 161–62.
⁴³ *O.R.*, Serial No. 58, p. 634.
⁴⁴ Warner, *Generals in Gray*, p. 284.
⁴⁵ Fisher, "Life on the Common Level," p. 77. For the influence of Sawney Webb and the Webb School experience on young postwar Tennesseans, see Laurence McMillin, *The Schoolmaker: Sawney Webb and the Bell Buckle Story* (Chapel Hill: University of North Carolina Press, 1971), pp. xi–xvii, 152–163 passim. With respect to a measure of academic achievement at Webb School, the author of *The Schoolmaker* states that during the school's first fifty years, it produced more Rhodes scholars than any other American secondary school. See *ibid.*, pp. 9, 156–57.

On July 18, 1928, Lillian Boone Fentress, Howard's aunt, and Anna Maude Smith opened The Anna Maude, an upscale cafeteria which built an impressive reputation for food, service, and decor in Oklahoma City. Smith and Fentress were co-owners and partners in the business, which survived the Depression and continues today.

Lillian Boone Fentress (1876–1954) was a sister of Thomas Fisher's wife, Lula Boone, as well as sister of Howard H. Boone, Mary Fisher Boone's husband. Mary was Thomas Fisher's daughter. Beginning in 1916, Lillian Fentress, Howard and Mary Boone, and Howard Fisher shared the same household, first in Clinton, Oklahoma, then (beginning in 1918) in Oklahoma City, according to the "Fact Sheet," by Howard B. Fisher, August 7, 1980, in the author's possession. A souvenir brochure, "Our 25th Anniversary: The Anna Maude," is a source of information about staff, operations, and beginnings of the cafeteria. It was produced by The Anna Maude in 1953.
⁴⁶ See *Confederate Veteran* (July 1923), p. 247.
⁴⁷ See Hinton Rowan Helper, *The Impending Crisis in the South* (New York: Collier Books, 1963), pp. 25–109 passim.
⁴⁸ See Connelly, *Autumn of Glory*, pp. 4–5, 15, 18–23, 69–92, 132, 149–50, 151–52, 153–62, 177, 184, 187–90, 211–20, 234, 235–67, 313, 318–21, 332, 418–20, 438. See also Woodworth, *Jefferson Davis and His Generals*, pp. 75–78, 156–61, 173–78, 187–99, 233–55.
⁴⁹ Ralph Henry Gabriel, *The Course of American Democratic Thought* (New York: The Ronald Press, 1940), p. 132.
⁵⁰ See Horn, *Battle of Nashville*, pp. v–xiii. Stanley Horn saw the Battle of Nashville as *the* decisive battle of the war by asking and answering the question: "Which battle by a contrary event [or outcome], would have influenced the final result of the war . . . ?" See also Connelly, *Army of the Heartland*, pp. 11–12; Connelly, *Autumn of Glory*, p. 6.

⁵¹ Fisher, "1915 Memoir," p. 9.
⁵² Fisher, "Life on the Common Level," pp. 33-34.
⁵³ *Ibid.* Although Fisher did not reveal the young woman's name in his memoirs, one might guess one of two neighbors from the Sixth Civil District of Marshall County based upon a detailed review of census records for the names of eligible females with proximity in ages and addresses. The Ninth U.S. Census in 1860 reveals a possibility, Sarah Davis, daughter of James and Elizabeth Davis, whose age was given as fourteen and her birthplace shown as Mon[tana?]. Fisher revealed in his 1921 memoir that the young woman to whom he was affianced had left the community and gone to live in Montana after she had terminated their relationship following the war. Had she gone to live in the territory of her birth? The possible Montana connection and the closeness of their ages, with Tom the elder by one to two years, elicit the guess that Sarah Davis might have been the first romantic love in his young life.

But when Fisher discussed in his memoir the termination of his relationship with the young woman, he wrote that, while away at school, he received a letter from his brother, Bascom, who wrote that he had just heard of the marriage of Miss A (the young woman in question) to Mr. M. If the unknown woman's maiden name really began with the letter A, the likely candidate, from census records, would have been Sally Adams, daughter of Joseph and Eveline Adams. Sally, whose father was a prosperous farmer, lived near the Fishers and was 16, also Thomas's age, in the 1860 census.

Whoever she was, Fisher last saw her in Nashville on a street railway trolley traveling from St. Thomas Hospital to the downtown transfer station. When he wrote in 1921, he revealed that she had died only a few weeks after he last saw her. But still he chose not to reveal her name. Fisher, "Life on the Common Level," p. 34

⁵⁴ James I. Robertson, Jr., "The Civil War" (Washington, D.C.: U.S. Civil War Centennial Commission, 1963), pp. 35-36.

⁵⁵ See Charles A. Beard and Mary R. Beard, *The Rise of American Civilization:* vol. 2, *The Industrial Era* (New York: Macmillan, 1930), pp. 105-10. Regarding government contractors in the Civil War, see Gustavus Myers, *History of the Great American Fortunes* (New York: Modern Library, 1964), pp. 188-89, 290-98, 400-6, 474-75, 520-22, 523n, 536-41, 546-52.

Epilogue

¹ See Folmsbee, Corlew and Mitchell, *Tennessee: A Short History*, pp. 385-88; C. Vann Woodward, *Origins of the New South, 1877-1913*, vol. 9 of *A History of the South* (Baton Rouge: Louisiana State University Press, 1951; Austin: The Littlefield Fund for Southern History of the University of Texas, 1951), pp. 180-88.

² See William B. Hesseltine, *The South in American History* (New York: Prentice-Hall, 1943), p. 557; Arthur Meier Schlesinger, *The Rise of the City, 1878-1898*, vol. 10 of *A History of American Life* (New York: Macmillan, 1933), pp. 13-14; Samuel Eliot Morison, Henry Steele Commager, and William E. Leuchtenburg, *The Growth of the American Republic*, seventh edition (New York: Oxford University Press, 1980), vol. 2, pp. 51, 55-60; Charles P. Roland, *The Improbable Era: The South since World War II* (Lexington: University Press of Kentucky, 1975), pp. 4, 26-29.

³ See Morison, Commager, and Leuchtenburg, *The Growth of the American Republic*, vol. 2, pp. 483-507, 620, 625, 628-30, 657-61, 665-66, 675-80, 685-91, 731-32, 759-63, 767-74.

⁴ See John E. Fisher, "Government Support for Economic Growth," *Business and Government Review* (September-October 1965), pp. 12-19.

⁵ Dates of birth and death of Jacob and Nancy Helm Fisher are on their common grave marker, Ganntown Cemetery, Johnson County, Illinois. See also Jones, *Fisher Scrap Book*, pp. 34, 35-36, 44.

⁶ *United States Census of Agriculture*, 6th and 16th civil districts, Marshall County, Tennessee, Ninth (1860) and Tenth (1870).
⁷ Fisher, "Life on the Common Level," pp. 7, 11, 26; Jones, *Fisher Scrap Book*, pp. 58, 59; *U.S. Census*, Tenth (1870) and Eleventh (1880).
⁸ *U.S. Census*, Eleventh (1880), Jones, *Fisher Scrap Book*, pp. 48-49, 79; See John R. Stewart, memoir of T.B. Fisher in Tennessee Conference *Journal* (1922), pp. 95-97.
⁹ Jones, *Fisher Scrap Book*, pp. 153-54; *U.S. Census*, Eleventh (1880); Certificate of Death, Tennessee State Library & Archives, Nashville. Bascom Hurt Fisher's dates of birth and death are on his grave marker in the Fisher Cemetery, Farmington-Verona Road, Marshall County, Tennessee.
¹⁰ Jones, *Fisher Scrap Book*, p. 50; *U.S. Census*, Eighth (1850), Ninth (1860), Eleventh (1880); R.M. Haggard memoir in Tennessee Conference *Journal* (1902).
¹¹ See Hesseltine, *The South in American History*, pp. 580, 589-90; Woodward, *Origins of the New South*, pp. 205-9; Lester C. Lamon, *Blacks in Tennessee, 1791-1970* (Knoxville: University of Tennessee Press, 1981), pp. 62-67.
¹² See Schlesinger, *The Rise of the City*, pp. 380-81; John E. Fisher, *The John F. Slater Fund: A Nineteenth Century Affirmative Action for Negro Education* (Lanham, Md.: University Press of America, 1987), pp. xviii, 119-20, 122-26.
¹³ Fisher, "Life on the Common Level," pp. 14-15; *U.S. Census*, Ninth (1860), Tenth (1870), Eleventh (1880).
¹⁴ Jones, *Fisher Scrap Book*, pp. 72-74; Fisher, "Life on the Common Level," pp. 8-9. James Wesley Fisher's dates of birth and death are on his grave marker in the Fisher Cemetery, Farmington-Verona Road, Marshall County, Tennessee.
¹⁵ Fisher, "1915 Memoir," pp. 1, 7; Fisher, "Life on the Common Level," pp. 8-9; Jones, *Fisher Scrap Book*, pp. 78-79. William Stratton Fisher's dates of birth and death are on his grave marker in the Fisher Cemetery, Farmington-Verona Road, Marshall County, Tennessee. His diary is contained in Jones, *Fisher Scrap Book*, pp. 81-95.
¹⁶ *U.S. Census*, Eleventh (1880); Jones, *Fisher Scrap Book*, pp. 98, 109; Fisher, "Life on the Common Level," p. 8; letter from Marshall W. Lovell to the author dated November 27, 1967.
¹⁷ Fisher, "Life on the Common Level," pp. 10-11, 26; Jones, *Fisher Scrap Book*, pp. 58, 59; *U.S. Census*, Eleventh (1880). Elisha Monroe Fisher's dates of birth and death are on his grave marker in the Fisher Cemetery, Farmington-Verona Road, Marshall County, Tennessee.
¹⁸ Jones, *Fisher Scrap Book*, pp. 48-49; Fisher, "Life on the Common Level," pp. 1-2; *Confederate Veteran* (April 1896), p. 131; William Waller (ed.), *Nashville, 1900 to 1910* (Nashville: Vanderbilt University Press, 1972), p. 340. John Franklin Fisher's dates of birth and death are on his grave marker in the Fisher Cemetery, Farmington-Verona Road, Marshall County, Tennessee.
¹⁹ Jones, *Fisher Scrap Book*, pp. 50, 55, 153.
²⁰ Fisher, "1915 Memoir," pp. 7-9; Fisher, "Life on the Common Level," pp. 17-18, 20. The households and occupations of John Jordan and William A. Ransom of Murfreesboro were reconstructed from the *U.S. Census*, Tenth (1870).
²¹ John E. Fisher, "Life on the Common Level: Inheritance, Conflict, and Instruction," *Tennessee Historical Quarterly* (Fall 1967), p. 321; *Eleventh* [1860] and *Twelfth* [1870] *Annual Catalogues of the Officers and Students of Union University, Murfreesboro, Tennessee* (Nashville, 1860 and 1870). Regarding the work of Adolphus Heiman, see James Patrick, *Architecture in Tennessee, 1768-1897* (Knoxville: University of Tennessee Press, 1981), pp. 135-38, 145-57; and James Patrick, "The Architecture of Adolphus Heiman," *Tennessee Historical Quarterly* (Summer and Fall 1979), pp. 167-187, 277-295.
²² See Fisher, "Life on the Common Level," pp. 23-92 passim.
²³ *Ibid.*, pp. 21, 33-34.
²⁴ Fisher, "1915 Memoir," pp. 20-21, 31; see Benjamin F. Byrd, Jr., "Dr. Paul Eve, 1806-1877" in *Send for a Doctor* (Nashville: The Public Library of Nashville & Davidson

County, 1975), pp. 108-25; see also William Waller (ed.), *Nashville, 1900 to 1910*, pp. 239-42.

25 Fisher, "1915 Memoir," pp. 36, 37-38, 40; Fisher, "Life on the Common Level," p. 92; letter to author from Lucian H. Boone of Dallas, Texas, June 24, 1981. Dates of marriages and deaths verified by cemetery records, newspaper notices, and memorials published in Tennessee Annual Conference *Journals*.

26 Fisher, "Life on the Common Level," p. 14.

27 See Ralph E. Morrow, *Northern Methodism and Reconstruction* (East Lansing: Michigan State University Press, 1956), pp. 29-57.

28 Fred Arthur Bailey, *Class and Tennessee's Confederate Generation* (Chapel Hill: University of North Carolina Press, 1987), pp. 78-79, 99, 100. Another student of the Tennessee Civil War Veterans Questionnaires finds Bailey's conclusions relative to class-consciousness among respondents to the questionnaires less than convincing. See Jennifer K. Boone, "'Mingling Freely': Tennessee Society on the Eve of the Civil War," *Tennessee Historical Quarterly* (Fall 1992), pp. 137-46.

29 Stephen V. Ash, *Middle Tennessee Society Transformed, 1860-1870*, pp. 84-96, 131, 163-67, 197-200, 202, 203-5. For a lucid view of racial discrimination and black responses thereto in a segregated America, see Charles S. Johnson, *Background to Patterns of Negro Segregation* (New York: Thomas Y. Crowell, 1972).

30 Fisher, "Life on the Common Level," pp. 74-75.

31 *Ibid.*, p. 14. See William A. Dunning, *Reconstruction, Political and Economic, 1865-1877* (New York: Harper & Row, 1962), pp. 109-23. Dunning's treatise was originally published in 1907.

32 Fisher, "Life on the Common Level," p. 10. See Ralph Henry Gabriel, *The Course of American Democratic Thought* (New York: The Ronald Press, 1940), pp. 308-30 passim.

33 Fisher, "1915 Memoir," p. 22; Fisher, "Life on the Common Level," pp. 75, 86.

34 Georgia Harkness, *The Methodist Church in Social Thought and Action* (Nashville: Abingdon Press, 1964), pp. 99-102. A rediscovery of John Wesley as theologian has given a Wesleyan cast to American Methodism's love affair with theological liberalism for over fifty years. See Richard P. Heitzenrater, "The Present State of Wesley Studies," *Methodist History* (July 1984), pp. 221-33.

35 T.B. Fisher, "Sermons." Fisher's sermons and sermon notes were written tightly in a fine well-crafted script on sheets of paper of differing size and quality. In the pulpit, he referred to them with the aid of spectacles with magnifying lenses set low on the bridge of his nose. Fisher gave each sermon a scriptural reference and sometimes a title. A few are dated. They remain in manuscript form. His homilies were preserved after Fisher's death by Will Stratton and Estelle Carr Fisher and are in the author's possession.

36 Fisher, "Life on the Common Level," p. 15.

37 See Theodore T. Munger, *Horace Bushnell: Preacher and Theologian* (Boston: Houghton, Mifflin and Company, 1900), pp. 67-87 passim.

38 Fisher, "Sermons."

39 Fisher, "Life on the Common Level," pp. 14-15.

40 Fisher, "Sermons."

41 Hesseltine, *The South in American History*, p. 508; Foster Rhea Dulles, *Labor in America: A History* (New York: Thomas Y. Crowell Company, 1949), pp. 114-25.

42 Fisher, "Sermons."

43 Fisher, "Life on the Common Level," p. 14. See Bertram Wilbur Doyle, *The Etiquette of Race Relations in the South: A Study in Social Control* (New York: Schocken Books, 1971), pp. 146, 147, 232.

44 Fisher, "Life on the Common Level," pp. 62, 72.

45 Related to the author by Harold H. Hughes of Arlington, Virginia, and J. Manning Potts of Nashville, students of John Roberts Fisher at Randolph Macon College. See editorial tribute to W.P. Fisher, *The Nashville Tennessean*, Monday, October 16, 1950.

⁴⁶ Fisher, "Life on the Common Level," p. 11; Fisher, "1915 Memoir," pp. 14, 17.

⁴⁷ Fisher, "Life on the Common Level," pp. 71-73. See reactions of clerics to being objects of charity, enduring poverty and a declining professional status in post-Civil War America in Richard Hofstadter, *The Age of Reform: From Bryan to F.D.R.* (New York: Alfred A. Knopf, 1955), pp. 148-52. Reactions often took the form of embracing the social gospel and later, by the 1890s, political progressivism, according to Hofstadter.

⁴⁸ Fisher, "Life on the Common Level," pp. 62-64; Fisher, "1915 Memoir," p. 12; Hunter Dickinson Farish, *The Circuit Rider Dismounts: A Social History of Southern Methodism, 1865-1900* (New York: Da Capo Press, 1977), pp. 321n, 349; Walter T. Durham, *Nashville: The Occupied City* (Nashville: Tennessee Historical Society, 1985), p. 144; Kelley in 1890 was the gubernatorial candidate of the Prohibition Party, which endorsed measures enhancing industrial democracy and had the most liberal and progressive platform of the three parties backing a candidate in 1890. See Paul E. Isaac, *Prohibition and Politics: Turbulent Decades in Tennessee, 1885-1920* (Knoxville: University of Tennessee Press, 1965), pp. 64-67.

⁴⁹ Robert Watson Sledge, *Hands on the Ark: The Struggle for Change in the Methodist Episcopal Church, South, 1914-1939* (Lake Junaluska, N.C.: Commission on Archives and History, The United Methodist Church, 1975), pp. 70, 136-37, 219-20.

⁵⁰ Fisher, "Sermons."

⁵¹ Paul K. Conkin, *Gone with the Ivy: A Biography of Vanderbilt University* (Knoxville: University of Tennessee Press, 1985), p. 97.

⁵² Edwin Mims, *Chancellor Kirkland of Vanderbilt* (Nashville: Vanderbilt University Press, 1940), pp. x, xi, xii, 268.

⁵³ In a letter dated January 2, 1992, to his daughter Mary, Fisher refers to and quotes a poem, "Go Little Line," written by Tillett, which the latter had sent him. Letter in the possession of Betsy Hammonds Fisher; Conkin, *Gone with the Ivy*, p. 175.

⁵⁴ Trinity College officially became Duke University in 1927. See Edwin Mims, *The Advancing South: Stories of Progress and Reaction* (Garden City, N.Y.: Doubleday, Page & Company, 1926), pp. 157-71; *To Give the Key of Knowledge: United Methodists and Education, 1784-1976* (Nashville: National Commission on United Methodist Higher Education, 1976), pp. 46, 47, 65-66.

⁵⁵ It is noted, of course, that Trinity had survived its refusal to dismiss historian John Spencer Bassett in 1903 pursuant to attacks on Trinity and Bassett for Bassett's unbiased views on race which were revealed in his article in the *South Atlantic Quarterly*. In the same year, Emory had dismissed Professor Andrew Sledd following attacks on Sledd's article dealing with race which appeared in the *Atlantic Monthly*. Sledd later rejoined the Emory faculty. In 1921, theologian John A. Rice's resignation from Southern Methodist University was accepted following attacks on his Old Testament writings by Texas fundamentalists. But the failure and disappearance of most such attacks indicated that interest by disaffected churchmen in suppressing heresy, free discussion of issues occasioned by new knowledge and social change, and converting the Methodist Church into a narrowly ideological church lacked consensus and conviction. See Edwin Mims, *The Advancing South*, pp. 145, 147-57; Robert Watson Sledge, *Hands on the Ark*, pp. 144-50.

⁵⁶ Sledge, *Hands on the Ark*, p. 66.

⁵⁷ Fisher, "Sermons." Fisher's views of scripture are illuminated by but distinguished in degree and substance from those of George Santayana who wrote in his *Introduction to The Ethics of Spinoza* (1910) that "the Bible is literature, not dogma."

⁵⁸ For a life sketch of Haygood, see Fisher, *The John F. Slater Fund*, pp. 39-41.

⁵⁹ Harold W. Mann, *Atticus Greene Haygood: Methodist Bishop, Editor, and Educator* (Athens: University of Georgia Press, 1965), pp. 182-84; Fisher, *The John F. Slater Fund*, pp. 81, 124, 137; John Patrick McDowell, *The Social Gospel in the South: The Woman's Home Mission Movement in the Methodist Episcopal Church, South, 1886-1939* (Baton Rouge: Louisiana State University Press, 1982), pp. 88-91; Farish, *The Circuit Rider Dismounts*, pp. 187, 199, 205.

⁶⁰ John J. Tigert IV, *Bishop Holland Nimmons McTyeire: Ecclesiastical and Educational Architect* (Nashville: Vanderbilt University Press, 1955), pp. 162, 182–86, 189–203 passim, 212–27; Wheaton J. Lane, *Commodore Vanderbilt: An Epic of the Steam Age* (New York: Alfred A. Knopf, 1942), pp. 315–17; Conkin, *Gone with the Ivy*, pp. 21–22.

⁶¹ Fisher, "Life on the Common Level," pp. 59–60.

⁶² *Ibid.*, pp. 56–57, and family oral tradition.

⁶³ T.B. Fisher to Mrs. H.H. [Mary] Boone, January 2, 1922; letter and subsequent referenced correspondence of T.B. Fisher are in possession of Betsy Hammonds Fisher.

⁶⁴ T.B. Fisher to Mrs. H.H. [Mary] Boone, August 18, 1919; Fisher, "Life on the Common Level," pp. 91–92; *Journal* of the Tennessee Annual Conference (1920), pp. 30, 59, 64–65.

⁶⁵ T.B. Fisher to Mrs. H.H. [Mary] Boone, October 4, 1920. A brief biographical sketch of Thomas's son, Will Stratton Fisher, is found in an advertising brochure, "The Ambrose Spirit," published by Ambrose Printing Company of Nashville in 1947.

⁶⁶ T.B. Fisher to Howard B. Fisher, December 21, 1920; T.B. Fisher to Mrs. H.H. [Mary] Boone, March 5, 1921; Fisher, "Life on the Common Level," pp. 91–92.

⁶⁷ Certificate of Death, Tennessee State Library & Archives, Nashville; *Nashville Banner*, Friday, March 2, 1922; *Nashville Tennessean*, Saturday, March 3, 1922. Teachout erred in recalling the date of death as March 3. Best evidence indicates the date was Friday, March 2. Teachout and the obituary writer in the *Banner* agreed on the time of day, 6:35 A.M.

⁶⁸ *Dallas Morning News*, Sunday, April 21, 1991.

Bibliography

Primary Sources

Alderson, William T., ed. "The Civil War Reminiscences of John Johnston, 1861-1865." *Tennessee Historical Quarterly* vol. 13, nos. 1-4 (March-December 1954); vol. 14, nos. 1, 2 (March, June 1955).
Annual Catalogue of the Officers and Students of Union University, Murfreesboro, Tennessee. Nashville: 1860 and 1870.
Annual Report of the Adjutant General of the State of Illinois. Springfield: Baker & Phillips, 1863.
Battles and Leaders of the Civil War. 4 vols. New York: Thomas Yoseloff, 1956. Edited by Robert Underwood Johnson and Clarence Clough Buel. Originally published in New York by The Century Company, 1884-1887.
Cannon, Newton. *Reminiscences.* Jackson, Tenn.: McCowat-Mercer Press, 1963.
Clark, Sam L. and H.D. Riley, Jr., ed. "S.H. Stout: Outline of the Organization of the Medical Department of the Confederate Army and Department of Tennessee." *Tennessee Historical Quarterly* vol. 16, no. 1 (March 1957).
Clayton, W.W. *History of Davidson County, Tennessee.* Philadelphia: J.W. Lewis Company, 1880.
Confederate Veteran. Nashville. 1893-1932.
Davis, Jefferson. *Rise and Fall of the Confederate Government.* 2 vols. New York: D. Appleton and Company, 1881.
Duke, Basil W. *Reminiscences of General Basil Duke, C.S.A.* Garden City, N.Y.: Doubleday, Page & Co., 1911.
Fisher, Thomas Burr. "Life on the Common Level." Unpublished manuscript, 1921. Collection of John Thomas Fisher.
_____. Untitled memoir, 1915. Collection of John E. Fisher.
_____. Sermons and sermon outlines. Manuscripts from collection of John E. Fisher.
Fisher, William Stratton. Diary. *The Fisher Scrapbook, 1730-1972.* Compiled by William L. Jones. Milan, Tenn.: Privately printed, n.d.
Grant, U. S. *Personal Memoirs.* 2 vols. New York: Charles L. Webster & Company, 1886.
Guild, George B. *A Brief Narrative of the Fourth Tennessee Cavalry Regiment.* Nashville: Privately printed, 1913.
Helper, Hinton Rowan. *The Impending Crisis of the South.* New York: Collier Books, 1963. Originally published in 1857.
Henry, Robert Selph, ed. *As They Saw Forrest: Some Recollections and Comments of Contemporaries.* Jackson, Tenn.: McCowat-Mercer Press, 1956.
History of Tennessee. Nashville: Goodspeed Publishing Company, 1887.
History of Tennessee with an Historical and Biographical Sketch of Maury, Williamson, Rutherford, Wilson, Bedford and Marshall Counties. Nashville: Goodspeed Publishing Company, 1887.
Horan, James D., ed. *C.S.S. Shenandoah: The Memoirs of Lieutenant Commanding James I. Waddell.* New York: Crown Publishers, 1960.

Lindsley, John Berrien, ed. *The Military Annals of Tennessee.* Nashville: J.M. Lindsley & Company, 1886.
Lipscomb, Andrew A., ed. *The Writings of Thomas Jefferson.* 20 vols. Washington, D.C.: The Thomas Jefferson Memorial Association, 1905.
Official Records of the Union and Confederate Navies in the War of the Rebellion. 31 vols. Washington: Government Printing Office, 1894–1927.
Report of the Adjutant General of the State of Illinois, Containing Reports for the Years 1861–1866. Vol. 8. Springfield: Journal Company, 1901.
"Revolutionary War Pension Records." National Archives and Records Administration. Washington, D.C.
Robertson, James I., Jr., ed. *James Longstreet: From Manassas to Appomattox: Memoirs of the Civil War in America.* Bloomington, Ind.: Indiana University Press, 1960. Originally published in Philadelphia by J.B. Lippincott Company in 1895.
"Service Records of Union and Confederate Soldiers." National Archives and Records Administration, Washington, D.C.
Sherman, William T. *Memoirs of General William T. Sherman, By Himself.* 2 vols. New York: D. Appleton & Company, 1875.
Taylor, Richard. *Destruction and Reconstruction.* New York: Longmans Green, 1955. Originally published in 1879.
United States Census of Population. Eighth (1850), Ninth (1860), Tenth (1870), Eleventh (1880), Thirteenth (1900). National Archives and Records Administration, Washington, D.C.
"The United States on the Eve of the Civil War." Washington: U.S. Civil War Centennial Commission, 1963. A condensation of a descriptive report based upon the Ninth Census submitted to the United States Senate in May 1862.
War of the Rebellion: A Compilation of the Official Records of the Union and Confederate Armies. 69 vols. and index. Washington, D.C: War Department, 1880–1901.
Watkins, Sam R. *"Co. Aytch": A Side Show of the Big Show.* Wilmington, N.C.: Broadfoot Publishing Co., 1987. Originally published in 1882.
Williamson, J.C., ed. "The Civil War Diary of John Coffee Williamson." *Tennessee Historical Quarterly* vol. 15, no. 1 (March 1956).
Wilson, James Harrison. *Under the Old Flag.* 2 volumes. New York: D. Appleton and Company, 1912.
Wyeth, John Allan. *Life of General Nathan Bedford Forrest.* New York: Harper, 1899. Republished as *That Devil Forrest.* New York: Harper & Brothers, 1959.

Secondary Sources

Ash, Stephen V. *Middle Tennessee Society Transformed, 1860–1870: War and Peace in the Upper South.* Baton Rouge: Louisiana State University Press, 1988.
———. "Sharks in an Angry Sea: Civilian Resistance and Guerrilla Warfare in Occupied Middle Tennessee, 1862–1865." *Tennessee Historical Quarterly* vol. 45, no. 3 (Fall 1986).
Ayers, Edward L. *The Promise of the New South: Life after Reconstruction.* New York: Oxford University Press, 1992.
Bailey, Fred Arthur. *Class and Tennessee's Confederate Generation.* Chapel Hill: University of North Carolina Press, 1987.
Bakeless, John. *Spies of the Confederacy.* Philadelphia: J.B. Lippincott Company, 1970.
Ballard, Michael B. *A Long Shadow: Jefferson Davis and the Final Days of the Confederacy.* Jackson: University Press of Mississippi, 1986.
Barrett, John G. *Sherman's March through the Carolinas.* Chapel Hill: University of North Carolina Press, 1956.

Beard, Charles A., and Mary R. Beard. *The Rise of American Civilization*. Vol. 2, *The Industrial Era*. New York: Macmillan, 1930.
Berringer, Richard E., Herman Hattaway, Archer Jones, William N. Still, Jr. *Why the South Lost the Civil War*. Athens: University of Georgia Press, 1986.
The Book of Discipline of the United Methodist Church, 1972. Nashville: The United Methodist Publishing House, 1973.
Boone, Jennifer K. "'Mingling Freely': Tennessee Society on the Eve of the Civil War." *Tennessee Historical Quarterly* vol. 51, no. 3 (Fall 1992).
Bowman, Virginia McDaniel. "Historic Williamson County: Old Homes and Sites." Nashville: Privately printed, 1971.
Brownlee, Richard S. *Gray Ghosts of the Confederacy: Guerrilla Warfare in the West, 1861–1865*. Baton Rouge: Louisiana State University Press, 1958.
Byrd, Benjamin F., Jr. "Dr. Paul Eve, 1806–1877." In *Send for a Doctor*. Nashville: The Public Library of Nashville and Davidson County, 1975.
Carter, Samuel, III. *The Siege of Atlanta, 1864*. New York: St. Martin's Press, 1973.
"Chickamauga and Chattanooga Battlefields." Washington, D.C.: National Park Service, 1956.
Civil War Centennial Commission. *Guide to the Civil War in Tennessee*. Nashville: Division of Information, Department of Conservation, 1960.
Civil War Naval Chronology. Washington: U.S. Naval History Division, 1971.
Clark, Blanche Henry. *The Tennessee Yeomen, 1840–1860*. Nashville: Vanderbilt University Press, 1942.
Clark, James C. *Last Train South: The Flight of the Confederate Government from Richmond*. Jefferson, N.C.: McFarland & Company, 1984.
Coffin, Henry Sloane. "Religion in the Last Hundred Years." *A Century of Social Thought*. Durham: Duke University Press, 1939.
Conkin, Paul K. *Gone with the Ivy: A Biography of Vanderbilt University*. Knoxville: University of Tennessee Press, 1985.
Connelly, Thomas Lawrence. *Army of the Heartland: The Army of Tennessee, 1861–1862*. Baton Rouge: Louisiana State University Press, 1967.
———. *Autumn of Glory: The Army of Tennessee, 1862–1865*. Baton Rouge: Louisiana State University Press, 1971.
———. *Civil War Tennessee*. Knoxville: University of Tennessee Press, 1979.
Cook, Raymond Allen. *Fire from the Flint: The Amazing Careers of Thomas Dixon*. Winston-Salem, N.C.: John F. Blair, 1968.
Cunningham, H.H. *Doctors in Gray: The Confederate Medical Service*. Baton Rouge: Louisiana State University Press, 1957.
Davidson, Donald. *The Tennessee: The New River, Civil War to TVA*. New York: Rinehart & Company, 1948.
Dictionary of American Biography. Edited by Allen Johnson, et al. 22 vols., 7 supplements. New York: Charles Scribner's Sons, 1928–1981.
Dillahunty, Albert. "Shiloh." Historical Handbook No. 10. Washington, D.C.: National Park Service, 1955.
Doyle, Bertram Wilbur. *The Etiquette of Race Relations in the South: A Study in Social Control*. New York: Schocken Books, 1975. Originally published in 1937.
Doyle, Don H. *Nashville in the New South, 1880–1930*. Knoxville: University of Tennessee Press, 1985.
Dulles, Foster Rhea. *Labor in America: A History*. New York: Thomas Y. Crowell Company, 1949.
Dunning, William A. *Reconstruction, Political and Economic, 1865–1877*. New York: Harper & Row, 1962. Originally published by Harper & Brothers in 1907.
Dyer, John P. *From Shiloh to San Juan: The Life of "Fightin' Joe" Wheeler*. Baton Rouge: Louisiana State University Press, 1961.
Farish, Hunter Dickinson. *The Circuit Rider Dismounts: A Social History of Southern*

Methodism, 1865-1900. New York: DaCapo Press, 1969. Originally published by the Dietz Press in 1938.
Ferm, Vergilius, ed. *An Encyclopedia of Religion.* New York: Philosophical Library, 1945.
Fisher, John E. "Government Support for Economic Growth." *Business and Government Review* vol. 6, no. 5 (September–October 1965).
_____. *The John F. Slater Fund: A Nineteenth-Century Affirmative Action for Negro Education.* Lanham, Md.: University Press of America, 1987.
_____. "Life on the Common Level: Inheritance, Conflict, and Instruction." *Tennessee Historical Quarterly* vol. 26, no. 3 (Fall 1967).
Folmsbee, Stanley J., Robert E. Corlew, and Enoch L. Mitchell. *Tennessee: A Short History.* Knoxville: University of Tennessee Press, 1969.
The Fundamentals: A Testimony to the Truth. 12 vols. Chicago: Testimony Publishing Company, 1910-1912.
Gabriel, Ralph Henry. *The Course of American Democratic Thought.* New York: The Ronald Press, 1940.
Gildrie, Richard P. "Guerrilla Warfare in the Lower Cumberland River Valley, 1862-1865." *Tennessee Historical Quarterly* vol. 49, no. 3 (Fall 1990).
Gill, Frederick C. *The Romantic Movement and Methodism: A Study of English Romanticism and the Evangelical Revival.* London: Epworth Press, 1937.
Govan, Gilbert E., and James W. Livingood. *A Different Valor: The Story of General Joseph E. Johnston, C.S.A.* Indianapolis: Bobbs-Merrill, 1956.
Hargrave, Hondon B. *Black Union Soldiers in the Civil War.* Jefferson, N.C.: McFarland & Company, 1988.
Harkness, Georgia. *The Methodist Church in Social Thought and Action.* Nashville: Abingdon Press, 1964.
Hartje, Robert G. *Van Dorn: The Life and Times of a Confederate General.* Nashville: Vanderbilt University Press, 1967.
Hattaway, Henry and Archer Jones. *How the North Won: A Military History of the Civil War.* Urbana: University of Illinois Press, 1983.
Heitzenrater, Richard P. "The Present State of Wesley Studies." *Methodist History* vol. 22, no. 4 (July 1984).
Henry, Robert Selph. *"First with the Most" Forrest.* Indianapolis: Bobbs-Merrill, 1944.
_____. *The Story of the Confederacy.* Garden City, N.Y.: Garden City Publishing Company, 1931.
Hesseltine, William B. *The South in American History.* New York: Prentice-Hall, 1943.
_____, ed. *Civil War Prisons.* Kent, Ohio: Kent State University Press, 1972.
History of American Methodism. Edited by Emory Stevens Bucke. 3 vols. Nashville: Abingdon Press, 1964.
Hofstadter, Richard. *The Age of Reform: From Bryan to F.D.R.* New York: Alfred A. Knopf, 1955.
Hopkins, Charles Howard. *The Rise of the Social Gospel in American Protestantism, 1865-1915.* New Haven: Yale University Press, 1940.
Horn, Stanley. *The Army of Tennessee: A Military History.* Indianapolis: Bobbs-Merrill, 1941.
_____. *The Decisive Battle of Nashville.* Baton Rouge: Louisiana State University Press, 1956.
_____. *Gallant Rebel: The Fabulous Cruise of the C.S.S. Shenandoah.* New Brunswick, N.J.: Rutgers University Press, 1947.
_____. *Invisible Empire: The Story of the Ku Klux Klan 1866-1871.* Boston: Houghton Mifflin Company, 1939.
Hurst, Jack. *Nathan Bedford Forrest: A Biography.* New York: Alfred A. Knopf, 1993.
Isaac, Paul E. *Prohibition and Politics: Turbulent Decades in Tennessee, 1885-1920.* Knoxville: University of Tennessee Press, 1965.

Jessup, John E., Jr. and Robert W. Coakley. *A Guide to the Study and Use of Military History.* Washington: Government Printing Office, 1982.
Johnson, Charles S. *Backgrounds to Patterns of Negro Segregation.* New York: Thomas Y. Crowell, 1972. Published as *Patterns of Negro Segregation* by Harper & Brothers in 1943.
Jones, James Pickett. *Yankee Blitzkrieg: Wilson's Raid Through Alabama and Georgia.* Athens: University of Georgia Press, 1976.
Jones, William. "Land Grant in Fisher Family for 186 Years." *The Lewisburg Marshall Gazette*, November 18, 1969.
Jones, William L., comp. *The Fisher Scrap Book 1730-1972.* Milan, Tenn.: Privately printed, n.d.
Lamon, Lester C. *Blacks in Tennessee, 1791-1970.* Knoxville: University of Tennessee Press, 1981.
Lane, Wheaton J. *Commodore Vanderbilt: An Epic of the Steam Age.* New York: Alfred A. Knopf, 1942.
Lewis, Lloyd. *Sherman: Fighting Prophet.* New York: Harcourt, Brace and Company, 1958. Originally published in 1932.
Literary Market Place: LMP, 1995, The Directory of the American Book Publishing Industry with Industry Yellow Pages. New Providence, N.J.: R. R. Bowker, 1994.
Long, E.B. *The Civil War Day by Day: An Almanac, 1861-1865.* Garden City, N.Y.: Doubleday & Co., 1971.
Lufkin, Charles L. "'Not Heard from Since April 12, 1864': The Thirteenth Tennessee Cavalry, U.S.A." *Tennessee Historical Quarterly* vol. 45, no. 2 (Summer 1986).
McBride, Robert M., and Dan M. Robison. *Biographical Directory of the Tennessee General Assembly.* Vol. I, *1796-1861.* Nashville: Tennessee State Library and Archives and the Tennessee Historical Commission, 1975.
McDonough, James Lee. *Chattanooga — A Death Grip on the Confederacy.* Knoxville: University of Tennessee Press, 1984.
———. *Stones River: Bloody Winter in Tennessee.* Knoxville: University of Tennessee Press, 1980.
———, and Thomas L. Connelly. *Five Tragic Hours: The Battle of Franklin.* Knoxville: University of Tennessee Press, 1983.
———, and James Pickett Jones. *War So Terrible: Sherman and Atlanta.* New York: W.W. Norton & Company, 1987.
McDowell, John Patrick. *The Social Gospel in the South: The Woman's Home Mission Movement in the Methodist Episcopal Church, South, 1886-1939.* Baton Rouge: Louisiana State University Press, 1982.
McMillin, Laurence. *The Schoolmaker: Sawney Webb and the Bell Buckle Story.* Chapel Hill: University of North Carolina Press, 1971.
McMurry, Richard M. *John Bell Hood and the War for Southern Independence.* Lexington: University Press of Kentucky, 1982.
McPherson, James M. *Ordeal by Fire: The Civil War and Reconstruction.* New York: Alfred A. Knopf, 1982.
McWhiney, Grady. *Braxton Bragg and Confederate Defeat: Field Command.* New York: Columbia University Press, 1969.
———, and Perry D. Jamieson. *Attack and Die: Civil War Military Tactics and the Southern Heritage.* University, AL: University of Alabama Press, 1982.
Maness, Lonnie E. "The Fort Pillow Massacre: Fact or Fiction." *Tennessee Historical Quarterly* vol. 45, no. 4 (Winter 1986).
Mann, Harold W. *Atticus Greene Haygood: Methodist Bishop, Editor, and Educator.* Athens: University of Georgia Press, 1965.
Mathews, Donald G. *Slavery and Methodism: A Chapter in American Morality, 1780-1845.* Princeton, N.J.: Princeton University Press, 1965.

Mims, Edwin. *The Advancing South: Stories of Progress and Reaction.* Garden City, N.Y.: Doubleday, Page & Company, 1926.
――――――. *Chancellor Kirkland of Vanderbilt.* Nashville: Vanderbilt University Press, 1940.
――――――. *History of Vanderbilt University.* Nashville: Vanderbilt University Press, 1946.
Mitchell, Reid. *Civil War Soldiers.* New York: Viking, 1988.
Montgomery, James Riley, Stanley J. Folmsbee, and Lee Seifert Greene. *To Foster Knowledge: A History of the University of Tennessee, 1794-1970.* Knoxville: University of Tennessee Press, 1984.
Moore, John Trotwood. *Ole Mistis and Other Songs and Stories from Tennessee.* Nashville: Cokesbury Press, 1925. Originally published by the John C. Winston Company in 1909.
Morison, Samuel Eliot, Henry Steele Commager, and William E. Leuchtenburg. *The Growth of the American Republic.* Seventh edition. 2 vols. New York: Oxford University Press, 1980.
Morrow, Ralph E. *Northern Methodism and Reconstruction.* East Lansing: Michigan State University Press, 1956.
Munger, Theodore T. *Horace Bushnell: Preacher and Theologian.* Boston: Houghton, Mifflin and Company, 1900.
Myers, Gustavus. *History of the Great American Fortunes.* New York: Modern Library, 1964.
National Cyclopedia of American Biography. 75 vols. New York: James T. White & Company, 1893-1984.
Owsley, Frank L. *Plain Folk of the Old South.* Chicago: University of Chicago Press, 1965. Originally published in 1949.
Parks, Joseph Howard. *General Leonidas Polk, C.S.A.: The Fighting Bishop.* Baton Rouge: Louisiana State University Press, 1960.
――――――. *John Bell of Tennessee.* Baton Rouge: Louisiana State University Press, 1950.
Patrick, James. *Architecture in Tennessee, 1768-1897.* Knoxville: University of Tennessee Press, 1981.
――――――. "The Architecture of Adolphus Heiman." *Tennessee Historical Quarterly* vol. 38, nos. 2, 3 (Summer, Fall 1979).
Robertson, James I., Jr. "The Civil War." Washington, D.C.: United States Civil War Centennial Commission, 1963.
――――――. *Soldiers Blue and Gray.* Columbia, S.C.: University of South Carolina Press, 1988.
Roland, Charles P. *The Improbable Era: The South since World War II.* Lexington: University Press of Kentucky, 1975.
Rowe, Kenneth E. *United Methodist Studies: Basic Bibliographies.* Nashville: Abingdon Press, 1987.
Schlesinger, Arthur Meier. *The Rise of the City, 1878-1898.* Vol. 10 of *A History of American Life.* Edited by Arthur M. Schlesinger and Dixon Ryan Fox. 12 vols. New York: Macmillan, 1933.
Sensing, Thurman. *Champ Ferguson: Confederate Guerilla.* Nashville: Vanderbilt University Press, 1985. Originally published in 1942.
Short, Roy Hunter. *Chosen to Be Consecrated: The Bishops of the Methodist Church, 1784-1968.* Lake Junaluska, N.C.: Commission on Archives and History, 1976.
Sificas, Stewart. *Who Was Who in the Civil War.* New York: Facts on File Publications, 1988.
Simpson, Matthew. *Cyclopedia of Methodism.* Philadelphia: Everts & Stewart, 1878.
Sledge, Robert Watson. *Hands on the Ark: The Struggle for Change in the Methodist Episcopal Church, South, 1914-1939.* Lake Junaluska, N.C.: Commission on Archives and History, The United Methodist Church, 1975.
Starr, Stephen Z. *The Union Cavalry in the Civil War.* Vol. 3, *The War in the West, 1861-1865.* Baton Rouge: Louisiana State University Press, 1985.
Steinkraus, Warren E. *Representative Essays of Borden Parker Bowne.* Utica, N.Y.: Meridian Publishing Company, 1980.

Stevens, John K. "Hostages to Hunger: Nutritional Blindness in Confederate Armies." *Tennessee Historical Quarterly* vol. 48, no. 3 (Fall 1989).
Sumner, William Graham. *Folkways: A Study of the Sociological Importance of Usages, Manners, Customs, Mores, and Morals.* New York: Mentor Books/The New American Library, n.d.
Tennesseans in the Civil War: A Military History of Confederate and Union Units with Available Rosters of Personnel. Part 1, *Military Histories.* Part 2, *Rosters.* Nashville: Civil War Centennial Commission, 1964.
Tigert, John J. *Bishop Holland Nimmons McTyeire: Ecclesiastical and Educational Architect.* Nashville: Vanderbilt University Press, 1955.
Titus, Harold H. *Living Issues in Philosophy.* New York: American Book Company, 1946.
To Give the Key of Knowledge: United Methodists and Education, 1784–1976. Nashville: National Commission on United Methodist Higher Education, 1976.
Tucker, Glenn. "Forrest — Untutored Genius of the War." *Civil War Times* vol. 3, no. 3 (June 1964).
Turner, Arlin. *George W. Cable: A Biography.* Baton Rouge: Louisiana State University Press, 1966. Originally published by Duke University Press in 1956.
Walker, Williston. *A History of the Christian Church.* New York: Charles Scribner's Sons, 1959.
Waller, William, ed. *Nashville, 1900 to 1910.* Nashville: Vanderbilt University Press, 1972.
Warden, Margaret Lindsley. *The Belle Meade Plantation.* Nashville: Nashville Chapter, Association for the Preservation of Tennessee Antiquities, 1979.
―――――. "Belle Meade's Glory Days." *Nashville Magazine* vol. 5, no. 8 (November 1977).
Warner, Ezra J. *Generals in Blue: Lives of the Union Commanders.* Baton Rouge: Louisiana State University Press, 1964.
―――――. *Generals in Gray: Lives of the Confederate Commanders.* Baton Rouge: Louisiana State University Press, 1959.
Welch, Herbert. *Selections from the Writings of the Rev. John Wesley, M.A.* Nashville: Abingdon-Cokesbury, 1942.
Wiley, Bell Irvin. *The Life of Johnny Reb: The Common Soldier of the Confederacy.* Indianapolis: Bobbs-Merrill, 1943.
―――――. *The Plain People of the Confederacy.* Baton Rouge: Louisiana State University Press, 1943.
Wilkinson, Warren. *Mother, May You Never See the Sights I Have Seen: The Fifty-Seventh Massachusetts Veteran Volunteers in the Army of the Potomac, 1864–1865.* New York: Harper & Row, 1990.
Wills, Brian S. *A Battle from the Start: The Life of Nathan Bedford Forrest.* New York: HarperCollins, 1992.
Wills, Ridley, II. *The History of Belle Meade Mansion, Plantation, and Stud.* Nashville: Vanderbilt University Press, 1991.
Womack, Bob. *Call Forth the Mighty Men.* Bessemer, Ala.: Colonial Press, 1986.
Woodward, C. Vann. *Origins of the New South, 1877–1913.* Vol. 9 of *A History of the South*, edited by Wendell Holmes Stephenson and E. Merton Coulter. 10 vols. Baton Rouge: Louisiana State University Press, 1951; and Austin: The Littlefield Fund for Southern History of the University of Texas, 1951.
Woodworth, Steven E. *Jefferson Davis and His Generals: The Failure of Confederate Command in the West.* Lawrence: University Press of Kansas, 1990.

Index

Abbeville, S.C. 137
Abingdon, Va. 116
Abrahams, Lot 139
Absalom Thompson house 155
Acworth, Ga. 77, 78, 112
Adams, Daniel W. 189, 193
Adams, Samuel J. 255
Adams, Silas: brigade 92
Adams, Theodore Riggs 31, 183, 257
Adams, Wirt: brigade 189, 193, 200
Agincourt, Battle of 26
Aiken, S.C. 127
Alabama 1, 11, 37, 44, 67, 93, 96, 104, 112, 142; residents 92, 103, 109, 132
Alabama River 197
Aldridge, J.M. 24, 257
Alexander, E. Porter 61
Alexander, Will W. 250
Alford, J.H. 257
Allatoona, Ga. 77, 112
Allen, J.G. 47, 53, 257
Allen, Thomas J. 255
Allen, William Wirt 131; brigade 74, 77, 92, 132–33
Allin, Phil T. 32
Allison, R.D.: squadron 56
Allston, Benjamin 16
Alston, S.C. 129
Altgeld, John Peter 242
Alton, Ill., military prison 24, 75
American Medical Association 235
Anderson, Charles W. 146, 206
Anderson, Francis M. 255
Anderson, J. Patton 132
Anderson, James 255
Anderson, John 30, 255
Anderson, Paul F. 15, 59, 114
Anderson, S.C. 73
Anderson, Samuel R. 93, 191

Andersonville Prison 91, 110, 111, 118
Andrews, James J. 37
Angell, James R. 246
Antietam, Battle of 145
Antioch, Tenn. 29
Appomattox Courthouse 134, 135
Arkansas 49, 54
Arlington National Cemetery 142
Armistead, Charles B.: brigade 189
Armistead Burt home 137
Armstrong, Frank C. 54, 61, 67; brigade 53, 55, 56, 153, 155, 160, 164, 173–74, 179, 189, 193, 196; division 58, 59, 66, 68
Armstrong, James B. 170
Armstrong, Samuel 255
Ashby, Henry M. 131; brigade 93
Asheville, N.C. 73
Ashland City, Tenn. 29
Ashworth, T.J. 68, 257
Athens, Ala. 67
Athens, Ga. 73
Athens, Tenn. 98
Atkins, James 253
Atlanta 37, 75, 79, 80, 82–83, 85–88, 105, 111, 112, 120, 122; Battle of 87; siege of 89, 94, 95; occupied 106–7; campaign losses 109
Atlanta & West Point Railroad 106
Augusta, Ga. 79, 120, 122–23, 130
Augusta & Savannah Railroad 123
Augusta Railroad 85, 91
Averasborough, N.C. 132

Bailey, John 34, 189, 257
Bailey, Robert 189, 257
Bainbridge, Ala. 38, 178
Baird, Absalom 123
Baird, W.H. 254

Baldin, William 20, 255
Baltimore 31, 34, 260n
Baptists, Tennessee 234
Barnes, John 101, 255
Barnwell, S.C. 127
Bartlett, Andrew J. 255
Bartlett, James M. 34, 67, 255
Bascom, Henry Bidleman 5
Bass, Thomas 134
Bate, William B.: division 154–55, 162–63, 169, 216
Bean's Station, Tenn. 68, 69
Beaufort, S.C. 126
Beauregard, P.G.T. 22, 120, 130, 134, 187, 188, 218
Beck, Calvin B. 255
Bedford County, Tenn. 14, 16, 26, 31, 47, 67, 99, 234
Beechlawn 151, 156, 176
Bell, John 9, 11, 12
Bell, Mattie 72
Bell, Tyree H. 205; brigade 150, 153–54, 163, 203, 213
Bell Buckle, Tenn. 99
Belle Meade 188
Bell's Mills 162, 168
Belmont, Mo. 14
Belmont estate 167
Benjamin, Judah P. 135
Bennett, Augustus G. 129
Bennett farmhouse 135
Bentonville, N.C. 132; Battle of 132–33
Berlin, Tenn. 5
Bethesda, Tenn. 35
Bickman, J.M. 189–90, 257
Biffle, Jacob B. 32, 33, 67, 68; brigade 69, 113, 160, 165, 173–74, 179; regiment 152, 181
Big Creek Gap 18, 19
Big Hill, Ky. 18
Big Shanty, Ga. 112
Billington, Joseph A. 31, 257
Bills, Gashan, A. 72, 255
Bills, John A. 66, 255
The Birth of a Nation 147
Black Creek 133
Black Warrior River 41, 204
Blackman, Felix H. 32
Blackstock, S.C. 131
Blaine's Crossroads, Tenn. 68
Blakemore, J.M. 255

Blanton, W.H. 114, 255
Blant's Hill 70
Bledsoe County, Tenn. 15
Blount's Plantation 42
Blountsville, Ala. 41
Bogler's Creek 195
Bomar, John 189, 257
Bon Air, Tenn. 52
Boone, Howard H. 217
Boone, Mary Fisher 217
Booth, Lionel F. 145
Boston University 6
Boulwares & Cox Wharf 82
Bowling Green, Ky. 15
Bowne, Borden Parker 6
Boyce, William M. 50, 257
Boyd, Thomas A. 64, 257
Braden, William W. 81, 151, 257
Bradford, W.F. 145
Bradley, J.B. 189, 257
Bradley County, Tenn. 139
Bragg, Braxton 19, 21, 24, 29, 43, 66, 68, 73, 79, 83, 111, 130, 137–38; Kentucky campaign 15, 18, 22; assessment of Forrest 24, 26; at Murfreesboro (Stones River) 27–28; relations with his top staff 32–33; retreats to Chattanooga 37, 47, 50, 52; follow up to Chickamauga 55; Battle of Chattanooga 61, 63; transferred to Richmond 59; in Augusta 121
Brannan, John M.: division 53
Breckenridge, John C. 9, 11, 28, 135, 136, 137–38, 218; and Bragg 33; at Chickamauga 54
Breckenridge, William C.P. 137; brigade 92, 127, 134
Brentwood, Tenn. 34–35, 112, 161, 168
Brentwood Church 254
Brice's Crossroads, Battle of 143, 210
Brightman, Edgar Sheffield 6
Brisbin, James S. 115
Bristol, Tenn. 100
Brittain, J.F. 257
Broad River 126
Brooklyn, N.Y. 142
Brotherton, George 101, 255
Browder, Simeon E. 140
Brown, James 136
Brown, John C., division 154–55
Brown, Joseph E. 111

Brown, Samuel C. 20, 255
Brownlow, James D. 104
Brown's Creek 162, 168
Bruce, J.W. 47, 80, 189, 257
Bruce, John H. 31, 47, 80, 257
Brush Mountain 78
Bryan, Jesse N. 24, 257
Bryant, Larry 24
Bryant, R.H. 19, 255
Bryant, Thomas J. 19, 255
Buck Head Church 123
Buell, Don Carlos 16, 19, 22
Buena Vista, Miss. 190
Buford, Abraham 148, 152, 153, 155, 158, 160–66, 173–76, 177, 189, 193
Bugg, John E. 255
Bugg, Joseph 69, 257
Bull's Gap, Tenn. 68, 69
Burnside, Ambrose 8, 98; at Knoxville 61, 63, 64
Burr, William 5, 24
Burrow, Hiram W. 50, 255
Bushnell, Horace 239
Butler, M.C. 129; division 136–37

Cable, George W. 146
Cahaba, Ala. 197
Cahaba River 35, 193–94, 199
Calfkiller River 52, 117–118
Calhoun, James M. 107
Calhoun, Ga. 96
Call, Henry C. 19, 255
Call, P.B. 189, 257
Cameron, Simon 11
Camp Chase 50, 53, 64, 68, 82, 100, 104, 163, 190
Camp Cheatham 14, 34, 72
Camp Douglas 53, 75, 148
Camp Morton 50, 58
Camp Nelson 115
Campbell, Given 138
Campbell County, Tenn. 67, 68
Campbellsville, Tenn. 150, 211
Campbellton, Ga. 92
Canby, E.R.S. 204–5, 212
Caney Fork River 15
Cannon County, Tenn. 100, 104
Cape Fear River 132
Caperton's Ferry 52
Capron, Horace 151; brigade 92, 150, 160

Carpenter, John 255
Carrollton, Ga. 112, 200
Carter, John 30, 257
Carter, Nathan W. 32
Carter house 160
Carter's Creek Pike 158
Cartwright, A.W. 50, 257
Cassville, Ga. 77, 96
Cathey, T.J. 80, 257
Cave Spring, Tenn. 36, 71, 177, 211
Cedar Bluff, Ala. 37, 43
Celina, Tenn. 117–18
Centerville, Ala. 194, 199, 200
Central Presbyterian Church 80
Chalmers, James R. 112, 193–94; division 148, 150, 151, 152, 155, 158, 160–62, 165–66, 168, 170–71, 174–77, 179, 181, 183, 189, 197
Chapel Hill, N.C. 134
Chapel Hill, Tenn. 21, 26, 36, 151, 177
Chaplin River 19
Chapman, T.M. 50, 257
Charleston, S.C. 11, 33, 129–30
Charleston, Tenn. 98
Charleston Railroad 126
Charlotte, N.C. 130, 137, 139
Charlotte Pike 162, 167
Chattahoochee River 80, 81, 82, 85, 92, 94, 111, 112
Chattanooga, Tenn. 15, 16, 18, 22, 28, 37, 38, 47, 48, 49, 50, 51, 52, 53, 55, 59, 66, 96, 97, 98, 102, 104–5, 113, 120, 149; Battle of 61, 68, 220
Chattooga River 42
Cheairs, Nat, home of 154
Cheatham, Benjamin Franklin 85–86, 133, 152, 153–55, 158, 158, 160–61, 167–68, 174, 188, 218; and Bragg 33
Cheraw, S.C. 130
Chester, S.C. 129, 130
Chevis's plantation 124
Chicago, Ill. 53, 75, 148, 242
Chickamauga, Battle of 51–55, 61, 71, 84
Chickamauga Creek 52
Chickasaw, Ala. 192
Chrisman, W.D. 31, 257
Christian Advocate 5
Christian Century 238
Chucky River 71
Cincinnati 5, 53, 120
Citronelle, Ala. 205

City Point, Va. 24, 34, 50, 64, 133, 166
The Clansman 147
Clanton, James M. 189
Clarksville, Tenn. 13
Clay County, Tenn. 117
Cleburne, Patrick 53-54, 218; at New Hope Church 77; at Atlanta 86; at Spring Hill 154-55; death 161
Cleveland, Tenn. 74, 98, 139
Clifton, Tenn. 19
Clinch Mountain 114
Clinch River 51, 67, 98-99; valley 16
Clinton, Okla. 235
Clinton County, Ky. 117
Cobb, Howell 92
Cobb, Joseph T.: Texas scouts 188
Coburn, John 33, 107
Cocke County, Tenn. 71
Coffee, A.N. 255
Coffee, Chatham 63
Coffee, Thomas W. 255
Coffee County, Tenn. 50, 151
Cole, Andrew Jackson 163, 257
Coleman, David 166, 168
Coleman, E. 102
Coleman, R.H. (Bob) 88
College Grove, Tenn. 23
Collins, William H. 72, 255
Collins, Willis M. 16, 255
Columbia, S.C. 126, 129
Columbia, Tenn. 29, 31, 32, 35, 104, 150, 151, 158, 175
Columbia University 238
Columbus, Ga. 198, 203
Columbus, Ky. 13, 14
Commission on Interracial Cooperation 250
Columbus, Ohio 50, 68
Confederacy, Southern 9, 22, 68, 179
Confederate Congress 13, 70, 202-3; Provisional 92, 220
Confederate States of America 11, 21, 111, 117
Confederate Veteran 82, 231
Connelly, Thomas Lawrence 151
Connesauga River 74, 119, 139
Constitutional Union Party 9
Conyers, Ga. 85, 138
Cook, James F. 47, 255
Cook, Thomas 255
Cooke, Gustave 94

Cooper, Douglas Hancock 212
Cooper, Samuel 43, 70, 188, 263n
Coosa River 119
Corinth, Miss. 37, 121, 181
Corlett, David R. 104, 257
Cornersville, Tenn. 20, 24, 99
Cottonport, Tenn. 57, 97
Courtland, Ala. 38, 39
Covington, Ga. 87, 91, 95, 122
Cowan, George 196
Cowan, J.B. 59, 179
Cowan, Marion 117
Cowper, J.T. 19, 255
Cox, Jacob D.: division 150
Cox, Nicholas N.: regiment 33, 59
Crabtree, William 20, 255
Crafton, G.H. 257
Cranston, Earl 237
Crawford, Frank 250
Crittendon, George B. 21
Crittendon, T.L.: corps 52
Crockett, J.E. 45, 47, 80, 257
Cromer, Joseph P. 189, 257
Crook, George H. 58
Crosser, Joseph K. 189, 257
Crossland, Ed 193
Croxton, John T. 53, 94, 160, 171, 192, 198, 199, 200, 205
Crutcher, T.R. 257
Culpeper, Va. 145
Cumberland, Army of the (U.S.A.) 31, 36, 220; advances on Chattanooga 49, 52; and Battle of Chattanooga 61; at Nashville 159
Cumberland City, Tenn. 167
Cumberland County, Ky. 117
Cumberland Gap 16, 19, 22, 66
Cumberland Gap road 65, 66
Cumberland Law School 52
Cumberland Mountains 18, 50, 52
Cumberland Plateau 99, 250
Cumberland River 29, 37, 162, 167, 173, 250
Cummings, James F. 80
Cunningham, W.M. 47, 255

Dallas, Ga. 77, 112; Battle of 77-78
Dalton, Ga. 37, 62, 68, 71, 73, 74-75, 96, 97, 112, 119
Dandridge, Tenn. 69, 71

Darnell, Allen 20, 255
Davidson, Elija A. 255
Davidson, H.B. 52, 255
Davidson, Henry B.: brigade 56, 58, 62
Davidson County, Tenn. 29, 151
Davis, J.B. 257
Davis, J.T. 24, 257
Davis, Jefferson 59, 61, 66, 79, 84, 95, 111, 113, 120, 134–38, 187, 263n; assessment of Forrest 26; intervenes for Forrest 60; captured 138–39, 198
Davis, Jefferson C. 31
Davis, N.C. 101–2, 255
Davis, Sam 102–4
Davis, W.G. 45, 47, 81, 257
Davis, W.H. 48, 257
Davis's Ford 152
Dawson's Bluff 131
Day's Gap 39
Decatur, Ala. 38, 119, 149, 178, 181
Decatur, Ga. 81, 85, 87
Decherd, Tenn. 66
Degenfeld, Charles M. 116
Democratic Party 9, 11, 13
Department of North Carolina, C.S.A. 130
Department of South Carolina, Georgia and Florida, C.S.A. 122, 130
Department of the Cumberland, (U.S.A.) 80, 112
Devan, D.W. 47, 257
Dibrell, George G. 32, 39, 58, 66, 67, 99; brigade 50, 51–52, 53, 55, 56, 63, 68, 69, 71, 74, 77, 78, 80, 81, 85, 93, 95, 97, 99–100, 101, 104, 113–15, 117, 120, 121, 124, 127, 131, 134, 136; surrendered, paroled 139–40
Dillard, Francis M. 189, 257
Dillard, Issac V. 189, 257
Dillard, J.J. 189, 257
Dillard, John L. 189, 257
Dixon, Thomas 147
Dodge, Grenville M. 37–38, 87, 103
Douglas, Richard 235
Douglas, Stephen A. 9, 11
Douglass, D.C. 1, 24, 30, 31; battalion 24, 29, 31, 31–32
Dover, Tenn. 29, 30, 51
Dowdey, J.M. 189, 257

Doyle, Eli J. 255
Drake, Henry T. 175, 257
Drummond, Henry 238
Drumwright, James T. 64, 257
Duck River 1, 36, 150, 151, 175
Duck River mill 163, 185
Duke, Basil W. 137–38
Duke, James Buchanan 248
Duke University 6, 248
Duling, John A. 50, 255
Duncan, William Wallace 244
Dunham, Cyrus L. 20
Dunning, William A. 238
Durham, N.C. 130, 135
Dwiggins, H.C. 95, 255
Dysart, Alfred A. 34, 255
Dysart, George D. 81–82, 255
Dysart, James M. 127, 255
Dysart, John H. 255
Dysart, Robert A. 127, 255
Dysart, Thomas J. 127, 255
Dysart, William A. 101, 255

East, Edward H. 245
East Point, Ga. 89
East Tennessee 8, 9, 19, 22, 31, 47, 51, 69, 98–99, 114; Department of 15, 16, 18, 137; upper 16, 63, 71, 114, 216
East Tennessee & Georgia Railroad 16
East Tennessee & Virginia Railroad 16
Eastport, Miss. 37, 190, 210
Eaton, Thomas Treadwell 234
Ector, Matthew D. 54, 166, 168
Edgefield, Tenn. 162, 166–67
Edgefield & Kentucky Railroad 118
Edmundson, James H. 1, 32, 38, 51
Eighteenth Illinois Infantry, U.S.A. 37
Eighteenth Tennessee Cavalry Battalion, C.S.A. 54, 58
Eighth Confederate Cavalry Regiment 74, 93
Eighth Michigan Cavalry Regiment, U.S.A. 92
Eighth Tennessee Cavalry Battalion, C.S.A. 1; Companies A and D 14
Eighth Tennessee Cavalry Regiment (Dibrell's), C.S.A. 32, 52, 55, 56, 58, 60, 66, 67, 68, 74, 76, 123, 124, 127, 134, 136; Company I 97

Eighth Tennessee Cavalry Regiment (Smith's/Anderson's), C.S.A. 15
Eighth Texas Cavalry Regiment, C.S.A. 71, 74, 94, 133
Eleventh Arkansas Cavalry Regiment, C.S.A. 188
Eleventh Kentucky Cavalry Regiment, U.S.A. 64, 92
Eleventh Tennessee Cavalry Regiment, C.S.A. 32, 58, 60, 67, 119, 213, 216; Company C 1, 24, 30, 34, 44, 45, 47, 50, 53, 62, 63, 67, 68, 69, 71, 74–75, 77, 78, 89, 96, 104, 111, 112, 121, 142, 152, 163, 175, 179, 181, 183, 185, 188, 189, 190, 198, 200, 203, 213; at Thompson's Station 33, 34; at Brentwood 34–35; pursues Streight 38, 39, 40, 41; at Post Oak Springs 51; at Sparta 52; at Chickamauga 53–54, 56; besieges Chattanooga 55; with Longstreet 63, 65, 68, 69, 71; Company H 63; at Resaca 75–76; in North Georgia 78, 79–83, 89, 94, 95–96; evacuation of Atlanta 107; Company G 112; in Middle Tennessee 150, 151; last fight, 198–200; Company C casualties 207–10; marching home 210–11
Eleventh Texas Cavalry, C.S.A. 71
Elliott, Washington Lafayette 66
Ellis, Thomas M. 127
Emory and Henry College hospital 115–16, 118
Emory College, University 6, 248
Endsley, Alexander M. 20, 255
Epperson, J.P. 189, 257
Epperson, James T. 257
Epperson, Thomas J. 64, 257
Etowah River 76, 77, 96
Eve, Duncan 234–35
Eve, Paul 234–35
Eve, Paul, Jr. 235
Ezell, G.W. 257
Ezell, Hugh Frank 75, 257
Ezell, J.B. 257
Ezra Church, Battle of 89, 94

Farmington, Tenn. 1, 26, 57–58, 99, 227
Farragut, David Glasgow 22
Farver, James E. 189, 257

Fayetteville, Ga. 92, 93
Fayetteville, N.C. 131–32
Fayetteville, Tenn. 22, 32, 72, 234
Featherston, Winfield S. 176
Feild, Hume R. 83, 176, 178
Fentress, Lillian Boone 217, 277n
Fentress County, Tenn. 117
Ferguson, Champ, and family 115–18
Ferguson, Samuel W. 137; brigade 85, 87, 109
Ferguson, W. 146
Ferrell, C.B. 39; battery 43
Fifteenth Pennsylvania Cavalry Regiment, U.S.A. 181
Fifteenth U.S. Colored Infantry Regiment 118
Fifth Georgia Cavalry Regiment 93
Fifth Mississippi Cavalry Regiment, C.S.A. 183
Fifth Tennessee Cavalry Regiment, C.S.A. 59, 60, 63, 68
Fifth U.S. Colored Cavalry Regiment 115
Fifty-First Indiana Infantry 36–37
Fifty-Third Tennessee Infantry Regiment, C.S.A. 78
Finney, James J. 228, 233
Finn's Point National Cemetery 64
First Confederate Cavalry Regiment, C.S.A. 54, 181
First Illinois Light Artillery, U.S.A., Battery E 8; Battery K 8
First Kentucky Cavalry Regiment, U.S.A. 92
First Middle Tennessee Cavalry Regiment, U.S.A. 37
First Minnesota Infantry Regiment, U.S.A. 145
First Tennessee Cavalry Regiment (Carter's), C.S.A. 58, 62
First Tennessee Infantry Regiment, C.S.A. 83
First Texas Infantry Regiment, C.S.A. 145
Fisher, Addie Ewing 227
Fisher, Bascom Hurt 221, 227–28, 229, 233; children 227–28
Fisher, Commodore Bascom 248, 259n
Fisher, Elisha Monroe 1, 3, 5, 9, 35, 96, 185, 227, 230–31, 233, 255, 257; enlists 14, 34; elected lieutenant,

resigns 15; reenlists 21; sick 78, 80; at home 220–23
Fisher, Elizabeth (sister) 5
Fisher, Elizabeth (cousin) 31
Fisher, Estelle Carr 253, 259n
Fisher, Fannie Ellen (Nellie) 230
Fisher, Franke 248
Fisher, Franklin A. 8
Fisher, Frederick 3
Fisher, George H. 16
Fisher, George W. 72
Fisher, Howard Boone 217, 238, 254
Fisher, Jacob 5, 8, 16, 226
Fisher, Jacob C. 14, 71–72, 255
Fisher, James Wesley 1, 5, 9, 15, 30, 49, 56, 79, 101–2, 114, 130, 185–86, 206–7, 227, 229, 231, 255; enlists 14, 19, 34; wounded 35–36; children 229
Fisher, John (father) 3, 4, 6, 36, 184–85, 221, 225; as slaveholder 3–4, 7, 228; farm 1, 3–4, 58, 226–27; sons 9, 31, 96, 184–85, 227–28, 231, 233; servant, Melinda, and her children 227, 228–29
Fisher, John (great uncle) 7
Fisher, John Franklin 5, 9, 21, 35, 79, 185, 211, 214–15, 221, 231, 233, 257
Fisher, John Roberts 243, 246, 252, 254
Fisher, Letitia (Lula) Boone 235, 238
Fisher, Margaret Marshall 230
Fisher, Mary 5
Fisher, Michael R. 14, 49
Fisher, Mildred Stratton 6, 31, 36, 221, 226–27; sons 9, 227–28
Fisher, Mollie Craig 227–28
Fisher, Mollie Dryden 229, 231
Fisher, Mollie Eastham 234–35, 238, 243
Fisher, Nancy Helm 5, 8, 226
Fisher, Olivia Williamson 230–31
Fisher, Robert W. 8
Fisher, Sallie Roberts 234–35, 238, 251
Fisher, Sally Hill 227
Fisher, Sarah Hurt 5, 72, 152, 229, 231
Fisher, Thomas Burr 1, 3, 5, 7, 9, 35, 44, 56, 127, 152, 170–71, 184, 206, 214, 220, 227, 229–30, 257; marries Sallie Roberts 15; enlists 21, 23; on slavery 23; at Thompson's Station 34; and health 45, 48; on Walden's Ridge 51; detailed as courier 65; becomes company sergeant 96; at home 220–23, 278n; post-war life 233–54
Fisher, Thomas Waterston 254
Fisher, Turner M. 14, 16, 49
Fisher, Will Stratton 243, 252, 253, 254, 282n
Fisher, William Stratton 5, 9, 35, 44, 80, 83, 95, 111, 112, 184, 221, 227, 257; enlists 21; captured and hospitalized 31; failing health 31, 72, 177, 211, 216, 229–30
Fisher, Wilson Phillips 243, 246, 254
Fishing Creek, Battle of 22
Flat Rock, Ga. 91
Flint River 106
Florence, Ala. 38, 39, 104, 148
Florida 110, 111; secedes 11
Fonville, Josh 255
Fonville, Simm. 81–82, 255
Forrest, Jesse 190
Forrest, Mary Ann Montgomery 59
Forrest, Nathan Bedford 1, 15, 19, 21, 31, 95, 101, 113–14, 118, 139, 142, 181, 183–84, 186, 187, 189–91, 192; Old Brigade 15, 32, 33, 35, 53, 57, 58, 60, 113, 121; and Bragg's Kentucky campaign 15; in West Tennessee 19–20, 24; assessments of 24, 26; and Bragg 26; at Fort Donelson 29; at Thompson's Station 33; at Brentwood 34–35, 112; at Douglas Church 35; pursues Streight 38–44; covers retreat to Chattanooga 49, 50; at Kingston 51; at Chickamauga 53–55; moves into Chattanooga 55; moves to confront Burnside 55; break with Bragg 59–60; detached from Army of Tennessee 58, 60; thanked by Congress 70–71; returns 143, 148; and Ft. Pillow 143–47; and the Ku Klux Klan 147; beliefs about him 147–48, 271n; leads advance into Tennessee 148–56, 158, 160–63; at Murfreesboro 162, 163–65; marches to rejoin Hood 175–75; commands rear guard 175–80; consolidates cavalry remnants 181, 186, 189; assumes new command 188; tries to counter

Wilson 193–97; in camp 202–7; farewell address 206
Forrest, William H. 1, 32, 39
Forsyth, Ga. 122, 200
Fort Delaware 50, 64, 139
Fort Donelson 15, 22, 29, 32
Fort Henry 15, 22, 37
Fort McAllister 125
Fort McHenry 31, 44
Fort Pillow 22; massacre 143–47
Fort Pulaski 125
Fort Sanders 66
Fort Sumter, fall of 9, 11, 14
Fortress Monroe 31, 133, 139
Fortress Rosecrans 163–64
Forty-Fourth U.S. Colored Infantry Regiment 119
Fosdick, Harry Emerson 238
Foster, John Gray 66
Foster, Robert C., III 14
Fouche Springs, Tenn. 150
Fourteenth Illinois Cavalry Regiment, U.S.A. 92
Fourteenth Tennessee Cavalry Regiment, C.S.A. 153
Fourteenth U.S. Colored Infantry Regiment 100
Fourth Alabama Cavalry Regiment, C.S.A. 32
Fourth Iowa Cavalry Regiment, U.S.A. 139
Fourth Regiment of Michigan Cavalry, U.S.A. 138
Fourth Tennessee Cavalry Regiment (Murray's/Smith's), C.S.A. 15, 58, 59, 63, 114–15, 140, 185, 215
Fourth Tennessee Cavalry Regiment (Starnes'/McLemore's), C.S.A. 1, 18, 19–20, 55, 58, 60, 62, 63, 74, 113–14, 121, 123, 124, 132, 134, 179, 216, 229; organized 15; early action 15–16, 169; Company D of 16, 19, 20–21, 30, 34, 44, 47, 48, 49, 50, 52, 53, 66, 67, 71, 72, 81, 95, 100, 101, 114, 126, 127, 130–31, 142, 186; Company A of 16, 49, 134; at Thompson's Station 33; at Brentwood 34–35; pursues Streight 39, 40, 41; rear guard of retreat to Chattanooga 49; at Sparta 51–52; Company F of 52; at Chickamauga 53, 56; with Longstreet 63, 67, 68, 70, 71; in North Georgia 78, 81–82; in Tennessee raid 95, 99; divided 99; Company K 101; Company C of 134; surrendered, paroled 139–140; Company D casualties 207–10
Fourth U.S. Regular Cavalry 35, 196–97
Frankfort, Ky. 18–19
Franklin, Ga. 94
Franklin, Tenn. 13, 33, 34, 49, 104, 149, 156, 158, 169, 227, 230, 234; Battle of 1, 159–61
Franklin County, Tenn. 16, 34, 49
Franklin Road 162, 167, 169
Freeman, James H. 255
Freeman, Samuel L. 32, 33, 35, 60, 196
French, Samuel G.: division 112
French Broad River 69, 70, 71, 73, 98
Fulton County Courthouse 83
The Fundamentals: A Testimony to the Truth 238

Gabriel, Ralph Henry 220
Gadsden, Ala. 41, 42, 43, 112, 120
Gainesville, Ala. 202, 206, 210
Gallatin, Tenn. 100, 185, 234, 237, 244
Galloway, Charles B. 250
Gantt, George: battalion 181
Gardner, William H. 115–16
Garfield, James A. 37
Garland, Landon Cabell 199
Garrard, Israel 92
Garrard, Kenner 91
Gates, L.C. 257
Gates, Woodson C. 20, 255
Gentry, William C. 255
Georgia 11, 69, 73, 84, 92, 105, 111, 113, 118–19, 121, 176; state militia 85, 111, 121
Georgia Railroad 85, 86
Gettysburg, Battle of 84, 145
Gibbs, R.T. 255
Giles, Thomas P. 67, 257
Giles County, Tenn. 20, 24, 50, 58, 102, 142, 151, 211, 234
Gilgal Church 78
Gist, States Rights 53–54
Glasscock, Henry H. 20, 255
Glasscock, Nathan 47, 255
Godwin, M., house 196

Goldsboro, N.C. 35, 132-34
Goodrich, J.T. 257
Goodwin, George W. 142, 255
Gordon, Ga. 122
Govan, Daniel C.: brigade 54
Grahamville, S.C. 131
Grainger County, Tenn. 67, 68
Grand Army of the Republic, New Orleans post 170
Granger, Gordon 149
Granny White Pike 167-69
Grant, Nancy 4
Grant, Ulysses S. 24, 66, 112, 120, 125, 126, 133, 135, 165-67, 174-75; occupies Paducah 13; at Belmont, Mo. 13-14; in Nashville 22; at Shiloh 22; at Chattanooga 61, 63, 68; on Forrest 143, 146
Grantsburg, Ill. 8, 226
Grass, Daniel 165
Gravelly Springs, Ala. 192
Graves, James K. Polk 81-82, 255
Greene County, Tenn. 73
Greeneville, Tenn. 114
Greensboro, Ala. 203
Greensboro, N.C. 130, 134, 135-136, 139
Greenville, S.C. 73
Grenada, Miss. 190
Griffin, Ga. 121
Griswoldville, Ga. 122
Guild, George B. 58, 114, 118, 140, 185, 215
Guild, Jo Conn 118
Guilford Courthouse, Battle of 7
Guntersville, Ala. 40

Hagan, James 131; brigade 132
Haggard, Barbara 228
Haggard, Bettie 227
Haggard, Mary Charlotte Fisher 228, 229, 233
Haggard, Robert M. 184-85, 228
Haggard, William Thomas 229
Halleck, Henry W. 111, 166-67
Hamblen County, Tenn. 66
Hamburg, Ala. 200
Hamilton, Edward G. 73, 189, 257
Hamilton, Oliver P. 55, 56, 117, 118
Hammond, John H. 171
Hampton, Wade 70, 113, 129, 131, 135, 136-37

Hampton, Va. 31
Hampton Roads 139
Hancock County, Tenn. 16
Hannon, Moses W. 77, 96, 109, 131
Hanson, Charles S. 116
Hardee, William J. 27, 121-22, 125, 129-30, 132, 187; and Bragg 33; withdraws to Chattanooga 50; in North Georgia 75-76, 79, 84, 85-87; corps 106, 107
Hardee, William J., Jr. 133
Hardeeville, S.C. 124, 126
Hardeman County, Tenn. 48
Harding, William Giles 188
Harding Road 162, 167
Hardison, J.J. 257
Hardison's Mill 151
Hargrove, Robert K. 244
Harkness, Georgia 6
Harper, W.C. 51, 257
Harper's Ferry, Va. 132
Harpeth River 158, 160, 169
Harris, Isham G. 11-12, 14, 205
Harrison, Elisha P. 20, 255
Harrison, Richard A. 20, 255
Harrison, Thomas J. 61, 71, 94, 160
Harrison, William 255
Harrison, William H. 104
Harrison House 104
Hartje, Robert G. 49
Harvey, Addison: scouts 203
Hatch, Edward 148, 176; division, 150, 160, 171, 178
Hathaway, John C. 138
Hawes, Richard 18
Hawkins County, Tenn. 16
Hay, John H. 47, 257
Haygood, Atticus Greene 249
Hazelwood, W.R. 257
Heiman, Adolphus 234
Helm, James G. 8
Helm, Moses Watkins 8
Helm, Rebecca Fisher 7-8
Helper, Hinton Rowan 218
Henderson, W.N. 257
Hendrix, Eugene R. 247
Hendron's Ferry 124
Henryville, Tenn. 150
Hermitage 165-66, 173
Heth, Henry 16, 19
Higginbottom, R.M. 68, 257
Hill, James 45, 257

Hillsboro Pike 161, 162, 167, 170
Hillsborough, N.C. 136
Hillsborough Tenn. 50
Hilton Head Island 125
Hindman, T.C.: division 54
Hiwassee River 52, 64, 97
Hobbs, R.C. 127, 255
Hog Mountain 41
Hoke, Robert Frederick 132
Holeman, Alexander W. 92
Holland, R.T. 45, 257
Holland's Ford 152
Hollow Tree Gap 174
Holman, Daniel W. 1, 29, 51, 55, 63, 67, 71, 76, 78, 112, 119, 181
Holman, Josie 243
Holman's battalion 29, 32
Holston River 65, 67, 68, 98
Holt, Bitha 243
Holt, J.H. 45, 257
Holtsburg, N.C. 136
Homer, quoted 51
Hood, John B. 1, 109, 111, 112, 118–21, 133; division 61; in North Georgia 75–76, 83–86, 88, 95; evacuates Atlanta, 106–7; Tennessee campaign 148–72, 216; retreats 173–80; relieved of command 187
Hopper, Newton 255
Hopper, Thomas 255
Hornsborough, S.C. 131
Horton, John N. 255
Horton, William R. 34, 47
Hoss, Elijah Embree 247
Hot Springs, N.C. 73
Hotel St. Cloud 165
Houk, Leonidas C. 18
Houston, John L. 16, 20, 255
Howard, Oliver O. 89, 90, 122, 126
Hudson, Alfred B.: battery 193
Huey's Mill 152, 185
Huff's Ferry 64
Huger's Landing 124
Huggins Amariah L. 56
Hughes' Ford 160
Humboldt, Tenn. 19
Humes, William Y.C. 58, 67, 68, 80, 85, 93, 94, 96, 131
Hunter, Elihu 228
Hunter, Frances Elizabeth Fisher 233
Hunter, George W. 255
Hunter, J.Z.B. 31, 257

Hunter, T.H.M. 257
Hunter, Thomas 16, 255
Hunter, W.A. 101, 255
Hunter, W.L. 255
Huntsville, Ala. 22, 119
Hurlbut, Stephen A. 144
Hurt, W.S. 72
Hurt's Crossroads, Tenn. 72, 152
Huwald, Gustave, A. 63

Illinois 8, 9, 11, 14, 53, 67, 242
The Impending Crisis of the South 218
Indian Territory 212
Indiana 31, 33; troops 67
Indianapolis 50, 58
Irwinville, Ga. 138
Island No. 10 22
Iverson, Alfred C., Jr. 85, 92, 109, 111, 120, 123, 124

Jacksboro, Tenn. 67
Jackson, Alfred E. 116
Jackson, Andrew: his home 165
Jackson, William H. 75, 93, 109, 121, 148; corps 94; division 150, 152, 153, 154–56, 158, 160–63, 174–76, 178, 179, 188, 191–92, 193–94, 197, 198–99, 202, 203–4
Jackson, Tenn. 71; U.S. Army General Hospital at 24
Jacksonville, Ala. 112
James River 82, 133
Jarman, George W. 234
Jasper, Tenn. 50, 57
Jay's Saw Mill 53
Jefferson, Thomas, quoted 3
Jenkins, Micah 61
Jennings, Will 116
Johnson, Andrew 12
Johnson, Bushrod 54, 102
Johnson, Edward: division 152, 153
Johnson, J.M. 80, 257
Johnson, Lewis 119
Johnson, Richard W. 160, 171
Johnson, William H. 190
Johnson County, Ill. 7, 226
Johnson's Ferry 200
Johnsonville, Tenn. 148, 162
Johnston, Albert Sidney 14, 22

Johnston, Joseph E. 26, 38, 71, 73, 74, 76, 79–85, 95, 129, 130, 133–36, 218; assessment of Forrest 24
Joice, George W. 47, 80, 190, 257
Jones, David 16, 255
Jones, Fielder A. 94
Jones, J.B. 47, 257
Jones, Redding 257
Jones Bluff 204
Jones' Camp Ground 111
Jonesborough, Ga. 93, 106, 122
Jordan, J.W. 257
Jordan, John 214; household 233
Jordan, Thomas J. 100
Joyce *see* Joice
Judah, Henry Moses 140
Julian, W.R. 39, 40

Kelley, David C. 162, 168, 170–71, 190–91, 203, 244–45, 250
Kelly, John H. 59, 74, 75, 77, 78, 80, 85, 93, 96, 97, 104
Kelly's Ferry 50
Kemper Barracks 53
Kennesaw Mountain 78, 80, 81
Kentucky 8, 9, 12, 13, 14, 18, 19, 21, 22, 47, 59, 64, 83, 92, 120, 165
Kentucky brigade (Williams') 80; (Breckenridge's) 134
Kentucky River 19
Kerr, Marshall V. 53, 255
Killough, James M. 81–82, 255
Kilpatrick, Judson 121–24, 126, 127, 131, 134, 150
King, B.W. 257
King, Elias 69, 257
King, T.R. 68, 8l, 189, 257
King, W.T.C. 64, 257
King Henry V 26
Kings Hill, Tenn. 178
Kings Mountain, Battle of 3, 7
Kingston, Tenn. 18, 51, 65, 97, 99
Kingston Springs, Tenn. 151
Kirkland, James Hampton 246–47
Knoxville 8, 18, 37, 58, 63, 64, 65, 67, 68, 69, 71, 72, 97–99, 140
Knoxville & Clinton Railroad 65
Ku Klux Klan 147, 241

L.&N. Railroad shops 254
Ladies Repository 5

LaFayette, Ga. 120
LaGrange, Oscar H. 192, 194, 199
LaGrange, Ga. 93, 94
Laiboldt, Bernard 96
Lamb, J.M. 45, 47, 257
Lancaster, S.C. 129
Laughton, G.W. 189, 257
LaVergne, Tenn. 27, 28, 163, 165
Lawrence Farm 43
Lawrenceburg, Tenn. 211
Lawrenceville, Ga. 82
Lawwell, Ethan 50, 255
Lawwell, Henry 20, 255
Laws, G.C. 257
Layne, Jesse R. 255
Lay's Ferry 75
Lebanon, Tenn. 13, 52, 99, 234, 243
Ledford, W. Pinckney 20, 255
Lee, Robert E.: assessment of Forrest 24; surrenders 134, 135
Lee, Samuel P. 183
Lee, Stephen D. 89, 174; corps 90, 106, 107, 151, 152, 153, 158, 162, 167–71, 174, 187–88
Lenoir Station, Tenn. 98
Lents (Lentz) Benjamin F. 20, 255
Leonard, L.J. 257
Levy, William 204
Lewis, Joseph H.: brigade 124
Lewisburg, Tenn. 3, 57, 227
Lexington, Ky. 18, 52, 115–16, 118
Lexington, Tenn. 24
Leydon, A. 61
Libby Prison 38, 44
Lick Skillet Road 78, 90
Liddell, St. John R. 54
Lincoln, Abraham 9, 11, 12, 111, 133–34, 135, 165
Little, J.W. 31, 81, 257
Little River 65
Little Tennessee River 63, 98
Loftin, J.H.C. 257
Loftin, T.B. 257
Logan, John A. 166; corps 129
Logan, Joseph P. 79
Logan, T.M.: brigade 129
Logan's Crossroads, Battle of 22
London, Ky. 18
Lone Mountain 66, 67
Long, Benton W. 48, 255
Long, Eli: division 192, 195–96
Long, Richard T. 66, 255

Longstreet, James 8, 54, 68, 69, 70, 98, 218; sent to Knoxville 61, 63, 64; siege of Knoxville 65, 66, 67; thanked by Congress 71; returns to Virginia 73
Longview, Tex. 227
Lookout Mountain 55
Loper's Crossroads, S.C. 127
Loring, William W. 79
Lost Mountain 78, 111
Loudon, Tenn. 64, 72, 98
Loudon County, Tenn. 63
Louisiana 11, 18, 79, 113
Louisville, Ga. 123
Louisville, Ky. 18, 31, 53, 69, 81, 140
Lovejoy's Station 91, 93, 94, 107, 110
Lovell, William Henry 230
Loving, William R. 101, 255
Lumpkins Station, Ga. 123
Lynchburg, Va. 116
Lyon Hylan B. 167; brigade 193-94

Macbeth, Charles 129
McAdams, John J. 58, 255
McAdams, William J. 142, 255
McCann, Richard 32
McConnell, Francis J. 6
McConnell, Peter M.W. 31, 257
McCook, Alexander M. 27, 74
McCook, Edward M. 91-94, 192, 194; division 197, 199-200
McCord, H.G. 177, 257
McCown, John Porter 32-33, 218
McCulloch, Robert: regiment 189
McCullough, Allen P. 255
McCullough, C.R. 257
McCullough, Delliston S. 255, 257
McCullough, William W. 20, 255
McCurdy, William A. 127, 255
McDonald, Charles 32, 54, 58
McDonough, Ga. 91, 107, 122
McDonough Road 95
McFadden, W.H. 257
McFerrin, John B. 83
McKendree Church 254
McKendree College 201
McKenzie, George W.: regiment 59
McKinstry, Alexander 102
McLane, G.A. 255
McLaughlin, William 92
McLaws, Lafayette: division 61

McLemore, W.S. 15, 51-52, 113
McLemore's Cove 63
McMillen, William Linn 169-70, 217
McMinnville, Tenn. 52, 57, 99
Macon, Ga. 89, 91, 92, 94, 121-22, 139, 198, 200
Macon & Western Railroad 91, 94, 106, 107, 122
McPherson, James B. 74, 75, 81, 85-88
McReynolds, James W. 97
McTyeire, Holland Nimmons 250
Madison, Ga. 122
Magee's farm 204
Magoffin, Beriah 12
Magruder, John Bankhead 212
Manchester, Tenn. 49
Marietta, Ga. 73, 80, 81, 95, 96, 111
Marion, Ala. 194, 197, 200
Marion County, Tenn. 53
Marshall, Eliza 230
Marshall, William A. 230
Marshall County, Tenn. 1, 4, 5, 8, 9, 11, 14, 16, 21, 26, 47, 48, 64, 67, 72, 75, 81-82, 99, 101, 151, 189
Martin, Jacob T. 112
Martin, William T. 61, 66, 68, 70, 71, 77, 80, 96, 97, 104, 120
Maryville, Tenn. 64, 69
Maryville College 248
Mason City, Iowa 103-4
Massengill's Mills, Tenn. 68
Matthews, Joel E. 198
Matthews, Shailer 238
Maury, Dabney, H. 204
Maury County, Tenn. 31, 47, 48, 72, 79, 151, 191, 230
Maynardville, Tenn. 66
Meade, George 175
Meadows, William M. 20-21, 255
Mecklenburg County, N.C. 3, 226
Meharry Medical School 243
Meigs County, Tenn. 57, 97
Memphis, Tenn. 13, 15, 22, 32, 49, 88, 169
Methodism, influence of on Fisher family 5-7
Methodist Episcopal Church 245; Tennessee Conference of 5, 24, 83, 95; University Senate of 6
Methodist Episcopal Church, South 245, 249-50; Tennessee Conferences of 244, 253; Ministerial

Educational Aid Society of 234;
General Conferences of 244, 248
Methodist Protestant Church 245
Methodist Publishing House 5, 6, 83
Methodist Quarterly Review 6
Mexican War 113
Middle Tennessee 9, 12, 14, 19, 21, 47, 49, 58, 99, 101, 105, 113, 120, 121, 150, 185, 228, 234, 237, 254
Middle West 165, 179
Middleton, Tenn. 31
Military District of Texas, New Mexico, and Arizona 212; Indian Territory, C.S.A. 212
Military Division of the Mississippi, U.S.A. 22, 125, 139, 145, 190, 192, 201
Military Division of the West, C.S.A. 120
Mill Creek 29
Mill Springs, Battle of 22
Milledgeville, Ga. 92, 113, 121-22
Miller, T.C.H. 1, 21, 23, 26, 30, 31, 96, 112, 151, 177, 257
Millington, John 275n
Milroy, R.H. 164
Mims, Edwin 246-47
Minty, Robert H.G. 52; brigade 80
Missionary Ridge 55, 59, 68
Mississippi 8, 11, 26, 32, 48, 58, 60, 95, 97, 112, 176
Mississippi, Army of (C.S.A.) 74-75, 85
Mississippi, Army of the (U.S.A.) 220
Mississippi River 13, 22
Missouri 14, 149
Mitchell, Ormsby, M. 22
Mitchell, Robert B. 57-58
Mobile, Ala. 187
Mobile & Ohio Railroad 121, 202, 204
Mobile Bay 121
Moffatt, Jonathan 255
Monnigan, Daniel 19, 255
Monroe County, Tenn. 64
Monterey, Tenn. 99
Montevallo, Ala. 192
Montgomery, Ala. 11, 13, 89, 92, 106, 198, 220
Moon, James 38
Morehead City, N.C. 133
Morgan, John Hunt 114, 117

Morgan, John T. 70, 109, 120
Morgan County, Tenn. 117
Morganton, Tenn. 63
Morris, John A. 163, 257
Morris Island 130
Morristown, Tenn. 16, 69
Morton, John W.: battery 32, 39, 56, 58, 164, 188
Mott, John R. 7
Moulton, Ala. 38
Mt. Hope, Ala. 38
Mt. Pleasant, Tenn. 150
Mouzon, Edwin 247
Mower, Joseph Anthony 132
Munger, Theodore T. 238-39
Murfree, James B. 116, 118
Murfreesboro, Tenn. 13, 22, 23, 29, 30, 33, 49, 52, 57, 99, 100, 149, 162, 163-65, 173; Battle of 1, 27-28
Murray, John P. 15
Muscle Shoals 58
Muse, Melchisedec B. 20, 255

Nahunta, N.C. 133
Nancy, James 257
Naron, L.A. 103
Nashville 4, 6, 12, 13, 15, 19, 22, 27, 28, 29, 34, 50, 64, 67, 82, 83, 99, 100, 102, 104, 112, 116, 118, 120, 140, 149, 156, 158, 161-62, 166, 169, 179, 234, 244, 253-54; as Union command center 22, 174; Battle of 1, 8, 125, 167-72
Nashville & Chattanooga Railroad 36, 57, 95, 97, 98, 100, 151, 163, 167
Nashville & Decatur Railroad 36, 95, 104, 178
Nashville & Northwestern Railroad 148, 162
Nauvoo, Ala. 181
Neely, J.I. 257
Negley, James S. 19
Neill, John T. 255
Nelson, John W. 142, 255
Nelson, William 31
New Hope, Tenn. 53
New Hope Church, Ga. 77-78, 112
New Orleans 22, 142, 212
New York 5, 142, 241
Newberry, S.C. 130
Newnan, Ga. 93-94, 112, 200

Newport, Tenn. 70, 71, 72
Niles Ferry 63
Nineteenth Alabama Infantry, C.S.A. 41
Nineteenth Tennessee Cavalry Regiment, C.S.A. 33, 181
Ninety-Fifth Ohio Volunteer Infantry Regiment, U.S.A. 169, 217
Ninth Illinois Infantry, U.S.A. 67
Ninth Kentucky Cavalry Regiment, C.S.A. 138
Ninth Pennsylvania Cavalry Regiment, U.S.A. 100
Ninth Tennessee Cavalry Battalion, C.S.A. 181
Ninth Tennessee Cavalry Regiment, C.S.A. 32, 39, 40, 55, 56, 58, 68
Nixon, George H. 113, 163, 173
Nolensville, Tenn. 27, 50
Noonday Creek 80
North Carolina 3, 4, 35, 49; troops from 121; state troops 136
Northern Virginia, Army of 21, 61, 84, 134, 137; its priorities 219–20
Northwestern University 6
Nowlin, James O. 100, 255

Oak Ridge, Tenn. 99
Ocmulgee River 91
Ocoee River 97
Oconee River 122
Ogeechee River, Shoals of 123
Ohio, Army of the (U.S.A.) 61, 91, 133, 220
Ohio, Department of the (U.S.A.), Army of Kentucky 31
Ohio River 81, 179
Oklahoma 118
Oklahoma City, Ok. 277n
Oliver Hospital 80
Olmstead, Charles H. 165
O'Neal, H.M. 257
One Hundred Fifty-Sixth Illinois Infantry Regiment, U.S.A. 140
Oostenaula River 75, 76
Opelika, Ala. 93–94
Orangeburg, S.C. 129
Overton, John, home of 168
Owen, J.G. 67, 257
Owen, W.J. 257
Owen's Crossroads 161

Owen's Ford 152
Oxford University 6

Paducah, Ky. 13
Paine, Robert 191
Paint Mountain 73
Paint Rock, Tenn. 16, 20, 73
Palmer, Joseph B.: brigade 164, 176
Palmer, William J. 139, 181
Palmetto, Ga. 93, 111, 112, 118
Palmyra, Tenn. 37
Parkes, James H. 253
Parkhurst, John G. 191
Pate, William J. 67, 257
Patterson, S.H. 257
Patton, Elisha A. 255
Peachtree Creek 82, 85; Battle of 86, 89
Peachtree Road 82
Peavine Creek 82, 85
Pegram, John 19, 27, 53, 56
Pelham, Tenn. 50
Pendergrass, Jasper 50, 255
Pensacola, Fla. 194
Perryville, Battle of 19
Peters, George B. 48–49
Peters, Jessie Helen McKissack 48–49
Petersburg, Ga. 139
Petersburg, Va. 179; fall of 134
Pettus Flying Artillery 193
Peyton, John W. 50, 255
Philadelphia, Pa. 6, 260n
Phillips County, Ark. 49
Piedmont, Okla. 235
Pigeon River 69, 70
Pikeville, N.C. 133
Pillow, Gideon J. 13–14
Pine Mountain 78, 79
Plantersville, Ala. 195, 197
Pocotaligo, S.C. 126
Poindexter, J.W. 81, 257
Point Lookout Md. 75, 82
Pointer, Henry 43
Polk, James K. 191
Polk, Leonidas 13, 54, 74–76, 85, 147, 218; and Bragg 32; death 79
Polk County, Tenn. 139
Pope, John 22
Poplar Springs 82
Port Royal Ferry 126
Porter, David D. 135

Potomac, Army of the 135, 149, 179
Powder Springs, Ga. 111
Powell, James M. 255
Presbyterian Church in the U.S.A. 248
Preston, William 54
Prestonburg, Ky. 115
Price, Reuben S. 50, 255
Price, Sterling 8, 149
Primrose, Benjamin C. 31, 67, 257
Protestant Episcopal Church 79
Puckett, John W. 256
Pulaski, Tenn. 13, 50, 102-3, 149, 177-78, 244
Putman, D.V. 45, 47, 258
Pyland, J.H. 34, 256

Quarles, W.A. 78
Quarterly Review 6

Rainey, N.E. Frank 34, 80, 96, 258
Rain's cut 167
Raleigh, N.C. 35, 130, 134
Rally Hill, Tenn. 153
Rambo, M.V. 45, 47, 80, 258
Rambo, William C. 126, 256
Ramsey, J.L. 258
Ramsey, J.M. 189, 258
Ramsey, T.J. 47, 258
Randolph, Ala. 194
Randolph-Macon College 243
Rankin, R.S. 81-82, 256
Ransom, Richard P. 95
Ransom, Robert, Jr. 61
Ransom, Whitman 39, 44, 258
Ransom, William A. 233-34
Ratliff, R.W. 115
Rauschenbusch, Walter 238
Readyville, Tenn. 16, 100
Receiving and Wayside Hospital 82
Redman, J.H. 19, 256
Reeder, William H. 53, 256
Reed's Crossroads, Tenn. 67
Reese, Robert 50, 256
Reese, William B. 50, 258
Reid, L.W. 258
Republicans 11, 12, 222
Resaca, Ga. 73, 75, 119
Revis, Daniel 189, 258
Reynolds, Daniel H. 176, 178

Reynolds, Ezekiel E. 256
Reynolds, W.G. 31, 47, 258
Rhea County, Tenn. 47
Rice, Francis 35
Rice, Francisco 101
Richland Creek 177
Richmond, Ky. 18, 169
Richmond, Va. 38, 44, 59, 70, 82, 83, 84, 111, 116, 179, 220; fall of 134
Richmond & Danville Railroad 134
Rickman, W.C. 258
Rienzi, Miss. 191
Ringgold, Ga. 31
Roane County, Tenn. 16
Roberts, Sallie 15
Robertson, J.J. 138
Robertson County, Tenn. 14
Robertsville, S.C. 124, 126
Robertsville, Tenn. 100
Robinson, Aaron B. 81, 258
Robinson, William M. 101, 256
Rock Creek 131
Rock Island Prison 53, 67, 68, 69
Rockingham, N.C. 131
Rocky Creek 123
Rocky Face Ridge 74-75
Rocky Mount, S.C. 129
Roddey, Philip D. 38, 39, 40, 93, 178; brigade 181, 189, 193, 195-96
Rogersville, Tenn. 16, 100
Rome, Ga. 37, 40, 42, 43, 119, 120
Rone, W.N. 258
Rosecrans, William S. 27-28, 37, 49, 52, 55, 61
Ross, Lawrence S. 94, 164; brigade 153, 155-56, 174-75, 178
Roswell, Ga. 81
Rough and Ready, Ga. 106, 110, 111
Rousseau, Lovell, H. 104, 140, 149, 162, 164, 173
Rousseau, Richard Hilaire 140
Royster, Edward D. 31, 47, 81, 258
Royster, J.W. 47, 258
Rucker, Edmund W. 150, 165; brigade 170; loses arm 171
Russell, A.A. 32
Russell, Milton 42
Russell, Thomas E. 256
Russellville, Ala. 38, 181
Russellville, Tenn. 66, 69, 98
Rutherford County, Tenn. 16, 23, 27, 47, 151; its courthouse 164

Rutledge, James 256
Rutledge, Tenn. 68

Sacramento, Ky. 196
St. Louis, Mo. 8
St. Thomas Episcopal Church 142
St. Thomas Hospital 254
Salem, N.J. 64
Salisbury, N.C. 130
Salter, Francis 196
Saltville, Va. 100, 114; Battle of 99, 114–15, 117, 121
Saluda Gap 73
Sand Mountain 39–40
Sandersville, Ga. 122
Sandtown Road 90
Sanson, Emma 41
Santayana, George 281n
Savannah, Ga. 121, 124, 125, 126, 131; Sherman's campaign to capture 99, 113, 120–21
Savannah River 121, 124, 125, 139
Sawyer, W.P. 256
Schofield, John M. 88, 133, 173; corps 81–82, 85–86, 149, 151–56, 158, 166–67, 169
Scott, John S. 18; brigade 169
Scott County, Tenn. 117
Scottsville, Ala. 199
Sears, Claudius W., brigade 164
Second Kentucky Cavalry Regiment, C.S.A. 59
Second Missouri Cavalry Regiment, C.S.A. 189
Second Tennessee Cavalry Regiment, C.S.A. 58, 62
Second Tennessee Cavalry Regiment, U.S.A. 31
Seddon, James A. 70, 187
Selma, Ala. 35, 139, 191–92, 195–96
Selph, Duncan H. 234
Semple, James A. 138
Seneca River 73
Sequatchie Valley 48, 52, 57
Seventeenth Arkansas Cavalry Regiment, C.S.A. 188
Seventeenth Regiment of Indiana Cavalry, U.S.A. 195
Seventh Alabama Cavalry Regiment, C.S.A. 181, 183

Seventh Iowa Infantry Regiment, U.S.A. 103
Seventh Kansas Cavalry Regiment, U.S.A. 102
Seventh Tennessee Cavalry Regiment, C.S.A. 170
Seventy-Third Indiana Infantry Regiment, U.S.A. 37
Sevierville, Tenn. 69, 70
Sewanee, Tenn. 50
Shakespeare, William, quoted 26
Shaw, Henry B. 102
Shaw, Joseph 55, 56, 124, 127, 134
Shawneetown, Ill. 201
Sheffield, E.V. 258
Sheffield, E.W. 258
Shelbyville, Tenn. 13, 22, 28, 31, 47, 49, 50, 57, 72, 73, 75, 82, 99, 101, 118, 152, 163, 183, 253
Shelton, W.D. 81, 258
Shenandoah, C.S.S. 212
Shepherd, R.L. 80, 258
Sheridan, Philip H. 33, 175
Sherman, W.T. 22, 66, 92, 95, 105, 111, 112–13, 120, 143–44, 165; assessment of Forrest 24, 183, 205–6; Atlanta campaign 73, 74, 88, 89, 91, 96, 106, 107; banishes civilians 109–10; his Savannah campaign 120–26, 220; Carolina campaign 126–27, 129–36
Shiloh, Battle of 22, 59
Ship's Gap 74
Shoal Creek 148
Shook's Gap 69
Short, James A. 134
Shy, William, and Shy's Hill 170
Sinking Cane, Tenn. 100
Sipsey River 198
Sister's Ferry 124, 126
Six Mile Creek 193–94
Sixth Tennessee Cavalry Regiment, C.S.A. 58, 62, 181
Sixty-First Regiment of Illinois Infantry, U.S.A. 165
Skagerag, Ga. 93
Slater Fund 249
Slocum, Henry W. 107, 112, 122, 126
Slucer, John 19, 256
Smith, A.J. 149
Smith, Alfred T. 140
Smith, Andrew Jackson 167

Smith, Anna Maude 277n
Smith, Baxter 15, 59
Smith, Benjamin A. 127, 256
Smith, Edmund Kirby 16, 18, 31, 211-12, 218
Smith, Ezra C. 116-18
Smith, George 20, 256
Smith, Gustavus J. 256
Smith, Gustavus W. 85, 107
Smith, Henry I. 103
Smith, J.C. 258
Smith, J.G. 20, 256
Smith, James A.: brigade 165, 174-75
Smith, Samuel A. 31, 81, 198, 258
Smith, Sarah Ann 117
Smith, Thomas Benton 216-18, brigade 164; at Shy's Hill 169-70
Smith, William R. 20, 256
Smithfield, N.C. 130, 133-34
Smith's Springs, Tenn. 151
Smotherman, James M. 189, 258
Smotherman, R.N. 258
Smyrna, Ga. 81
Smyrna, Tenn. 99, 102
Snake Creek Gap 119, 120
Sneedville, Tenn. 100
Snell, A.R. 189, 258
Snell, James T. 258
Snell, Thomas J. 189, 258
Somerset, Battle of 22
Sope Creek 81
South Carolina 3, 11, 73, 113, 124, 125, 136
Southern Association of Colleges and Schools 246
Southern Education Board 246
Southern Methodist University 248
Sparta, Tenn. 52, 99, 100, 101, 117
Speruce, J. Jackson 256
Springfield, Tenn. 14, 118, 244
Spring Hill, Tenn. 33, 34, 38, 39, 42, 45, 47, 50, 151-56, 158, 174, 178
Standing Stone, Tenn. 99
Stanley, David S. 36, 149
Stanton, Edwin M. 165-66
Starke, Peter B. 203; brigade 189, 193, 197
Starnes, James W. 49, 51-52, 113
State hospital, Nashville 170, 217
Steedman, James B. 36, 96-97, 104, 149, 167, 169, 178
Stegall, Douglas M. 256

Stegall, Milton C. 20, 256
Stegall, P.M. 258
Stevenson, Ala. 165
Stevenson, Carter L. 16, 174
Stewart, Alexander P. 54, 78, 79, 84, 86, 90, 106, 107, 112, 133, 152, 153, 155, 158, 160-61, 167-68, 188
Stewart's Landing, Tenn. 98
Stilesboro, Ga. 77
Stillwell, J.W. 81, 183, 258
Stone Mountain 85
Stoneman, George 74, 77, 91-92, 93, 140-41
Stones River 163; Battle of 1, 27-28
Strange, J.P. 164, 203
Stratton, William 5
Strawberry Plains, Tenn. 69, 98-99, 104
Streight, Abel D. 176; raid 36-44
Strong, Josiah 238
Sugar Creek 178
Sugar Tree, Tenn. 58
Sullivan, Jeremiah C. 20
Sulphur Springs, Tenn. 47
Sumey, A. Franklin 34, 49, 256
Sumterville, S.C. 127
Sutt, J.W. 19, 34, 256
Sutton, Samuel J. 20, 256
Swanson, Edward 72
Swanson, Felix Z. 112
Swanson, Ira 112
Swanson, John J. 112
Sweeney see Swiney
Sweetwater, Tenn. 64, 140
Swiney, Adolphus N. 256
Swiney, Littlebury J. 20, 256
Swiney, Warren L.D. 16, 256
Swiney, William D. 20, 256

Talladega, Ala. 44, 202
Tanner, Robert 189, 258
Tarver, Benjamin 243
Tarver, Susan 243
Taylor, J.A. 189, 258
Taylor, J.D. 195
Taylor, N.R. 45, 47, 258
Taylor, Richard 113-14, 120, 138, 183, 186, 187, 189, 191, 195, 197, 199, 201, 202-3, 204-5 213
Taylor, W.C. 47, 258
Taylor, W.R. 81, 258

Taylor, Zachary 113
Teachout, Stanley R. 254
Tennessee 4, 8, 9, 11-13, 22, 32, 68, 97, 100, 112, 113-14, 116, 118, 176
Tennessee, Army of, C.S.A. 1, 28, 33, 49, 51, 58, 60, 63, 69, 73, 95, 105, 111, 120, 130, 132-33, 137, 179; and Battle of Chattanooga 61; in North Georgia 74; changes commanders 83-85; Forrest returns to 143; to North Carolina 187-88; its leadership 218-19; its priorities 219-20
Tennessee, Army of the (U.S.A.) 220
Tennessee, Provisional Army of 13, 14
Tennessee River 19, 36, 37, 38, 40, 50, 51, 52, 58, 61, 63, 64, 65, 95, 97-98, 104, 119, 140, 162, 178, 181, 192, 210; Great Valley of 98
Tennessee State Supreme Court 247
Tennison, Hiram 81-82, 256
Tennison, J.F. 256
Tenth Confederate Cavalry Regiment 93
Tenth Tennessee Cavalry Regiment, C.S.A. 33, 55, 56, 59, 60, 67, 68, 188, 213
Texas: secession of 11; troops 176
Third Arkansas Cavalry, C.S.A. 71
Third Confederate Cavalry Regiment 93
Third Ohio Infantry Regiment, U.S.A. 37
Third Tennessee Cavalry Regiment, C.S.A. 15, 162, 170
Third Tennessee Cavalry Regiment, U.S.A. 31
Third Tennessee Volunteer Infantry Regiment, U.S.A. 18
Thirteenth Regiment of Kentucky Cavalry, U.S.A. 117; Company C 115
Thirteenth U.S. Colored Infantry Regiment 169
Thirtieth Kentucky Infantry Regiment, U.S.A. 115
Thirty-Ninth North Carolina Infantry Regiment, C.S.A. 166
Thirty-Seventh Kentucky Volunteer Infantry Regiment, U.S.A. 116
Thirty-Third Indiana Infantry Regiment, U.S.A. 107

Thomas, Christopher C. 47, 256
Thomas, George C. 127, 256
Thomas, George H. 22, 81, 120, 125, 140-41, 149, 162, 165-67, 173, 192; and the XIV Army Corps 54, 85-86; and Battle of Nashville 167-69, 171-72, 174-75, 176, 179-80
Thomas, Isaac A. 34, 256
Thomas, Jonathan 7, 228
Thomas Station, Ga. 123
Thompson Ford 68
Thompson's Chapel 161
Thompson's Station 33-34, 49, 112, 158
Tillett, Wilbur Fisk 247
Tilton, Ga. 96
Tinsley, H.B. 19, 35, 256
Tombigbee River 202, 210
Torrey, William H. 94
Town Creek, Ala. 38, 39
Transmississippi 137, 138, 211
Transylvania College 5, 52
Trice, John 189, 258
Trinity Church 239, 245
Trinity College 248
Trinity Methodist Episcopal Church, South 83, 95
Trion, Ala. 200
Triune, Tenn. 34, 49, 173
Tugaloo River 73
Tullahoma, Tenn. 32, 37, 49, 50
Tunnel Hill 74
Tupelo, Miss. 130, 181
Turner, J.C. 47, 258
Tuscaloosa, Ala. 80, 192, 199-200
Tuscumbia, Ala. 38, 104, 113-14, 118, 120, 148
Twelfth Confederate Cavalry Regiment 93
Twelfth Ohio Volunteer Cavalry Regiment, U.S.A. 115, 138; Company I 116
Twelfth U.S. Colored Infantry Regiment 169
Twentieth Tennessee Infantry Regiment, C.S.A. 23
Twenty-First Tennessee Cavalry Regiment, C.S.A. 153
Twenty-First Tennessee Infantry Regiment, C.S.A., Company A of 88
Twenty-First U.S. Colored Infantry Regiment 129

Index

Twenty-Second Tennessee Cavalry Regiment, C.S.A. 113
Tyner's Station 55

Unaka Mountains 73
Union University 233-34
Unionism 11, 12, 13, 14
Unionists 16, 18, 21, 22, 40, 65, 102, 143, 147, 185
Unionville, Tenn. 31, 67
United States of America: casualties 222-23; post-war economy 225-26
United States Army Corps: IV 149, 150, 153; XIV 54, 85-86, 120, 122, 123-24, 132; XV 122, 127, 129; XVI 102-3, 145; XVII 122, 132; XX 112, 122, 129, 132; XXI 54; XXIII 149, 150
United States Congress 5, 142
Unitia, Tenn. 63
University of Alabama 192, 199
Upton, Emory 139, 192, 194-95
Usry (Ussery), William, and family 211
University of Tennessee 66, 265n
University of the South 50

Vanderbilt, Cornelius 250
Vanderbilt, William H. 250
Vanderbilt University 6, 199, 246-48, 250; medical department of 235; board of trust 245
Van Dorn, Earl 32-33, 48, 58
Varnell's Station, Ga. 74
Vaughn, John C. 63, 137, 139
Verona, Miss. 188, 189, 190, 210
Verona, Tenn. 1, 26, 72
Versailles, Ky. 19
Villa Rica, Ga. 112
Virginia 22, 61, 67, 99, 120, 176

Waco, Tex. 82
Wagner, George Day: division 153
Walden's Ridge 52, 57
Walker, George W. 256
Walker, W.H.T. 53, 54
Walker, William W. 20, 127, 256
Walthall, Edward C. 54, 158, 176-77
Walton, Edwin S. 193
Walton Road 99

Warfield, Cornelia Francis 151, 176
Warner, Samuel 64, 183, 258
Warren County, Tenn. 151
Warrensburg, Tenn. 73
Wartburg, Tenn. 100
Wartrace, Tenn. 16, 28, 57
Washburn, C.C. 170
Washington, D.C. 75, 111, 179; Grand Review 211
Washington, Ga. 36, 137-38
Waterloo, Ala. 192
Waters, Shelah 99
Watkins, Sam 83-84
Waynesboro, Ga. 123-24, 131
Webb, Francis M. 49, 256
Webb School 217, 277n
Wesley, Charles 5
Wesley, John 5
West Mississippi, Army of 212; Military Division of (U.S.A.) 212
West Point, Ga. 112, 119, 203
West Point, Miss. 188, 190, 194, 198
West Point, N.Y. (U.S.M.A.) 79, 88, 104, 113, 121, 201
West Tennessee 8, 9, 19, 22, 24, 47, 58, 59, 71, 121
Western & Atlantic Railroad 40, 74, 77, 78, 81, 85, 95, 106, 111
Western Military Institute 102
Wharton, John A. 27, 58, 61-63
Wheeler, James T. 54, 140, 181
Wheeler, Joseph 1, 32, 51, 59, 70, 74, 95, 101, 113-14, 117, 118-19, 142, 186, 214, 215-16, 218; appointed to command Bragg's cavalry 24, 56; at Murfeesboro (Stones River) 26-28; attacks Ft. Donelson 29; covers to retreat to Chattanooga 50; conducts raid of Middle Tennessee 56-58; in siege of Knoxville 61, 64, 65; commands Johnston's cavalry 75, 77, 80, 81; commands Hood's cavalry 85-87; defeats Stoneman and McCook 91-94; second Tennessee raid 95-101, 104-5, 109, 121; follows Sherman to Savannah 120-24; in the Carolinas 127, 129-34, 136-38; captured 138; post-war career 142
Whigs 9, 11, 12, 222
White, John H. 20, 256
White County, Tenn. 117-18
Whitefield, George 5

Whitthorne, W.C. 191
Wiggins, J.H. 127, 134
Wiggs, William W. 66, 256
Wild Cat Creek 52
Wilhoit, J.B. 258
Wilkinson Pike 163–64, 173
Wilkinson's Crossroads 173
William and Mary, College of 243
Williams, James Chesley 31, 258
Williams, John Stuart 80, 85, 98, 99, 100, 104, 113–14, 120
Williamson, C.B. 230
Williamson, F.M. 71, 81, 258
Williamson, J.J. 230
Williamson, Wesley H. 31, 71, 258
Williamson County, Tenn. 23, 35, 49, 51, 67, 104, 112, 151, 227
Willis, Joseph G. 256
Willis, Leonidas: battalion 188
Wilmington, N.C. 133
Wilson, Alpheus Waters 245
Wilson, Andrew L.: regiment 153
Wilson, Ewing A. 14, 15, 251–52
Wilson, James H. 139, 149, 152, 153, 160, 161–62, 165, 166, 167–68; pursues Hood 174–79; his Alabama campaign 191–201
Wilson, John H. 81, 258
Wilson, Joseph 45, 47, 80, 258
Wilson Pike 161
Winchester, Tenn. 16, 28, 127

Winn, Alexander 23
Winn, George W. 244
Winnsboro, S.C. 129
Winstead's Hill 158
Wirz, Henri 118
Wisdom, J.H. 42
Wolford, Frank 56; brigade 64, 69
Wolseley, Viscount: assessment of Forrest 26, 210
Wood, D.T. 258
Wood, Thomas J. 37, 54, 167
Woodall, W.P. 258
Woodbine 167
Woodbury, Tenn. 100
Woodward, Thomas G. 59
World War I 240–41, 244
Wright, Marcus Joseph 190
Wright, R.V. 134
Wyeth, John Allen 55, 186–87, 213
Wynn, Joseph B. 64, 258
Wynn, W.S. 258

Yale College and Divinity School 239
Yale University 113, 246
Yellow River 138
Yopp, Jeremiah 101, 256
Yorkville, S.C. 137
Young, G.C. 256
Yunt, Thaddeus 19, 256

www.ingramcontent.com/pod-product-compliance
Ingram Content Group UK Ltd.
Pitfield, Milton Keynes, MK11 3LW, UK
UKHW041924140426
5217IPUK00014B/307